JOHN CARTER

AND THE

GODS OF HOLLYWOOD

1ST EDITION

MICHAEL D. SELLERS

JOHN CARTER AND THE GODS OF HOLLYWOOD

It took 100 years to bring Edgar Rice Burroughs' *John Carter of Mars* to the big screen. It took Disney Studios just ten days to declare the film a flop and lock it away in the Disney vaults. How did this project, despite its quarter-billion dollar budget, the brilliance of director Andrew Stanton, and the creative talents of legendary Pixar Studios, become a calamity of historic proportions?

Michael Sellers, a filmmaker and Hollywood insider himself, saw the disaster approaching and fought to save the project – but without success. In *John Carter and the Gods of Hollywood*, Sellers details every blunder and betrayal that led to the doom of the motion picture – and that left countless Hollywood careers in the wreckage.

John Carter and the Gods of Hollywood is a must-read for every fan of John Carter and Edgar Rice Burroughs, and every film buff intrigued by the "inside baseball" aspects of modern Hollywood.

RICHARD A. LUPOFF
Author of *Edgar Rice Burroughs: Master of Adventure*
and *Barsoom: Edgar Rice Burroughs and the Martian Vision*

DEDICATION

John Carter and the Gods of Hollywood is respectfully dedicated to the memory of Edgar Rice Burroughs and to all those who are working to keep that memory alive, and legacy intact.

PREFACE

In 1912 struggling Chicago businessman Edgar Rice Burroughs wrote *A Princess of Mars*, the tale of John Carter, a Virginia cavalryman mysteriously transported to Mars where he would find adventure and meaning in life alongside Dejah Thoris, the incomparable Princess of Helium. The story would lead to an eleven book series and become the cornerstone of modern science fiction. Burroughs went on to write *Tarzan of the Apes* and, at the time of his death in 1950, was the best-selling author of the 20th century, with his books translated into 58 languages and outselling his contemporaries Hemingway, Faulkner, and Fitzgerald combined. His creation Tarzan was then, and remains today, the single most globally recognized literary character ever created.

In the 1960s, countless minds of my generation encountered the extraordinary imagination of Edgar Rice Burroughs through the Ace and Ballantine paperback reprints that were published monthly, and which could be found in every drug store and corner newsstand throughout America. Already half a century old, the books felt as current as if they had been written yesterday, and we collected them all, 40 cents a copy for the Ace Books, 50 cents for Ballantine, and read them multiple times.

Discovering Burroughs was not a lonely or isolated pursuit — the fans were legion. Gradually a long list emerged of scientists and storytellers, politicians and spiritual leaders, all of whom said that it was Burroughs who had caught their imagination, and inspired them in their youth, among them Ray Bradbury, Arthur C. Clarke, Carl Sagan, Ronald Reagan, Jane Goodall, Billy Graham, George Lucas, Steven Spielberg, and James Cameron.

Burroughs' writing was extraordinarily vivid and detailed. The planet that he created seemed so real that many of us felt almost as if we had lived there, or could live there–more than that, it induced a yearning to be there and experience the world of our dreaming, and thus it was that for decades Barsoom played as a movie in our minds, while Hollywood attempted to create a real movie. But Hollywood couldn't quite pull it off — the imagination of Burroughs, for decade after decade after he wrote *A Princess of Mars* in the fall of 1911, continued to exceed Hollywood's capacity to create. Meanwhile some of our greatest filmmakers made liberal use of scenes, images, and ideas from Burroughs' Barsoom: *Star Wars* and *Avatar* in particular drew heavily upon Burroughs, mining it for creative inspiration.

But they were not the original, and we still yearned for that.

Then in 2008 Disney announced that Andrew Stanton, Director of *Wall-E* and *Finding Nemo*, would be directing a film version of *A Princess of Mars* and in January 2010 filming began — and all of those who had been waiting for decades through one false alarm after another knew that at long last this cherished source-work of imaginative fiction would finally make it to the screen. We owed Stanton and Disney a deep debt of gratitude for bringing a film such as this to the screen, and to the world.

But then the dream slowly and inexorably turned to a nightmare.

Everyone who has followed Disney's *John Carter* now knows the basic outline of what happened. The film cost at least $250M to make and $100M to market; it opened poorly in the US, better overseas, and 10 days into the theatrical run Disney announced it was taking a $200M write-down due to its high cost, which meant that even with $280M in global box office gross, it was still a financial failure. *John Carter* was declared to be a failed enterprise. It was game over.

Fans, meanwhile, rallied to support the continuation of the series, and the film began to grow a steadfast and persistent cult following. While Disney has not officially ruled out a sequel nor returned the rights to the Edgar Rice Burroughs estate, it is generally considered to be settled knowledge in "the industry" that Disney has no intention of continuing the series.

Against this background, *John Carter and the Gods of Hollywood* says "Not so fast!" and attempts to achieve an in-depth understanding of what really happened with a view toward keeping open the question of whether continuation of the series is justified. It asks:

1) What is the true value of the literary property? What was it about Edgar Rice Burroughs' 1912 story that caused it to be so wildly popular and influential in the first place? Why, exactly, did scientists and storytellers from Carl Sagan to Ray Bradbury to George Lucas to James Cameron find inspiration in the works of Edgar Rice Burroughs? Why has it been in print continuously for 100 years? What was his particular genius? And have the film adaptations and borrowings from Burroughs fully harvested the value the old master presents, or is there untapped value there?

2) What is the full story of what went wrong with the release of *John Carter*? It is generally acknowledged that the marketing was ineffective -- what, exactly, happened with the marketing? Why was it not only ineffective, but *inactive* in ways that are possible to document? How much of an impact did this have on the final performance? How much of a difference would effective marketing make?

3) *John Carter* earned close to $300M -- a figure which, for example, puts in the range of fellow 2012 sci-fi adventure *Prometheus*, which earned a sequel. The difference is the high cost of production for *John Carter*. How did such a high cost of production come about? Would sequels necessarily cost as much?

4) A fan movement has grown up supporting the continuation of the *John Carter* series. What is the actual relevance, if any, of the fan movement? In the age of social media, what does the presence of such a movement mean to any possible sequel or reboot by Disney or another studio?

5) Given all factors, is there a bona fide business case for continuation of the series? How would it alter the equation if cost savings could be achieved by producing films 2 and 3 concurrently? What are the prospects of bringing in foreign coproduction partners

from China and/or Russia -- the two largest overseas markets where, in both cases, *John Carter* was a success? What other strategies could be employed to reduce risk for Disney and increase the likelihood of success?

To make the case that I have set out to make requires that I provide a detailed, critical look at all aspects of the film enterprise including the development, production, and the marketing campaign. This is not an exercise in simply finding fault and casting blame. The purpose is to show how certain mistakes and assumptions, compounded by other mistakes and assumptions, created a "perfect storm" of errors that resulted in a film that fell vastly short of its potential. Under these circumstances, making a final judgment as to sequels needs to proceed from a clear understanding of what went wrong, and how it might be corrected, to arrive at valid conclusions about the worth of the film asset that has been created, and the potential for a series.

In documenting damaging mistakes, inexplicable lapses in marketing activity, and the like, I have confined myself almost entirely to verifiable data with attribution that can be accessed through footnotes that have been provided, or in some cases via social media and marketing research software that is readily available. I have provided full attribution from articles and public and private interviews. In the case of some private interviews which comprise a small percentage of the overall content, I agreed to respect the privacy requirements from interviewees who are under current and ongoing nondisclosure agreements, principally with the Walt Disney Studios. There are a relatively small number of occasions where attribution has not been possible. Recognizing the importance of providing credible, verifiable sourcing, I have minimized the reliance on such non-attributable information.

My hope is that the "takeaway" of a reasonably openminded reader after reading this book will be a) that the underlying literary property truly is a treasure that has great value left in it; b) that correctable mistakes in the marketing of *John Carter* plus the presence now of a motivated fan base means that second and third films can reasonably be projected to do substantially better in their theatrical runs than the first film did; and c) that with smart, savvy efficiencies in production and the use foreign financing/coproduction options from territories where the film did well, a business case for successful continuation can be made.

Finally, I acknowledge and embrace the fact that this is personal for me. The imagination and storytelling genius of Edgar Rice Burroughs inspired me in countless ways in my youth. It gave me the confidence to pursue a life that has had its share of adventures and misadventures, first in service to my country, and later in pursuit of dreams that I believed in. I have had failures and made more than my share of mistakes, but it was Burroughs who taught me to give my all to things that I believe in, and my life has been richer for it. It was the old master who taught me to believe in the power and possibility of the human spirit. I and others of like mind "pledge our metal" to his. If you think we'll give up easily, consider the spirit of John Carter as it comes through in this passage:

> "I knew though that it was but a question of minutes before their greater numbers would wear me down, or get around my guard. I must go down eventually to certain death before them. I shuddered at the thought of it, dying thus in this terrible place where no word of my end ever could reach my Dejah Thoris. .....
>
> Then my old-time spirit reasserted itself. The fighting blood of my Virginian sires coursed hot through my veins. The fierce blood lust and the joy of battle surged over me. The fighting smile that has brought consternation to a thousand foemen touched my lips. I put the thought of death out of my mind, and fell upon my antagonists ......"

Or, in the words of Andrew Stanton's John Carter:

> "Find a cause ... fall in love ... write a book."

ACKNOWLEDGEMENTS

I would like to acknowledge the goodwill and encouragement of Jim Sullos, Cathy Wilbanks, Janet Mann, Willie Jones, and Tyler Wilbanks of Edgar Rice Burroughs, Inc., as well as the support of the many fans, bloggers, and scholars within the Edgar Rice Burroughs fan community, and the emerging global community of fans of the film *John Carter*. I would also like to thank Danton Burroughs for his life's work on behalf of his grandfather's legacy, and Danton's wife Linda Burroughs and her daughters Dejah and Llana Jane Burroughs for their support and inspiration. I would like to thank Richard A. Lupoff for his many kindnesses and wise mentoring; and Jack Scanlan for his indefatigable support as *pro bono* publicist to *The John Carter Files* and the *Back to Barsoom Facebook Group*. I want to thank Bob Zeuschner, Scott Tracy Griffin, Mike Shaw, and Jerry Schneider of the LA SubERBS for their fellowship and Jeff Elmo Long of the Burroughs Bibliophiles for his editorial coaching; Roland Trenary and Bob Couttie for help with the editing, Andrew Stanton for giving his all to the film and for "the tweet," and Taylor Kitsch for being a stalwart not just onscreen but off. I want to thank Valerie Sellers for her help and expertise in revealing the mysteries of modern social media monitoring; Don Barton for 10 years of friendship and wisdom; and Dr. Stanley Galloway for patience and thoroughness is pointing out "nits" both big and small, in the manuscript. I especially want to thank all of those from the film crew and studio who agreed to be interviewed and in so doing took the leap of faith and trust that I could receive your information and maintain your privacy. I would like to thank my own Dejah Thoris, Rena Sellers, who has stood by me far beyond what I could reasonably expect, and Khanada Taylor, and Jan Austin for their leadership and inspiration to the fans of the film. I would like to offer a special thank you to Dick Cook for green-lighting the film, and in spite the disappointments on many levels, I am thankful to Disney Studios for actually producing a screen version of Burroughs' classic tale – something others tried to do and failed for the better part of a century.

CONTENTS

PROLOGUE: A FIRST INKLING OF TROUBLE

On November 30, 2011, the day that Walt Disney Studios was set to debut the trailer for the Andrew Stanton film *John Carter* on *Good Morning America*, I was eagerly waiting. It would be the best glimpse yet of a film that I'd been anticipating since my childhood.

I had discovered the Martian tales of Edgar Rice Burroughs at the library at Patch Barracks in Stuttgart Germany during a rainy Little League summer when I was 12, and by the time I reached adulthood I had read all the Burroughs books multiple times, and been inspired by them. I could sketch from memory an accurate map of Barsoom, recite the full history of the Tharks and John Carter's relationship with them, and draw accurate renderings of all the creatures and cultures of that mystical planet.

Now, decades later, the movie that had existed only in my mind all these years was finally about to become a reality on cinema screens worldwide. The release date was March 9, 2012, exactly 100 days from the November unveiling, and I was looking forward to watching the climax of the campaign unfold over the coming twelve weeks.

Finally the trailer played, and the campaign was launched.

But ... what had been hyped in advance as debut of the full theatrical trailer didn't turn out to be that at all. Rather, it was a 45 second TV spot, with the first 11 seconds consisting of having the camera zoom in slowly on the Times Square giant screen, only cutting to the actual spot ten seconds into it.[1] The spot itself seemed disjointed and unfocused. The full trailer finally did premiere sixteen hours later on Jimmy Kimmel and thankfully it was better than the cut-down version shown that morning, but it still seemed to miss the mark. Who was John Carter? Why was he leaping hundreds of feet into the air and battling apes in an arena? And where was all this taking place? Of course I knew the answers to all these questions, but I had read the books. What would I think if I just came across this trailer without knowing any of the history?

I wonder what people are saying about it?

I checked online and saw that the trailer, and Disney marketing, were taking a shellacking. *The Film Stage* wrote:[2]

> After Disney botched the trailer release of the one film that needs all the good buzz it can get, by releasing just 49 [sic] seconds of it early this morning on GMA, we now have the full thing thanks to IGN.... I held some hope after the disappointing first trailer, and the latest one is definitely an improvement, but still not what I hoped for coming from such a great storyteller (also visually speaking) as Stanton....

Collider.com, a top entertainment outlet, offered the following:[3]

> *Good Morning America* had a sneak peek of the new *John Carter* trailer earlier today, which probably wasn't the best way to present a hard sell to an unfamiliar audience, not to mention a critical group of fans ready to tear into the film adaptation that dropped the most interesting half of Edgar Rice Burroughs' *John Carter of Mars* . . .

Troubled, I decided to do a little more checking. Until this point I had only been paying intermittent casual attention to the campaign --

---

[1] Robin Roberts, "Friday Night Lights Star Taylor Kitsch Shows Official Trailer for John Carter" *Youtube "ABC News" Channel*, 30 Nov 2011, 2 Sep 2012 <http://www.youtube.com/watch?v=Swf9pVGVW30>. Comment: The trailer was variously reported in the media as being from a low of 42 seconds to a high of 49 seconds long. On the ABC News link provided, the trailer begins at 1:01 with the zoom-in to the Times Square giant screen. At 1:12 it cuts to the continuation of the trailer. The trailer ends at 1:46. The correct figure is 45 seconds.

[2] Jordan Roup, "Full Second Trailer For John Carter," *The Film Stage*, 1 Dec 2011, 3 Jun 2012 <http://thefilmstage.com/trailer/full-length-second-trailer-for-john-carter/>.

[3] Brendan Bettinger, "Full Trailer For John Carter Starring Taylor Kitsch," *Collider.com*, 30 Nov 2011, 3 Jun 2012 <http://collider.com/john-carter-movie-trailer-2/129710/>.

what had I missed? Was I witnessing a one-time stumble, or an ongoing problem?

On *IMDB Pro*,[4] I checked *John Carter's* "MovieMeter" ranking. It was ranked 986 as of November 27, the most recent ranking, meaning 985 movies were receiving more hits and *IMDB* message board activity than *John Carter.* This seemed low for a $250M tentpole film 100 days out from its release date. It should be higher, I thought. A lot higher.

I decided to compare *John Carter* to two comparable upcoming "tentpole" films -- Lionsgate's *The Hunger Games*, slated for release two weeks after *John Carter* on March 23, and Disney's *The Avengers* slated for release two months after *John Carter* on May 4. *John Carter* didn't need to be ranked higher or even as high as either of these two -- but it should be in the same general vicinity and seeing how these films rank would give an "order of magnitude" indication of where the other high profile films slated for a spring release were ranked.

The results? *The Hunger Games* was ranked 17,[5] while *The Avengers* was ranked 26.[6]

I pulled up the *IMDB Pro* Data Table View for each film,[7] which includes a week by week summary of ranking and links to each article on

---

[4] Internet Movie Data Base Pro, (*IMDB Pro*), "John Carter The (2012)," 30 Nov 2012, 30 Nov 2012 <http://pro.imdb.com/title/tt0401729/> Information courtesy of Internet Movie Data Base <http:IMDB.com>. and is used by permission..

[5] *IMDB Pro*, "*The Hunger Games* (2012)," 30 Nov 2012, 30 Nov 2012, <http://pro.imdb.com/title/tt1392170/>.

[6] *IMDB Pro*, "*The Avengers* (2012)," 30 Nov 2012, 30 Nov 2012, <http://pro.imdb.com/title/tt0848228/>.

[7] *IMDB Pro*, "*John Carter* (2012) MovieMeter: Data Table View," accessed 2 Sep 2012 <http://pro.imdb.com/title/tt0401729/graph-data> ; *IMDB Pro*, "*The Avengers* (2012) MovieMeter: Data Table View," accessed 2 Sep 2012 <http://pro.imdb.com/title/tt0848228/graph>; *IMDB Pro*, "*The Hunger Games* (2012) MovieMeter: Data Table View," accessed 2 Sep 2012 <http://pro.imdb.com/title/tt1392170/graph-data>. The *IMDB Pro* MovieMeter, Data Table View, is available for each film released, and contains a table with links to a comprehensive list of articles on a given movie updated weekly. In maintaining this database, the *IMDB* monitors all of the major recognized US media outlets reporting regularly on movies, as well as a large and representative selection of international media outlets regularly reporting on movies. Unless otherwise stated, all comparisons between the publicity output for *John Carter* and other movies' publicity are based on information derived from the *IMDB Pro* MovieMeter Data Table for each film.

the film that appeared in entertainment media outlets for the week. These articles don't just happen – they are seeded by the publicity team who release to the media stills, concept art, interviews, etc, all according to a predetermined plan and schedule.

I picked a random week, October 9, and compared *John Carter*, *The Hunger Games*, and *The Avengers* side by side. *The Hunger Games* publicity team had generated 72 articles placed for the week; *The Avengers* had placed 149 articles; the *John Carter* team had generated a total of 9 article placements.

Nine?

I then looked at the entire month of October and compared the article output as monitored by *IMDB Pro*. The score for October?

Avengers 640, *Hunger Games* 224, *John Carter* 31.

Taking the entire period from the end of August until the end of November, the disparity remained the same -- both *Avengers* and *Hunger Games* were well over 1,000 articles, and *John Carter*?

A whopping 45 articles.

Or, stated differently: *IMDB* was monitoring a little over four articles per week about *John Carter*, versus well over 100 per week for the other two.

What did it mean?

Unless there was something I was missing -- it seemed clear that the *John Carter* promotional campaign was being severely and inexplicably out-hustled and outworked by each of the other two films. If there were a ten point scale for ranking effort expended to promote, *The Avengers* would rate a 9.4, *The Hunger Games* would rate an 8.9 for its promotional effort, and *John Carter* would be lucky to rate a 3.0.

Complacency? Impossible.

Because of its $250M price tag, the "bar" that *John Carter* had to get over was higher than the bar for either *The Avengers*, which had a reported cost of $220M, or *The Hunger Games*, with a budget of $80M. Plus *John Carter* was closer to its release date than either of the other two -- meaning it was deeper into its promotional campaign and should be operating with a greater sense of urgency than either of the other two, not lesser.

I tried to imagine any scenario under which it would make sense for *John Carter*, during a critical period just months before its release, to go silent like this. Could there be some artful "lie low" rationale that would explain *John Carter* being silent while other "tentpole" releases were grinding out the "buzz fodder"?

I couldn't think of any.

It made no sense.

No sense at all.

Clearly something was seriously amiss.

PART ONE

THE FIRST 95 YEARS

A Gift for "Damphool" Narrative

In the summer of 1911, Edgar Rice Burroughs was a desperate man, and defeat was at his doorstep. He would later calculate that before his circumstances changed for the better, he had slogged through 18 jobs and business schemes without success. At 35, he was able to keep his family of four fed and clothed only through regular visits to a nearby pawnshop and the occasional largesse of his wife's wealthy and generous family. He had pawned his wife's jewelry and his watch and now there was nothing left to pawn. Burroughs needed a solution.

Again and again he answered blind newspaper ads but no salaried jobs materialized. He eventually cobbled together a few dollars which allowed him to buy agency rights for a company selling pencil sharpeners. He borrowed office space, recruited a team of subagents, and set out once again to make a go of it as an entrepreneur -- only this time, fate intervened.

Frequently alone in the borrowed office space while his subagents were out making calls, he began reading the pulp magazines of the Frank A. Munsey company -- *Argosy*, *All-Story*, and others. The pulps had evolved out of the dime novels of the previous century, and had formed a key place in the culture of America since 1896 when *Argosy*, the first pulp, began publication. The magazines delivered 192 pages of all-fiction entertainment for the bargain price of 10 cents. *All-Story* liked to boast: "192 pages -- All stories--stories of rapid action and stirring adventure, stories with sweep and go to them. Stories without tiresome descriptions or baffling dialect."[8]

As he read the tales of adventure, romance, and mystery, he became convinced that he could replicate and probably improve upon the stories he was reading. He famously said of his entry into the writing arena: "...if people were paid for writing rot such as I read in some of those magazines, that I could write stories just as rotten. As a matter of fact, although I had never written a story, I knew absolutely that I could write stories just as entertaining and probably a whole lot more so than any I chanced to read in those magazines."[9]

In attempting imaginative fiction for the pulps, Burroughs had substantial personal experience to draw on. Before settling down in Chicago he had attended various military schools and academies; he had volunteered for the Rough Riders; he had panned gold and carried the mail on horseback in Idaho; he had served as a cavalryman chasing the last Apache holdouts in Arizona; and he had served as a detective for a railroad company in Salt Lake City.

For his first literary effort, he chose to pose a highly imaginative "what if" scenario: What if a Virginia civil war cavalryman was mysteriously transported to Mars, there to find himself captive among a warlike tribe of fifteen-foot tall, six-limbed Tharks, only to later find

[8] Sam Moskowitz, *Under the Moons of Mars, A History of the Scientific Romance* (Holt Rinehart Winston, 1970) 308, 5 Sep 2012 <http://ia600801.us.archive.org/5/items/ UnderTheMoonsOfMars_768/ UnderTheMoonsOfMarsEditedBySamMoskowitz1970.pdf>.

[9] Edgar Rice Burroughs, "How I Wrote the Tarzan Books," *Washington Post and New York World Sunday Supplement*, October 27, 1929, 3 Sep 2012< http://www.erbzine.com/ mag0/0052.html#>.

himself caught up in an epic war between nations of humans including Dejah Thoris, the incomparable Princess of Helium, with whom he falls in love and for whom he would lay down his life?

He initially titled the story: *My First Adventure on Mars*, then retitled it *The Green Martians*, before finally submitting under the title *Dejah Thoris, Martian Princess* using the pseudonym "Normal Bean."

"I had never met an editor, or an author, or a publisher," Burroughs would later write in his autobiography. "I had no idea how to submit a story or what I could expect to get in payment. Had I known anything about it at all I would not have thought of submitting half a novel."[10]

Securing a supply of onionskin stationery of *The American Genealogical Society*, Burroughs began to write.[11]

THE STORY

As Burroughs commenced writing in the summer of 1911, he had no inkling that the words he first wrote would begin a process that would see him transformed in a few short years from a desperate, failed entrepreneur to the most popular author on the face of the planet.

What was his unique appeal?

A close examination of the opening pages of his first published story provides clues to a genius that is more psychological than literary -- a sly and natural sense of how to vividly evoke his settings and engage readers with his characters.

---

[10] Irwin Porges, *Edgar Rice Burroughs, the Man Who Created Tarzan*, (Brigham Young University Press, 1975) p110.

[11] It is recommended to be at least minimally exposed to the actual text of *A Princess of Mars* in order to weigh the discussion which will follow throughout the remainder of *John Carter and the Gods of Hollywood*. The text of *A Princess of Mars* is readily available through Project Gutenberg at <http://www.gutenberg.org/ebooks/8748>. An excellent free eBook version is Art Mayo, *Best Edition of John Carter*, (Mousecatcher Media, 2012), text available online at <http://thejohncarterfiles.com/2012/02/cosmic-knight-errantry-why-i-love-princess-of-mars-by-art-mayo/> Additionally, the Library of Congress has an excellent online "First Edition" simulation at <http://read.gov/books/pageturner/princess_mars/>.

DEJAH THORIS, MARTIAN PRINCESS

by Normal Bean (Edgar Rice Burroughs)

FOREWORD

To the Reader of this Work:

In submitting Captain Carter's strange manuscript to you in book form, I believe that a few words relative to this remarkable personality will be of interest.

My first recollection of Captain Carter is of the few months he spent at my father's home in Virginia, just prior to the opening of the civil war. I was then a child of but five years, yet I well remember the tall, dark, smooth-faced, athletic man whom I called Uncle Jack.

He seemed always to be laughing; and he entered into the sports of the children with the same hearty good fellowship he displayed toward those pastimes in which the men and women of his own age indulged; or he would sit for an hour at a time entertaining my old grandmother with stories of his strange, wild life in all parts of the world. We all loved him, and our slaves fairly worshipped the ground he trod.

He was a splendid specimen of manhood, standing a good two inches over six feet, broad of shoulder and narrow of hip, with the carriage of the trained fighting man. His features were regular and clear cut, his hair black and closely cropped, while his eyes were of a steel gray, reflecting a strong and loyal character, filled with fire and initiative. His manners were perfect, and his courtliness was that of a typical southern gentleman of the highest type.

The frame story would become one of the signatures of Burroughs' narrative strategy. Knowing that he would be taking the reader on what he would later term a "damphool species of narrative,"[12] Burroughs always hastened to convey to the reader that he was acting in the role of messenger only, delivering a narrative that had in some fashion been delivered to him by a third party. It was an affectation of course - but an effective one.

In this case, he uses the character Burroughs in the frame story to offer an objective if somewhat idealized portrait, quickly sketching Carter

---

[12] Bill Hillman, Erbzine, "Edgar Rice Burroughs Bio Timeline 1910-1919", Erbzine, 2 Sep 2012, <http://www.erbzine.com/bio/years10.html>, citing March 6, 1912 Letter from Edgar Rice Burroughs to Thomas Newell Metcalf, editor of *All-Story*.

as a man who embodies the characteristics that every virtuous man would like to possess, from the "splendid specimen of manhood," to "loyal character, fire, and initiative." This segment sets up Carter as a man worthy of respect and admiration, but intentionally does not allow us to see inside the character of the man.

Burroughs then describes how Captain Carter was absent for "15 or 16 years" during which the war was fought and lost, and when Carter returned, he was genial as before, but did not seem to have aged appreciably. Burroughs also observes: "when he thought himself alone I have seen him sit for hours gazing off into space, his face set in a look of wistful longing and hopeless misery; and at night he would sit thus looking up into the heavens, at what I did not know until I read his manuscript years afterward."

Soon Carter begins to narrate his own story:

> I am a very old man; how old I do not know. Possibly I am a hundred, possibly more; but I cannot tell because I have never aged as other men, nor do I remember any childhood. So far as I can recollect I have always been a man, a man of about thirty. I appear today as I did forty years and more ago, and yet I feel that I cannot go on living forever; that some day I shall die the real death from which there is no resurrection. I do not know why I should fear death, I who have died twice and am still alive; but yet I have the same horror of it as you who have never died, and it is because of this terror of death, I believe, that I am so convinced of my mortality.

> And because of this conviction I have determined to write down the story of the interesting periods of my life and of my death. I cannot explain the phenomena; I can only set down here in the words of an ordinary soldier of fortune a chronicle of the strange events that befell me during the ten years that my dead body lay undiscovered in an Arizona cave.

As soon as Carter himself begins to speak, the reader is drawn in by the carefully implanted contradictions between the third-person physical description by Burroughs, and the inner monologue of the actual character John Carter. The "splendid specimen of manhood" tells the reader he is actually a "very old man" who does not know how old he is, and has always appeared "about thirty." He claims to have "died twice and am still alive" -- but knows he is mortal and has a very human "terror of death." Because of this, Carter tells us, he has decided to write down a narrative of the (adroitly understated) "interesting periods of my life and death", acknowledging that "I cannot explain the phenomena", and then promising to tell the story as an "ordinary soldier of fortune" -- although the reader knows instinctively that this is an extraordinary man, yet one who seems quite real, is compellingly spiritual, and does not, evidently, have all the answers in spite of all the superlatives heaped on him by the Burroughs character.

It was Thornton Wilder who said: "There is something mysterious about the endowment of the storyteller. Some very great writers possessed very little of it, and some others, lightly esteemed, possessed it in so large a measure that their books survive down the ages, to the confusion of severer critics."[13] Burroughs was a natural storyteller, and the opening paragraphs of *A Princess of Mars* confirmed it.

In a few words Burroughs introduces a mysteriously alluring character. As Lance Salvosa would put it 100 years later: "Best of all was the timeless mystery and white-hot courage of John Carter himself. He didn't know how old he was; he only knew what mattered. And there was something stirring and meaningful about that."[14]

A few paragraphs later Carter infuses his narrative with sly, ironic humor:

> At the close of the Civil War I found myself possessed of several hundred thousand dollars (Confederate) and a captain's commission in the cavalry arm of an army which no longer existed; the servant of a state which had vanished with the hopes of the South. Masterless, penniless, and with my only means of livelihood, fighting, gone, I determined to work my way to the southwest and attempt to retrieve my fallen fortunes in a search for gold.

His travels take him to Arizona, where, pursued by Apaches, he takes shelter in a cave where he is overcome by drowsiness, so that a sense of "delicious dreaminess" overcomes him, and is at the point of giving in to

---

[13] Thornton Wilder, "Thornton Wilder on Playwriting," DoodleMeister.com, 5 Oct 2010, 2 Sep 2012 <http://doodlemeister.com/2011/10/05/thornton-wilder-on-playwriting. > .

[14] Lance Salvosa, Weblog Comment, "Readers Describe How They Discovered John Carter," The John Carter, Comment by Lance Salvosa, 19 Jul 2012, 5 Nov 2012 <http://thejohncarterfiles.com/2012/07/readers-describe-how-they-discovered-john-carter-what-about-you/>.

his desire to sleep when he hears horses approaching and attempts to spring to his feet, only to be "horrified to discover the my muscles refused to respond to my will." He then notices a vapor filling the cave, and concludes initially that he has been overcome by poisonous gas. The sound of horses are revealed to be Apaches, who climb to the entrance of the cave, look at Carter's prostrate body, and recoil in fear, leaving him where he lies.

Then, with the Apaches gone, a new terror -- from the cave, out of sight to Carter's rear, the sound of a "low, distinct moaning." Carter hears it approach, yet he cannot move - he is paralyzed. He ponders his predicament:

> To be held paralyzed, with one's back toward some horrible and unknown danger from the very sound of which the ferocious Apache warriors turn in wild stampede, as a flock of sheep would madly flee from a pack of wolves, seems to me the last word in fearsome predicaments for a man who had ever been used to fighting for his life with all the energy of a powerful physique.

He lies still, unable to move, until near midnight, when suddenly he hears the moaning again.

> The shock to my already overstrained nervous system was terrible in the extreme, and with a superhuman effort I strove to break my awful bonds. It was an effort of the mind, of the will, of the nerves; not muscular, for I could not move even so much as my little finger, but none the less mighty for all that. And then something gave, there was a momentary feeling of nausea, a sharp click as of the snapping of a steel wire, and I stood with my back against the wall of the cave facing my unknown foe.

Carter stands above the "lifeless clay" of his former body, and wonders "Have I indeed passed over forever into that other life?" But he can feel his heart pounding; he can feel the cold sweat.....At the entrance to the cave he looks into the Arizona moonlit landscape.

> My attention was quickly riveted by a large red star close to the distant horizon. As I gazed upon it I felt a spell of overpowering fascination—it was Mars, the god of war, and for me, the fighting man, it had always held the power of irresistible enchantment. As I gazed at it on that far-gone night it seemed to call across the unthinkable void, to lure me to it, to draw me as the lodestone attracts a particle of iron.

My longing was beyond the power of opposition; I closed my eyes, stretched out my arms toward the god of my vocation and felt myself drawn with the suddenness of thought through the trackless immensity of space. There was an instant of extreme cold and utter darkness.

Next, under the Chapter title "My Advent on Mars," Carter relates:

I opened my eyes upon a strange and weird landscape. I knew that I was on Mars; not once did I question either my sanity or my wakefulness. I was not asleep, no need for pinching here; my inner consciousness told me as plainly that I was upon Mars as your conscious mind tells you that you are upon Earth. You do not question the fact; neither did I.

I found myself lying prone upon a bed of yellowish, mosslike vegetation which stretched around me in all directions for interminable miles. I seemed to be lying in a deep, circular basin, along the outer verge of which I could distinguish the irregularities of low hills.

He is naked, and his attempts at locomotion produce "a series of evolutions which even then seemed ludicrous in the extreme." He finds that he must learn to walk all over again due to the lower gravity. In spite of the difficulty with walking he is determined to explore a walled structure, about four feet in height, which is adjacent to where he finds himself. That structure turns out to be an incubator, filled with eggs of uniform size, about two-and-one-half feet in diameter. He then describes the creatures that are emerging from the eggs:

Five or six had already hatched and the grotesque caricatures which sat blinking in the sunlight were enough to cause me to doubt my sanity. They seemed mostly head, with little scrawny bodies, long necks and six legs, or, as I afterward learned, two legs and two arms, with an intermediary pair of limbs which could be used at will either as arms or legs. Their eyes were set at the extreme sides of their heads a trifle above the center and protruded in such a manner that they could be directed either forward or back and also independently of each other, thus permitting this queer animal to look in any direction, or in two directions at once, without the necessity of turning the head.

The ears, which were slightly above the eyes and closer together, were small, cup-shaped antennae, protruding not more than an inch on these young specimens. Their noses were but longitudinal slits in the center of their faces, midway between their mouths and ears.

14

There was no hair on their bodies, which were of a very light yellowish-green color. In the adults, as I was to learn quite soon, this color deepens to an olive green and is darker in the male than in the female. Further, the heads of the adults are not so out of proportion to their bodies as in the case of the young.

The iris of the eyes is blood red, as in Albinos, while the pupil is dark. The eyeball itself is very white, as are the teeth. These latter add a most ferocious appearance to an otherwise fearsome and terrible countenance, as the lower tusks curve upward to sharp points which end about where the eyes of earthly human beings are located. The whiteness of the teeth is not that of ivory, but of the snowiest and most gleaming of china. Against the dark background of their olive skins their tusks stand out in a most striking manner, making these weapons present a singularly formidable appearance.

Carter then acknowledges that he made most of the reported observations later, for he is warned by the rattling of accoutrements of an advancing adult warrior of the same species, riding upon an 8-legged thoat and bearing down on him with a lance that would have impaled him had his reflexes and newfound jumping ability not allowed him to leap high and out of harm's way. This technique -- giving a detailed physical description of each new creature upon its first appearance -- is one that Burroughs repeats throughout the story and indeed through all of his subsequent John Carter stories, and is a unique technique. While using this almost scientific descriptive technique, as opposed to a more impressionistic one, slows the narrative down momentarily, it has the effect implanting the fully described alien image vividly on the imagination of the reader, and may represent at least one piece of the puzzle to Burroughs' accomplished ability to make Barsoom come alive in the mind of the reader.

As Carter leaps out of the way of the oncoming lamp, flinging himself thirty feet into the air, his remarkable ability to "sak" ('jump' in Barsoomian) provokes Tars Tarkas, the leader of the group of "Tharks", the green Martian adults, to come forward and make gestures of peace, which Carter reciprocates, and he is then taken peacefully by the Tharks to their encampment, where the next phase of his adventure begins.

This opening sequence reveals much about Burroughs' style and peculiar narrative gifts. Much has been made of the fact that he dispenses with any attempt at scientific explanation of John Carter's passage to Mars, and this is often referred to as a liability. Very little has been written about the very spiritual nature of how Burroughs engineers the passage; how John Carter experiences death or at least a deathlike state in the cave in Arizona; how he is unsure whether he has passed into the afterlife; and how he then feels an intense longing for Mars before being drawn there and awakening naked, a newborn, among the newborn Tharks.

With images of death and rebirth; of peculiar creatures at the first moment of their lives paired with Carter at the first moment of his advent on Barsoom, Burroughs has deftly propelled the reader through time and space to a moment of rebirth with Carter -- a moment of spiritual and corporeal renewal on a new world. Earth is left behind; Carter does not mention it, he does not think of it; he does not yearn for it. He is, by implication, precisely where he is meant to be, and the reader is right there with him, ready to explore, ready to be immersed in a world which thus far has just begun to be revealed only in one small way -- an ochre desert, and an incubator, and fifteen foot high green warriors.

Continuing the story.....

Tars Tarkas and the Tharks take Carter to the foot of nearby mountains and into a ruined city, where in and around the central plaza are encamped as many as 1000 Tharks. Carter the observer provides detailed -- but never so lengthy as to interrupt the force of the narrative -- descriptions of what he sees; the males, the females, the children, the city.

Carter is taken by Tars Tarkas, whom Carter discerns is vice-chieftain of the community, to Lorquas Ptomel, the chieftain. Carter encounters difficulty walking and as a result finds himself "skipping and flitting about among the chairs and desks like some monstrous grasshopper." This results in one of the warriors grabbing him:

> I was roughly jerked to my feet by a towering fellow who laughed heartily at my misfortunes.
>
> As he banged me down upon my feet his face was bent close to mine and I did the only thing a gentleman might do under the circumstances of brutality, boorishness, and lack of consideration for a stranger's rights; I swung my fist squarely to his jaw and he went down like a felled ox. As he sunk to the floor I wheeled

around with my back toward the nearest desk, expecting to be overwhelmed by the vengeance of his fellows, but determined to give them as good a battle as the unequal odds would permit before I gave up my life.

My fears were groundless, however, as the other Martians, at first struck dumb with wonderment, finally broke into wild peals of laughter and applause. I did not recognize the applause as such, but later, when I had become acquainted with their customs, I learned that I had won what they seldom accord, a manifestation of approbation.

Having proved his mettle, Carter is granted status as an "honored prisoner." This scene too hints at one of Burroughs' unique gifts. The physical challenge met by John Carter is predictable; the reaction of the Tharks is not. Burroughs intrigues the reader as he allows the exposition -- in this case the Thark code of honor and ethics -- to spring from the action and create in Carter a moment of epiphany. Think how much more effective this is than simply having Carter explain that the Tharks so respect fighting valor that it trumps their notion of friend or foe? It is vivid, and Carter's epiphany is shared by the reader, and Thark culture comes alive.

Carter is turned over to Sola, a Thark female, for training in the language and ways of the green Martians. She takes him to her quarters, then calls in the creature that will be Carter's watchdog and guardian, Woola, the calot:

It waddled in on its ten short legs, and squatted down before the girl like an obedient puppy. The thing was about the size of a Shetland pony, but its head bore a slight resemblance to that of a frog, except that the jaws were equipped with three rows of long, sharp tusks.

Sola stared into the brute's wicked-looking eyes, muttered a word or two of command, pointed to me, and left the chamber. I could not but wonder what this ferocious-looking monstrosity might do when left alone in such close proximity to such a relatively tender morsel of meat; but my fears were groundless, as the beast, after surveying me intently for a moment, crossed the room to the only exit which led to the street, and lay down full length across the threshold.

And so within a few short chapters, Burroughs has established John Carter's narrative voice and with it his character; transported him to Mars through a death/rebirth scenario; and twice through a combination of wit and physical skills, Carter has not only survived threat -- he has made an impression and won allies. This is a pattern that is essential to Burroughs' approach -- Carter is threatened occasionally, each threat proves a trial which advances him on the scale of Thark culture, allowing him to win additional allies, gain stature, and progress in his new world. The narrative does not rely on major action sequences; rather the reader is pulled forward with astonished delight as each new detail of the strange world of Barsoom is revealed, and John Carter reveals different aspects of his intelligence, courage, and humanity.

Most importantly, the reader is on the journey with Carter -- for the most part the reader encounters Barsoom as Carter encounters it, with the only concession to exposition being that Carter frequently reveals knowledge of Thark culture out of sequence--drawing on later-acquired knowledge when describing his first encounter with different aspects of the society. Burroughs' choices in how he layers in the exposition are extraordinarily deft--he repeatedly finds just the right mixture of current scene description; latter-acquired knowledge; and character response to the surroundings.

Burroughs, the first time author dealing with creation of an entire planet and host of planetary cultures, is off and running with a narrative that matches the same deftness that John Carter manages in his achieving a special status among the Tharks.[15]

Half a continent away from Burroughs' Chicago home, in New York, the vividly compelling early chapters of his story quickly caught the eye of Burroughs' first publisher.

THE SALE

Burroughs had made his first submission of the story when it was a little more than half finished. On August 14, 1911, he mailed the partially finished 43,000 word manuscript to *Argosy* Magazine, 175 Fifth Avenue, New York City. It was only 10 days later when Thomas Newell

---

[15] For a complete summary of *A Princess of Mars*, I suggest: <http://www.erblist.com/erblist/pomsummary.html>.

Metcalf, the managing editor of *All-Story* (a sister publication of *Argosy*), replied with a provisional approval and notes requesting that Burroughs speed up the beginning so as to get John Carter to Mars without delay. Burroughs responded immediately, completing the story and mailing in a 63,000 word manuscript on September 28, 1911.

There followed a period of impatient waiting for Burroughs, until on November 4 Metcalf made an offer of four hundred dollars for first serial rights only--Burroughs would retain all other rights.   Burroughs accepted, with the caveat the he hoped to earn better rates for future stories, and on November 17th Burroughs received a check in the amount of $400, representing the equivalent of six months' salary. While falling short of full salvation, Burroughs fortunes, it seemed, had finally taken a turn for the better.[16]

To Burroughs, it all seemed very easy. He made the decision to make writing his career, but was, as he put it, "canny enough not to give up my job." [17]

FIRST PUBLICATION

The story appeared in the February 1912 edition of *All-Story* as *Under the Moons of Mars*.   *All-Story* promoted it to the readers as "a surprisingly vivid interplanetary romance."   The theme of "romance" would again be emphasized as Part 1 of the series was entitled: "Under the Moons of Mars: Part I, the Romance of a Soul Astray." [18]

---

[16] Bill Hillman, "The Business Correspondence of Edgar Rice Burroughs and Thomas Newell Metcalf, Editor of *All-Story* Magazine, Part 1," 2 Sep 2012, <http://www.erbzine.com/mag28/2832.html>.

[17] Edgar Rice Burroughs, Washington Post and New York World Sunday Supplement, "How I Wrote the Tarzan Books," 27 Oct 1929, <http://www.erbzine.com/mag0/0052.html#>.

[18] The exact meaning of the word "romance" in 1912 still retained connotations of its medieval meaning of a narrative in one of the Romance dialects (i.e. not in Latin) "treating of heroic, fantastic, or supernatural events"<http://dictionary.reference.com/browse/romance>, and not necessarily promising a "romance" novel in the sense that we understand it today.

The story thrilled the readers of *All-Story*, hundreds of whom wrote in to praise it, and its serial run, which began in February 1912 and ran for six months, including April, when America was convulsed over the story of the sinking of the *Titanic*. It concluded in July with the story ending on a cliffhanger note, with Carter marooned on Earth and Dejah Thoris left behind on Mars:

> I can see her shining in the sky through the little window by my desk, and tonight she seems calling to me again as she had not called before since that long dead night.
>
> I think I can see, across that awful abyss, a beautiful black-haired woman standing in the garden of a palace, and at her side is a little boy who puts his arm around her as she points to the sky toward the planet earth.
>
> I think I see them, and something tells me that I shall soon know.

All-Story circulation jumped, and the magazine was flooded with letters of approbation.   These came at a time when the entire pulp industry was under pressure to evolve, as rising costs were threatening the viability of the 10 cent, 192-page formula.   So strong was the response to Burroughs' story, that Munsey decided to use it as the launch pad for a long-contemplated experiment that was necessary to the magazine's survival -- a price increase from 10 to 15 cents per issue.[19] Such an increase needed the strongest possible launch position, and the readership increase experience by *All-Story* during the five month run of *Under the Moons of Mars* was just that boost, and thus is was in July of 1912 that the increase in price from 10 to 15 cents, and an increase in pages from 192 to 240, was implemented.

That Burroughs' first effort had made a huge impact was undeniable, but what differentiated it from the other stories of the day?

Sam Moskowitz writes in his "History of the Scientific Romance":[20]

> Those who have gained a stereotyped concept of Burroughs as a writer who conveys his plot line on a nonstop Jetstream of action, moving his characters along so swiftly that readers cannot react to his laws, are in great error. The fascination of Burroughs rests in

---

[19] Moskowitz, 303.

[20] Moskowitz, 336.

the careful delineation of the *setting* in which he has placed his characters and the sharpness with which he etches them, presenting their weaknesses as well as strengths, their eccentricities, philosophies, and environmental shapings. A character may be villainous in motivation, but nevertheless strikingly courageous. A hero may do a foolish or unbecoming deed through pride or vanity. Political expediency may turn enemies into allies and then into firm friends.

The "careful delineation" that Moskowitz refers to is indeed one of the particular aspects of genius that Burroughs displays, for it includes two competing components--completeness on the one hand, and brevity on the other. Burroughs carefully seeded his stories with exposition of the world encountered by parsing the details in manageable doses, always doing so without derailing the forward momentum of the story, and never in such large doses as to overwhelm the audience.

The result of Burroughs' artful expertise in this area is that his world of Barsoom ultimately contains more detail of flora and fauna, natural history, cultural and political history, and geography than virtually any imaginary world, and yet all of this is created within the spare confines of novels that ran from 60,000 to 90,000 words. (For reference -- *Lord of the Rings* novels average more than 200,000 words each.)

In Donald Maas' acclaimed analysis of the techniques of best selling authors, *The Fire In Fiction*, he writes of setting:[21] "You must instill the soul of a place into your characters' hearts and make them grapple with it as surely as they grapple with the main problem and their enemies." This formulation seems to precisely capture the manner in which Burroughs created an instant and ever evolving bond between John Carter and Barsoom -- a bond that begins with the spiritual nature of his transport there, and the yearning that accompanies it. Carter is drawn to Mars; he feels his destiny is there and, with it, a solution to the emptiness of his life on Earth. Once there, each succeeding revelation increases his, and the readers', fascination with the history and culture that he encounters.

But vivid settings aside, Burroughs also found a way to speak to the heart of his readers in a way that some have described as "wish-fulfillment" fantasy, wherein the protagonist becomes the avatar of the

---

[21] Donald Maas, *The Fire In Fiction*, Writer's Digest Books, 2009, Chapter 4 (Ebook)

reader in exploring and experiencing worlds, relationships, and adventures that feed a deeply felt and undernourished need.

Writing about the wish-fulfillment component of Burroughs' stories, Abraham Sherman notes that the reader feels "safe" with a protagonist he or she can trust in an environment of extreme risk and challenge, and this is fundamentally different from "serious literature" and its focus on character growth and development. While ERB's heroes have unique personality and enough foibles to feel real -- they are without a doubt role models with a sort of mythic goodness and unbeatable resolve that is deeply satisfying. Writes Sherman:[22]

> The idea of being presented with an ennobling example of the good to inspire readers upward in their thinking is considered by some critics today as idealistic and merely a distraction from the seriousness of "real life." Those critics think that people who dwell too much on "impossible" goodness will do themselves a disservice by not grappling with reality.....if Burroughs was an iconoclast against any idea, he was against the human tendency to let other human beings define what is possible. His unmatched imagination was practically one big protest statement against letting others limit us.

Art Mayo would speak of Carter as embodying a kind of "cosmic knight errantry" and in this he was onto something. Indeed, after accepting *A Princess of Mars*, Metcalf solicited from Burroughs a "serial of the regular romantic type, something like, say, Ivanhoe, or at least of the period when *everybody* wore armor and dashed about rescuing fair ladies."[23] Metcalf too had discerned that beneath the interplanetary surface of Burroughs story beat the heart of a tale of chivalry and honor, or love and sacrifice.

Mayo writes:[24]

[22] Abraham Sherman, Weblog Comment, *The John Carter Files*, 19 Jul 2012, 2 Sep 2012 <http://thejohncarterfiles.com/2012/07/a-teacher-takes-on-john-carter-the-storytelling/#comments>.

[23] Porges, 115-118, <http://www.erbzine.com/mag36/3601.html>.

[24] Art Mayo, *Best Edition of John Carter*, (Mousecatcher Media, 2012), Introduction, <http://thejohncarterfiles.com/2012/02/cosmic-knight-errantry-why-i-love-princess-of-mars-by-art-mayo/>.

With its beautiful maiden, its swordplay, and its faithful hound; its horsemanship (albeit upon 'thoats'), its seamanship (albeit upon the air), its clashing of rival kingdoms – it makes romance a thing alive once more. Six hundred years after the close of the age of knights, it furnishes the possibility of new vistas for chivalrous deeds – and in the modern age. John Carter is, in the words of Princess Dejah Thoris, "a queer mixture of child and man, of brute and noble." And in this he is little different to the ideal knight described by C. S. Lewis: "a man of blood and iron, a man familiar with the sight of smashed faces and the ragged stumps of lopped-off limbs; [as well as] a demure, almost a maidenlike, guest in hall, a gentle, modest, unobtrusive man.

If the "knightliness" of John Carter resonated with readers of the day as something familiar and appealing, there was an aspect to Burroughs characterization that was unique -- and that was the "superpowers" that Carter possessed once being transported to Mars, where the lesser gravity rendered him stronger, and faster, and able to leap thirty-five feet into the air and 100 feet distant. An ordinary mortal on Earth, Carter was the prototypical Superhero on Mars, and his added strength and agility, coupled with his honor and loyalty, made him into a character who provided wish fulfillment gratification to readers who sought escape from drab lives, and ordinary circumstances.

Many years after Burroughs first wrote, the concept of "escape fiction" would be advanced -- literature which allowed the audience to escape its workaday world and enter a realm of adventure, excitement, and romance -- and Burroughs clearly was a leader of the emerging tradition, fed by the pulps, of this type of world.

But Burroughs' writing, beginning with *A Princess of Mars*, proved capable of striking a response more deeply felt than simple escape. Burroughs seemed to inherently grasp the diminishment of the grandness of America that came with the closing of the frontier a mere decade earlier. He had participated in the final death throes of the Indian Wars, chasing Geronimo and the last Apache stragglers through an Arizona that matches that which John Carter found himself in, and implicit in his prose was not just the escape from ordinariness, but also what Thomas Bertonneau terms a "conservationist" streak: "The

Burroughsian landscapes are less "escapist" than "conservationist," preserving in memory the primitive live of everyone's ancestors."[25]

And so in the early months of 1912 a new star of the pulps was born, and Burroughs would soon tower as the strongest force in the pulps, a purveyor of "scientific romance" that would soon evolve into science fiction later in the century -- a century whose first half would be dominated by Burroughs.

---

[25] Thomas Bertonneau, "Edgar Rice Burroughs and the Masculine Narrative," *Brussels Journal*, 27 Aug 2009, 2 Sep 2012 < http://www.brusselsjournal.com/node/4066>.

BURROUGHS AND HOLLYWOOD 1912-1950

In a letter on March 6, 1912, shortly after *Under the Moons of Mars* had been published, Burroughs described a new novel he was working on:[26]

> The story I am now on is the scion of a noble English house -- of the present time -- who was born in tropical Africa where the parents die when he was about a year old. The infant was found and adopted by a huge she-ape, and was brought up among a band of fierce anthropoids . . .

Burroughs completed the 98,000 word story, which he called *Tarzan of the Apes*, on May 14, 1912, and sent it immediately to Metcalf. Meanwhile Burroughs, out of money and not able to support his family from his primary position at Coleman's Stationery, took a second position as manager for the Bureau of Systems: The Magazine of Business Efficiency. *Tarzan* would so please Metcalf that he paid Burroughs $700 for serial rights, with the much needed check reaching Burroughs on June 26, and devoted an entire *All-Story* edition, October 1912, to the publication of the full story.

---

[26] Porges, 123.

Yet even though Burroughs was a smashing success with both *Under the Moons of Mars* and *Tarzan*, with readers clamoring for a sequel to both, Metcalf objected to the approach Burroughs took with the sequel, *Return of Tarzan*, and turned it down. Burroughs, exhibiting hardheadedness for the first time, stuck to his version and sold it to rival Street and Smith for $1000, which was $300 more than Metcalf had paid for the serial rights to Tarzan. Metcalf was in trouble with Bob Davis, his managing editor, for letting the most successful author in the *All-Story* stable go to a rival publisher with the sequel to the most successful story ever published by *All-Story*. Soon thereafter Metcalf informed Burroughs that he was being reassigned, and from that point on it was Davis who would handle Burroughs.

The dustup with Metcalf behind him, Burroughs began to churn out stories at a remarkable pace. In 1913 alone Burroughs, by his own reckoning,[27] wrote and submitted stories totaling 413,000 words including *At the Earth's Core*, the first Pellucidar novel of an inner world within the Earth; *The Return of Tarzan; The Cave Girl; Number Thirteen; The Girl from Harris; The Mucker;* and *Warlord of Mars*, the third installment and completion of the initial Martian Trilogy.

But even as his pulp career flourished, Burroughs efforts to get his serialized novels published as books met obstacle after obstacle. Throughout 1913 and into 1914 Burroughs submitted *Tarzan of the Apes* and *Under the Moons of Mars* to book publishers -- but there were no takers. Aside from the blow to Burroughs' ego, this meant that there was no royalty stream of income -- only the payments from the pulps for first serial rights -- and that meant that the money flowed only as long as Burroughs remained productive, which he did.

As the fall of 1913 arrived, and the Chicago winter approached, Burroughs felt the lure of the warm sunshine of California, and in September the author and his family of five left Chicago for California with the expectation that they would spend the winter there, and return to Chicago in the spring.

---

[27] Edgar Rice Burroughs, *Washington Post and New York World Sunday Supplement*, "How I Wrote the Tarzan Books," 27 Oct 1929, 3 Sep 2012 <http://www.erbzine.com/mag0/0052.html#>

With the move to California would come the first steps toward the century-long journey of John Carter, gentleman of Virginia, from pulp pages to cinema screens.

The Burroughs family spent the fall and winter of 1913-1914 in San Diego. Although he was unsuccessful in getting his stories published as novels, Burroughs encountered more success in arranging secondary serialization with newspapers and magazines. By the time the family arrived in California, *Tarzan of the Apes* had been successfully serialized in the *New York Evening World Magazine* Newspaper. Other stories ran in the *Evening World,* and more newspapers began to pick up Burroughs' output. Burroughs and family returned to Chicago, and remained there for two more years -- but the lure of California remained strong.

During the summer of 1916, Burroughs took his entire family, including an Airedale named Tarzan, on a 6,000 mile journey which Burroughs called "auto-gypsying" and lasted three months, ending with the family alighting in Los Angeles, where they took up residence for the winter at a rented house on Hoover Street, a scant four miles from Hollywood. Burroughs continued his prodigious writing output, logging 277,000 words published in spite of the lengthy "gypsying" respite, while also continuing his efforts to get his works produced as motion pictures. Once in Hollywood, he redoubled those efforts.

Hollywood's first Edgar Rice Burroughs story to be released as a film, *The Lad and the Lion,* premiered in May of 1917, less than a month after the US had declared war on Germany and entered World War I. Aside from *The Lad and the Lion,* progress was being made toward the first *Tarzan of the Apes* movie, and in August of that year, trade magazines reported that National Film's Los Angeles studio was in preparation for the production of *Tarzan of the Apes.* For the rights, Burroughs was paid $5,000 cash and given a $50,000 equity share in the movie.

During the fall of 1917, National Film went into production of *Tarzan of the Apes,* principally in Louisiana. It was a grand scale production that included 11,000 extras, 40 aerial acrobats, four lions, six tigers, several elephants, and 18 apes.[28] The struggles of the production were extraordinary and Burroughs, unhappy with the casting of Elmo Lincoln and script of the movie, became disgusted with the motion picture industry in general. He dumped his 10,000 shares of motion picture stock in December, and in January 1918 declined to attend the premiere. The film was a huge success, becoming one of the first motion pictures to gross one million dollars. A year later a second Tarzan movie, *The Romance of Tarzan*, was released, and was also successful.

In spite of his unhappiness with the National Film production of *Tarzan of the Apes*, Burroughs decided that he wished the family to live permanently in California. Eventually in 1922, Burroughs purchased for the then princely sum of $125,000 the legendary Mil Flores country estate -- 540 acres in the foothills of the Santa Monica Mountains in the San Fernando Valley a few miles north of Hollywood. Burroughs re-christened the estate, which included a spectacular Spanish style villa overlooking the mountains to one side and the valley to the other, as "Tarzana." The grand house stood atop a hill and had eighteen rooms and six baths. The hill on which is was situated contained fifteen acres set in flowers, shrubs and trees. Half a mile up the canyon there was a foreman's house, bunkhouses, barns, and corrals.

By all accounts, Burroughs thrived at the Tarzana ranch. Early mornings he would ride into the Santa Monica Mountains; the gardens and pools surrounding the property were delightful for the children, and the proximity to Hollywood was convenient, as evidenced in a letter to Herbert T. Weston dated May 8:[29] "There have been three motion picture men up in the past two days.....I guess our move to sunny Southern Cal will provide profitable from the m.p. standpoint, as I am nearer to where they do it." Burroughs also wrote that "a guy bobbed up day before yesterday with the plan of a whole village he wished to plant in my front

---

[28] For an excellent account of the travails of the production, see Tarzan, Lord of the Louisiana Jungle, a documentary film produced by Al Bohl and Allison Bohl. See: <http://www.tarzanlordlajungle.com/>

[29] Burroughs, Edgar Rice, and Herbert T. Weston, *Brother Men: The Correspondence of Edgar Rice Burroughs and Herbert T. Weston*, (Duke University Press, 2005) 89.

<yard -- school, city hall, banks, business houses, motion picture theater, and it was labelled: City of Tarzana, which sounds like a steamboat."

By 1919, *The Romance of Tarzan* had been completed and successfully released to cinemas. On the Barsoomian front, his Martian trilogy consisting of *A Princess of Mars*, *The Gods of Mars*, and *Warlord of Mars*, was complete, but he had yet to get any bites from Hollywood for the series. Interest remained high in Tarzan, and in 1921 Burroughs' involvement in motion picture production increased with *The Son of Tarzan*, a 15-episode serial by National Film, the same company that had aroused Burroughs' ire with their handling of *Tarzan of the Apes*. Burroughs himself, using his Tarzana Ballroom Theater as editing studio, cut the 15-episode serial into a single feature length picture.

Later that year Burroughs sent a scenario, *Angels' Serenade*, to Century Film Corporation in Hollywood, only to be rejected. Another Tarzan movie -- this one again starring Elmo Lincoln -- followed, entitled *The Adventures of Tarzan*.

Attesting to the popularity of Tarzan, in 1922 the film rights to *Jungle Tales of Tarzan* and *Tarzan and the Jewels of Opar* were sold for what was then an astronomical price of $40,000 to the Stern Brothers and Louis Jacob, who a few months later and partly on the strength of the acquisition of the rights, formed Universal Pictures.

Still no Mars project.

By 1926 the last of the Tarzan silent movies, *Tarzan and the Golden Lion*, was in production, but when Burroughs saw the final product his only comment was that he wished he knew enough about film production to have directed it himself.

Still no Mars project.

Meanwhile, Burroughs fame, and for the most part, his wealth, continued to grow. By the early 1920s, his annual domestic royalties topped $100,000 a year and that was in addition to his first serial rights payments. He became an advocate for author's rights, and he was the first author to self-incorporate, creating Edgar Rice Burroughs, Inc., the company that remains active today and continues to administer his rights. The offices for Edgar Rice Burroughs, Inc., a small bungalow and warehouse built in the style of Spanish farm architecture, were created in

1926 at 18354 Ventura Boulevard and remain the offices of the company today, where a small staff continues to administer the rights and look after the interests of the works of Edgar Rice Burroughs.

THE FLASH GORDON FIASCO

There would always be two strands of the story of how Burroughs' imagination arrived on screens and in the public consciousness -- the direct route, through adaptation of Burroughs material with attribution to Burroughs, and the indirect route, where Burroughs' imaginative output would be mined (some would say strip-mined) by others. The first major incidence of the latter would take place in the early 1930s, and would concern Flash Gordon.

In 1931, at a time when the Tarzan comic strip was hugely popular, Edgar Rice Burroughs approached United Feature Syndicate, who distributed the *Tarzan* strip, and pitched the idea of a *John Carter* Martian comic strip series to them. Among Burroughs' letters is a 1932 response from George Carlin of United Feature Syndicate indicating that UFS was not on board, and considered the idea as one that could potentially damage their interests in the *Tarzan* strip. "I cannot emphasize too strenuously my own personal feeling that the production of the Martian strips would seriously handicap the *Tarzan* feature."[30]

Two years later, in 1933, Burroughs was in correspondence with King Features Syndicate, a main rival to United, about a *John Carter* strip. That effort progressed encouragingly, with King Features hiring artist Alex Raymond and writer Don G. Moore to develop the script. Burroughs was enthusiastic, but by this time was very savvy about the value of the rights he was offering, and negotiations bogged down. Burroughs insisted on retaining all spin-off rights to the serial, including radio, move serials, TV -- even Big Little Books.

Finally, on January 4, 1934, Burroughs received a letter: "I am sorry to say that at this writing it seems impossible for us to arrange syndication under terms which would suit you." Three days later the

---

[30] Robert R. Barrett, "How John Carter Became Flash Gordon," *Burroughs Bulletin* #60 (19-23) Undated, Accessed 3 Sep 2012 at <http://www.erbzine.com/mag33/3393.html>.

"Flash Gordon" series, a King Features production, began its run. Burroughs' explanation for what happened is found in a letter written a year later, in 1935:[31]

> As to the syndicate that was dickering for the Martian strips, this was the King Features. They approached us, and sample material was sent them which included art work. The New York office okayed everything as well as the terms, but when the idea was submitted to Mr. Hearst for the final stamp of approval it was quickly disapproved, probably because Mr. Hearst felt that a Martian strip could be gotten out cheaper by not having to pay royalties to us. Shortly thereafter 'Flash Gordon' made his appearance in the comics, and this no doubt was the upshot of the matter.

There can be no doubt that Flash Gordon, which went on to huge success as not just a comic strip, but eventually serialized with major success in radio and film, was based in large part on John Carter. Indeed, many of the plot lines are lifted from Edgar Rice Burroughs' Mars and Venus novels, and Flash himself is described as being a superb swordsman operating in places where swordplay is a key form of combat, with powerful earth-man muscles which allow him to make giant leaps.

In 1934 Burroughs formed "Burroughs Tarzan Enterprises" with Ashton Dearholt, an actor who managed after several tries to persuade Burroughs to finance a production company with offices in Hollywood and New York. The first film produced by the company was *The New Adventures of Tarzan* starring Herman Brix (who later changed his name to Bruce Bennett) as Tarzan.[32] Additionally, the company pitched dozens of Burroughs' completed novels and scenarios to various studios. While the company did not prosper, Burroughs' familiarity with Hollywood increased.

---

[31] Barrett, 26

[32] Bill Hillman, "Edgar Rice Burroughs, Film Producer," *Angelfire.com*, 2 Sep 2012, <http://www.angelfire.com/trek/erbzine6/erbz287.html>

CLAMPETT, ERB, AND MGM - THE ANIMATED JOHN CARTER

Bob Clampett was born in 1913 and had grown up next door in Hollywood to Charlie Chaplin, and in 1931 had gone to work as a cartoonist at Harman-Ising Studio, a company who had an output arrangement with Warner Brothers, churning out cartoons that included the very first Merry Melody, which Clampett worked on as a young cartoonist.

Clampett knew his place, up to a point, and that included quietly learning the craft of animating, and only gradually getting involved in generating the story ideas for cartoons, and even then, the idea of contributing ideas for new characters or new series of cartoons was still out of bounds. He was years away from being viewed as senior enough to create new characters or do what he really wanted to do, which was to direct animated shorts and features.

Clampett believed that animation offered far richer possibilities than just the kind of slapstick farm and animal humor that Harman-Ising was outputting to Warner Brothers. Growing up in the twenties, he had eagerly devoured all of Burroughs books, especially the Barsoom series, and saw in it an opportunity for an ambitious realistically drawn fantasy series that would skew more toward adults, but still be accessible to children, and would capture the spirit of adventure and wonder that he had felt when reading the Barsoom novels.

He knew where to find Burroughs -- Tarzana Ranch was by then a landmark in Southern California -- and so he journeyed to the estate and met with Burroughs and told him of his idea to create a series of animated cartoons based on the John Carter character and series.

For his part, Burroughs was immediately interested. One of his great frustrations was that Hollywood, while obsessed, it seemed, with Tarzan, was hesitant to tackle Mars, or any of other Burroughs fantastical other worldly works. Burroughs well understood the reasoning, that the special effects of the day just couldn't match the imagination of what Burroughs had created. Lions, and elephants, and tigers -- yes; banths, and thoats, and ulsios -- not so much.

Perhaps animation was a solution....

Burroughs had another reason for reacting positively. Burroughs' son John Coleman had just graduated from college and had artistic inclinations. He saw in the young Clampett someone who could teach John Coleman a thing or two -- and so he encouraged the project and introduced John Coleman into the mix as a collaborator with Clampett.

Clampett and John Coleman Burroughs worked diligently for months -- nights and weekends for Clampett, since he continued his full-time work for Warner Brothers through Harman-Ising. John Burroughs created detailed colored sketches and sculptured models. Clampett's idea was that the stories would break down into a series of 9 minute installments that could either stand alone as serial installments, or could be combined into a feature length movie.

That Burroughs was enthusiastic was evidenced by the fact that he went out of his way to talk to MGM about it--MGM being the studio of the Johnny Weismuller Tarzan films which were then hugely popular, beginning with *Tarzan the Ape Man* in 1932 and continuing with *Tarzan and His Mate in 1934*, and *Tarzan Escapes* in 1936. The movies, which were the equivalent of the James Bond series of the day, had quickly become a major source of revenue and profits for MGM, so it was logical that Burroughs would look to them -- and logical that they would be open to his approach.

To sell the idea to MGM, Clampett and the younger Burroughs settled on creating six minutes of test footage, to be accompanied by a pitch portfolio that included artwork, selling points, and illustrations from the Barsoom novels.[33]

A cover letter, carefully double-spaced on the letterhead of Edgar Rice Burroughs, Inc, read:

> For twenty-five years we have been awaiting a medium that could properly depict on the screen the highly imaginative Martian creations of Edgar Rice Burroughs.

> In the recently greatly improved cartoon animation technique in color we see that medium, which, in connection with the

---

[33] Bill Hillman, "John Carter Folio," *Erbzine*, 3 Sep 2012 at http://www.erbzine.com/mag21/2175.html.

increasing demand for motion picture shorts, suggests that this is the opportune time to offer the animated cartoon rights in our series of nine Edgar Rice Burroughs Martian novels recording the adventures on the Red Planet of

JOHN CARTER, WARLORD OF MARS

The following pages give a brief summary of a few of the reasons why such a series of animated cartoon shorts in color should produce outstanding results at the box office.

In addition to the nine Martian novels and the magazine publication of these stories, there is now appearing in a cartoon magazine, with a circulation of 500,000 copies a month, a series of four pages of *John Carter of Mars* cartoons in colors, which give this character still wider circulation and publicity. You will find several of these cartoons mounted elsewhere in this brochure.

EDGAR RICE BURROUGHS INC
TARZANA, CALIFORNIA

The text of the presentation pitch, which was hand-drawn on a large spiral portfolio with graphics and illustrations much in the manner of a Powerpoint Presentation today, read:

The name EDGAR RICE BURROUGHS needs no introduction to theater goers.........because during the past 25 years the public has bought more than 20 MILLION COPIES of his adventure novels.

And because MILLIONS OF PEOPLE have seen the 18 motion pictures based on his stories.

So! EDGAR RICE BURROUGHS means BOX OFFICE SUCCESS anywhere!

25 Years ago, EDGAR RICE BURROUGHS created GREAT characters: JOHN CARTER OF MARS ... whose amazing adventures are told in nine popular novels which have sold millions of copies.

WHY has the public THRILLED to the Mars books for 25 years?

Why?/Because ACTION and ROMANCE are the keynotes of the BURROUGHS name.

Because the MARS stories are CHOCK-FULL of ACTION and ROMANCE

Why have the MARS STORIES been translated into MANY DIFFERENT LANGUAGES AND DIALECTS?

Because every GENERATION in EVERY RACE thrills to a HERO who fights 4 armed GREEN men 10 feet High astride 8 legged mounts!

Because PEOPLE GASP AT THE MAN who crosses swords with humans whose heads scamper away from dead bodies.

A HERO who matches wits with PHANTOM BOWMEN, the mental warriors of MASTERMIND OF MARS.

The MARS STORIES have held MILLIONS spellbound because their hero FIGHTS for and LOVES an incomparably EXOTIC MARTIAN PRINCESS.

Do YOU know the FINAL REASON why the MARS STORIES have years of sound publicity behind them?

Here is why: Because the HERO of the MARS books is the HANDSOME, THRILLING, JOHN CARTER OF MARS.

In terms of technique, the test footage created by Clampett and John Coleman Burroughs was different than anything previously seen at the time, and even today looks unusually realistic in his use of color and movement.[34]   Clampett used oil painting to achieve the side shadowing so as to create a different look from the harsh outlining that defined the look of the typical animated film to date.   The test footage included scenes of John Carter running, engaging in a sword-fight, and riding an eight legged thoat.

"We would oil paint the side shadowing frame-by-frame in an attempt to get away from the typical outlining that took place in normal animated films. In the running sequence, for example, there is a subtle blending of figure and line which eliminated the harsh outline. It is more like a human being in tone. We were working in untested territory at that time. There was no animated film to look at to see how it was done," Clampett said.[35]

By all accounts, the presentation to MGM went well.   Burroughs' support to the project, and MGM's success with the Tarzan property, both created a strong predisposition on the part of MGM executives to green-light the project -- and in the presentation meeting, a green light is what Clampett and the younger Burroughs thought they got.

Clampett, convinced he had a deal with MGM for an animated *John Carter, Warlord of Mars* that would become the first animated feature, years ahead of *Snow White* which was then being developed at Disney, quit his job animating for Warners and readied himself for his new adventure on an animated Barsoom.

Then it all fell apart.

"I had already given notice to Warners and was preparing to start on the *John Carter* series when MGM's change in decision came down," Clampett said.   "The studio said, 'No, we do not want the *John Carter* thing; we want *Tarzan.*' Aesthetically, Jack Burroughs and I were very inspired by the Mars project. And the idea, as much as I like Tarzan, to do the alternate series was simply not the same."

---

[34] Youtube Channel "TJStuff1", "John Carter of Mars Animation (Rare) Bob Clampett," *Youtube*, 14 Jul 2008, 2 Sep 2012, <http://youtu.be/bTAlgZlqwnQ>.

[35] Jim Korkis, "Lost Cartoons: The Animated John Carter of Mars," *Jim Hill Media*, June 2003. 2 Sep 2012 <http://www.erbzine.com/mag9/0934.html>.

The exact reasons for MGM backing out of the deal are not fully known, although the reason given to Clampett and Burroughs is that throughout the midwest and south, MGM booking agents responsible for booking theaters for the studio expressed concern that the audiences were not yet ready for adventures on Mars by John Carter or anyone else.

Clampett would end up staying with Warner Brothers, where he would go on to become a legendary animator and animation director, helming dozens of classic Porky Pig, Daffy Duck, Bugs Bunny, and other Merry Melodies cartoons.

John Coleman Burroughs evolved into an excellent illustrator, taking on the job of illustrating some of the later Edgar Rice Burroughs Martian novels -- illustrations which benefited from the extensive work done in support of the Clampett animation project.

After the Clampett episode, efforts to get *John Carter of Mars* on the screen in Hollywood went quiet for a time.

THE SUPERMAN-JOHN CARTER CONNECTION

Even before Burroughs was engaged in the negotiations for a *John Carter* strip that would eventually break down and yield Flash Gordon instead, two young men in Cleveland -- writer Jerry Siegel and artist Joe Shuster, were at work creating the character who would eventually be sold the DC Comics and appear nationally in syndication as Superman in 1938. As recently as 2011, Superman placed Number 1 on IGN's list of top comic Superheroes -- and Superman, like Flash Gordon, owed much to John Carter and Burroughs.

In their early conceptions, Superman's powers were more limited than they would be when the series came to ultimate fruition in 1938. Siegel cited John Carter: "Carter was able to leap great distances because the planet Mars was smaller than the planet Earth; and he had great strength. I visualized the planet Krypton as a huge planet, much larger than Earth."[36]

---

[36] Andrae Nemo, "Superman Through the Ages: The Jerry Siegel and Joe Shuster Interview, Part 8 of 10," *The Classic Comics Library Issue #2*, August 1983, 6-19.

But unlike the Flash Gordon wholesale appropriation of the John Carter character, Siegel found a way to make it unique, and different, while building on the same premise that Burroughs had initially put forward. Superman, unlike John Carter, is not a warrior -- he doesn't kill as a routine part of his existence. His history is that he is the son of a scientist, then is raised by a couple of kindly farmers, and finally finds himself on a planet filled with warring tribes, but rather than becoming part of it first, then rising above it, Superman protects without becoming part of the societies he is protecting. His "otherness" is maintained throughout.[37]

BURROUGHS' FINAL ACT

Burroughs continued to write, pursue his business interests, and dabble in Hollywood. He started a production company and produced his own Tarzan movie, in Guatemala, with decidedly mixed creative, financial, and personal results. He lost money; the movie was disappointing; and the episode played a key role in a divorce from his wife Emma Hulbert Burroughs.

By the time World War II broke out, Burroughs was living in Hawaii, where he witnessed the attack on Pearl Harbor while playing tennis. He was 64 years old at the time, and had accomplished more than the 35-year old failed businessman in Chicago who took up pen to paper in 1911 could have ever dreamed.

After Pearl Harbor, Burroughs signed up to become the oldest War Correspondent in U.S. history, deploying with the troops to the Pacific theater from which he sent dispatches throughout the war.

An article by Lloyd Shearer in Liberty Magazine in 1945 summed up Burroughs profile and global posture in a narrative that has the ring of a Fox Movietone Newsreel in its writing and cadences:[38]

---

[37] For an excellent discussion of John Carter vs Superman see <http://www.sequart.org/magazine/10693/john-carter-vs-superman/>

[38] Lloyd Shearer, "Tarzan and the Man Who Made Him," *Liberty Magazine*, 14 Jul 1945, accessible 3 Sep 2012 at <http://www.erbzine.com/mag31/3159.html>.

Today the more than 30,000,000 copies of his novels in 58 languages and dialects make him the most widely read author on earth. Tidy sales of other items include some 21 Tarzan motion pictures, 364 radio programs, more than 60,000,000 ice-cream cups, 100,000,000 loaves of Tarzan bread, countless numbers of Tarzan school bags, pencils, paint books, penknives, jungle costume, toys, and sweaters. In addition there are the famous Tarzan comic strips, carried by 212 newspapers with a circulation of more than 15,000,000.......In short, in one form or another, Tarzan is known to more people on earth than any other fictional character.

Over the years Burroughs, while gaining wealth and attention, had never achieved "literary" acceptance and while he made a great show of not minding this at all, indications abound that he experienced frustration over the lack of respect afforded him for his efforts. Once, miffed that he had not been included in a "Top Ten" list of authors even though that year he was the third top-selling author in the country, he wrote a letter complaining about it. His frequent complaints about the screen depiction of Tarzan, beginning with the 1918 Elmo Lincoln version but including many of the other productions, ran counter to his protestations that he was in it for the business of it all. And finally, the fact that he suffered throughout his career from a variety of stress induced maladies, none completely debilitating due to his strict work ethic, but troubling nonetheless, provide ample evidence that all was not completely rosy for Burroughs as he continued to grind out his novels, manage his real estate and business interests, and finally pursue one last adventure in the Pacific.

After the Clampett near miss of 1936, the *John Carter* series continued to sell books, but Hollywood took a back seat: *Tarzan* yes, *John Carter* no. Animation had been an option; live action was beyond Hollywood's capability and would remain so for many years.

Burroughs died on March 19, 1950. The New York Times wrote of Burroughs in his obituary:[39]

---

[39] New York Times Staff, "E.R. Burroughs, 74, Created Tarzan," *The New York Times*, 20 Mar 1950: 21.

E.R. Burroughs, 74, Created Tarzan

35,000,000 Books Sold

LOS ANGELES: March 19 - Edgar Rice Burroughs, the novelist, who created the apeman "Tarzan," famed in books and films, died this morning at his Encino home of a heart ailment. His age was 74. The author, who had been ill for three months, had eaten an early breakfast, and was lying in bed reading when death came. His daughter, Joan, and his two sons, John and Hulbert, were at the bedside. Mr. Burroughs had been a shut-in for several years. Confined to a wheelchair by a series of heart attacks, he still derived great pleasure from creating the action necessary for the Tarzan books....

140,000,000 SAW EACH FILM
Creator of the most widely known jungle character of this century, Mr. Burroughs never considered himself in a class with Kipling. That each Tarzan movie was seen by 140,000,000 persons or that his books had sold 35,000,000 copies did not alter his conviction that his success was due to an uncanny faculty for avoiding intellectual precincts. In fifty-six languages vast multitudes read of the tribulations of the Englishman reared by apes in Africa. Two hundred newspapers, forty of them foreign, told, with pictures, how Tarzan fought alongside his animal friends against cruelty and avarice. On the radio and in children's games the loud but limited vocabulary of the jungle monarch was in constant rehearsal.

According to Burroughs' grandson John Ralston Burroughs, who was with him often near the end, Burroughs, who had evolved into an opponent of organized religion, said in his final weeks:[40]

"If there is a hereafter, I want to travel through space to visit the other planets."

His ashes were buried without a marker at the base of a large tree in the front yard of the Spanish cottage housing the offices then, and now, of Edgar Rice Burroughs, Inc..

---

[40] Bill Hillman, "Edgar Rice Burroughs - L. Ron Hubbard Connection, Part IV," Erbzine, 2 Sep 2012 < http://www.erbzine.com/mag23/2344.html>

HARRYHAUSEN TO LUCAS 1950-1980

In the decade after Burroughs' death in 1950 the ERB "brand" went into one of the few declines it has experienced over the full 100 years since *Princess of Mars* was first published in 1912. The attention to the business of Edgar Rice Burroughs, Inc., lapsed, and copyright renewals were not attended to, allowing many of the books to prematurely fall into the public domain. This encouraged more "strip-mining" of the content without attribution or royalties, and many of the great science fiction writers of the day freely mined Burroughs for ideas. The books were gradually going out of print, although most libraries had a reasonable supply. Editions that were available at the time of Burroughs' death included the original A.C. McClurg first edition from 1917, a variety of Grosset and Dunlap reprints issued from 1918 through 1940, and an ERB, Inc. edition, issued in March 1948, two years before the author's death.

During that same decade, Hollywood legend Ray Harryhausen became interested in the Barsoom Series. In the late 1950s Harryhausen, coming off *Jason and the Argonauts* and other successful films, began a campaign to bring *John Carter of Mars* to cinema screens, but even with all his success, the prospect of the visual effects that would be required proved daunting for studios and Harryhausen moved on to other pastures.

In the 1970s an effort to develop the film was mounted in the UK by Raymond Leicestshire. Extensive character and set design studies were completed before the project "went sideways" and was mothballed.

But it was what would become known as the great "Burroughs Revival" of the 1960s that brought the book and all of Burroughs work to a new generation.

THE 1960'S BURROUGHS REVIVAL

Soon after Burroughs' death in 1950, Editor in Chief of Ace Books, Donald A. Wollheim, began pursuit of paperback rights but was unsuccessful. Cyril Rothrund, administrator of Burroughs' estate, simply didn't have interest in pursuing the literary rights, preferring instead to concentrate on the more lucrative film and comic book licenses, as well as the exploitation of Burroughs' real estate investments. Eventually Ace, Ballantine Books, and hardcover publisher Canaveral Press were all interested in securing the rights to publish Burroughs. Recounting the situation in *The Great American Paperback*, Richard A. Lupoff, who edited the Canaveral Burroughs edition and emerged as one of the key figures in the revival, writes:[41]

> In the early 1960s a flaw in the Burroughs copyrights was discovered, and several companies leaped to publish new editions of old Burroughs titles. Wollheim, at Ace, was quick to do so. He obtained a series of glorious cover paintings, many of them by artists who had cut their teeth in the comic-book industry. These included, most notably, Roy G. Krenkel and Frank Frazetta. These Ace singles are among the most beautiful and highly sought of 1960's paperbacks.
>
> Caught sleeping at the switch, members of the Burroughs family finally took action. Hulbert Burroughs, a surviving son, came to

---

[41] Richard A. Lupoff, *The Great American Paperback*, Collector' Press, 2001, Chapter 8

New York to meet with various publishers. The result was an arrangement with Canaveral Press to produce hardcover editions of Burroughs' books. Paperback rights would be divided between Ace and Ballantine Books, with Ballantine getting the more desirable Tarzan and Martian series. Ace had to settle for Burroughs' "hollow earth" and Venusian series. Other one-off's were divided between the two.

The combined output of the three publishing houses resulted in the vast majority of Burroughs' novels becoming available with high visibility and at an affordable price point for a decade beginning in 1963. Suddenly available in every drug store and newsstand, the Ace and Ballantine paperbacks would thrill an entire wave of leading edge Baby Boomers born between 1946 and 1955 -- among them, George Lucas and James Cameron, who would later draw heavily on Burroughs, Lucas in his *Star Wars* series, and Cameron in *Avatar*.

During the 1970s, as George Lucas was emerging as a "name" director in Hollywood, he signed a two-picture deal with Universal Studios to make *American Graffiti*, followed by *Star Wars*. As successful as *American Graffiti* was, it was not enough to persuade Universal to stay the course with Lucas' planned Space Opera, and it was dumped. In coming up with the idea for *Star Wars*, Lucas was later quoted a saying that he had in mind Flash Gordon as a prototype and explored getting the rights to the Gordon franchise, but when that proved elusive he turned to the source material for Flash Gordon - the novels of Edgar Rice Burroughs in particular -- for inspiration.

In its final onscreen iteration, *Star Wars'* six films contain many, many elements that Lucas borrowed from Burroughs, although the overall vision clearly contains a variety of influences. Barsoomian words like Jed, banth, and others were liberally incorporated into the Lucas' universe. *Return of the Jedi*, of all the *Star Wars* episodes, was the most derivative of Burroughs, with its emphasis on swordfights (albeit laser); Jedi knights; and Princess Leia in a Dejah Thoris-styled wardrobe ensemble. The coliseum scene from *Attack of the Clones* was lifted almost wholesale from *A Princess of Mars*, and would become iconic in its own right -- so much so that when Disney's *John Carter* trailers began appearing in late 2011 featuring the original coliseum scene -- it was the "original" that seemed derivative of the copy, not vice versa.

James Hoare, writing in Sci-Fi Now identifies six points of strong similarity:[42]

1. That gold bikini
This can't be anything other than a deliberate tip of the hat, Leia's gold bikini from 1981's Return Of The Jedi is clearly inspired by the skimpy outfits of Dejah Thoris, the Princess Of Mars herself, depicted in the Seventies Marvel comics (as above, obliging chained up for added similarity on the cover of *Warlord Of Mars* issue 11, April 1978) or lurid Frank Frazetta book covers. Oh, and they're both princesses, obviously.

2. Banthas
Great beasts of burden, Bantha are found on Tatooine in the *Star Wars* universe – in Edgar Rice Burroughs' Barsoom stories, Banths are lion-like carnivores that hunt the low hills of Mars

3. The Sith
An ancient and mysterious order of Dark Side Force Users of whom Darth Vader and Darth Maul are members, over in Barsoom the Sith are large predatory insects that have been hunted to the brink of extinction.

4. Jabba's sail barge
Jabba The Hutt's armada of luxury flying platforms, skimming low across the surface of Tatooine wouldn't look out of place in Edgar Rice Burroughs books – the Martians use gravity-defying 'flying boats' to zip across the Mars' otherworldly deserts as depicted above on the 1973 Ballantine Books edition of second book *The Gods Of Mars.*

5. Coliseum battle
Attack Of The Clones' Jedi versus monsters in the great red rock arena of Geonosis has clearly been cribbed directly from the battle with the white ape in *A Princess Of Mars*, even the pics from Disney's *John Carter* (above) look eerily similar. Although, both scenarios were stolen from Ancient Rome so perhaps Edgar Rice Burroughs' supporters should just let that one go.

6. The Jedi
Another noise George clearly liked to hear rattling around in his eardrum, the monarchs of Mars are called Jed (king), Jeddak (emperor) and Jeddara (empress) – it's worth noting that in Barsoom a padwar is a low-ranking officer.

---

[42] James Hoare, "*John Carter* versus *Star Wars*," *Sci Fi Now*, 15 Dec 2011, 2 Sep 2012 <http://www.scifinow.co.uk/blog/john-carter-versus-star-wars/>.

Yet for all the elements that Lucas borrowed, the overall "feel" of his universe clearly was different from that of Burroughs and also incorporated elements ranging from the samurai movies of Akira Kurosawa to the adolescent science fiction of Robert Heinlein, Isaac Asimov, and the other sci-fi icons of the 1950s.

He made liberal use of Burroughs.

But it wasn't Burroughs.

DISNEY AND PARAMOUNT 1986-2006

In 1986 Disney Studios, looking for a new franchise that could compete with rival Fox Studios' *Star Wars* franchise, optioned the rights to *A Princess of Mars* through Carolco with producers Andrew Vajna and Mario Kassar.   The duo was coming off the very successful *Terminator 2: Judgment Day*, and had also produced multiple *Rambo* films, which had also achieved excellent results.   Writer Charles Pogue, who had previously written *The Fly* was selected by Disney to write the adaptation.   At the time, Pogue said of the project:[43]

> The story has a wonderful 'fish-out-of-water' thematic quality, with Carter barging through this archaic society and working his way to the top by breaching every rule in the book.
>
> "What I would like to do with this novel is to bring, if not the literal adaptation, then at least the spirit and tone of Burroughs, to the screen," he added. "We all know in 1987 that there's nothing on Mars, and that's another reason why I think it's important to keep the hero in the 1800s when people still believed that there was life there…or could be life. This is, essentially, Errol Flynn on

---

[43] Jim Korkis, "The Disney John Carters That Never Were," *i09*, 9 Jan 2012, 3 Sep 2012 <http://io9.com/bob-gale/,>

Mars. He's a very human character thrust into a very strange and bizarre world. Basically, it's what movies should be.

Disney found Pogue's script in need further work, and a year later hired Terry Black to do a rewrite. In an interview in the LA Times in 1988, Black described what he faced, and how he saw the project:[44]

> Three-quarters of a century and the book is still popular, which says something. Even at that, the studio wanted to change the whole story around. At one point, they wanted me to throw out the whole book—which I thought was foolish advice. ....The stories are good enough. The only reason [they haven't been made] is because it would be so fantastically expensive to animate all the creatures and do the special effects. .....Actually, they (Disney) want this to be the next *Star Wars*.

Next, still not ready to pull the trigger, Disney hired Terry Rossio and Ted Elliot to do a rewrite. Rossio and Elliot would go on to fame for, among other films, *Pirates of the Caribbean*, *Shrek*, and *Aladdin*.

By the time Rosso and Elliot's script was complete, John McTiernan, who was coming off *Predator*, *Die Hard* and *The Hunt for Red October*, was selected to direct. Another rewrite followed, this one by Bob Gale, whose main credential was *Back to the Future*. Gale completed his draft in January 1991, after which McTiernan and Disney attached Tom Cruise to play John Carter, and Julia Roberts to play Dejah Thoris.

But Cruise wasn't satisfied with the script, so in 1992 another rewrite was ordered, with McTiernan being given the writer he wanted, Sam Resnick. who was coming off the Patrick Bergin *Robin Hood* TV Movie that had been produced by McTiernan.

Resnick's script turned out to be acceptable to all parties, so at this point Disney ordered the Resnick script to be budgeted, and the result that came back -- $120M by several accounts -- meant that the film would be the most expensive film ever to that point. A key issue affecting the budget--other than the casting of A list talent like Cruise and Roberts -- was how to accomplish the look of the film, and in particular the creatures that would be needed. Disney had proposed using disguised elephants, camels, and other animals to achieve the Barsoomian creatures,

---

[44] Jim Korkis, "The Disney John Carters That Never Were," *i09*, 9 Jan 2012, 3 Sep 2012 <http://io9.com/bob-gale/,>.

but McTiernan had become convinced that Computer Generated Imagery (CGI) was the better , albeit more expensive, alternative. A bottleneck developed, and was exacerbated by the fact that Carolco, the production company of producers Vajna and Kassar, had fallen on hard times after years of success, further complicating the financing plan for the film.

Finally, in 1993, McTiernan -- who was the beneficiary of a "pay or play" deal that meant he got paid whether the film was made or not -- left the project. Disney brought in George R.R. Martin and Melinda Snodgrass to do another revision. Martin would later write *Game of Thrones*, while Snodgrass was the successful writer for *Star Trek: The Next Generation*. Nothing came of this final attempt -- and in 2000 Disney allowed the project to revert to Edgar Rice Burroughs, Inc.

In all, Disney had spent 14 years developing the film; 7 writers had produced 5 distinct drafts; but once again *John Carter of Mars* had failed to make it to the screen.

In late 2001, Producer James Jacks, coming off *The Mummy* and *The Mummy Returns*, read the autobiography of uber-geek blogger Harry Knowles in which Knowles included *John Carter of Mars* as one of the most significant sci-fi properties never to be made into a movie. Jacks bought in to Knowles' vision and convinced Paramount to go for the project, which they secured in 2002 after a bidding war with Columbia Pictures. Paramount's deal with Edgar Rice Burroughs, Inc included a $300,000 upfront payment against $2,000,000 if the film were to go into production.

Jacks brought the Austin, Texas based Knowles on board to the project as an advisor, and eventually an executive producer, and hired Mark Protosovich (*The Cell*) to write the screenplay, and Robert Rodriguez (also based in Austin) signed on to direct after fellow Austinite Knowles showed him the script.

Unlike the tortured Disney production, Paramount moved quickly and by 2005 had a full production plan in place that centered on Rodriguez using his all-digital stages in Austin which had been built originally for Sin City. Rodriguez announced that he was planning to hire

Frank Frazetta, who had created dozens of iconic Burroughs and Barsoom illustrations in the 1970s, as the designer. However, just as the film looked like it was about to go forward, Rodriguez become embroiled in a dispute with the Director's Guild over his decision to award co-director status to Frank Miller for *Sin City*. Miller was not a member of the Director's Guild, who in any event does not allow co-director credits, and the subsequent conflict led to Rodriguez resigning from the director's guild. This in turn meant that Paramount, who was a signatory to the DGA Agreement and thus had to use DGA talent, had to find another director for the project.

Paramount Chose Kerry Conran *(Sky Captain and the World of Tomorrow)* and hired Ehren Kruger to rewrite the script. Conran's tenure is notable for a thirteen minute "pitch video" he created for Paramount, bootleg copies of which have remained in circulation on the internet and which include compelling art images, plus live action depiction of John Carter in a swordfight with a motion capture Thark. Conran wanted to shoot the film in the Australian outback, and scouted for locations there -- but in late 2005 Conran opted out of the film and was replaced by Jon Favreau.

Favreau brought in Mark Fergus to rewrite the Kruger screenplay. A key change that Favreau implemented was to abandon the present day setting that Kruger and Conran had come up with, and revert to the a Civil War era. Favreau also re-conceptualized the film around the use of practical locations and effects rather than the extensive CGI envisioned by Conran, citing *Planet of the Apes* as his inspiration. He envisioned the Tharks being created via a combination of prosthetic makeup and CGI. A budget was created, and again, as had previously happened, the budget was so high as to give the studio pause.

Finally, in 2006, Paramount, as Disney had before them, threw in the towel and allowed their option to lapse, with the rights reverting yet again to Edgar Rice Burroughs, Inc. Once again, the on again, off again march of *John Carter of Mars* to cinema fruition went on hold.

As soon as Paramount released the rights, the *Hollywood Reporter*, *Variety*, and the other trade publications reported the reversion of rights back to its owners.

One of those who read the articles was an animation director, Andrew Stanton, then in the midst of directing *Wall-E* for Pixar. Stanton had been following the development of *John Carter of Mars* for years. He had been a fan of the comic books, and the novels, during his childhood, and the news that the rights to the Burroughs property were available triggered the beginning of a chain of events that would lead, finally, to Burroughs hundred year old property making it to cinema screens worldwide.

PART 2

JOHN CARTER OF MARS
2007-2011

COOK AND STANTON

Andrew Stanton's entry point into the world of Edgar Rice Burroughs and Barsoom was through the brief run of *John Carter* Marvel Comic Books that appeared in the 1970s, when Stanton was in elementary and junior high school. He describes his first experience with the stories:[45]

> It was the comic book form—short run of it in the '70s—and like most of the set, my best friend was a latchkey kid and had all these older brothers and it was nothing but a comic heaven in their attic. I remember being introduced to this. They all used to draw, and they would draw these Tharks all the time. From there, turned out to find out about the books that they were from, and I started to read them. I decided to read them from cover to cover from my junior high school years bleeding into my high school years. My friends that were girls used to tease me and call them my romance novels.

Stanton feasted on the comics and drew his own Tharks and Barsoomian fliers, absorbing the story and lore of Barsoom first in comic form -- then in novels, a fact that would play a key role in his

---

[45] Steve Weintraub, "20 Things to Know About John Carter," *Collider*, 11 Jul 2011, 3 Sep 2012 < http://collider.com/andrew-stanton-interview-john-carter/101272/>.

interpretation of the two central characters, John Carter and Martian Princess Dejah Thoris.

In both the comics and the books, John Carter was a master warrior, "the greatest swordsman on two worlds," but in the comics he was a trash-talking modern superhero with lines like: 'I'm coming for you Kan, to wring your filthy neck until you spit out what I must know. Speak, scum! Where are you hiding Dejah Thoris!"[46]

As Stanton would later say, quoting Steve Jobs, "You only get one first impression," and Stanton's first impression of John Carter, Dejah Thoris, and Barsoom came from the Marvel comics, not the books. And although he did graduate to the books, in the end, it was the Marvel depiction of the world of Barsoom, and the situation of a human dropped in among the warring factions and tribes there, that captured his imagination more than the characters of the two central figures or other elements that were derived exclusively from the Burroughs novels.

Thirty-five years later, in 2005, during the awards run for his first feature, *Finding Nemo*, Stanton was at the Vanity Fair Oscars after-party where he ran into fellow director Robert Rodriguez, who was then in advanced development for Paramount's version of John Carter. Stanton was seething with friendly jealousy, so he sidled up to Rodriguez, and in what he would later describe as a 'loving' way, looked Rodriguez in the eyes:[47]

"Don't f--k it up."

Rodriguez gave him a stare.

"John Carter. Don't screw it up. I just really, really want to see it done right!"

"Oh, no, no, no."

"Here's how I would open it. You can have it!"

"Lay it on me," Rodriguez replied.

---

[46] *John Carter, Warlord of Mars*, Marvel Comics, Issue #3, 3 Aug 1977

[47] Matt Patches, "Andrew Stanton Interview," UGO, 9 Feb 2012, 3 Sep 2012 < http://www.ugo.com/movies/john-carter-andrew-stanton-interview>.

Whereupon Stanton explained to Rodriguez his ideas about how to open the story. Shortly after his conversation with Rodriguez, the *Sin City* director was out due to his dispute with the DGA, and Kerry Conran took over the ultimately ill-fated Paramount project.

A month later, at Pixar, Stanton was having a story meeting with Mark Andrews, head of story on *Incredibles* and *Ratatouille*.[48] Andrews was describing a shortlist of projects for the future that he had in mind for development at Pixar, and Stanton responded to one with: "That's like *John Carter of Mars*." The comment stopped Andrews dead in his tracks; then the two discovered that they shared a childhood fascination for the Burroughs series, even going so far as to sketch Barsoomian characters. The two ended up doing a mock 'pinkie-swear' that if either ever ended up working on a *John Carter of Mars* project, they would work together.

A year later, Stanton was deep into the production of *Wall-E* when he read in August 2006 that Paramount had relinquished the rights to *A Princess of Mars*. His first reaction, as a fan, was disappointment -- but disappointment quickly turned int a fixation. He had been following the ragged path of Burroughs' Mars series to the screen since 1986, and had witnessed all the disappointments -- Mctiernan, then a series of misfires under Paramount -- Rodriguez first, then Kerry Conran, then Jon Favreau.

Now it was available.

An idea began to form.

A week later Disney studio chief Dick Cook gave Stanton a "check-in" call, just to see how the director was progressing with *Wall-E*.[49] After giving Cook an update on the status of *Wall-E*, which was still two years out from its release date, Stanton brought up the suddenly available Burroughs property: "Maybe when I finish 'WALL•E', if I'm not a one-hit-wonder, would you consider letting me make it? It's just a crime that

---

[48] Roth Cornet, "Director Andrew Stanton Talks About His Passion for 'John Carter'," *Screen Rant*, March 2012, 3 Sep 2012 < http://screenrant.com/andrew-stanton-john-carter-interview-rothc-158510/ >.

[49] Roth.

it's not going to get out there. Regardless of whether I'm the one to make it, you should get the rights."

Cook said he would look into it. A 2003 Business Week article famously described him as the "nicest guy in Disney's jungle" and indeed, by the time Stanton approached him in 2006 he was probably the best liked senior executive in Hollywood, with extraordinary relationships and a history that included conceptualizing *Pirates of the Caribbean* with Johnny Depp in a one-on-one meeting.[50]

At the time Stanton came forward with the proposition to direct *A Princess of Mars*, the status of Pixar within Disney was such that Cook had to take the request seriously. Stanton was the number two at Pixar, second only to Lasseter, and his first directorial effort, *Finding Nemo*, had become the highest grossing animated film ever, bringing in $867M globally. He was a creative force to be reckoned with.

Cook, the veteran of 36 years of Disney corporate politics, knew instantly that this could not be treated as any other director pitching a project; it had strategic implications for Disney Studios and Disney Corp overall.

A month later Disney acquired the rights to the first three books in the 11 book series, and shortly thereafter Cook and Disney signed Stanton to direct.

Today, with the benefit of hindsight, many commentators have questioned the viability of the material, which would prove expensive to produce, did not have a large current fan base, and had been strip-mined for the better part of a century via everything from Superman to *Flash Gordon* to *Star Wars* to *Avatar*. Would the original inspiration for all these classics — coming out after the clones had already had their run in the public consciousness, result in the paradox of the original seeming to be derivative of the imitator? If Cook was worried about this, he never went on record as having such concerns.

After Disney announced that it had acquired the rights and Stanton would direct, one of the first calls Stanton got was from Jon Favreau,

---

[50] Ronald Grover, "The Nicest Guy in Disney's Jungle," *Business Week*, 4 Dec 2003, 3 Sep 2012 < http://www.businessweek.com/stories/2003-12-04/the-nicest-guy-in-disneys-jungle>.

who had been set to direct the Paramount version when the studio decided to pull back. "I'm so bummed to have lost the property, but if it had to go to anybody I'm so glad it went to you."[51]   Stanton was touched, and at the same time felt, for one of the first times, the pressure that would come with this project that had been 100 years in development. "Well, then I'll try to do good by you."

Favreau had a request: "I want to be a Thark."

Stanton laughed, and agreed, and eventually made good on the promise with Favreau playing a brief but memorable role as the "Thark Bookie" taking bets on whether Helium or Zodanga would win the air battle that introduces Dejah Thoris to Carter in the story.

---

[51] Harry Knowles, "Harry Interviews Andrew Stanton about John Carter, Gods of Mars, and Warlord of Mars," *Aint It Cool News*, 14 Feb 2012, 3 Sep 2012 < http://www.aintitcool.com/node/53561/>.

ADAPTING A CLASSIC

As he set out to adapt Burroughs novel, Stanton was given all the various screenplays created under the previous Disney development effort. Cook had obtained rights to the first three novels -- and all options were open: Stanton could largely stick to the same structure that Burroughs had created, making the first movie conform substantially to *A Princess of Mars* -- or he could take another approach. Cook left it up to Stanton to work out the details.

It was the story that came first for Stanton:[52]

> I actually am superstitious about getting too much, if any visual stuff for awhile until I have an outline that works, because you can get really seduced by visuals and they can sometimes hide that you actually need to change the story or that your story's not good enough. It's like I should be able to pitch you the story without any visuals and it should hold your attention. And so I do that almost to myself . . . I won't reward myself with creating visuals until I've got at least an initial outline . . . once it works, I will pull the trigger immediately on development artists, and I will have a long list of stuff I want them to create.

---

[52] German Lussier, "Andrew Stanton Outlining 'John Carter' Sequel, Would Consider Directing and Much More," *Slashfilm*, 13 Feb 2012, 3 Sep 2012 < http://www.slashfilm.com/andrew-stanton-outlining-john-carter-sequel-directing/>.

To get started, Stanton pulled in Mark Andrews, making good on the "pinkie swear" from 2005. Pulling in a collaborator was partly a necessity due the ongoing work with *Wall-E* that still constituted a more than full-time job, but it also reflected Stanton's need for collaboration. He didn't like to write alone, and in fact he'd had a harrowing experience with *Finding Nemo* that made collaboration an even greater necessity.

Prior to his first directorial effort with *Finding Nemo*, Stanton had been of the opinion that the original Pixar Brain Trust, consisting of Lasseter, Stanton, Pete Docter, and Joe Ranft, worked together in a synergistic way that he likened to the Beatles: The collective output was far better than the work any one of them could do solo. And because, like the Beatles, the work came out under the "team" brand -- in this case "Pixar" -- it kept egos in check. "Our movies get famous, not the moviemakers."[53]

But Stanton had a hankering to find out what he could do on his own, and *Finding Nemo*, while not exactly that -- it was still a Pixar film -- was his first chance to direct. He easily got the project green-lit -- but in the execution, there were problems. The film wasn't working, and Stanton knew it. "I just felt -- I suck. Really suck, and they're going to replace me. It's coming."[54] Stanton's anxieties were driving him batty, yet he remained fiercely independent, even though he felt the pressure that this was the film -- his film -- that was going to do what no other Pixar film had done, and that was to fail.

At his lowest point, he woke up one morning came to a realization: "I'm not an auteur. I need to write with other people, I need people to work against. It's not about self-exploration--it's not about me--it's about making the best movie possible."[55] He allowed himself to admit that he didn't have every answer, and needed the help of those around him --

[53] R.J. Heijmen, "Finding Freedom in Finding Nemo: When Andrew Stanton Tried to Get Fired," *Mockingbird*, 11 Nov 2011, 3 Sep 2012, < http://www.mbird.com/2011/11/finding-freedom-in-finding-nemo-andrew-stanton-tries-to-get-fired/>.

[54] Tad Friend, "Second Act Twist," *New Yorker*, 17 Oct 2011, 3 Sep 2012< http://www.newyorker.com/reporting/2011/10/17/111017fa_fact_friend>.

[55] Friend, *New Yorker*.< http://www.newyorker.com/reporting/2011/10/17/111017fa_fact_friend>

and when he did that, the team rose up and problems began to be solved. With *Finding Nemo*, things began to fall into place and the film went on to massive success, both critically and at the box office. But Stanton had learned the he needed collaboration, thrived on it, and could get lost in the weeds without it.

Stanton and Andrews reread the books and then compared their reactions.

First, there was the matter of determining an overall attitude or approach toward the original material. Cook had given Stanton full latitude to approach the material the way he wanted to, so there was no pressure from that area. Nor was there, in Stanton's view, pressure from the kind of huge and demanding fan base that, say, a filmmaker adapting Harry Potter would face: "The harsh truth is that the Burroughs fans are slowly, slowly fading. I don't have some big Harry Potter problem where everybody is going to be offended if I change anything. It was the opposite. I was afraid it was going to fall down the sewer grate of history and no one was going to find it again."[56]

So as a starting point, Stanton felt that he had considerably more latitude than he would if he were adapting a currently wildly popular literary property -- moreover, he felt that the series had ceased garnering new, youthful adherents at least in part because of certain aspects that, in spite of the wealth of imaginative value in the books, were out of synch with modern sensibilities. Stanton felt he understood what the problem was -- and he had a plan for dealing with it in a way that he thought would update the material, while still remaining true to the spirit of Burroughs' original, and without changing the world of Barsoom in anything other than minor ways. Stanton's intention was that viewers of the movie would find themselves immersed in a richly detailed, fully realized rendering of Burroughs' Barsoom that was populated by the peoples, cultures, creatures, and history as Burroughs had imagined it.

Not only would Stanton retain the post Civil War period setting on Earth -- he would stay true to Burroughs' era in terms of design concepts and execution, offering in effect a period appropriate

---

[56] Yana Umerova, "Andrew Stanton: I Wanted to Hide the Heroic John Carter," *Kinopoesk*, 13 March 2012, 3 Sep 2012 < http://www.kinopoisk.ru/level/73/interview/1838137/>

"Steampunk" version of Barsoom. All of this would be fully in synch with the books. The changes would come not to the world, but to some of the characters and certain elements of the story which Stanton felt he could improve upon while making sure that the movie produced in the viewer the same feeling at he'd had as a kid when reading the books -- a feeling of wonder, a bit of awe, and delight and extraordinary world of Burroughs' Barsoom.

Problem number one in Stanton's view was what Stanton perceived as the "episodic" nature of the material. He was aware that *A Princess of Mars* had originally appeared a five part serial in *All-Story* Magazine, and Burroughs, and he made various comments that suggested that he believed the original story had been written in episodes designed to fit the five part serialization -- each with their own climax, each ending with a cliffhanger that pulled the reader forward and kept them waiting for the next installment.

Stanton's assessment accurately reflected the fact that the neophyte writer Burroughs' *A Princess of Mars* was not as finely structured, particularly in the final third, as Stanton needed it to be. But the notion that it had been written as a series of segmented episodes was little more than a myth -- Burroughs had written the first 43,000 words and submitted them, then submitted the final 60,000 + word version without knowing how it would be published, or in how many segments. (Tarzan, after all, would be published in its entirety in one edition.)

Stanton's assessment:[57]

> There's a whole air factory kind of climax at the end that really had no connection to anything from the beginning of the movie. It was very disconnected. You're so used to -- when you see a well told story in a movie -- things you learn about in the front have some significance in the back end of the story. And the book isn't like that. It was a real problem. Because the book was written as a serial in a magazine -- each chapter had to have its own cliffhangers. You wanted to have a problem that was resolved by the end of the chapter. So as a novel, it looks like train cars all

---

[57] Mike Ryan, "Andrew Stanton, 'John Carter' Director, On the Trials and Tribulations of Bringing the Film to Life," *Moviefone*, 7 Mar 2012, 4 Sep 2012, <http://news.moviefone.com/2012/03/07/andrew-stanton-john-carter_n_1327070.html>.

attached together with no attachment from the caboose to the engine. So we had to take the parts off of the car and remake a new car and use as many parts from the car and repurpose them.

In Stanton's view, a subcomponent of the problem of the novel being too episodic was that there was no main antagonist or villain -- it shifted throughout the story, and that, Stanton was sure, would not work for a single 2 hour film. He would unify the story around a villain who had some heft, and would be there for the duration.

Second, there was the problem of making the two main characters -- John Carter and Dejah Thoris -- relevant and relatable to 2012 audiences. Stanton acknowledged that what had drawn him to the stories in the first place had been the alien world Burroughs had created (and which Stanton first experienced through the Marvel comic books) -- the vividness and strangeness of it all. He had never, even in his youth, fully bought into the John Carter character, who even then he had found to be a bit too bland.[58]

Stanton felt that Burroughs' John Carter was in most respects a Prince Valiant-like figure -- "perfect knight" who lacked the complexity, and a hint of darkness, that modern audiences were looking for: [59]

> A character who is iconic like John Carter can be very vanilla, very boring, like 'I am the hero'. He reads like that in the book. I wanted someone where all the novel stuff--justice, 'have to save the day', 'take that risk,' 'be crazy'--where all of that is all on the inside. And what would make it more interesting, he didn't want to be attached to that anymore."

Stanton's John Carter would still have the inner code, the inner need to do right and act honorably -- but it would be submerged beneath an exterior that rejected those things.

---

[58] Among the Burroughs faithful, Stanton's comments about Carter and his decision to change the character's demeanor and objectives would become a matter of impassioned debate once the film came out. Many felt that Stanton, coming to Burroughs via the Marvel comic books, never gave Burroughs' John Carter and Dejah Thoris a chance. Many intensely preferred Burroughs John Carter to Stanton's, whom they criticized as being sulky, sullen, and self-centered through most of the movie.

[59] Yana Umerova, "Andrew Stanton: I Wanted to Hide the Heroic John Carter," *Kinopoesk,* 4 March 2012, 4 Sep 2012, http://www.kinopoisk.ru/interview/1838137/. >.

Stanton's perception of Dejah Thoris in the books was that she was too passive, too much a "damsel in distress" for modern day audiences. As a result, the books turned too much on what Stanton would term "rescue heroism" and not enough on characters who had the kind of arc that Stanton, and the modern audiences whom he felt his own inner fanboy represented, would need. Dejah would need to be updated and given a more active storyline.

Again, it seems that Stanton's perception may have been skewed by the comic books being his original source. Dejah Thoris of the novel *A Princess of Mars* is hardly a wilting damsel in distress. In that novel, ERB's Dejah leads a scientific expedition into hostile territory and when taken prisoner makes a bold, impassioned speech to Lorquas Ptomel, leader of the Tharks.; upon seeing Sarkoja attempt to blind Carter with a mirror during a duel, launches herself "like a young tigress" on the 12 foot high Sarkoja; when Carter stays behind to hold off the Warhoons, she dismounts her thoat and tells Sola she will not leave John Carter to die; and finally agrees to sacrifice her happiness for the safety of Helium by entering into an arranged marriage with Sab Than.[60]

Besides addressing the episodic nature and adjusting the characters, there was a third issue that Stanton considered to be a serious deficiency -- how does John Carter get to Mars? In Stanton's view, the Burroughs approach which involved virtually no discernible science would simply not be acceptable to a 2012 audience. "Even when I was a young kid and I read it. That was the weakest thing in the book. I was like -- what? How did he get to Mars? Everybody I ever met that was always your connective moment, your shibboleth ....like ...yeah...how does he get there? I don't get it. It was really just a hole that needed to be filled .... it was kind of unaddressed. so it was a perfect thing, just from a story construction standpoint, make it a fly in the ointment ....make him, just

---

[60] Michael D. Sellers, "John Carter: In Defense of Dejah Thoris -- "Heroic Daughter of a Heroic World," The John Carter Files, 4 Apr 2012, 4 Sep 2012, <http:// thejohncarterfiles.com/2012/04/john-carter-unsheathing-a-sword-in-defense-of-dejah-thoris/>.

by accidentally coming across what he does, it's a harbinger of the problem he's going to be for everything."[61]

Stanton knew he would face recriminations for the Burroughs fan base for many of these changes, but he was banking on the fact that the Burroughs core fans were few and becoming fewer as the years passed:[62]

> It's very obvious to me, nobody knows. It's few and far between you can find people...with each generation...the older people are, the more likely they know, the younger, less likely, so I had to write this in the same way the marvel comics people wrote it in the 70's...the same thing with the movie...I don't expect you to know about the material...this is not like "this novel is finally come to the screen for all you fans." I don't know if there are any fans out there, but the novel has been made into a film.

Stanton of course knew that there were, in fact, fans of the original material -- typically Baby Boomers who had discovered the Burroughs through the Ace and Ballantine paperback reprints in the 60s. But these were simply not numerous enough to make pleasing them a priority.

One person Stanton did feel he needed to get on board with the changes was Danton Burroughs, the grandson of Edgar Rice Burroughs and the keeper of the flame of the Burroughs legacy. On October 2, 2007, Stanton, co-writer Mark Andrews, and producer Jim Morris visited the offices of Edgar Rice Burroughs, Inc, where they were briefed and shown archival materials by Burroughs. Stanton explained his intentions regarding the character of John Carter and according to both Stanton and Jim Morris, obtained Burroughs' enthusiastic approval.[63]

There was another potential problem with the material, and this one was not of Burroughs making -- the strip-mining of Burroughs

[61] Empire Magazine Youtube Channel, "Andrew Stanton Interview - John Carter," *Youtube*, 9 Mar 2012, 4 Sep 2012 <http://www.youtube.com/watch?v=A1357M3WS9g>

[62] Peter Sciretta, "John Carter Set Interviews: Andrew Stanton, Taylor Kitsch, Willem Dafoe, Lynn Collins, and Thomas Hayden Church," *Slashfilm*, 9 Feb 2012, 4 Sep 2012 <http://www.slashfilm.com/john-carter-set-interviews/>.

[63] Bill Hillman, "Pixar's John Carter Team Visits Tarzana," *Erbzine*, 2 Oct 2007, 8 Sep 2012 <http://www.erbzine.com/news/news22.html>; also "Jim Morris Explains the Details of His Role in John Carter," *The John Carter Files*, 6 Aug 2012, 4 Sep 2012 <http://thejohncarterfiles.com/2012/08/jim-morris-explains-the-details-of-his-role-in-john-carter/>.

imagination. For 100 years everyone from Flash Gordon to *Star Wars* and *Avatar* had been making liberal use of Burroughs' creativity, and there was a very real risk that the original, finally making it to the screen at the end of the "100 years in the making" development, would feel derivative of the imitators. Stanton accepted this and felt on the one hand that it reinforced the need for him to seek ways to "refresh" the material without losing the essential feel of it, while on the other hand it stood as an element in the equation that would never completely be conquered. Stanton said:[64]

> "There's this weird familiarity with it, you feel like, do I know these people, have I been there before? And that's unavoidable, but I knew that nobody has ever done the specifics of the books, nobody has ever captured the exact DNA, like you spent all this time in the world meeting people that kind of looked like this person, but nobody has that person's--the real person's--personality. And that's what we really tried to capture was that specific personality of the book."

Although Stanton consciously did not allow himself to go too deeply into the "world-build" aspect of the development at this early stage, preferring to concentrate on story first, then design, he nevertheless also made one key design related decision that impacted the storytelling and structure.

A film such as this could be undertaken with a wide range of visual styles. At the one end was the largely "fantastical" approach, filmed against green screens and emerging with the look of something like *300*, or *Sky Captain and the World of Tomorrow*, while at the other end was something which, while still fantastic due to the subject matter, would have a more realistic texture to it.

In contemplating this, Stanton looked into his own reaction as a reader and came away with the realization that while Burroughs' world of Barsoom was indeed fantastic, one of the key components of Burroughs writing style had been to make it feel real -- so much so, that as a reader it felt more like a plausible adventure to another, very exotic

---

[64] Amy Nicholson, "'John Carter' director Andrew Stanton on Staying True to His 12-Year-Old Self," *BoxOffice.com*, 28 Feb 2012, 3 Sep 2012 <http://www.boxoffice.com/articles/2012-02-john-carter-director-andrew-stanton-on-staying-true-to-his-12-year-old-self>.

country, than a pure fantasy journey to someplace that clearly could never exist unless laws of physics and reality were reversed. There was no sorcery in Burroughs' books; and things that appeared to be fantastic did so according to laws of science and physics. Because of this, Stanton felt, the essential feeling of reading the books was different from reading other fantastic fiction: "When you read the books, you forget you are on a different planet in space, you feel like you're in another country with another culture.......and that's what I felt was more interesting about it.....that sort of adventurer explorer aspect of it."[65]   It would be, as producer Lindsey Collins would later put it, "Master and Commander in the skies above Mars."

In the end, Stanton concluded that the key was to recreate the feeling of an extraordinary but ultimately real place -- a world rich in history and culture; a world with laws of science and physics that made logical sense even when they involved different rules than earth; a world that the audience could sink its teeth into and a where those who, like Stanton, had read the books, would feel was indeed the Barsoom they had loved. Beyond that, many changes would be needed and Stanton and Andrews set about writing the screenplay confident that they had a plan that made sense -- now it was a matter of implementing it.

CHANGING THE CHARACTER OF JOHN CARTER

In both the book and the movie, John Carter is a former Virginia cavalryman who is searching for gold in Arizona when he is inexplicably transported to Mars.   In both cases he is a talented swordsman; accomplished fighting man and principled human being operating under a "code" that is grounded in a sense of what is honorable and what is not.   And in both cases he ends up identifying with Barsoom and adopting it as his home planet.   But his path in getting there is vastly different in the two treatments.

John Carter of the novel *A Princess of Mars* is a spiritually whole fighting man who is given an air of mystery by the fact that he does not

---

[65] Matt Patches, "John Carter Andrew Stanton Interview HD," *Hollywood.com Youtube Channel 'Hollywoodstreams'*, 29 Feb 2012, 4 Sep 2012 <.http://www.youtube.com/watch?v=4WnmrA-9RpM>.

age, and does not remember his childhood. He is drawn to Mars in a moment of profound personal transition (he believes his earthly self has died) and accepts that he is on Mars as a matter of destiny. Given a second chance at life in a new world with which he feels a special kinship, he relishes his new life and new world, learning the culture and winning respect and allies from the culture where fate has cast him, living by his own code of honor at all times. He knows his own heart and knows his "ideal" woman when fate brings him together with her, even though she was "hatched from an egg" and is not even of his own species.[66] He impulsively and effectively defends first himself, then Woola, then Dejah Thoris' honor and places himself in her service, making sure that she is safe and properly cared for, repeatedly displaying self-denial in favor of her well being. Though never referred to as a "knight" — Carter is everything that the chivalric code demands: courageous, honorable, gentle, courteous, and spiritually aware. He treats Dejah Thoris in a manner consistent with courtly love, placing his service to her above his personal desires, inwardly committing himself to her in a deep and spiritual fashion without demanding that she love him in return.

John Carter as drawn by Burroughs was a character who captured the imagination of readers in its day, evoking the "I want to be like him" emotional response in males, and "I want to be with him" emotional response in females, in a deeply archetypal way. For male readers who came upon Burroughs' creation in adolescence, John Carter was the embodiment of the "better self", the "masculine man" who was everything one could hope to be. For women readers, he was the elusive man of dreams – the reason to not "settle" for the ordinary, because out there somewhere is a John Carter.

Was Burroughs' Carter too bland, as Stanton believed? Did he really need to be made more conflicted, more flawed? Certainly to do so was a legitimate choice, but was it a choice made necessary by a deficiency in Burroughs' Carter, or by a reluctance on Stanton's part to delve into and explore what Burroughs had provided?

---

[66] An interesting attitude for a Civil War veteran Virginia cavalryman!

Robert McKee, in his much cited Hollywood screenwriting tome, *Story*, writes:[67]

> The Law of Conflict is more than an aesthetic principle; it is the soul of story. Story is metaphor for life, and to be alive is to be in seemingly perpetual conflict. As Jean-Paul-Sartre expressed it -- the essence of reality is scarcity, a universal and eternal lacking. There isn't enough of anything in this world to go around. Not enough food, not enough love, not enough justice . . .

Burroughs' Carter may not have been conflicted in the manner of the now familiar modern flawed hero -- but he was the epitome of the character for whom conflict is scarcity. Lost on Earth, a man without a past, searching for meaning, he reaches an end in the Arizona cave -- is it death? Or something else? He's not sure, but then he break free of that, and is filled with yearning, and from the moment he arrives on Barsoom the eternal lacking is there, but now with the promise of fulfillment -- and his quest to find that which is lacking is the "conflict" that pulls the reader forward. Reborn, he first seeks respect among the Tharks, building an alliance of Woola first, then Sola, then Tars Tarkas. Then Dejah Thoris arrives and awakens within him an even more intense scarcity, a scarcity of love -- not just romantic love, but knightly love -- allegiance first to Dejah Thoris, but eventually, through her, to Helium and as the series of books progresses, to Barsoom. Burroughs' Carter evoked the emotions that William Faulkner spoke about in his classic Nobel Prize acceptance speech: "The poet's, the writer's duty is to ... help man endure by lifting his heart, by reminding him of the courage and honor and hope and pride and compassion and pity and sacrifice which have been the glory of his past."[68] Burroughs' hero may have harkened back to that glory of man's past; he may have framed Carter in line with Faulkner's "the old verities and truths of the heart."

But to Stanton's sensibility this was a risk -- unless tempered by a "damaged goods" status at the outset of the book. He concluded that a 2012 audience, 98% of whom had never been exposed to the books, were likely to be far more familiar with the "damaged goods" flawed

---

[67] Robert McKee, Story, Harper Collins/Reganbooks, (1997), 210

[68] William Faulkner, "Nobel Prize Banquet Speech," NobelPrize.org, 10 Dec 1950, 4 Nov 2012 <http://www.nobelprize.org/nobel_prizes/literature/laureates/1949/faulkner-speech.html>.

hero and better be able to relate to a hero who progresses from that state to a state, near the end of the story, that approximated Burroughs' character.

STANTON'S JOHN CARTER

Stanton's Carter is haunted by the past but at the outset, we don't know exactly what, or why. When Powell attempts to press him into service for the Union Cavalry, he resists with a sullen demeanor and the reckless fearlessness of someone who has nothing to lose. He makes is clear that no external cause has meaning for him; "whatever you think I owe......I have already paid." After saying this, Carter looks at his hand where two wedding bands--a man's and a woman's--are visible. Carter's message: *Leave me alone!* He is a widowed man whose purpose in life has evaporated, and who is going about his quest for gold with an almost zombie-like sense of leaden persistence.

This external package of John Carter as the damaged loner is comfortingly familiar to the 98% of viewers whose frame of reference is not the Burroughs books, but rather the accumulation of expectations gleaned from movie heroes of the last several decades. Reluctant, self-absorbed, resisting the call to action, yet skilled and capable, it could be argued (and would be, by Stanton and his creative team) that Stanton's John Carter of 2012 is as familiar and easy to root for to modern audiences as Burroughs more classic rendering was to audiences in 1912.

Meanwhile, to those familiar with the John Carter of the novels, it is a dramatic change and one that alters some of the basic chemistry of the story.

Interestingly, however, while Stanton's Carter may have a radically different demeanor than Burroughs' Carter, the argument can be made that the character as revealed through choices and actions shows many more similarities than differences to Burroughs' John Carter.

1. In Arizona, Stanton's Carter finds himself in a moment where Powell has been shot by Apaches. He has no allegiance to Powell; in fact Powell is his antagonist at that point in the story. But at great personal risk, Carter returns and saves Powell — an act worthy of

ERB's John Carter and a character defining moment which Stanton clearly expects the audience to note.

2. In the movie, as in the book, Carter attempts to elude Woola. As in the book, Woola is injured, although in the movie it is the Tharks, not white apes, who injure the Calot. Carter defends Woola, in the process showing compassion.[69] This is another clue to the fact that Stanton's Carter in spite of his refusal to acknowledge any loyalty or allegiance, is nonetheless operating from a code of honor very similar, if not identical to, to that of the novel's John Carter.

3. Next comes the arrival of the warring Zodangan and Heliumite warships. Carter: "That don't look like a fair fight," another evidence of his sense of a code of honor. Then he sees Dejah Thoris, realizes there are humans, and intervenes in the conflict, first to save Dejah Thoris (chivalrous behavior), and then to conclude the conflict in favor of Helium — the party who was on the receiving end of the "not a fair fight" comment.

4. Next he is awarded Dejah Thoris, as in the book, and then is given the name Dotar Sojat with Tars Tarkas exulting, "he will fight for us!" As in the case with Powell, Carter immediately rejects fighting for anyone, and says no, he does not fight for the Tharks. But when he is told that unless he does so and becomes a Thark chieftain, the safety of "your red girl" (Dejah Thoris) cannot be guaranteed–he does the chivalrous thing and accepts appointment as a Thark chieftain, for no reason other than to protect Dejah Thoris. Again, in spite of "I don't fight for anyone" words — John Carter's choices and actions are largely consistent with the book.

5. Up until this point — Carter has displayed courage by trying to escape Powell; displayed honor by saving Powell; courage and chivalry by saving Dejah Thoris and taking on Sab Than's airpower; and chivalry by accepting a Thark chieftainship purely to protect Dejah Thoris. His protestations that he doesn't want to take up a cause are meant to be read not as true expressions of Carter's

---

[69] This moment is almost lost in the way the scene is mounted, as Carter has barely finished protecting the wounded Woola when Tars says "You killed him with one blow", and Carter responds with "I understand you!" – and so the impact of Carter's defense of Woola is somewhat lost.

character — rather that are the conscious expression, while his actions those of a chivalrous warrior, same as John Carter of the novel.

To those who grew up with Burroughs' "perfect knight" John Carter, it doesn't "feel" quite like John Carter. Yet when it is finally revealed what the source of the "damaged goods" nature is — it turns out that it is precisely the honor and loyalty that defined Burroughs' Carter that is devastating the conscious portion of Stanton's Carter. It is his loyalty and love of his wife and family that has left Carter damaged–and it is loyalty and love of the wife and child that impedes his ability to connect with his new circumstances.

In the end, Stanton's John Carter and Burroughs' John Carter are largely the same--it is just that Stanton's John Carter arrives there at the end of the story, while in Burroughs' version he is there from the beginning.

PRE-PRODUCTION: FATEFUL DECISIONS

In the earliest stages of pre-production, Andrew Stanton indicated in several interviews that he was unsure whether and to what degree *John Carter of Mars* would be live action, animated, or a combination of both, nor was it clear whether it would be brought into the marketplace branded as Pixar, Disney, or something else.

Stanton's first comments on the project came in Toronto in June 2008 at a June 8, 2008 roundtable interview promoting the June 29 release of *Wall-E*. In that session, Stanton provided the first acknowledgment that *John Carter of Mars* would be his next film, and that he was in active development of the project.[70] The reports across the internet spawned by this first report all described the upcoming *John Carter of Mars* as a Pixar film, although there is no indication that this was any more than an assumption, given that it was, at this point, an all-Pixar operation consisting of Stanton, Pixar writer Mark Andrews, and Pixar General Manager Jim Morris as producer.

---

[70] Mike Bastioli, "Exclusive: Andrew Stanton Confirms John Carter of Mars," Big Screen Animation, *Big Screen Animation*, 6 Jun 2008, 8 Sep 2012 <http://www.bigscreenanimation.com/2008/06/exclusive-andrew-stanton-confirms-john.html>.

On June 19, 2008, Alex Billington, writing in *FirstShowing.net* quoted Stanton on the issue of whether *John Carter of Mars* would be live action of animated:[71]

> One of the biggest questions surrounding the project is whether they're planning on staying CGI or integrating live action. Stanton starts off by saying that "we honestly don't know," but adds that "it's clearly got to be a hybrid of some sort." As for what to expect, I suggest you don't even *begin* to start guessing what that might mean. Pixar always tends to push the limits of our imagination and I think that's what we can expect here. He explains that this first year is all spent "worrying about the story" and asserts that thinking about the visuals and figuring out how the film will look is a distraction from the actual writing. Instead, "this year is just about writing the script to make it as good as it can possibly be."

Stanton's next comments came in a June 25 interview with "Capone" of *Ain't It Cool News*, also part of the *Wall-E* roll-out. In that interview Stanton said:[72]

> We've learned from the Pixar Methodology: don't get distracted about how [you are going to do it] and all these things everybody wants to ask; just make a great story and everything else wants to fall into place. So in all other specifics we aren't even going to decide upon until next year, once we have a script that we think i worth making.

As to how it would be distributed, Stanton told *Slashfilm's* Peter Sciretta in an interview published June 27, 2008:[73]

> There's been no discussion about exactly how it will be distributed or what moniker it will be under. Everything is going to be derived based on whatever we end up with script-wise, so this whole year is just about the script. In 2009 will be much more involved in the OK, exactly how is this going to get made? And exactly how are

---

[71] Alex Billington, "Andrew Stanton Briefly Updates on John Carter of Mars," FirstShowing.net, 19 Jun 2008, 12 Sep 2012 <http://www.firstshowing.net/2008/andrew-stanton-briefly-updates-john-carter-of-mars-adaptation/>.

[72] Capone, "Andrew Stanton gives up the goods on Wall-E and John Carter of Mars to Capone," *Ain't It Cool News*, 25 Jun 2008, 8 Sep 2012 <http://www.aintitcool.com/node/37209>.

[73] Peter Sciretta, "Interview: Andrew Stanton," *Slashfilm*, 27 Jun 2012, 8 Sep 2012 <http://www.slashfilm.com/interview-andrew-stanton/>.

we going to present it? Nobody is worrying about that until there's a script.

Although Stanton professed uncertainty as to whether the film would be live action, animated, or a combination of both, at least within Disney's legal department it was understood that the film was, per contract with Edgar Rice Burroughs, Inc., to be a minimum of 60% live action. Disney legal was also aware that Disney had licensed the first three books, and had three years after the first film was released to launch a sequel, or the rights would revert to the Burroughs estate.

By January 2009 Stanton was certain enough of the answers to the questions about live action versus animation, and distribution label, that he was able to give an interview to Sci-Fi Wire's Fred Topel, after which Topel wrote:[74]

> Stanton confirmed that *Carter*, based on the books by Edgar Rice Burroughs, will be live-action. "Yeah, I think that's the only way," he said. "I mean, there are so many creatures and characters that half of it's going to be CG whether you want it to be [or not], just to realize some of these images that are in the book. But it will feel real. The whole thing will feel very, very believable . . .

Asked if it would be a Pixar film, Stanton answered:

> Well, it's not being done by the Pixar crew. It's being done by Disney, and I'm sort of being loaned out. We're sort of using any element that we need to make the film right. We're not being purist with Pixar, but Pixar's a brand that you have to trust that's for all ages. This story of *John Carter* is not going to be an all-ages film.

Perhaps Stanton's most intriguing comments came in a lunch with "Quint" of *Ain't It Cool News* and Todd McCarthy of *Variety* in Santa Barbara on January 24, 2009, where Stanton was to be a member of the "Writer's Panel." Quint reported in *AICN*:[75]

> I was able to attend a luncheon before the panel and sat with Tom McCarthy and Andrew Stanton. Of course *John Carter of Mars* had to come up . . . here's what's going on with JOHN CARTER OF

[74] Fred Topel, "Wall-E Helmer Andrew Stanton talks John Carter of Mars," Blastr.com, 13 Jan 2009, 8 Sep 2012 <http://blastr.com/2009/01/wall-e-helmer-andrew-stanton-talks-john-carter-of-mars.php>.

[75] "Quint", "SBIFF: Quint Has News on John Carter of Mars from Andrew Stanton," Ain't It Cool News, 25 Jan 2009, 8 Sep 2012 <http://www.aintitcool.com/node/39879>.

MARS:
- It is live action.
- [Stanton]:"It is huge, it is exciting, it scares the crap out of me. It's either going to make me or break me."
- It is NOT a Pixar movie, rather a Disney film. However Stanton's creative team from Pixar are all still involved.
- The style is going to be very real, not highly stylized. He said that 20 some years ago that version could have been made, but since Star Wars and a whole glut of science fiction and fantasy films have ripped off giant portions of *JCOM* over the years the only option he sees is doing a straight up, realistic version of the story. He described it as if it was a National Geographic crew that stumbled across a preserved civilization while exploring a cave. Very real, but awe-inspiring . . .
- He has his second draft done and will be casting soon.

Thus as Stanton moved from "the year of the screenplay" in 2008, to early pre-production in 2009, the emphasis shifted from the relentless focus on the story, to questions of design, technology, casting, and -- ultimately and crucially -- budget.

Why did *John Carter* cost so much to produce?

And what was the path through the production investment ended up where it did? Was it, as the press widely reported, a function of an inexperienced director and "costly reshoots" to correct mistakes? Or something else?

First, as is typical, at the time Dick Cook optioned the property for Disney neither he nor anyone had more than a general "back of the napkin" assumption about what it would cost to produce, and he pegged that number at $150-175M, which would put it a notch below the most expensive Hollywood tentpole productions like *Pirates of the Caribbean*, but still in the upper reaches of production investment. Was this a reasonable assumption as of 2007-2008 when he made it?

The film was a mix of live action and animation and as far back as the 1990s the budget for the McTiernan version of *John Carter of Mars* had topped out at $120M. But a large portion of that had been to pay the A-List fees of Tom Cruise and Julia Roberts and there was little likelihood that Stanton would demand, or even want, that level of star. With Stanton directing and throwing Pixar style animation into the mix, it was hard to estimate what the outcome might be. Pixar films then in production were Ratatouille ($120M), *Wall-E* ($180M), and Up ($200M). But how much animation would there be? How much live action?

At the outset, $150-175M was an assumption, not a budget. No real budget could even be attempted until a screenplay was complete. Only then could the exhaustive exercise of preparing a film budget be accomplished, a process that includes breaking down each page of the script into its component parts--which cast members are on screen; what sets, props, and other elements are required; what special effects are needed to depict what is on the page; what stunts; what special equipment; etc. Once the breakdowns were completed, a shooting schedule would have to be produced. And only then could actual budgeting be attempted -- and even that would have only assumptions for key elements like the cost of onscreen talent, since typically (although perhaps not in the case of *John Carter*) most of the cast are not be signed until after the first thorough budget is complete.

So the project moved forward through drafts and redrafts of the screenplay in 2009, and casting was initiated, before a true thorough budget could be completed. In March 2009 Stanton learned the Pulitzer Prize winning author Michael Chabon--whose 'beat' as a writer was comic books and the like anyway--had been as big a Burroughs fan as Stanton and Andrews were in their youth. Ever the collaborator, Stanton approached Cook about bringing him on board as a writer to rewrite the script that Stanton and Mark Andrews had been working on to that point. Cook agreed. It brought in a top-level writing talent; however, it also had the effect of delaying the completion of the screenplay and hence left the budget unfinalized. A true final budget would now have to await Chabon's rewrite. Michael Chabon only began his revisions to the screenplay in April 2009, and Taylor Kitsch was signed a month later -- and when it was announced in June 2009 that Kitsch and Lynn Collins had been signed, the budget figure floated by Disney was $150M.[76]

---

[76] *IMDB Pro*, "Taylor Kitsch Lands on Mars," *IMDB Pro* 16 June 2009, 4 Sep 2012, <http://thejohncarterfiles.com/wp-content/uploads/2012/09/IMDb-Pro-Taylor-Kitsch-Lands-John-Carter-Of-Mars.pdf>; also 16 June 2009, 4 Mar 2012 http://www.hollywoodnorthreport.com/article.php?Article=7297.

CAST DESIGN

From the beginning, the issue of who would be cast in the lead role of John Carter was a front burner item, with Hugh Jackman put forward early on as a prime candidate. But Stanton wasn't interested. In his first public interviews about the project in January 2009,[77] Stanton acknowledged he was actively seeking to cast the film, but Jackman wasn't on his radar: "I know everybody wanted Hugh Jackman forever. But he's only getting older and more exposed now, so it's a tough call. I'm your typical filmmaker, I want to find the next best unknown." Names that were being discussed, Stanton acknowledged, included Josh Duhamel and Jon Hamm -- but it was "wide open."

Then there was the matter of how to animate the 9-12 foot high Tharks. Burroughs had written the Tharks to be 15 feet high; however to make the Tharks that tall would eliminate the possibility of shooting them using the CGI motion capture technology that Stanton wanted to use -- technology that would allow real actors, working on stilts and wearing motion capture cameras and suits, to interact with the human actors rather than forcing the human actors to act to a designated spot, with the CGI characters filled in later.

On the casting front, Stanton became interested in Taylor Kitsch immediately after seeing him in an episode of Friday Night Lights. He felt that Kitsch carried the kind of "troubled soul" complexity that he needed for John Carter -- yet had the physicality to pull off the heroic aspect of the character that would be needed as well.[78] "I wanted to hide the heroic John Carter .... That's what I saw in Taylor when I saw him in Friday night lights. I saw this character who was trying to hide a lot and I thought he made that so interesting . . . and there are just some actors, they are more interesting to watch as they listen than the other actor who is talking. that's a rare gift. and that was one of the reasons I knew I wanted him. A character as iconic like John Carter can be very vanilla, very boring, like "I am the hero." I needed someone to counter that.I wanted someone where all the novel, justice, have to save the day, take

---

[77] Total Film, "Andrew Stanton Talks John Carter of Mars", *Total Film*, 13 Jan 2009, 4 Sep 2012, < http://www.totalfilm.com/news/andrew-stanton-talks-john-carter-of-mars>.

[78] Yana Umerova, "Andrew Stanton: I Wanted to Hide the Heroic John Carter," *Kinopoesk*, 13 March 2012, 3 Sep 2012 < http://www.kinopoisk.ru/level/73/interview/1838137/>

that risk, be crazy, all on the inside. and what would make it more interesting, he didn't want to be attached to that anymore. That's what made it interesting for Taylor ..."

For Dejah Thoris, Stanton was taken in by the audition performance of Lynn Collins, a Texas born, Juilliard trained actress who brought to the part not only her classical training, but a black belt in an Okinawan style of karate. Collins had spent her summers growing up in Japan, where her father was an expert in Samurai swordsmanship, and afforded Collins an opportunity to become familiar and comfortable with swordplay.

Stanton's decision to cast relative unknowns in the lead roles was the kind of decision that, under "normal" circumstances, would be subject to highly focused critical review by either a senior producer on the show, or by the studio chief or head of production supported by the head of marketing. The casting of leads is, after all, as much a business decision as a creative one since stars are a principal means of branding a film.

But perhaps because the budget had not yet been set and Cook was still thinking in terms of $150M; or perhaps because iStanton and Pixar equities made Cook inclined to give him what he wanted; or perhaps because Cook was distracted by the fact that at this point he was under pressure--attack, almost--from Disney CEO Bob Iger -- for any or all of these reasons, neither Cook nor anyone else outside the immediate production team subjected Stanton's choices to critical review.

While it is easy to criticize this decision in retrospect, the fact was that Stanton had been extraordinarily successful with *Wall-E*, an unlikely sci-fi animated picture in which even the voice talent was largely composed of "no-name" talent. If Stanton, coming off *Wall-E* and *Finding Nemo* before that, wanted fresh faces in the leads, there would be little or no resistance.

Finally by late summer 2009 Chabon's pass on the script was complete, and a true budget could be set.

The budgeting process was even more complicated than normal because in the case of *John Carter*, relying so heavily on special effects -- the VFX category is expanded into its own sub-breakdown sheets delineating the particular VFX required for the particular scene.

Although the breakdowns sheets are normally prepared by a producer, line producer and/or a production manager, the director's involvement is required because the script is typically ambiguous on many points, and the director must clarify how many extras; details about the set, etc.

As for Stanton - he had no clue about what the budget would be and wasn't ashamed to admit it. Budgeting wasn't his thing, and later he would admit that he never gives much consideration to budget, since both *Finding Nemo* and *Wall-E* had been expensive to make, and had turned out successfully.

When it came time for a budget to be created, producer Jim Morris, whose "day job" was General Manager of Pixar, took the lead. Morris had come to Pixar from George Lucas' *Industrial Light and Magic*, where he had a long history going back to the early 1990s and had worked as a production executive or "senior staff" on a long list of films. After coming to Pixar, he was credited as Production Executive on *Ratatouille*, then as Producer on *Wall-E*. *John Carter* would be his second film as producer, and he would be the senior producer on the project. Lindsey Collins, also from Pixar who had worked with Stanton for 10 years, was brought on board as a second producer. And Colin Wilson, who had been an executive producer on *Avatar* and would bring that expertise to the project, was also added into the producer mix early on.

For a first time director, this was an unusually "friendly" arrangement -- meaning that the producers were handpicked by the director who would look to them to enable the production. There was no "studio cop" in the equation, reflecting Cook's decision to accommodate and enable the production rather than try to tightly control it. It was an all-Pixar team, except for Wilson, and although it was not released as "the first Pixar live action film" it was largely produced as such.

The script that Stanton wanted to shoot contained plenty of production value elements -- aerial battle, action set pieces -- that are traditionally associated with driving a budget higher, but more than any of these elements, it was the huge amount of screen time occupied by the 3D Thark characters -- Burroughs' fifteen foot high (reduced to twelve in the movie), six limbed green Martians -- that was the budget buster. Stanton intended to accomplish the Tharks using 3D motion capture techniques much as James Cameron had used to film the "Na'vi" in Avatar -- but in the case of *John Carter*, the "Thark screen time" was greater, and almost all the scenes involved combining humans and Tharks in the same frame, something that only rarely occurred in Avatar. Achieving a Pixar level of characterization for the Tharks--as well as all the other CGI required for the film--was the main factor driving the budget and when Morris came back to Stanton with a budget, it was substantially higher than Cook's target.

The hard reality was that the film as envisioned by Stanton included more animated shots than either *Wall-E* or *Finding Nemo* — and that was just the animation. While *Finding Nemo* had cost a relatively modest $94M, *Wall-E* had ended up as a $180M production investment -- and so with more animation shots than either of these films, plus a full complement of live action material, Morris, Collins, and Stanton came to the conclusion that there was no reasonable way to shoot this script and contain the budget within the $150-175M range.

Was consideration given to rewriting the script in such a way as to reduce the budget? There is no indication that such a course of action was ever considered. Should it have been? With the benefit of hindsight, seeing the difference in outcomes of *John Carter* and *Prometheus*, the question lingers -- what would have happened if a focused effort to contain the budget at a maximum of $200M had been made?

As it was, the decision made by producing team was that the budget needed to be defended, not reduced. The film, at a cost of around $250M, was only 30% higher than *Wall-E* and obviously consisted of an infinitely larger and more complicated production scenario. Plus no one was getting paid exorbitantly: It was the cost of an army of 3D visual effects artists and animators working for three years, coupled with the wind and grind of a large scale live action shoot, that drove the budget to $250M.

And so it was that the producers went back to the studio with its budget in hand and said this is what it will take — we can't make the movie you hired Andrew to make with anything less.

Cook could have drilled down into the budget to figure out what was driving the budget so high, and required rewrites to bring it down, but there are no indications that this happened. If Stanton could hit *Wall-E* numbers or, better yet, *Nemo* numbers, the budget wasn't a problem.

Was the timing of the budget decision a factor in Cook's willingness to go along with the higher-budget, no-name cast formulation?

All indications are that the budget decisions took place after May, 2009, which marked a watershed in Cook's relationship with Disney CEO Bob Iger, with Iger openly criticizing Cook on the conference call announcing the Q2 financials.[79] The months after that watershed were the months in which *John Carter* budget and casting decisions were being made -- and they were also, as it would turn out, the final months of Cook's tenure as studio chief. Did the likely knowledge that he was on his way out affect Cook's decision-making regarding *John Carter*?

Whatever the reasons, one key element in Cook's legacy was that Stanton was allowed to cast two relative unknowns in the lead roles of John Carter; and he was allowed budget "breakage" prior to the start of filming that took the agreed upon budget all the way up to $250M, putting *John Carter* on a par with the most expensive films ever made.

As with the decision to acquire the property in the first place, it seems likely that the Disney-Pixar relationship entered into Cook's analysis. In a sense, Disney owed Pixar one — the animation studio had certainly brought in Disney infinitely more rewards than the "budget gap" that was now under consideration.

After the casting of Kitsch and Collins was announced on June 12, 2009, the next casting decisions came in quick succession. On June 14 Thomas Haden Church was announced; then on July 19 came the announcement that Willem Dafoe would play Tars Tarkas, John Carter's Thark ally. Meanwhile a start date of November 2009 was announced. On September 6, Disney announced Samantha Morton as Sola, Dominic West as Sab Than, and Polly Walker as Sarkoja.

The start date was then moved to January 4, 2010.

---

[79] Nikki Finke, "Exclusive! Dick Cook Fired From Disney; Hollywood Registering Shock at News," *Deadline Hollywood*, 18 Sep 2009, 4 Sep 2012 <http://www.deadline.com/2009/09/exclusive-dick-cook-fired-from-disney/>.

JCOM was heading into production with a budget of $250M that envisioned a 100 day principal photography shoot, and 6 days of reshoots. Disney did not announce the budget, and as it turned out it would not be until August 2011, more than a year after principal photography was complete, that anyone from Disney would speak of the budget having reached $250M--but it reached that point in pre-production, as part of the production plan drafted by Morris and approved by Cook.

SHAKEUP AT TEAM DISNEY

On May 5, 2009, on the heels of a quarter that had included the release of *Confessions of a Shopoholic*, *Race to Witch Mountain*, and *The Jonas Brothers: 3D Concert*, Bob Iger took the microphone at the quarterly conference call with Disney investors and analysts and began with a startling slap at Studio Chief Dick Cook: "Our second quarter performance reflected the weak global economy, as well as disappointing results at our movie studio."[80] The criticism of Cook was a break from protocol, and he reiterated it slightly later in his presentation: "Studio performance was disappointing, something they would be the first to admit."

Iger's presentation contained other indications that change was in the wind:

---

[80] Walt Disney Company Staff, "Q2 FY09 Earnings Conference Call", *Disney Corporate Events and Presentations*, 5 May 2009, 5 Sep 2012 <http://cdn.media.ir.thewaltdisneycompany.com/2009/q2/2009_05_05_q2-fy09-earnings-transcript.pdf>.

As we look ahead, we see a blend of new and traditional media and business models utilizing both established and new distribution marketing and platforms. The movie theater isn't going away. Neither is broadcast television, but the same can also be said of new media. It isn't going away and we expect it to grow in size and significance to people's lives. For that reason, we absolutely must be where our consumers are going.

In the conference call, Iger established two critical narratives: First, that Cook's choices were subject to open questioning, not just within the halls of Disney Studios, but publicly by the highest officer of the Disney parent corporation, and second, that new media was here to stay and learning to deal with it effectively was a top priority for the company and the studio division.

What Iger didn't mention in the conference call was that he was closing in on the completion of a deal to acquire Marvel -- an acquisition that would have profound implications for 'boy franchise' starter *John Carter of Mars*. Three months later in August 2009, Disney announced the acquisition of Marvel with Iger emphasizing that the acquisition gave Disney "5,000 characters." In reporting the acquisition, Brooks Barnes writing in the New York Times note: "The brooding Marvel characters tend to be more popular with boys — an area where Disney could use help." Barnes also noted, ominously for *John Carter of Mars*: "As Disney's film division becomes suddenly crowded, the company may find its new partnerships bumping into one another."[81]

Barnes was exactly right. Cook, as the conference call had foreshadowed, was history and his selected vehicle for achieving a "boy franchise' -- *John Carter of Mars* -- was about to be swamped in the Marvel tsunami. The Marvel deal had been a major focus of Iger's attention, and now that it was done -- it was only a matter of time for Cook, and by extension, *John Carter of Mars*. After all, Marvel characters had a large, active, existing fan base that went to movies, while the *John Carter* existing fan base following was limited for the most part to the boomer contingent that included George Lucas and James Cameron who, like the boomer fans, had become followers of the Mars novels during the

---

[81] Brooks Barnes, "Disney Swoops Into Action, Buying Marvel for $4B," New York Times, August 9, 2009, 4 Sep 2012 <http://www.nytimes.com/2009/09/01/business/media/01disney.html>.

Burroughs reboot in the 1960's and 70's when paperback versions of Burroughs' books were widely available.

A little more than a month later, on September 19, 2009, it was over. According to some sources the end came without warning, Cook was called into a meeting with Iger and told that his services were no longer needed — that the studio "wanted to go in a different direction." Other sources claim that Cook did in fact know the end was coming; that he was given an opportunity to chart a course more in line with Iger's vision and opted not to – even choosing the date of his departure.[82] Either way, after 38 years at Disney, Cook was gone, and *John Carter* was suddenly and completely an orphan.

Weeks later, in October 2009, Rich Ross, head of global operations for the Disney Channel and thus a consummate Disney insider who had Iger's trust based on the exemplary performance of the TV unit, took over as Chairman of Disney Studios with a mandate to apply the lessons learned from his global TV operation to the Studio and drag Disney Studios operations, kicking and screaming if necessary, into the 21st century.

Ross, who was 46 at the time he took over as Studio Chief, was a curious choice for the studio chief position. Lanky, with a smile that brought comparisons to the iconic Disney character Goofy, Ross had been immensely successful as the head of Disney's global TV operations, overseeing worldwide hits such as *Hannah Montana*, *That's So Raven*, and *Lizzie Mcguire*, causing Jacques Steinberg to write in the New York Times that Ross had an uncanny ability to encase "old fashioned themes in a modern sensibility" that resonated worldwide. He also had demonstrated what the Times called a "shrewd ability to coordinate different parts of the Disney machine, from radio stations to Disney-branded magazines to Web sites, and his uncanny connection to young people's sensibilities."[83]

---

[82] Nikki Finke, "Exclusive! Dick Cook Fired From Disney; Hollywood Registering Shock at News," *Deadline Hollywood*, 18 Sep 2009, 4 Sep 2012 <http://www.deadline.com/2009/09/exclusive-dick-cook-fired-from-disney/>.

[83] Jacques Steinberg, "Oh, Grow Up Mr. Ross," *New York Times*, 22 Oct 2006, 3 Sep 2012, <http://www.nytimes.com/2006/10/22/arts/television/22stei.html?_r=1&pagewanted=print>.

Ross promptly fired more than a dozen senior staff including the heads of production, marketing, and distribution, as well as the head of Miramax. The heads of physical production and casting were also let go, as was the president of the Disney Studios Motion Picture Group. He then made a string of unorthodox hires -- starting with young producer Sean Bailey to run production, then non-Hollywood marketing chief M T Carney. In an article entitled "New Team Alters Disney's Path" Brooks Barnes wrote in the New York Times:[84]

> The overhaul reflects the Walt Disney Company's belief that the blueprint for running a movie studio needs to be redrawn to reflect a landscape where DVD sales are sputtering, social media is changing film marketing and consumers are demanding to watch films when and where they want.

> "We're not saying that everything is going to change, like we're no longer going to do TV ads or something," Ms. Carney said. "But we are also not afraid to try new things, to try daring things."

> Even the kinds of movies Disney makes has changed. Mr. Ross is no longer interested in developing projects, big or small, that cannot be squarely branded under one of three banners — Disney (family), Pixar (animation) or Marvel (superheroes) — the better to cut through the marketplace clutter.

Of particular significance was the brand solidification behind Disney as the "family" brand and phasing out the more adult brands Touchstone, and Buena Vista. This would prove significant for *John Carter of Mars*.

From the perspective of insider Hollywood, Ross had one huge negative in the view of most observers: He was a "TV guy" with no hands on experience in either picking a slate of movies, or bringing them to the marketplace. Clearly Robert Iger felt that the success in television programming would transfer over to developing a slate of movies that matched Disney's aesthetic, and successfully appealed to Disney's market, but the jury was out as to whether his experience in TV could be transferred to the peculiar discipline of motion picture marketing.

One thing for sure was that Ross understood the role of the studio in the larger Disney scheme. It had been many years since the studio

---

[84] Brooks Barnes, "New Team Alters Disney Studios' Path," *New York Times*, 26 Sep 2010, 4 Sep 2012 <http://www.nytimes.com/2010/09/27/business/media/27disney.html>.

was the most profitable of Disney divisions -- but it had the distinction of being the intellectual property "wave-maker" -- with hit properties having the capability to quickly generate demand for everything from sequels to merchandise, products, soundtracks, games, digital devices, theme parks, cruise lines, stage adaptations, and more.

From Ross's perspective *JCOM* came with many red warning flags attached to it. At $250M it was very pricey; it didn't have a built-in fan base sufficient to justify such a budget; and it was a distraction from what at that point seemed a far more promising set of properties — the Marvel collection, and the Pixar portfolio. Had Marvel been in the fold in early 2007 when Cook acquired the rights to *A Princess of Mars*, it is highly unlikely that such a green light would ever have been given.

Iger himself was negative about *JCOM* and let Ross know it. He openly criticized Cook's decision to green light, and the decision to let the budget increase to $250M, and made it clear to Ross that the *JCOM* production was more of a problem to be addressed, than an opportunity to be realized.

Andrew Stanton, continuing with his prep for the movie's start of principal photography in January, waited for the shoe to drop with a shutdown of the production. "I thought, 'Are we gonna lose the green light?' In the very beginning I assumed it would be like that, cause who's gonna give me the keys to a Ferrari if I've never driven before?"[85]

But the project was all but mounted. It was scheduled to begin shooting in January; all the principal cast had been signed; all contracts with major suppliers had been set. Above all--and this was, in the end, what carried the day and caused Iger and Ross to allow *JCOM* to proceed --there was the reality that *John Carter of Mars*, even though it wasn't officially a Pixar project, was in fact a "Pixar baby"-- meaning it was a passion project of Andrew Stanton who was supported and believed to be "owed the opportunity" by Pixar chief John Lasseter.

The decision was made. *JCOM* would be allowed to proceed.

---

[85] Rebecca Keegan, "Director Andrew Stanton looks back on 'John Carter' rocky path," Los Angeles Times, 8 Sep 2012, 8 Sep 2012 <http://www.latimes.com/entertainment/movies/moviesnow/la-et-mn-john-carter-director-20120908,0,1996908.story>.

HALF-MEASURES IN MARKETING

A second decision was also made which all but sealed the fate of the film. *JCOM* and Stanton would be offered full production support in the form of the necessary financing to complete the movie, but -- and this was a huge 'but' -- *JCOM*, a film that was "too big to fail" due to its enormous budget, would be allowed to do just that. Marketing support would be limited to that afforded a "normal" release; there would be no major push to obtain the merchandising, licensing, and co-promotion deals that would normally be deployed to create the kind of "event" atmosphere that a film at the highest level of budget ever seen in Hollywood would need.

Production financing, yes.

All-out marketing support? No so much.

Recipe for disaster? You bet.

Meanwhile, Ross promptly put on ice the next tentpole project in the pipeline approved by Cook -- *"Captain Nemo: 20,000 Leagues Under the Sea."* Nemo was scheduled for a February production start. Disney's announcement went to pains to state that "event pics like *20,000 Leagues*, *John Carter of Mars* and *Tron"* were still a priority under new chief Rich Ross.

Through the remainder of the fall and into the first quarter of 2010 Ross worked to put in place a team whom he felt would respond to his vision and be able to implement the mandate to shake things up in the film division.

One of his first hires was Sean Bailey, producer of *Tron: Legacy*, to take over as head of production, a role that would make Bailey responsible for overseeing the production of *John Carter of Mars*. Commenting on the appointment, the L.A. Times noted: "Bailey, who has no experience as a studio executive, faces a steep learning curve in assembling slates of movies and managing dozens of executives and filmmakers."[86]

---

[86]Claudia Eller and Dawn C. Chmielewski, "Disney Studios Chief Rich Ross names Sean Bailey Head of Production," LA Times, 15 Jan 2010, 5 Nov 2012 <http://articles.latimes.com/2010/jan/15/business/la-fi-ct-disney15-2010jan15>

Bailey came on board in January 2010, the same month that *JCOM* began principal photography. Bailey was a young producer with no experience as a studio executive. He had been slated to be the producer of the canceled *Captain Nemo* as well as *Tron Legacy*, and it had been a smart, hi-tech presentation he had made to Ross concerning that movie that had caught Ross's eye and ultimately resulted in the appointment. Bailey would not, however, take a hands-on involvement in the production of John Carter; rather he would delegate that primarily to production executive Brigham Taylor, who had been on the project since inception.

A key position that was unfilled as of January 2010 was the head of marketing job. Ross made it clear from the outset that, although he would interview some industry insiders for the job, his preference-- supported by Iger--was to look outside the pool of Hollywood veterans .

THE SEARCH FOR A MARKETING CHIEF

In Hollywood, veteran marketers who specialize in theatrical movie marketing consider themselves to be a unique breed, and are skeptical of the idea that an outsider can prosper in their universe. History supports their view: In the 1990s, both Disney and Warner Brothers experimented by hiring an outsider to head their marketing divisions. For Disney, the choice was Burger King's John Ciwnyski, while for WB it was Brad Ball of Macdonalds. Neither proved to be a good fit for the unique discipline of movie marketing, and neither lasted long.

The challenge of movie marketing is singular: Typically in the "normal" world of marketing, brands are built over a number of years, with multiple campaigns, attempted, some of which work better than others, and with the marketers having the ability to engage in a certain degree of trial and error to find the best way to grab an audience and get them to try the product. Not so with movie marketing. Movie marketers only get one shot to develop a globally recognized brand name that, in a matter of weeks, goes from being unheard of by the vast majority of the general public, to a must-see event that with a call to action" has extremely high requirement -- a requirement that the target audience not only get up off the couch and go stand in line to spend $10 or more to watch the movie -- it has to get them to do this on precisely the same weekend -- the opening weekend when a movie earns as much as 40% of its total and defines itself as either a hit or a flop. With movie marketing, there are no second chances, and course corrections have to be deft and quickly handled. Virtually no other marketing discipline features this type of pressure to orchestrate all elements of a campaign according to a schedule with a single end point that is both daunting and unforgiving.

Disney CEO Robert Iger was fully aware of the unique demands of theatrical film marketing, and of the history of failure of bringing in outsiders, but in 2009 when he appointed Rich Ross as studio chief he made clear that he expected Ross to shake things up in the movie marketing arena, where Iger believed that the studio had been out of synch with a film business that was rapidly evolving towards a global digital future. Iger didn't buy the argument that only "movie guys" could crack the code of movie marketing, and he was against the idea of continuing to draw from a pool of entrenched insiders at a time when rapid change through digitalization and global reach was changing the landscape.

For his part, Ross felt that much of what he had learned in building a hugely successful global TV operation could be applied to the studio division, and this was part of it. He set out to find someone who could think strategically and globally, and who could look at the marketing of a movie not just from the perspective of its theatrical release--but from the larger perspective of its entire lifespan as an entertainment product. He wanted someone who was savvy when it came to optimizing social networking and making good use of emerging technologies to promote products, in the process diminishing the heavy reliance on the traditional types of advertising -- TV spots, billboards, print ads, and the like.

Ross did not go it alone in his search; rather in the early part of the process he worked with ML Search, a top executive search outfit, and as finalists were identified, each went before a committee of Disney executives and top producer clients like Jerry Bruckheimer, and Dreamworks CEO Stacey Snider. Although they were not part of the panel, Ross also sought inputs from Steven Spielberg, Pixar's Jon Lasseter, and Marvel's Kevin Feige.

Scottish born MT Carney was a candidate who stood out in terms of the search criteria. She had been worldwide planning director at Ogilvy

& Mather before moving on to become founding partner of Naked Communications. Naked was a communications strategy company who motto was: "The Agency Model Stripped Naked" and the company had developed a reputation for brand building that relied less on traditional advertising, and more on emerging technologies. Clients included Coca-Cola, Nokia, and tissue giant Kimberly Clark.

Carney had coined phrases like "Mapping the Customer's Journey," "Fleet of Foot, Pure of Heart," and "Four dimensional storytelling," and "it's time to rethink how products, services, and brands are connected to their consumers."[87] She had become a highly articulate proponent of the view that many traditional ad agencies were faltering when it came to adapting to the changing landscape of marketing and communications.

The announcement of Carney's hiring came on April 20, 2010, as *JCOM* was on Day 53 of principal photography. In an internal memorandum Ross told studio execs: "the film business is changing before our very eyes, and we must all rise to the occasion to meet our consumers' changing needs."

AVATAR SHAKES UP THE MARKETING EQUATION

On December 18, 2009, as *JCOM* was in the final stages of pre-production, James Cameron's *Avatar* was released and quickly was on its way to becoming the all-time top box office performer in history. In a variety of interviews Cameron freely admitted to being inspired by Burroughs and *John Carter of Mars*:[88]

> With 'Avatar,' I thought, Forget all these chick flicks and do a classic guys' adventure movie, something in the Edgar Rice Burroughs mold, like *John Carter of Mars*—a soldier goes to Mars.

---

[87] Nikki Finke, "Disney Picks Movie Marketing Chief (Her Motto? 'The Agency Model Stripped Naked')," *Deadline Hollywood*, 20 Apr 2010, 4 Sep 2012 < http://www.deadline.com/2010/04/disney-picks-new-movie-marketing-chief/>

[88] Michael D. Sellers, "Heady Days for Edgar Rice Burroughs Fans: *Avatar*, ERB, and John Carter of Mars," *Erbzine*, 8 Jan 2010, 4 Sep 2012 <http://www.erbzine.com/mag30/3038.html>.

That wasn't the only time he said it -- in at least five interviews Cameron openly identified Edgar Rice Burroughs and *John Carter of Mars* not only as inspiration for Avatar, but as an overall model for it.

Avatar struck a responsive chord with audiences from its first day in theaters, and digital word of mouth was phenomenal. For its first weekend it was initially reported to have grossed $72M, a figure released on Sunday morning that, in line with standard studio practice, included an estimate for Sunday. That estimate had to be revised upward when actuals came in on Monday to $77M -- an indication of exceptionally strong word of mouth. Still, by "normal" patterns and standards, a $77M opening weekend would typically, even for a blockbuster with good word of mouth, project to a domestic total of $220M to $240M, so few were prepared for what happened next. On its second weekend, instead of dropping 35-40%, it dropped just 1.8% and logged $75.6M en route to a lifetime domestic gross of $760.5M and global gross of $2.8B, landing it in the Number 1 All Time spot.

For *JCOM*, the implications were significant. On the one hand, Avatar showed the potential that existed for a film with the same general outlines as *JCOM*--as Cameron had said, a soldier goes to Mars (or in this case, Pandora) and makes his adventurous way there.

But while it highlighted the possibility, it also illustrated and heightened the the potential problem of perception. Now it was no longer *Star Wars* that would be cited as coming first before *John Carter of Mars*; it was *Avatar* as well, and *Avatar* would be extremely fresh in the minds of viewers who were observing the rollout of *JCOM*.

What were the similarities?

The Basic Setup: Burroughs was the master of the story of a man--a warrior--dropped into a foreign and typically very dangerous culture, who must survive on his wits and skills, and who by virtue of his wits and skills wins the love of a worthy woman and rises to a position of greatness in the society. This aspect of Avatar resonates completely with Burroughs.

The World Created: With Avatar, the vividness with which Burroughs created Barsoom, Amtor, Caspak, Pellucidar, and Tarzan's jungle has been captured for the first time cinematically. This meant that the experience of viewing Avatar was, arguably, as immersive as was the experience of reading Burroughs tales and getting lost in the worlds he created--made more vivid by the execution.

The Creatures: The six-legged horselike "Pa'li" controlled by thought (with the help of a plug-in) seemed to be almost a direct lift of Burroughs' Barsoomian thoats -- even down to the fact that they were guided by telepathy. The Thanotaur that chases Jack Sully at the beginning, and aids Neytiri at the end, reminded of the Barsoomian banth.

Neytiri: There was no doubt that the beautiful Neytiri fills the bill as a love interest with as pivotal a role as Dejah Thoris, and creates the romantic drive that was central to virtually every Burroughs novel, or at least to all the novels that were a "first" novel about a given character.

The Level of Action: Complete, over-the-top action was a hallmark of Burroughs stories and from the moment Jake Sully and company exit their helicopter in the jungle of the Na'Vi, the action is every bit as exhilarating as that written by Burroughs.

The differences?

Aspects of the Setup: No Burroughs sci-fi novel included a setup wherein large numbers of humans were present on the planet the hero visits -- and certainly none in which the conflict between the humans and the natives is a central facet of the story.

Jake Sully: The paraplegic ex-marine is a bit different from any Burroughs hero. Burroughs' heroes were always, without exception, exceptional physical specimens. The closest parallel would be *Mastermind of Mars* in which the hero, Ulysses Paxton, lies dying (and possibly maimed with legs destroyed) in a trench in World War I when he looks into the sky, sees Mars, and finds himself transported to Barsoom.

A Human, Quatrich, as the Main Antagonist: This is definitely different from the Burroughs setup for 'planetary romances' -- and resonates more with other sci-fi authors.

Avatar, released in 2009, represented the last of the "strip-mining" of Burroughs, and whether this would be an asset or liability to *John Carter of Mars* remained to be seen.

A $250M Production Experiment?

As the start date of Principal Photography approached, Stanton knew that he was in for as grueling an experience as he had ever had in his life. Live action, location film-making would be completely unlike the work Stanton was used to at Pixar. He would be on his feet, and need to be on his game, for 12-14 hours a day, no down time, no opportunities for mistakes.

As filming began, he found that besides the pressure to get the shot and move on, the experience was familiar:[89]

> A lot of people think that when you're on an animated CG movie, you're working with computers. I have to keep telling people, 'No, I work with human beings.' I work with 200 human beings. I have conversations with at least 50 human beings a day about the art form, about why a character would do this or what a set should look like. Why we should use the color red or the motivation or the plot. The conversations I'm having here are absolutely no different. It's just real and you can actually touch it. That's probably the biggest difference. But the intellectual, artistic and

---

[89] Matt Patches, "John Carter: Andrew Stanton Interview," *UGO*, 9 Feb 2012, 4 Sep 2012 <http://www.ugo.com/movies/john-carter-andrew-stanton-interview>.

even practical conversations on a lot of things hasn't been as huge a transition as I had thought. Which is good. I don't feel as out of my element as I thought I might be.

The issue of Stanton's ability to adapt from animation to live action filming would become one of the major focuses in the controversy that would eventually envelope the project.

Traditionally, the Hollywood approach to live action film-making emphasizes a lengthy pre-production that yields a "blueprint" for the film, followed by a single period of "principal photography" whose objective is to get *everything* "in the can", followed by editing and post-production. Under the traditional model, reshoots in excess of a "pickup day" or two are considered remedial and are an indication that something was missed the first time around. Under the conventional system, the existence of reshoots is perceived to signify that something went wrong during the principal photography and "costly reshoots" are necessary as a remedial and unplanned exercise.

But while this traditional view is understood to be the norm, most directors acknowledge that a period of reshoots (which are more properly thought of as "additional shooting" since the object is often not to reshoot what you already shot, but rather is to get additional shots and scenes that clarify and enhance the story) can be invaluable because, at the point where the film has been assembled, instead of shooting 10 times what will actually show up in the film, the shots that are executed can be very carefully calibrated to fit within the actual edited film. Director Bill Condon, explaining re-shoots for *Breaking Dawn*, said: "A film is a lot like a puzzle, with each piece – each shot, no matter how brief – needing to fit exactly with the ones around it. Our Part Two puzzle is finally coming into full view, and in a few weeks we'll be heading back north to pick up some additional shots – the last tiny missing pieces."[90]   *Red Tails* Director Bill Hemingway, describing re-shoots for his film about Tuskegee Airmen, said: "We all knew there was going to be additional photography. It wasn't a surprise."   He described

---

[90] THR Staff Report, "Director Bill Condon Confirms 'Twilight: Breaking Dawn Part 2 Reshoots," *The Hollywood Reporter*, 14 Apr 2012, 4 Sep 2012 <http://www.hollywoodreporter.com/news/twilight-breaking-dawn-kristen-stewart-robert-pattinson-bill-condon-312197>.

the reshoots as "little character moments and effects-driven scenes that were needed to "make things clear; to strengthen individual characters."[91]

Stanton went on record as being more passionately committed to re-shoots than almost any other live-action director, so much so that he viewed his approach as revolutionary for live action, yet grounded in what has been termed the "Pixar process":[92]

> You know, I planned reshoots for after I got an assembly, so I had real objectivity about what it needed.
>
> That's all we do at Pixar. The truth is, we rip down and put up our movies a minimum of four times over four years. How I learned to make a movie by shooting it four times. That's how we make them. People wonder what the magic elixir of Pixar is. It's this: we shoot the movie four times!
>
> To me, that's just how art is formed....It's like me saying to you, you can all go and write a piece about what we talked about today, but you only get to write it once. You don't get to change a word once it's set down. And that's how movies are made, and it's fucked up. It should be that you should somehow be able to balance economics and let the artist be an artist, and not be afraid of failure or trial and error.

In an interview just before the release of the film, Stanton's producer Lindsey Collins says: "It's the way we've always worked and certainly at Pixar that's how we work – we get it all up there and put it up and we watch it and go, 'That's not working, let's move that over here.....So it doesn't surprise me at all that that's how Andrew worked on this one."[93]

---

[91] Tambay Obenson, "Red Tails Director Anthony Hemingway Talks the Film, George Lucas, Rumors, More ... ," *Indiewire*, 3 Aug 2011, 4 Sep 2012 <http://blogs.indiewire.com/shadowandact/
red_tails_director_anthony_hemingway_talks_the_film_george_1>.

[92] Brendan Connelly, "Andrew Stanton Tells Me It's on his Agenda to Completely Change the Way Movies Are Made," *Bleeding Cool.com*, 30 Nov 2011, 3 Sep 2012, <http://www.bleedingcool.com/2011/11/30/andrew-stanton-tells-me-its-on-his-agenda-to-completely-change-the-way-movies-are-made/>.

[93] Jen Yamato, "'A Complete and Utter Lie': The Fact, Fiction, and Fury Behind John Carter's Woes," *Movieline.com*, 9 Mar 2012, 4 Sep 2012 <http://movieline.com/2012/03/09/a-complete-and-utter-lie-the-fact-fiction-and-fury-behind-john-carters-woes/>.

The 100 days of principal photography went off smoothly and were accomplished on schedule and within budget, with no studio representative on the set. Back at Disney, new chief of production Sean Bailey started his tenure at about the same time the production launched, and left Stanton and the production team to their own devices.[94]

The hands off nature of the studio's involvement was unusual given Stanton's status as a first time live action director, and the huge risk that the budget of $250M represented. But Stanton's own comments shed some light on what Disney would have faced had the studio decided to tangle with him:[95]

> I was pretty hardball. To be honest nobody ever fought me, but it was the fan in me that gave me the guts. That, and I have a day job [as Head of Story at Pixar]. I just felt like if anybody had a chance of making this without it being fucked up by the studio, it might be me. They're too afraid of me – they want me happy at Pixar. So I thought I should use this for good, and make the movie the way I always thought it should be made. If at any one of these points if they were going to push back, I would have pulled out. It's the best way to buy a car – I don't mind walking away. So it pretty much got me through to the end. I never saw a studio person on the set until the reshoots.

"Make your mistakes early," Stanton would repeatedly tell his team, echoing the Pixar philosophy that it is only through "getting it up there" and seeing its flaws, that the character and story will be revealed. There is no doubt whatsoever that Stanton came into *John Carter of Mars* with a production philosophy grounded in the "Pixar Process" of film-making, a process which emphasizes trial and error.

But while Stanton would repeatedly sing the praises of the Pixar process–would the film-making team in fact have the latitude to execute the film according to such a process? Objective reality would seem to say no — at least not in a very complete way. The production plan that Stanton and company agreed to called for 100 days of principal photography and only six days of reshoots — hardly comparable to the

---

[94] Devin Faraci, "Andrew Stanton Explains Why It's Still JOHN CARTER OF MARS ... Technically," *Badass Digest*, 29 Feb 2012, 4 Sep 2012 < http://badassdigest.com/2012/02/29/andrew-stanton-explains-why-its-still-john-carter-of-mars-technically/

[95] Faraci.

"reshoot it four times" system that applied at Pixar for *Wall-E* and *Finding Nemo*. Even with the reshoots expanded to 18 days, the production scenario still falls far short of the kind of repeated "reshoots" that a Pixar film goes through. To even come close to the "Pixar process", the plan would have to called for several extended reshoot periods as the film gradually revealed itself through successive renderings. Recognizing the impossibility of such an approach in live action film-making, Stanton never suggested anything of that sort, and Disney surely would never approved such a plan which would have driven the costs of production even more into the stratosphere.

And so the production was mounted with a general commitment to the philosophy of the Pixar process, but without the actual structure that such process required. It would be a hybrid production whose 100 day main shoot, 6 day reshoot arrangement was 90% "old school" but whose spirit of collaboration and "building on errors" would be 90% Pixar.

Did the expansion of the reshoot schedule from 6 to 18 days materially affect the budget? The answer would appear to be no. The reshoots were for the most part accomplished as local "green screen" days in Los Angeles at the Playa Vista stage, and were inexpensive enough to be covered by the contingency allocation within the approved budget.

How did the creative team respond to the approach? "Stanton was amazing to work for," one top creative participant in the production said in a private interview. "His interpersonal skills are among the best. He has a way of making you feel you're on his level even if it's unlikely that you really are. He encourages you to try things and constantly reassures you that no ideas are bad ideas, and that the process is an open, collaborative one–guided by Stanton's overall vision to be sure, but really empowered by the rest of us." Another put it this way: "It felt a little 'scrambled' at times, not as button downed as I've experienced with other director, but there was an underlying confidence that if there was a sense of things being slightly unfocused — that sense was on the surface, and underneath the surface there were processes at work that would yield something more profound than our usual way of working was likely to. So we bought into it."

While the question of reshoots has for the most part been a "part of the conversation" about *John Carter* as it pertains to the effect the reshoots had on the budget, a more relevant question is, did Stanton get enough reshoots and re-tweaking of the film in post production to complete his own creative process?

Stated differently, did Stanton in fact get to pursue the film to the result that he would normally have been able to achieve had it been a Pixar film, or did the result represent something closer to film that had still had several Pixar iterations to go -- but which had to be brought to "completed" status prematurely due to the exigencies of live action film-making.

Was the marriage of the Pixar process to live action film-making a success, a failure, or a mixed bag?

Time would tell, but one thing was clear, and that was that the price tag of $250M did not come from an out-of-control production. The production itself adhered to the plan that was approved except for 12 extra reshoot days which were not a material factor in the budget being as high as it was.

THE BRAIN TRUST SCREENING

Principal Photography on *JCOM* wrapped in July 2010, and for the next four months Stanton worked on creating his first assembly of the movie at Barsoom Studios in Berkeley. By December, he had completed his first 170 minute assembly of the movie. As is often the case for VFX-heavy films, the first assembly, while instructive to the actual team immersed in editing the film, was difficult for "outside eyes" to view because of the many incomplete VFX shots — shots which in this case included many of the shots of the 3D animated Tharks whose characters were essential to the story. Hand drawn images would serve as stand-ins for many of the elements that would only be available to see later.

But the time had come to share the film with 'outside eyes' and get feedback, and so it was that Stanton showed the 170-minute rough cut at Pixar to his "Brain Trust" group, consisting of Lasseter, Brad Bird, Morris, Collins, and other Pixarians. Sean Bailey and Brigham Taylor from Disney were also shown the same cut. By multiple accounts, the reaction to the material was mixed. There were concerns that the opening was too long and confusing; the middle sagged; and the character of Dejah Thoris was too aggressive and needed recalibration. The criticism came almost exclusively from the Pixarians. The studio executives, Bailey and Taylor, provided notes but there is no indication that they were in any way disturbed by what they had seen, or were really major players int he evaluation process.

For Stanton's part, he had not expected rave reviews -- the Pixarians had worked together before and gone through the long road to a successful movie, and "tough love" was the norm. For the group to react with unqualified raves would have been distinctly out of character; moreover, the entire purpose of the exercise was to get feedback that could help improve the movie, not simply to get affirmation that it was good.

Key elements in the feedback:

The Character of John Carter: Importantly, one area of consensus was wholehearted endorsement of Stanton's transformation of John Carter's character from the Galahad-like "perfect knight" of the Burroughs books, to a conflicted, war-damaged widower who is lost and who eventually finds purpose on Barsoom. This was a change that would prove highly controversial among the small but intense group of lifetime Edgar Rice Burroughs fans, but pleasing the core fan group was not high on the list of priorities. Said one production professional with a front row seat to the creative decision-making: "It was a $250M gamble to get modern audiences who have no knowledge of the source material to buy into it; pleasing a few thousand lingering fans from the sixties who are passionate advocates of the original material in all its specificity just couldn't be a major consideration. Be respectful, yes. Let them dictate the treatment of the story, no."

The Character of Dejah Thoris: When it came to Lynn Collins' Dejah Thoris, there was concern. Stanton had been adamant from the beginning that he wanted to strengthen Collin's character, including presentation of her as a warrior capable of holding her own in hand to hand combat, and Collins, who was both a Juilliard trained actress and a lifelong martial arts student, had "the right stuff" to fulfill the more aggressive side of her character. But Dejah Thoris is also intended to be the "incomparable" princess — the most desirable woman on two worlds

— and the calibration of feistiness on the one hand, and feminine allure on the other, had skewed too much toward the former.

The Confusing Opening: Another area that came in for criticism included the opening Barsoom scene, which centered on Dejah Thoris displaying her ninth ray machine and included what the Brain Trust collectively felt was too much exposition for the audience to absorb — Barsoomian politics and science, mostly. It was suggested that this be simplified or even cut — with the latter suggestion being that Stanton consider following Edgar Rice Burroughs' lead and have the view experience Barsoom only through John Carter — traveling there with him, and learning about it as he learns about it. Stanton was strongly against this:[96] "That's lazy thinking, guys," Stanton replied. "If I do that, then thirty minutes in I'm going to have to stop the film to explain the war, and Dejah, and who everyone is, and we're going to have even bigger problems."

But while Stanton resisted changing the opening in such a major way, he proved generally responsive to the other suggestions as to how to "plus" the film — "plus" being the Pixar term for the process by which a film is relentlessly improved as it moves from stage to stage in the journey from development to a finished film.

After the holidays Stanton went back to work. Each morning there was a teleconference with the UK based VFX team, with Stanton's animation background coming into play as he issue extremely detailed instructions and suggestions to 'plus' the animation and effects. Afternoons were spent with the editing team headed by Eric Zumbrunnen, working out the shots and scenes that would be included in the reshoot.

Meanwhile, at Disney, the first big marketing decision that would affect *John Carter of Mars* was about to be made.

---

[96]Tad Friend, "Second Act Twist," *The New Yorker*, 11 Oct 2011, 4 Sep 2012, <http://www.newyorker.com/reporting/2011/10/17/111017fa_fact_friend>.

INFLUENCING THE INFLUENCERS

With a major theatrical release motion picture, some degree of marketing is present from the moment the picture is approved to go into production. Typically this early activity takes the form of press releases announcing the green-lighting of the project; announcements of the signing of director and stars, the beginning of principal photography, and other milestones. This is also the period in which decisions are made regarding what level of cross-promotional tie-ins, and which merchandising deals, and licensing arrangements will be pursued. If these are to be pursued, the effort to identify partners and develop deals -- which can often require substantial lead time--is launched.

Increasingly, studios also use this period to get an early head start on building 'buzz' for the film through social media platforms like Twitter, and *Facebook*, and through outreach and reputation/relationship management with key "influencers" who track movies and write about them from the time they are announced until well after they are released. Effective management of the pool of influencers and the key social media platforms is significant to a studio both as a means of generating buzz -- and equally important, as a way of monitoring reactions to the marketing materials and messages that are released. Notes Pete Blackshaw, Executive VP of the Nielsen Online digital strategic services:[97]

> The name of the game for the studios is to take full advantage of all early signals. The downside for them is a movie can be damaged really quickly — the flow of information on these platforms, and degree to which influencers are tapping into those signals is quite profound.

Thus there are two functions for the influencer media and social media platforms -- one, to "spread the word" and generate buzz, and two, to provide a feedback loop that allows the studio to monitor what Blackshaw calls "all early signals" and right the ship when it needs to be righted, early in the game when the audience is small and mistakes, if corrected, can be minimized.

For *John Carter of Mars*, mechanisms of influence that were available and relevant at the early stage of the *John Carter* campaign were:

1) *Traditional Trade Publications*: *Variety* and *The Hollywood Reporter*, plus Hollywood pulse-o-meter *Deadline Hollywood*. These are the "traditional" source of influence from the mainstream trade media, and remain important. Not widely read by the public, they are nevertheless monitored closely by key blogs and entertainment outlets ("2" below) who replay information derived from the trades.

2) *Key Entertainment Bloggers and Websites*: About 40 key blogs and entertainment sites collectively reach as much as 80% of the audience for early reporting on movies-in-progress. Among the most active influencer media outlets with the largest audiences are *Movies.com*, *Hit Fix*, *MovieWeb*, *MTV Movies Blog*, *Slashfilm*, *i09*, *Ain't It Cool News*, (whose founder Harry Knowles had been attached as a producer on Paramount's *John Carter of Mars*), *ComingSoon.net*, *Filmsite.com*, *Collider.cm*, *Badass Digest*, *Joblo.com*, *Empire Online*, *Total Film*, *ScreenRant*, *Hollywood.com*, *Hit Fix*, *MovieWeb*, *Movieline*, *Indiewire/The Playlist*, *Dark Horizons*, *Topless Robot*, *Fused Film*, *Den of Geek*, *Film School Rejects*, *HeyUGuys.com*, *First Showing*, *Cinema Spy*, *Digital Spy*, *The Geek Files*, *Geek*

---

[97] Anthony Hamp, "Universal, Sony, Others Wrestle With How Social Media Affects Box Office," *Advertising Age*, 5 Oct 2009, 2 Sep 2012, <http://www.fabriqate.com/fabriqate-interactive-great-article-on-digital-marketing-on-movie/>

Tyrant, *Comic Book Movie*, *ReelzChannel*, *Cinema Blend*, *What Culture.com*, and as many as a dozen others.

3) *Key Social Media Platforms Twitter and Facebook*: These two social media platforms are of strategic importance and building a strong list of followers on each is important, keeping in mind that the early followers on these platforms are most likely to themselves be "mini-influencers" likely to tweet and comment about a film they are excited about. Many have their own personal blogs and/or have extensive networks of their own on *Facebook* and Twitter and thus one follower on Twitter or *Facebook* equals many hundreds or even thousands of "followers of the follower," who in turn have their own networks. Disney had available both the official *John Carter* Twitter and *Facebook* presence; and the official Walt Disney Pictures Twitter and *Facebook* presence.

4) *Disney Bloggers*: Disney maintains a "Disney Blogger" network which has as many as 500 blogs devoted to all things Disney. With names like *Disney For Life*, *Mouse Dreaming*, *Babes in Disneyland*, *The Disney Dork Blog*, *Disney Fan Ramblings*, *Stitch Kingdom*, *and Adventures By Daddy*, *Everything Walt Disney World*, the Disney bloggers are positioned to exert influence on Disney enthusiasts, but are generally not "in the same league" as the top entertainment blogsites in terms of audience reach and relevance to the potential *John Carter* audience.[98]

The task before Disney at this early stage was to manage their Twitter and *Facebook* profiles effectively, and to maintain a flow of good information and materials to this manageable "ecosystem" of "influencer" bloggers and journalists and "mini-influencers" who are the early adopters on *Facebook* and *Twitter*.

---

[98] Michael D. Sellers, "A Comparison of Key Entertainment Bloggers and Disney Bloggers," *The John Carter Files*, 10 Sep 2012, 10 Sep 2012 <http:// thejohncarterfiles.com/wp-content/uploads/2012/09/Comparison-of-Entertainment-and-Disney-Blogger-Sites.pdf>. A comparison of 10 Key Entertainment Blogsites shows an average of 53,152 *Facebook* Likes per Entertainment site and an average Google Page Rank of 6.1; whereas 10 Key Disney Bloggers show an average of 11,957 *Facebook* likes and an average Google Page Rank of 3.1. See

BREAKING DOWN THE INFLUENCER MEDIA

At the top of the Influencer ecosystem are corporate owned megasites like the Internet Movie Data Base (estimated 80M unique monthly visitors), Yahoo Movies (estimated 27M unique monthly visitors), Rotten Tomatoes (estimated 7M unique monthly visitors), and Fandango (estimated 6.8M unique monthly visitors).[99]

However, when it comes to tracking movies a year or more before their release, the influencers tend to be a more independent and colorful group, none moreso than Harry Knowles of *Ain't It Cool News*. In 1997, the second year that AICN was in existence, Bernard Weinraub wrote in the New York Times:[100]

> Harry Jay Knowles is Hollywood's worst nightmare. In an industry whose executives, agents and producers ferociously seek total control -- over information, over the media, over one another -- this 25-year-old college dropout and confirmed film geek is driving them crazy. His power comes from the bits and bytes of information and gossip spread over his rapidly growing Web site (http://www.aint-it-cool-news.com), which is averaging two million hits a month. He works out of his father's ramshackle home in Austin, Tex., but his impact in Hollywood is extraordinary--and instantaneous.

Of the influencers who focus on upcoming movies, *ComingSoon.net* is one of the largest, with an estimated 1.6M unique monthly visitors, while *MovieWeb*, *Movies.com*, and *Hollywood.co*m each have an estimated 500,000 unique monthly visitors.[101] *Slashfilm*, started by Peter Sciretta in 2005, has an estimated 510,000 unique monthly visitors counts 74,000 *Facebook* fans, carries a Google Page Rank of 7, and has won more than a dozen

---

[99] Ebizmba.com Staff, "Top 15 Most Popular Movie Websites (September 2012)," *EBizMBA.com*, 9 Sep 2012, 11 Sep 2012 <http://www.ebizmba.com/articles/movie-websites>.

[100] Bernard Weinraub, "The Two Hollywoods: Harry Knowles is Always Listening," *The New York Times*, 16 Nov 1997, 10 Sep 2012 <http://www.nytimes.com/1997/11/16/magazine/the-two-hollywoods-harry-knowles-is-always-listening.html>.

[101] Ebizmba.com Staff, "Top 15 Most Popular Movie Websites (September 2012)," *EBizMBA.com*, 9 Sep 2012, 11 Sep 2012 <http://www.ebizmba.com/articles/movie-websites>.

major awards.[102] *Collider.com*, with 32,000 *Facebook* Fans and a Google Page Rank of 7, is self-described by editor-in-chief Steve 'Frosty' Weintraub, as "an uncalled for, online barrage of breaking news, incisive commentary and irreverent attitude that will do for the internet what Art Modell did for the Cleveland Browns; i.e. move it to Baltimore."[103] Sci-fi site *i09* under editor-in-chief Annalee Newitz boasts 161,000 *Facebook* fans and a Google Rank of 7, and defines its beat as "science, science fiction, and the future."[104] UK based *Total Film*, with 125,000 *Facebook* fans, touts itself as "The Modern Guide to Movies" while *ScreenRant*, which was started in 2003 by Vic Holtreman "as a place to rant about some of the dumber stuff related to the movie industry," sports 140,000 *Facebook* Fans and a 7 Google Ranking. Other top influencers include *Hit Fix* (54,000 *Facebook* Fans and a 6 ranking), and *Digital Spy* (47,000 *Facebook* Fans and a 6 ranking).

These, plus a few dozen others, represent a critical mechanism through which a studio can lay a buzz foundation and, equally importantly, keep an ear to the ground for feedback on what is working, and what is not working, as they roll out a film.

DISNEY: THE VIEW FROM OUTSIDE LOOKING IN

For an outsider following the *JCOM* story, this "Preliminaries" phase was unusually long and characterized by sporadic press releases that began in January 2007 with the announcement that Disney was pursuing the Edgar Rice Burroughs Property *"A Princess of Mars."* There were then announcements that Andrew Stanton had been signed to direct the film, and that Michael Chabon had been hired to do a rewrite. Then came the announcement on June 15, 2009 that Taylor Kitsch and Lynn

---

[102] All *Facebook* Fan references refer to the number of "Likes" on the publication's *Facebook* page as of 11 Sep 2012. Google Page Rank index refers to the Google Page Rank as accessed on 11 Sep 2012 at <http://www.prchecker.info/>.

[103] Steve 'Frosty' Weintraub, "Collider.com - About Us", Accessed 12 Sep 2012 <http://collider.com/about/>.

[104] Annalee Newitz, "i09 -- About Us," i09, Accessed 12 Sep 2012 <http://io9.com/about/>.

Collins had been cast as the leads in the film. Some of the articles announcing the cast signing include reference to a budget of $150M:[105]

> Canadian film actor Taylor "Friday Night Lights" Kitsch has been cast as the lead in Disney's upcoming adaptation of author Edgar Rice Burroughs' *John Carter Of Mars*, to be directed by Andrew "Wall-e" Stanton in 2010. Stanton confirmed that the $150 million budgeted sci fi production, will be live-action. "There are so many creatures and characters that half of it's going to be CG," he said. "but it will feel real. The whole thing will feel very, very believable."

Later in the summer of 2009 there were more cast announcements.[106] There was silence in September (the month that studio chief Dick Cook was fired) and in October (the month that Rich Ross was hired as the incoming studio chief). In November, evidence that Ross was reviewing all projects came in the form of a press release that Disney had halted production on *Captain Nemo: 20,000 Leagues Under the Sea* -- a press release that included assurances that this did not mean that Disney was abandoning major event films under Ross, stressing "big event films like *20,000 Leagues*, *John Carter of Mars*, and *Tron* are still a priority."[107]

In the social media arena, on November 28, 2009, Disney created a *Facebook* page for *John Carter of Mars*, although no entries were posted

---

[105] *IMDB Pro*, "Taylor Kitsch Lands on Mars," *IMDB Pro* 16 June 2009, 4 Sep 2012, <http://thejohncarterfiles.com/wp-content/uploads/2012/09/IMDb-Pro-Taylor-Kitsch-Lands-John-Carter-Of-Mars.pdf>; also 16 June 2009, 4 Mar 2012 http://www.hollywoodnorthreport.com/article.php?Article=7297. Note that this casting announcement came three months before Dick Cook would leave Disney, and two months before Disney would announce the acquisition of Marvel. It was one month after Disney CEO Bob Iger had publicly criticized Dick Cook and Disney studios in a conference call with investors and financial journalists.

[106] These were the final elements of the campaign that unfolded under studio chief Dick Cook, who was fired by Disney CEO Bob Iger on September 18, 2009. Rich Ross replaced Cook on October 5, 2009, three months before *JCOM* was scheduled to begin principal photography. In the "house-cleaning" that would follow Ross's arrival, the heads of marketing, production, and the Walt Disney Motion Picture group were all fired.

[107] Michael Fleming, "Disney Docks '20,000 Leagues' Pic," Variety, 16 Nov 2009, 4 Sep 2012 <http://www.variety.com/article/VR1118011454?refCatId=13>.

until January 2010.[108]   Then as *JCOM* began principal photography in January 2010, more releases came, announcing additional cast acquisitions and eventually, on January 16, 2010, came the official announcement that principal photography had begun in London.

On *Facebook*, January 2010 saw Disney make its first social media efforts, posting four articles with links and posting the official synopsis for the first time:

> From Academy Award®-winning filmmaker Andrew Stanton (Finding Nemo, WALL-E), *John Carter of Mars* brings this captivating hero to the big screen in a stunning adventure epic set on the wounded planet of Mars, a world inhabited by warrior tribes and exotic desert beings. Based on the first of Edgar Rice Burroughs' "Barsoom Series," the film chronicles the journey of Civil-War veteran John Carter (Taylor Kitsch), who finds himself battling a new and mysterious war amidst a host of strange Martian inhabitants, including Tars Tarkas (Willem Dafoe) and Dejah Thoris (Lynn Collins).[109]

Then, from February 2010 onward, with the film in Principal Photography, Disney publicity and the still leaderless marketing department went silent. Apart from a brief announcement on March 12, 2010, that Michael Giacchino would score *JCOM*, no visible publicity or marketing efforts were logged by *IMDB Pro* publicity monitoring.[110]   The

---

[108] John Carter Official *Facebook* Page and Timeline, 28 Nov 2010, 4 Sep 2012, <https://www.facebook.com/JohnCarterMovie>

[109] This synopsis was later revised, after the arrival of MT Carney in April 2010, to:
From Academy Award®--winning filmmaker Andrew Stanton comes "John Carter"—a sweeping action-adventure set on the mysterious and exotic planet of Barsoom (Mars). "John Carter" is based on a classic novel by Edgar Rice Burroughs, whose highly imaginative adventures served as inspiration for many filmmakers, both past and present. The film tells the story of war-weary, former military captain John Carter (Taylor Kitsch), who is inexplicably transported to Mars where he becomes reluctantly embroiled in a conflict of epic proportions amongst the inhabitants of the planet, including Tars Tarkas (Willem Dafoe) and the captivating Princess Dejah Thoris (Lynn Collins). In a world on the brink of collapse, Carter rediscovers his humanity when he realizes that the survival of Barsoom and its people rests in his hands. The screenplay was written by Andrew Stanton, Mark Andrews and Michael Chabon.

[110] *IMDB Pro*, "*John Carter* (2012) MovieMeter: Data Table View," *Internet Movie Data Base*, accessed 2 Sep 2012 <http://pro.imdb.com/title/tt0401729/graph-data> also available for PDF download at <http://thejohncarterfiles.com/wp-content/uploads/2012/09/IMDb-Pro-John-Carter-MOVIEmeterData-Table-as-of-Aug-26-2012.pdf>.

Facebook page was not updated;[111] the Twitter account did not exist and would not be created until June 15, 2011;[112] there were no announcements, including no official announcement of the completion of principal photography in July -- a milestone that traditionally receives an announcement in the media.

This period of "media silence" coincided with MT Carney taking over as President of Marketing in April 2010, as *JCOM* was on Day 52 of a 100 day shooting schedule. The silence continued until finally on August 15, 2010, a few weeks after the completion of principal photography, came the first mention of *JCOM* during Carney's tenure -- an announcement that *John Carter of Mars* would be released on June 8, 2012.[113]

Again, "media silence" ensued after the release date announcement -- a silence which continued until the end of the year. Thus in all of 2010 the total output from Disney consisted of four *Facebook* updates in January 2010 followed by silence on *Facebook*;[114] plus (as monitored by Internet Movie Data Base) the announcement of Giacchino's signing in

---

[111] John Carter Official *Facebook* Page and Timeline, 28 Nov 2010, 4 Sep 2012, <https://www.facebook.com/JohnCarterMovie> Note: *Facebook*'s "Timeline" function chronicles the date the page was created, and includes each post by the page owner throughout the history of the page.

[112] Twitter, John Carter Official Twitter Account, 15 Jun 2011, 4 Sep 2012 <http://twitte.com/johncarter>.

[113] *IMDB Pro*, "*John Carter* (2012) MovieMeter: Data Table View," accessed 2 Sep 2012 <http://pro.imdb.com/title/tt0401729/graph-data> also available for PDF download at <http://thejohncarterfiles.com/wp-content/uploads/2012/09/IMDb-Pro-John-Carter-MOVIEmeterData-Table-as-of-Aug-26-2012.pdf>. The *IMDB Pro* Data Table publicity log for John Carter note 22 mentions of John Carter from February 2010 through August 8 2010. Other than the announcement of Giacchino being brought on board to score, all mentions appear to be unrelated to any Disney marketing efforts; for example Bryan Cranston mentioned John Carter during an interview about his appearance in Red Tails; John Carter was mentioned by Universal in its announcements that Taylor Kitsch had been cast for that movie, etc.

[114] John Carter Official *Facebook* Page and Timeline, 28 Nov 2010, 4 Sep 2012, <https://www.facebook.com/JohnCarterMovie>.

April 2010, and the August announcement of the release date being June 8, 2012.[115]

In reviewing the publicity and marketing output of Disney during 2010, the obvious inference to draw is that attention to *JCOM* was sporadic at best, with long periods of silence and no sign of any major engagement by Disney marketing. Such an inference would be consistent with the notion that *JCOM* suffered from Dick Cook's departure; the firing of the entire Cook executive team, and the instability that followed and continued until at least the hiring of MT Carney in April 2010.

In sum, based purely on the public record of the output of the campaign from inception in 2007 through the end of 2010, it is possible only to conclude that Disney did nothing special to draw attention to the film, and limited itself to the basic output of a very few media releases, with no other visible marketing efforts taking place.

THE VIEW FROM WITHIN DISNEY

MT Carney's first major creative decision concerned the tagline for *The Sorcerer's Apprentice* -- coming up with "It's the Coolest Job Ever." When the film flopped badly, the knives came out, with trade magazine *The Hollywood Reporter* labeling it "one of the hall-of-fame worst taglines ever."[116]

The fall and winter 2010-2011 would bring a number of films that looked relatively weak, and in need of some concerted attention. The summer of 2011 would bring *Pirates of the Caribbean: On Stranger Tides*, but it was already established that former Sony Marketing Co-President Valerie Van Gelder was running that show, at Jerry Bruckheimer's insistence.

---

[115]*IMDB Pro*, "*John Carter* (2012) MovieMeter: Data Table View," accessed 2 Sep 2012 <http://pro.imdb.com/title/tt0401729/graph-data> also available for PDF download at <http://thejohncarterfiles.com/wp-content/uploads/2012/09/IMDb-Pro-John-Carter-MOVIEmeterData-Table-as-of-Aug-26-2012.pdf>.

[116] Kim Masters, "Disney hires new marketing guru for 'Pirates 4'," *Hollywood Reporter*, 7 Sep 2010, 3 Sep 2012 <http://www.hollywoodreporter.com/news/disney-hires-new-marketing-guru-27524>

Farther out, Marvel's *The Avengers* was already being touted as a "can't miss" winner slated for release in May 2012, and the Marvel team had already, by the time the acquisition took place, put in place a long and varied list of corporate partners, creative cross promotions, and merchandising tie-ins. *John Carter of Mars*, slated for June 8, 2012 release, was next, followed by Pixar's *Brave*.

MT CARNEY'S BAPTISM BY FIRE

One of Carney's first acts was to reorganize the department into pods of focus rather than have everyone work on each movie. She ordered a study of Disney's ad-buying process; she got rid of more than a dozen staff members; and she implemented a chic redesign of the offices in Burbank where the marketing division operated. She also undertook a round of firings in which some of the senior staff were replaced with new, younger staff who in Carney's view were more digitally savvy than the oldsters she was letting go, and thus were more in line with Rich Ross's vision for the direction the marketing division should take.

But if Ross and Carney had an idea of transforming the department, the iconic producers relying on Disney marketing were not so sure and thus the early months of Carney's tenure were also marked by the hiring of marketing veterans who were assigned specifically to Disney's major "client producers" to handle their product. Valerie Van Galder was brought in to handle the upcoming *Pirates of the Caribbean: On Stranger Tides* for Jerry Bruckheimer; Kevin Campbell was brought in at the behest of Dreamworks CEO Stacey Snider to handle Dreamworks films; and Dana Precious was hired to handle Marvel. A senior media strategist, Michael Kassan, was also brought in to review all aspects of Disney's marketing strategy -- with the net result leaving Carney in a role that was bearing increasing signs of a coordinator -- with an exception to this being John Carter.

As the films began to roll out, Carney was forced to learn quickly about what Sharon Waxman, writing in the respected "The Wrap" would call "the shark-infested waters of major studio movie releases."[117]   The first major film in the pipeline, *The Sorcerer's Apprentice*, opened on July 14 to an anemic $17M domestically en route to a $63M domestic and $215 worldwide total. Her second major release, *Secretariat*, opened on October 7 to just $12.6M and was soundly beaten by *The Social Network* in its second week.

But while the "client producers" would all get their own marketing consultant, in what would turn out to be a fateful decision *John Carter of Mars* -- lacking a Bruckheimer, Spielberg, or Feige to please -- was not assigned an outside consultant. The in-house Disney team would handle the picture, headed by Carney herself.

While there was considerable interest in Hollywood in the Carney experiment, Carney herself gave few interviews and was rarely quoted. One exception: in the aftermath of the Secretariat opening in October, veteran Hollywood journalist Sharon Waxman got Carney to sit down for an interview and asked her tough questions about her early months in Hollywood. Carney's answers are revealing on multiple levels:[118]

> *On the hiring of consultants:* "I'm very respectful of the movie business and of people's experience. I feel the combination of my experience and their movie experience will be great. I have hired and I will continue to hire the absolute best people that I can find. I'm aware of the fact that I don't have tons of experience, so I hire around me the people that have experience that are really good. You'll see the people I'm going to hire over the next couple of months, it just keeps getting better. Do I think I can cut a better 30 second spot than Val Van Galder than Dana Precious? Of course I can't. That's why I hired them. I have other skills. And the combination of that together will be something really cool--if you people just give me a chance."
>
> *On the Secretariat marketing strategy:* "This one I look and can't think what we did wrong. We had huge buzz. We got more Internet

[117] Sharon Waxman, "Is Disney's MT Carney Ready for Hollywood's Shark-Infested Waters?," *The Wrap*, 10 Oct 2010, 3 Sep 2012 <http://www.thewrap.com/movies/column-post/education-disneys-mt-carney-she-ready-hollywoods-shark-infested-waters-21592>.

[118] Sharon Waxman, "Exclusive: Disney's MT Carney, Grilled -- 'A Baptism by Fire'," *The Wrap*, 10 Oct 2010, 3 Sep 2012 <http://www.thewrap.com/movies/article/mt-carney-grilled-21594?page=0,0>.

buzz than a whole lot of movies. In the heartland people are older, they don't run out to see a movie on its first weekend, and "Social Network" held on better than we thought. It took away a big chunk of our audience. I don't think we made any big mistakes in marketing campaign. I'm very proud of the campaign, and it's a shame it wasn't a massive rip-roaring success. Randall and Gordon McVeigh and Sean and Rich – everybody was completely on board. All the team. This was movie that Rich and Sean didn't greenlight, everyone really wanted it to do well. We did our best, put together great campaign."

On whether her experience in New York meant she could bring insight to Hollywood: "There are some simple fixes in the way things are put together in terms of process and structure which can make things much more effective. We just came from doing a four-day conference with marketing and distribution executives in Europe. We talked about planning further in advance, and taking into consideration the needs of individual markets further in advance so we're not doing just-in-time planning. The way it was done different [by Disney]. So people have marketing plans early, that is changing the way we work with non-domestic markets so we can start to become much more global. Movies are so global now. And we're trying to make sure that everything we do strategically we do for a reason, and not just because it's cool. There can't be any dead ends in what we do. Everything should link to something else. And everything should link to a sale. Getting everyone to work together in collaborative. It sounds kumbaya, but it's just very practical."

Carney, new to the industry and with a very full plate of other issues demanding her focus, would be directly in charge of the *JCOM* campaign. Her "strategic vision" as revealed in the interview with Waxman speaks for itself.

CHANGING THE JOHN CARTER RELEASE DATE

As it happened, it was not until January 2011 that something occurred that would bring *JCOM* fully onto Carney's radar. Tim Burton's *Frankenweenie*, scheduled for release on March 9, 2012, needed to be moved to a later release date. That left open the March 9 date -- the same weekend that had worked extremely well for *Alice in Wonderland* in 2010. It was already clear that the 2011 offering for that weekend, *Mars Needs Moms*, was in trouble and would not perform well -- but it was not a weekend, or month, that could be lightly cast aside; a film needed to be identified and placed in the March 9, 2012 slot.

Could *JCOM* be ready for a March 9, 2012 release?

The decision had to be made shortly after Sean Bailey and Brigham Taylor had viewed the 170 minute cut of the film that Stanton had shown to the "Brain Trust" at Pixar in December 2010. Normally, if Bailey as head of production felt that *JCOM* was in trouble, the idea of advancing the release by three months would make no sense, particularly with "tentpole dollars" at stake. But Bailey gave a thumbs up to *JCOM* being moved forward, with Morris, Collins, and Stanton all agreeing to the move.

Besides the fact that March is not blockbuster "primetime" in the way that June is, the other problem with March 9, 2012, was that Ridley Scott's Sci-Fi epic *Prometheus* was slated for that date. Did Disney really want to put *JCOM* up head to head against Fox's *Prometheus*? Or, if *JCOM* vacated June 8, could Fox be induced to move *Prometheus* from March to June, in effect swapping dates with the Disney film?

Ross, Carney, Bailey and President of Distribution Chuck Viane, a 25 year Disney veteran and a close ally of the departed Dick Cook, analyzed the situation. June 2012 was looking very crowded now. with *Snow White and Huntsman* and *GI Joe: Retaliation* all hitting, followed by a jam-packed July starting with *The Amazing Spiderman*. Could a case be made to justify moving *JCOM* to March to fill the slot vacated by *Frankenweenie?*

No one felt that Stanton's film would prosper from the swap if it meant going up head to head with *Prometheus*. As crowded as it was in June -- the total available box office in that month was far higher than March. The June "pie" was typically $1.1-$1.5B, while the March "pie" was typically $650-900M, although the previous year, 2010, with *Alice in Wonderland* having a surprisingly strong run, the March total had reached $1B. But without an *Alice in Wonderland*, March tended to be around $750M which meant that *JCOM* would need a much larger relative share of the market if it moved to March. *Prometheus* was a problem, and *The Hunger Games* on March 23 was also a problem.

But, assuming *Prometheus* would move to June, could it work?

On balance, *JCOM* would still be better off in June.   True, there would be more competition, but the adage that "every day is a weekend" in June meant that *JCOM* would prosper even with a relatively smaller share of the available audience, because the available audience was that much larger.

But while *JCOM* would benefit from sticking to the June release, the studio still had a problem -- it had a hole to fill in March because *Frankenweenie* simply wasn't on track to be ready.

A tentative decision was reached: As long as the Stanton didn't scream too loudly,   *John Carter of Mars* would take the vacated *Frankenweenie* spot and move to March 9, 2012, which would give it the exact same weekend that *Alice in Wonderland* had done so well with in 2010.

It was also the exact same weekend that the upcoming flop-in-the-making *Mars Needs Moms* would be released in 2011.

Planning began to make the announcement on January 19, 2011

The January 19, 2011 announcement of the release date change would be the first official announcement recorded by *IMDB* from Disney about JCOM since August 15, 2010, when the original release date of June 8, 2012 had been confirmed.   An interesting component of the announcement on August 15th is that the announcement made no mention of the film's budget (which had previously been announced as $150M, at the time Taylor Kitsch had been cast), and the press coverage of the announcement was uniformly positive.   *Empire Online*, for example, in announcing the June 8 date had referred to *John Carter of Mars* as "all kinds of exciting,"[119]   Brian Gallagher of *Movieweb* called it "highly anticipated,"[120] *Joey Paur* at Geek Tyrant talked of it as a film "I'm

[119] Empire Online Staff, "Release Date for John Carter of Mars; also Frankenweenie," *Empire Online*, 15 Aug 2010, 3 Sep 2012 <http://www.empireonline.com/news/feed.asp?NID=28599>.

[120] Brian Gallagher, "John Carter of Mars and Frankenweenie Set Release Dates", *MovieWeb*, 15 Aug 2010, 3 Sep 2012 <http://www.movieweb.com/news/john-carter-of-mars-and-frankenweenie-set-release-dates>.

very much looking forward to seeing," [121] and in all -- of more than 40 publications that covered the announcement, none offered any negative commentary. Also interesting is the fact that the reader comments reacting to the announcement contained less than 10% negative -- and that negativity was generally directed at the announcement's acknowledgment that the film, which had been shot with traditional 2D cameras, would be presented in post-modified Disney 3D.

A key feature of the *John Carter of Mars* promotional profile as of the time that the announcement was made was that, up until that time, while there had not been a great deal of publicity generated about the film, what publicity had been generated had been positive. There had been zero negative press coverage of the film -- it had a "clean sheet" as of January 19, 2011. Thus the "influencer" media was on board with *John Carter*, and the negativity that would later surface had not yet manifested itself.

Carney, whose expertise in modern digital media had been a key factor in hiring her over others who were more qualified in the traditional aspects of movie marketing, made sure that the journalists to whom the news of the change in release date were given the story as Disney wanted it to be played -- that the move was a bold one, pitting *JCOM* against Ridley Scott's presumed blockbuster *Prometheus*.

The "spin" worked as planned, up to a point. Typical of the coverage was *Deadline New York*, which in reporting the move, wrote: "there were definitely some raised eyebrows at Fox today at this aggressive *John Carter Of Mars* vs *Prometheus* scheduling move by Disney. Dogfight! *Prometheus* is that Ridley Scott film scripted with *Lost's* Damon Lindelof from Alien DNA. So now Disney's 3D *John Carter Of Mars* based on Edgar Rice Burroughs' fantasy series comes off its June 8th, 2012, date and onto March 9, 2012." [122]

---

[121] Joey Paur, "Disney Sets Release Dates for John Carter of Mars and Frankenweenie," *Geek Tyrant*, 15 Aug 2010, 3 Sep 2012 < http://geektyrant.com/news/2010/8/9/disney-sets-release-dates-for-john-carter-of-mars-and-franke.html>.

[122] Mike Fleming, "Disney Moves 'John Carter of Mars' to Same Date as Fox's 'Prometheus'," *Deadline New York*, 19 Jan 2011, 3 Sep 2012 < http://www.deadline.com/2011/01/disney-shifts-release-dates-on-john-carter-of-mars-and-frankenweenie/>.

But while Disney was generally successful in controlling the journalists through whom the story was released; it was less successful in controlling the comment threads in which readers -- who in marketing terms were key consumer "influencers" as well, since the comments become part of the article -- would react to the announcement. And it was here, in the comment threads, that the first bits of negativity toward *JCOM* began to surface: One typical comment, in response to the Deadline New York announcement: *"I certainly hope the move of John Carter of Mars from summer to pre-May is not indicative of the quality of the film being less-than expected."*

But although these comments were significant because they marked the first negativity, the negativity was mild and overall, the announcement was managed effectively enough that the comment never got out of hand; the ratio of positive/negative comments stayed at 90%/10% or better, and the universe that tracked movie release dates in advance generally accepted Disney's arguments as to why the move was a good, aggressive one, rather than a vote of 'no confidence' for the movie.

A week after Disney announced that *JCOM* was moving to March 9, Fox announced that *Prometheus* was moving its release date to June 8, 2012, in essence swapping with *John Carter*. This created the impression, desired by Carney on behalf of *JCOM* and Disney, that Disney's aggressive move had caused *Prometheus* to blink, and move, leaving the March 9 date to *JCOM*.

But while the announcement had been made without serious blowback, with the accelerated release date came a renewed urgency to ramp up the promotion and publicity. Disney had released nothing to the media about *JCOM* from August 15, 2010, until the January 19, 2011, announcement of the release date change.[123] Carney had assured Ross

---

[123] MDB Pro, *"John Carter* (2012) MovieMeter: Data Table View," accessed 2 Sep 2012 <http://pro.imdb.com/title/tt0401729/graph-data> also available for PDF download at <http://thejohncarterfiles.com/wp-content/uploads/2012/09/IMDb-Pro-John-Carter-MOVIEmeterData-Table-as-of-Aug-26-2012.pdf>. Note that *IMDB Pro* publicity monitoring noted 6 casual mentions of John Carter in articles principally about other topics between the August 2010 announcement that Principal Photography had wrapped and the January 19, 2011 announcement of the date change. All appear to be incidental mentions by third parties; none appear to have been generated by the John Carter campaign.

that the campaign could handle the earlier release date; now it was time to begin making good on that assurance.

But curiously, even after the accelerated release date was announced on January 19, 2011, the months of February, March, and April 2011 were as bereft of any coverage of *JCOM* as the previous six months had been.

The one exception: On January 31, 2011, in a brief interview which was not arranged by Disney publicity and which took place on the red carpet during his arrival at the MTV Movie Awards, Stanton provided what would be the only public update on the status of the movie during what would be a nine month period from the original release date announcement on August 15, 2010, until May 2011. Stanton's update, which was posted by MTV, was widely picked up across the entertainment spectrum, included:[124]

> I'm not in post-production — I'm in digital principal photography now, which goes on for the rest of 2011, so I'm only halfway through the movie........When you've made animated movies your whole life, it was pretty exciting to be outside for a day, let alone for months. For as cold and as hot and as hard as it was, which I knew it would be, I was up for it and it was a blast. It was the hardest thing I'll ever have done, but man, it was a great adventure. It was like sailing across the ocean, you know, everything that goes with that.
>
> Hopefully he'll [Taylor Kitsch] be another great face on the big screen, and hopefully he'll be John Carter to people and nobody else if we've done it right. ....I didn't try to make it [the film] look like anything else. I really tried to make it its own thing. I tried to make a very historically accurate Martian film if that makes sense, so I'll let you decipher that.

The interview prompted reactions on the various sites that published it. The following exchange, from the popular site Slashfilm.com, is significant for several reasons:[125]

[124] Josh Wigler, "'John Carter of Mars' Will Be a 'Historically Accurate' Martian Film,' Says Director Andrew Stanton," *MTV Movie Blog*, 31 Jan 2011, 3 Sep 2012 <http://moviesblog.mtv.com/2011/01/31/john-carter-of-mars-andrew-staton/>.

[125] Germain Lussier, "Andrew Stanton Offers 'John Carter of Mars' Update," *Slashfilm*, 31 Jan 2011, 3 Sep 2012<http://www.slashfilm.com/andrew-stanton-offers-john-carter-mars-update/>.

Daniel H: This is easily one of my most anticipated movies of 2012. It's interesting that there's been such a tight lid on this movie, there's not been a single image released of anyone in costume as far as I'm aware.

Corey A: FINALLY. That man has been in radio silence for like a year and a half. Great to hear things are moving along. Can't wait for *John Carter*.

Tobor 68: I was just thinking about this film and wondering where it's at! so good timing on the article! historically accurate Martians, well that sounds like they've done their research on sci-fi imagery of the era. probably what kind of imagery ERB was saturated with. so, for me, being a fan of that era. this will be astounding and/or amazing!!

JP Money: "historically accurate Martians, well that sounds like they've done their research on sci-fi imagery of the era."

Palmer S. It amazes me how under wraps they've managed to keep this whole production; can't wait to see the finished product.

FJ2036: Wow I forgot about this project, there hasn't been any buzz or articles on movie websites/magazines. Can't wait to see a official image!

This exchange of comments questioning the 'media silence' over *JCOM* was repeated on multiple sites that carried the Andrew Stanton interview, and is significant. Movie marketing in 2012 relies on social media chatter, and comments are monitored for the volume; the subject matter; and the positive/negative ratio.

At this moment, thirteen months before the release, the film had been "buried" for months with no effort being made to "prime the pump" with early articles, set visits, images, and interviews.

Why?

The fact was -- it was the sudden acceleration of the *JCOM* release schedule that finally brought the film to MT Carney's full attention. Previously the release was still 16 months out; now, suddenly, at was barely a year out and it was time to focus on it.

With that focus, a problem surfaced.

THE BRANDING PROBLEM

Like virtually all of the films in the pipeline, *John Carter of Mars* had been green-lit by the previous regime of Dick Cook, so that alone did not differentiate it. But the fact that its budget was a whopping $250M, and it was being produced by a Pixar team headed by Andrew Stanton but also including Pixar's general manager Jim Morris and Pixar producer Lindsey Collins, made it different. The word had come down from Iger through Ross to Carney that it was to be sold traditionally, without the kind of creative marketing and cross-promotional tie-ins that Marvel had dazzlingly arranged for *The Avengers*. Faced with the new release date of March 9, 2012, Carney conducted a strategic review of the project.

Challenge number one was what was known in brand strategy circles as "brand misalignment:" or "brand incongruency" -- a situation in which the product being promoted is not in alignment or congruency with the brand it is being sold under. Rich Ross had consolidated down to three brands: Disney (family), Pixar (animation), and Marvel (superhero/action).[126]

Was *JCOM* a good fit as a Disney-branded release?

Disney was one of the most storied brands in the world and it was perfectly well understood the "brand promise" of Disney was "fun family entertainment." Recently this had been officially revised internally at Disney to be "entertainment with heart" -- an attempt to broaden the brand promise. But while this broadening may have been understood within Disney, to the general public it was still "fun family entertainment."

Arrayed against this was the reality that for 100 years the Edgar Rice Burroughs Martian series of books had been sold not as family entertainment. Instead, it promised that the story within would be *heart-pounding romantic adventure in a richly imagined fantastical setting*. The imagery associated with the novels had always been that of sword-bearing John Carter protecting scantily clad Dejah Thoris from threat by fantastical creatures. The stories themselves -- told in first person by grown man of

---

[126] Brooks Barnes, "New Team Alters Disney Studios' Path," *The New York Times*, 26 Sep 2010, 2 Sep 2012 <http://www.nytimes.com/2010/09/27/business/media/27disney.html>.

in-determinant age who hacked his way to a substantial body count of dead Tharks and Zodangans as he pursued romantic acceptance by the Princess of the title--were clearly intended for adults at the time they were written. Indeed, the one essential ingredient in family friendly adventure -- the presence of teenage or younger characters -- was completely absent. There were no teen or child characters in Burroughs' books, nor would there be in Stanton's movie.

But what were the options?

Because the Disney brand is so strong and specific, and the brand promise so well understood, Disney had long ago realized that in order to participate in a wider range of films than the Disney brand allowed, it needed to have a non-Disney-branded way of participating with films that don't meet the very precise "brand congruency" or "brand alignment" requirements of a "Disney" branded film. Disney did this by creating three alternate labels under which it released films that didn't precisely meet the definition of a "Disney" film. These alternate labels include *Buena Vista*, *Hollywood Pictures*, and *Touchstone Pictures*. Recent examples of films released under the Touchstone label include *The Help*, *Step Up 3D*, *War Horse*, *The Tempest*, and sci-fi pictures *I Am Number Four* and *Real Steel*. Buena Vista Pictures has been used as the label for *Wild Hogs*, *Bridge to Terabithia*, *The Game Plan*, and *Ratatouille*, and even one of the *Pirates of the Caribbean* movies -- *Pirates of the Caribbean: At World's End*. Notably *20,000 Leagues under the Sea*, under development at the time *John Carter* went into production, was slated as a Buena Vista Pictures release. The Hollywood Pictures label was used for, among others, Michael Bay's *The Rock*.

But under Iger and Ross Disney had "semi-retired" the Buena Vista and Touchstone labels. *JCOM* would go out as a Disney branded film -- no other option was acceptable to Ross or Iger. After all, the argument went, the *Pirates of the Caribbean* franchise was PG-13 and did just fine as a Disney release. The counterargument was that the *Pirates of the Caribbean* films had been based on a wildly popular theme park ride, and had been carefully co-branded as Jerry Bruckheimer Films productions, which blurred any incongruence in a way that *JCOM*, without a co-brand, would not. This was crucial. Bruckheimer was a preeminent brand for adult action films with a storied history that included *Con-Air*,

Armageddon, Blackhawk Down, Pearl Harbor, Gone in Sixty Seconds, and *National Treasure.* Co-branding with Bruckheimer was a shrewd move which assured that adult audiences who might be put off by the Disney logo on an action film, would be reassured. *The Avengers,* in the pipeline behind *John Carter,* would go out as a "Marvel Studios" release with virtually no mention of Disney in the promotion.

But *John Carter* would, for better or worse, go into the market branded as pure Disney.

This left MT Carney with two choices -- sell it as what it really was and just let the misalignment with the Disney brand exist; or somehow try to make the square peg that was *John Carter* fit into the round hole that was the Disney brand. And in the end, that was the decision that was made: *John Carter of Mars* would be released as a Disney film, and Carney would build a campaign that kept it on the Disney brand reservation.

THE FIRST MARKETING BLUNDER

After the announcement on January 19, 2011 that *John Carter of Mars* would move its release date forward from June 8 to March 9, 2012, Disney went silent yet again on the publicity front. One reason was that MT Carney and her team were preoccupied first with the looming disaster that was *Mars Needs Moms*, and secondarily with Carney's efforts to come to grips with both the brand misalignment she saw in *JCOM*, and the recent history of films with "Mars" in the title doing poorly -- this last being a problem that was certain to be exacerbated when the anemic *Mars Needs Moms* reached theaters exactly one year ahead of *JCOM*.

In Carney's view, the pulpy, geeky, *John Carter of Mars* title unnecessarily excluded large portions of the audience that would be needed if the film was to avoid being as big a disaster as *Mars Needs Moms* was likely to be.

Carney's solution: drop "of Mars" from the title and go with the simple "*John Carter.*"

Carney organized focus group testing, the results of which supported her contention that a wider audience could be attracted by dropping "of Mars" from the title. She presented her findings to Rich Ross and got his concurrence.

That left Andrew Stanton to be convinced.

Carney found Stanton difficult to deal with, and so she proceeded cautiously. In late 2010, the first work on a what would eventually become the first trailer was begun, and members of the team visited Stanton and presented their work, which Stanton rejected on a number of occasions. One production team member familiar with the early trailers brought in said: "They were all one version or another of 'in a world where' generic trailers and Andrew was all about it not being generic. Then on January 27, 2011, a week after announcing the March 9 release date switch, Disney hired Frank Chiocchi, an EVP of marketing at Universal whom Hollywood reporter called "one of the best in the business in regards to trailers" as the new head of creative media for all live-action titles, reporting directly to MT Carney.[127] Chiocchi had come up through the ranks of the industry, staring in radio in Phoenix, then owning an ad agency there. He moved into film marketing in 1996 with top agency CmP (now called mOcean," then moved to Universal in 2002 where he oversaw both print and audio visual campaigns. He was assigned to deal with Stanton.

Chiocchi, with Stanton's blessing, brought in Joseph Tamusaitis, an award winning creative director whose previous work included the trailer for Pixar's "Up" and Disney's "Prince of Persia."

Over a period of several months Chiocchi and Tamusaitis struggled to find an approach to the trailer that Stanton would accept. Finally in March, during reshoots at the La Playa stage near LAX, Tamusaitis showed up with a completely new version using Peter Gabriel's "My Body is a Cage," and it was instantly "problem solved" for Stanton.

---

[127] Pamela McClintock, "Disney Hiring Marketing Maven Frank Chiocchi (Exclusive)," *The Hollywood Reporter,* 27 Jan 2011, 3 Sep 2012 <http://www.hollywoodreporter.com/blogs/risky-business/disney-hiring-marketing-maven-frank-84276>.

From that point forward, work on the teaser trailer went smoothly, at least from Stanton and the production team's standpoint. "It was a clear breakthrough moment and everyone felt it would work — and Andrew clearly felt justified in having been hardheaded about it," explained one of those present on the production side.

The trailer was clearly not the one that Carney had wanted to put out there; the earlier efforts which Stanton had nixed, and which were much closer to the eventual main theatrical trailer that would hit screens December, represented her take on what was needed.

So, who was in charge of the marketing?

Did Stanton have the power to veto the trailers that the marketing team were presenting to him?

Technically, no -- he did not have absolute veto power. As director he had what is defined contractually as "meaningful consultation" on trailers, key art, and so on, but he did not have absolute approval or formal control. In sending the trailer back to be reworked again and again, Stanton was treading a fine line, but he felt justified in pushing for the all important "first impression" to be different.

As for Chiocchi and Tamusaitis -- they were caught between their need to satisfy two bosses who had different views, Stanton and Carney. The dynamic of a first time director trumping a studio marketing chief was an unusual one -- but it was an unusual situation. The marketing chief was inexperienced and overloaded; Stanton had the Pixar "clout factor" working in his favor, and it was still early days so on the first trailer, Stanton was largely given his way. MT Carney and her team felt it focused too much on the love story, and there wasn't enough action in it, and especially not enough eye-popping special effects (even though this is a common problem with most "first trailers" for VFX laden films -- the major VFX shots often aren't ready by the time the first teaser trailer comes out). By late May 2011 the trailer had been approved and was set for a July debut.

After the prickly experience with the trailer, Carney left it to Rich Ross to break the news to Stanton about the title change. The meeting occurred soon after the trailer had been locked, and was one of the few face to face meetings between Ross and Stanton during production and completion of the film Ross explained Carney's theory that "of Mars" was narrowing the audience unacceptably, and that focus group testing confirmed that reducing the title to "*John Carter*" would open it up to a larger audience.

Stanton was taken aback. He had been the originator of the title change from "*A Princess of Mars*" to *John Carter of Mars*, claiming that he felt that "Princess" in the title of a Disney made movie would drive the male audience away. But he had never contemplated dropping "of Mars."

"Stanton bristled at first; he wasn't in love with the title change at all. But it was presented to him as a done deal, not an item for his approval, and his only option other than accepting it would have been to throw a tantrum and threaten to quit. He didn't do that. He accepted it, " said a production colleague who was among the early group to hear from Stanton about the meeting with Ross. "After giving it some thought, he eventually concluded that from a creative point of view John Carter becomes "John Carter of Mars" through the course of the first movie, and that helped him make his peace with it on a creative level."

When giving interviews in 2011 Stanton put forward a united front with the studio, giving the impression that he had been the author of the latest name change. But later he gave a more definitive explanation for what had happened, and how:[128]

> At the time there was panic about *Mars Needs Moms*. That wasn't convincing to me to do anything. Then they did all this testing and found out that a huge bulk of people were saying no off the title. You can't lie about that stuff, that's the response you're getting. I was like 'Eh, that's what the movie is.' But I don't want to hurt people from coming to the movie. Then I realized the movie is about that arc [of John Carter's character], and I said, 'I'll change it if you let me change it at the end. And if you let me keep the JCM logo.' Because it means something by the end of the movie, and if there are more movies I want that to be what you remember. It may seem like an odd thing, but I wanted it to be the reverse Harry Potter. With the latest Harry Potter they had Harry Potter

[128] Devin Faraci, "Andrew Stanton Explains Why It's Still John Carter of Mars ... Technically," *Badass Digest*, 29 Feb 2011, 2 Sep 2012 <http://badassdigest.com/2012/02/29/andrew-stanton-explains-why-its-still-john-carter-of-mars-technically/>

and the Blah Blah Blah Blah, but you just see the HP. I wanted the JCM to mean something.

Until now Stanton and the production team had been referring to the project as *JCOM*. Now that "of Mars" was gone, they would begin referring to it informally as *'Carter.*

At Disney, with the decision to change the title now in place, the focus shifted to the question of how and when to announce it -- and how to make sure that it was received positively.

In this, Carney's inexperience played a role.

A WATERSHED MOMENT -- THE ROOTS OF NEGATIVITY

The announcement of the title change was by far the biggest "marketing moment" of the campaign up to this point. It was a decision which, it could be reasonably assumed, would be second guessed by many of the influencers whom Disney needed to maintain as allies, and who had been following the movie for years, always as *John Carter of Mars*.[129]

The solution selected by MT Carney was to leak the information to Garth Franklin of *Dark Horizons*, who in turn tweeted about it: *"John Carter of Mars* is now just *John Carter."*[130]

Reaction to the title change was uniformly hostile across the dozen or so entertainment outlets that reported it. Adam Chitwood at *Collider.com* called it "disappointing,"[131] while at *CinemaBlend* Eric

---

[129] Both Paramount from 2000-2006, and Disney before that from 1986-2000, had settled on *John Carter of Mars* as the title for the film.

[130] Garth Franklin, Dark Horizons Twitter Feed, 23 May 2011, 2 Sep 2012, <https://twitter.com/darkhorizons/status/72573086767132672>.

[131] Adam Chitwood, "Title Changes: John Carter of Mars Becomes John Carter," Collider.com, 23 May 2011, 2 Sep 2012, < http://collider.com/john-carter-of-mars-title-in-time/92540/>.

Eisenberg called it "quite confounding,"[132] and *GeekTyrant's* Joey Paur called it "stupid" and a "brain fart," adding: "That's a boring title and it's just distanced itself even further from the Edgar Rice Burroughs classic novels from which the film was adapted. So how is that helping the movie? It's not."[133]

Slashfilm's Germain Lussier wrote:[134]

> Double Academy Award-winning director of Finding Nemo and WALL-E, Andrew Stanton, is currently working on his first foray into live action, an adaptation of the classic sci-fi fantasy novel *John Carter of Mars* by Edgar Rice Burroughs. For some reason, though, Disney has now changed the title from that to "Gary Carter," the Hall Of Fame catcher for the 1986 New York Mets. No, I'm sorry. I meant *John Carter.* That's the new official title. For real.

Clearly and unequivocally, the title change had landed with a thud.

It was time for a little damage control.

THE 'REPUTATION MANAGEMENT' THAT DIDN'T HAPPEN

As an executive familiar with digital marketing best practices, Carney's team would be expected to have been paying attention to not only the articles by entertainment journalists and bloggers -- but also the comments by readers, as well as comments on *Twitter, Facebook,* and other social networks and micro-blogs. Such monitoring, with quick response capabilities ready to be deployed, is a standard feature of what is most commonly referred to as "reputation management" -- the reputation being that of the brand that is in play, in this case, *"John Carter."*

---

[132] Eric Eisenberg, "John Carter of Mars Now Just John Carter; Andrew Niccol's Now Retitled In Time," *Cinemablend,* 23 May 2011, 2 Sep 2012 <http://www.cinemablend.com/new/John-Carter-Of-Mars-Now-Just-John-Carter-Andrew-Niccol-s-Now-Retitled-In-Time-24846.html>.

[133] Joey Paur, "Disney Changes the Title of John Carter of Mars to John Carter," *Geek Tyrant,* 23 May 2011, 3 Sep 2012 <http://geektyrant.com/news/2011/5/23/disney-changes-the-title-for-john-carter-of-mars-to-john-car.html>.

[134] Germain Lussier, "Title Changes for Former 'John Carter of Mars,' 'Now' and 'Still I Rise,'" *Slashfilm,* 23 May 2011, http://www.slashfilm.com/title-john-carter-mars-now-still-rise/

Echo Research,[135] one of the top Reputation Management providers, describes the tools normally employed to monitor reputation, include: "competitive benchmarking, reputation scorecards, key performance indicators, journalist surveys, media content analysis, new media measurement . . . reputation survey and analysis, PR and communications measurement and rating methodologies." Software programs that are readily available and used by studios and independent distributors allow the studio to monitor the chatter, assess how much buzz is being generated, and quickly determine the positive/negative ratio. It is widely considered to be an important marketing tool -- and particularly so when dealing with a theatrical release, where there are no "do-overs." Recognizing a "reputation problem" and taking steps to correct it is a critical function, and one which -- on something as sensitive as changing the name of a brand -- would normally be expected to be a high priority for any company, and especially so for a $250M theatrical film.

Aside from the negative comments by the influencers who posted their articles -- what sort of reader comments were appearing on the sites covering the name change?

The comments on the *Slashfilm* article typical of the reaction across the internet:[136]

> *Ken C* John Carter? That's the one where Samuel L Jackson plays a basketball coach, right?
>
> *Octoberist:* John Carter sounds generic while 'John Carter of Mars' sounds more pulpy and kinda bold. Bad move, and I hope Disney changes it back.
>
> *DNW:* The should, but they won't. Rapunzel became *Tangled*, The Bear & The Bow became Brave...it's a trend.
>
> *The Dead Burger:* I need to pay more attention to John Carter; I just noticed that Stanton directed my two favorite Pixar movies. Gotta put that one on my list.

---

[135] Echo Research 2012, 4 Sep 2012 <http://www.echoresearch.com/us/services/corporate-reputation-management/>.

[136] It is impractical to cite the comments from all 20 or so of the articles that appeared; however in researching this, each article and the comment threads were examined and the one chosen is typical of the totality of the response.

Marley L: In Andrew Stanton I Trust....

Andreas C: The only reason I can see to change the title of "John Carter of Mars" would be that simply "John Carter" could work better with sequels, but aside from that, the title change makes no sense at all. Very odd.

Monster Killed the Pilot: 'John Carter' will look lame on the movie poster.

Ian T: If I were at Disney, I'd be afraid people assumed John Carter was that guy from the Terminator movies.

Mudassir C: or the doctor from ER

VSK: Did they mean John Carter the ER doctor?

VL: The bad news just keeps rolling in. Andrew Stanton has done plenty to earn trust, don't get me wrong, but everything (except the Giacchino score) sounds like this is going in the wrong direction.

The net result? Carney had tried to reposition the film in a more favorable way for the millions of non-geek, non-influencer, non-fanboy viewers who would never hear of the film until much closer to the release date. In so doing, she had sowed the seeds of distrust and disappointment among the early influencer audience who tracked movies far in advance; commented on blogs; wrote about them on message boards, *Facebook*, and *Twitter*, and generally set the tone, positive or negative, that would become the "buzz foundation" long before the casual audience that was the target of the name change even started paying attention. It was an entirely predictable response.

The question then becomes -- was Carney and her team paying attention to the reaction? Once the negatives starting rolling in, what sort of countermeasures were taken?

An obvious move that not only would have helped as a countermeasure, but would have clearly been a much more effective way of rolling out the news in a way the preempted criticism, would have been to have director Andrew Stanton make the announcement in an interview or release that included an explanation for the reasoning behind it. Stanton was silent, however, and only was heard on the subject in "edit bay" interviews that took place a month after the title change was announced, and which were embargoed by Disney until July 11, by which time any ability to affect the flow of negativity had been lost.[137]

There is no evidence that Disney either actively monitored the response, or took any countermeasures. No one from Disney went on record with any explanation; no one from the production weighed in on the topic; and there was no second wave of articles from bloggers stating a more favorable attitude toward the name change (something that would typically reflect a 'reputation management' effort as Disney publicists reached out to bloggers and entertainment journalists).

Meanwhile the negative response to the name change was a watershed moment in the unfolding image of the film. It was a moment when a willing and cooperative audience of key influencers went from a positive orientation supportive of the film, to doubting naysayers who would, increasingly, question everything they saw or heard about the film.

Why was it handled so awkwardly?

Regardless of the "why" of it, the "what" was clear enough: MT Carney, hired in part because of her expertise in social media and new media marketing, failed to anticipate the negative reaction and when it came, apparently failed to value the influencers enough to even monitor them -- and for sure failed to employ reputation management best practices to control and minimize the damage.

Disney's status as a capable steward of the project had taken a hit, and the credibility of the entire enterprise had been knocked down a substantial notch. But the moment for countermeasures had passed. It was on to the next phase of the campaign -- one which would see the unveiling of the first poster, the first trailer, and many other firsts that would set the tone for the film's ultimate reception.

IGER AND LUCAS - THE DANCE BEGINS

Three days before Disney announced the *John Carter* title change, on May 20, 2011, Disney Chairman Bob Iger was in Orlando at Disney's Hollywood Studios theme park for the grand opening ceremony of Star

---

[137] Meredith Woerner, "Everything You Need to Know about Disney's John Carter Movie," *i09*, 11 July 2011, 2 Sep 2012 <http://io9.com/5819836/>.

Tours 2, a Star Wars Themed ride that, in its newest incarnation, was about to go 3D. Also present at the event was George Lucas, creator of Star Wars and the principal owner of Lucasfilm Ltd.

The ceremony brought the two men together with lightsabers in their hands, and according to Iger, "George had to show me how to use it."[138]

But it was substantially more than a bit of coaching in lightsaber technique that was on the agenda between the two men. Iger, fresh off the $4B acquisition of Marvel, had his eye on the *Star Wars* franchise and took advantage of the relaxed access to Lucas to begin a dialogue about the possibility that Disney would acquire Lucasfilm and the *Star Wars* franchise.

For Iger, *Star Wars* was a perfect acquisition target that reflected the core values and vision that he had nurtured during his tenure as Disney Chairman. Although Iger's official Disney bio lists "generating the best creative content possible" as the cornerstone of his vision for the company, his tenure had been marked more by the acquisition of creative content than the internal generation of it.[139] First it had been Pixar, then Marvel. "We proved with our Pixar and Marvel acquisitions that we know how to expand the value of a brand," Iger would later say in an interview. And it was this ability to take a stable and reliable brand and optimize it across multiple platforms and in every territory around the world that differentiated Disney and was, ultimately, the company's core competence in the Iger era.

John Carter, while not precisely part of that tradition, was an example of a film, and prospective franchise, being built from the ground up in the "old school" Disney way at a time when the "new model" for Disney that Iger had created and was continuing to develop was one of acquisition, not creation, followed by enhanced exploitation of the creative intellectual property acquired.

---

[138] Ronald Grover and Lisa Richwine, "Disney $4B Lucasfilm Deal Began With Light Sabres in Orlando", Reuters, 30 Oct 2012, 5 Nov 2012 <http://www.reuters.com/article/2012/10/31/disney-lucas-iger-idUSL1E8LUGV020121031>

[139] Walt Disney Company Staff, "Robert Iger, Chairman and Chief Executive Officer," accessed 5 Nov 2012, <http://thewaltdisneycompany.com/about-disney/leadership/ceo/robert-iger>

What did Iger's eye on the Star Wars prize mean for *John Carter*?

At the working level and even up to the level of MT Carney, it did not have a direct effect since the discussions between Iger and Lucas were very closely held. Rich Ross was aware of them, but it is unlikely the knowledge of the negotiations went further down the chain than that.

But while the closely held nature of the discussions meant that knowledge of the prospective acquisition did not reach troops in the field, it certainly became a factor affecting the attitude at the highest levels of Disney (Iger) and Disney Studios (Ross). Step by step, *John Carter* had become a very costly $250M "outlier" in the Disney universe, and was a project which did not fit the CEO's vision. In fact, with *Star Wars* in play, it had at least the potential to become an impediment to what Iger considered the far more important strategic acquisition of Lucasfilm. A deal with Lucasfilm would still be possible even if *John Carter* was a hit -- but Lucas had spent a lifetime building the Star Wars franchise and asking it to share studio focus with a nascent and successful *John Carter* would make any offer from Disney less attractive. Was this potential impediment enough to cause Iger or Ross to take active steps to scuttle *John Carter*? No. But did it lessen any remaining shred of motivation to "go the extra mile" for the Stanton film? Absolutely. It was one more piece to the puzzle of Disney's increasingly detached handling of the film.

Reshoots and Test Screenings

In the aftermath of the Brain Trust screening in December 2010, Stanton and the editorial team worked and reworked many of the scenes, identifying numerous spots within individual scenes where specific shots were needed to subtly adjust performances, change dialogue, and in some places provide alternate actions for the characters. In addition to the key insert shots to be added to existing scenes, there were a few newly written scenes, and a few previously shot scenes that would be reworked in their entirety.

An example of subtly re-working a scene with inserts and individual shots is a scene where John Carter discovers that Dejah Thoris is leading him not to the River Iss and passage back to Earth, but rather to Helium, where she hopes to enlist his support for her cause. Carter calls Dejah Thoris out, ejecting her from the thoat she is riding. Reactions to the scene in the Brain Trust screening centered on Carter appearing callous — and Dejah Thoris appearing willfully manipulative, neither of which were helpful reactions. In attempting to recalibrate the scene, Stanton and the editors came to the conclusion that making it clear that Carter was "conning" her into cooperation, rather than truly dumping her in the desert, would be helpful — and so they inserted the line "just play along." Then, to soften Dejah Thoris and provide a moment that would arguably help sell that Carter was beginning to fall for Dejah Thoris, they added a line for Dejah who, after explaining that the could not accept an arranged marriage to Sab Than, and run, and now might regret it: "I was afraid, weak—maybe I should have married, but I so feared it would somehow be the end of Barsoom."

The net effect of the two inserted moments was to adjust the audience "takeaway" from the scene in the desired manner -- Carter never intended to truly dump Dejah in the desert, and Dejah's apparent manipulation was motivated not by personal weakness, but rather by fear for her country and, ultimately, Barsoom.

Similar tweaks were implemented at various junctures throughout the film, plus the opening was re-imagined as, instead of a fully mounted scene introducing Dejah Thoris, more of a documentary style prologue with Willem Dafoe narrating as Tars Tarkas, the Thark Warlord. Strategies were also implemented to force the pace in the middle section of the movie.

THE PORTLAND TEST SCREENING

In June 2011, with 8 months to go until the release date, all of the key players from the film and from Disney Studios journeyed to Portland, Oregon for the first full-on test screening for Stanton's film. With any film, this is a critical juncture -- for *John Carter*, even more so.

The cut that would be shown incorporated the first round of reshoots from the La Playa stage, and although many of the VFX shots were still incomplete, the cut was watchable for "outside eyes." It also featured temp music, not the Giacchino score; the sound mix wasn't final or even near complete -- but it was a solid working cut that reflected all the work done until that moment, and the audience reaction would be an extremely important step in the process toward completion.

Altogether 5 Disney execs from production and marketing were there; plus Stanton, his key editorial crew, producers Lindsey Collins and Jim Morris, and a few others.

The audience was 400 Portland filmgoers, recruited by the A.C. Nielsen Corp. The format for the event was the standard one that Nielsen and other test screening outfits follow: There would be a brief introduction at the beginning designed to give the audience enough background on the film to approximate what they might be expected to know if they were viewing the film "normally" in a theater. They would also be warned that the film was still a work in progress and some shots will not be complete -- they would be seeing, for example, wireframes instead of fully articulated creatures, etc. After the screening, all viewers would fill out a detailed questionnaire that had been provided -- the key question on which were the first two check boxes -- one for "Excellent - Strongly Recommend" and the other for "Very Good - Recommend." The percentage score bandied about in Hollywood for any test screening is the percentage of people from the screening who check either of these two boxes.

There was a long list of additional questions, the most prominent of which was: "Was anything about the story unclear; were you confused?" Other questions addressed the characters, which scenes the viewer liked best, which scenes he/she liked least, and so on.

Stanton, like any filmmaker, was deeply nervous going into the screening, and frustrated by his inability to create fixes for problems as easily as he could in the all-digital universe of Pixar animation. He would later tell an interviewer:[140]

> If there's anything looming as a threat, it's this medium. Because if, worst-case scenario, there's some story line or motivation that seventy-five per cent of the people aren't getting, I don't have many options, other than cutting it out. If I can't cure the tumor, in a way I'd rather not know it's there. I'm only as good at solving problems as I have the ability to do something about them—and it makes me so mad.

Stanton, his gut twisting in spite of a tranquilizer, sat among the audience doing what filmmakers always do at such screening -- listening to the audience reactions rather than watching the film. He waited through the exposition scene of Barsoom, which had now been trimmed dramatically to the point that it was simply a two minute "teaser"

---

[140] Tad Friend, "Second Act Twist," *The New Yorker*, 17 Oct 2011, 3 Sep 2012 < http://www.newyorker.com/reporting/2011/10/17/111017fa_fact_friend#ixzz1v2uhBVRH >.

narrated by Willem Dafoe's character "Tars Tarkas." Stanton could detect no restlessness in the audience during this intro, but the real test would come when the first laugh was supposed to be delivered -- this would when he first would get a clear indication of whether the audience was truly with him or not. The laugh comes eight minutes into the film, when John Carter begins attempting to escape from Powell, who is attempting to impress him into service with the 7th US Cavalry in Arizona. The laugh came, and it was loud, more than the chuckle Stanton had hoped for:[141]

> I realized, O.K., they're with me. Then they laughed at anything that was meant to be a smile. There was no fidgeting in the air battle with Dejah, the least-finished part of the film, and I was thinking, O.K., just get them to the kiss, because I've always been very confident about the last third. And there was applause at the end!

When it was over, following Nielsen's standard procedure, 20 audience members reflecting various demographics were asked to stay for a focus group in which more detailed questions were asked. Stanton and his team lurked in the background and were ecstatic to hear responses that seemed to indicate the film had worked very, very well for those in the focus group. When asked if they would like there to be a sequel -- 19 out of 20 hands went up and it was high fives all around for the film-making team. Most of the other comments were positive.

Of particular significance--because this would later become an issue with critics -- was the question of whether the densely layered origins story at the beginning was confusing. The answer was not a simple no -- some of the focus group members acknowledged that that they had not been able to absorb all the detail from the opening narration about Barsoom, but they were quick to say that it didn't keep them from being intrigued by the story and wanting to know more, and clarity emerged later as the story progressed. Some indicated that they had never quite gotten the whole "Thern plot" angle, and would have appreciated a bit more clarification -- but the objections were mild and were vastly overshadowed by the obvious enthusiasm.

---

[141] Tad Friend, "Second Act Twist," *The New Yorker*, 17 Oct 2011, 3 Sep 2012 < http://www.newyorker.com/reporting/2011/10/17/111017fa_fact_friend#ixzz1v2uhBVRH >

For Stanton, this was crucial. He took the test screening reaction as confirmation that the fixes they had put in had worked, and that his theory of the audience not needing to fully "get" every aspect of the exposition in the opening was on target. He would later claim that he had always believed strongly that the opening narration need only establish that there are "these guy fighting these guys and there's a third force that's come into it" -- that was enough. He likened it to the way a child learns, picking up bits and pieces and gradually assembling it all, rather than having to fully understand everything from the beginning.

As soon as the focus group was over, the good news came down that the 75% had graded the film "Excellent" or "Very Good", a number that Disney marketers told Stanton should be rounded up to 80% given the unfinished nature of the film. This was a very high score -- good enough to cause everyone involved to breathe a sign of relief and know "we have something here."

Encouraged and relieved, Stanton headed back to Emeryville, visions of a trilogy now firmly implanted in his mind, and the Disney team headed back to Burbank.

One of the most important takeaways from the focus group -- and one that gave Stanton great comfort -- was that virtually all of the members of the focus group rated John Carter their favorite character. This, to Stanton, was vindication of his decision to "mess with" the iconic Burroughs character, updating it to make his "knightly" virtues submerged beneath a tormented exterior that kept him from being able to easily commit to a cause, even as his underlying integrity caused him to make a series of choices that, in Stanton's view, revealed the true nature of his character.

The focus group's favorite scene, almost to a person, was the scene that in the shorthand of the filmmaking team was referred to as the "Warhoon attack" -- the scene in which John Carter finally commits to his new identity on Barsoom and takes on a tribe that is bearing down on Dejah, intercut with flashbacks of him discovering his wife and child dead on earth, and burying them. This scene, more than any other, was a classic Stanton "make me care" moment -- and by the reckoning of all the focus group members, it had worked.

But even as he basked in the relief of knowing that the film was working, there was much work to be done. The film was far from perfect--the focus group had indicated that it sagged in the middle, a problem that Stanton agreed with and needed to be addressed. There was also a problem with the wedding scene at the end coming too quickly, without preparation, and on the flight back to Emeryville, Stanton was already thinking of a way to fix that problem. There were other minor problems, all manageable -- but all requiring attention.

Still, there was no way to regard the test screening as anything other than a major success, and a major step forward toward approval of a sequel. Stanton wondered if Disney might green-light a sequel based on the test screening, but then pushed the thought away. It had been good, but Disney would wait to see how the film fared in the crucible of the marketplace before committing.

Immediately after the test screening, Stanton went back to work, impressing Disney production executives with his desire to continue strengthening the film even after a very successful "opening." One executive who was in Portland said, "In spite of the fact that the screening had been a clear success, Stanton had zero complacency. He had a list of things he felt he could still 'plus', in 'Pixar speak', or improve."

At Disney, head of production Sean Bailey reported to Ross, and Ross reported to Iger, that the test screening had gone surprisingly well. Iger remained unconvinced, and no change was ordered to the decision, made previously, to deny *John Carter* the kind of all-out marketing support that *The Avengers* was getting. A theory began to develop that if Stanton was the filmmaker some thought him to be, all that was needed was the basic promotion package and the film would take over from there, selling itself through positive critical reviews and consumer word of mouth.

In his relentless Pixarian quest to "plus" the film, Stanton flew to London to film Dominic West, who played Zodangan leader Sab Than, having a conversation with Mark Strong about the Thern plot that

Stanton believed would clarify any confusion on that score. Then, back in the US, he flew to Los Angeles where a scene was shot in which John Carter proposes to Dejah Thoris, providing the missing beat between the wedding attack and defeat of Sab Than, and Carter's wedding to Dejah. Then, he went back again to London for a scene with Mark Strong. Then back to Emeryville.

Ramping up the Marketing

The preliminary phase of the marketing campaign would end on June 15 with the launching of the second phase -- the "Online Phase" -- during which the campaign would upgrade from sporadic efforts to a more sustained effort. The "battlefield" on which this stage of the campaign would be waged would primarily limited to the internet and consist of press releases; seeded article placements; interviews; the release of a poster, trailer, concept art, and still images; plus the building of a fan base via key social media mechanisms, in particular *Facebook* and *Twitter*. During this period there was one live promotional event, the Disney D23 conference in Anaheim, where the cast and director presented scenes from the film, took questions, and generated mostly online media coverage.

As Disney prepared to enter the Online Phase of the campaign, the "battle lines" had been drawn as follows: *John Carter* was now set for a March 9, 2012 release. Its main competition in the March frame was *The Hunger Games*, a futuristic Dystopian sci-fi film that had as its starting point a substantially stronger fan base than *John Carter* because it was based on the based on the immensely (and currently) popular young adults by Suzanne Collins. *John Carter* would have a two week head start on *The Hunger Games*, which opened March 23, so if typical patterns prevailed *John Carter* would have earned approximately 55% of its Domestic Gross prior to *The Hunger Games* opening -- but more generally it would be competing with *The Hunger Games* throughout Online Phase of the campaign for the early 2012 "buzz factor" and thus *The Hunger*

Games could have an effect on the entirety of the *John Carter* run, not just the period in which the two films were both in theaters.

Another combatant in the March release frame was Dr. Seuss' *The Lorax*, coming out on March 2, 2012, a week ahead of *John Carter*. While the demographic for *The Lorax* was different from either *John Carter* or *The Hunger Games*, this was a film which--particularly with *John Carter* being branded as a Disney release--could impact the fortunes of *John Carter*. Another film that was in a position to affect *John Carter's* fortunes was *21 Jump Street*, the reboot of the 1980's TV series, which would be released on March 16, one week into the *John Carter* run. A fourth film, *Wrath of the Titans*, would compete with *John Carter* and *The Hunger Games* in the general buzz arena.[142]

As Disney went into the active phase of the campaign, its digital assets via it website, *Facebook*, etc, were in place and thus an analysis of Disney's profile coming into the active campaign is useful in establishing what was the "digital DNA" of *John Carter* as the campaign launched.

JOHN CARTER -- DIGITAL DNA

What was the status of the new media component to the campaign as the active phase of the campaign began? The question is a valid one, keeping in mind that Carney had been hired with the intention of reallocating resources from traditional media to new media, and with a mandate to strengthen Disney's marketing performance in the new media arena. By June 2011 she had been on the job for over a year -- an eternity in digital terms. The question clearly emerges -- how did the *John Carter* digital campaign stack up?

There is an obvious template against which to measure *John Carter's* "digital DNA" and that is *Avatar*. The similarity in the films is obvious -- a human soldier goes to an alien planet and makes his way among the native people, falling in love with a beautiful alien and emerging as a leader of the planet where the action takes place. Cameron himself, in no less than 5 interviews, had said that his main inspiration for *Avatar*

---

[142] Relativity's *Mirror Mirror*, originally scheduled for March 9, was moved to March 30, and *Think Like a Man*, originally scheduled for March 9, was moved to May.

was *John Carter of Mars*. So, with *Avatar* grossing $2.8B worldwide, and with the sequel to *Avatar* not coming out until 2015 at the earliest, *John Carter* would be in a prime position to capture at least a substantial segment of the *Avatar* audience if it could position itself effectively.

THE AVATAR NEW MEDIA PROFILE

The *Avatar* website[143] was groundbreaking and designed to create excitement among the early adopters and influencers who would be visiting it during the long run-up to the release. Apart from the standard mix of trailers, gallery images, and background materials, the site features 14 side-scrolling square boxes which are designed to showcase the unique digital initiatives that made the film stand out.

Visitors had access to the story, detailed character biographies, music, a variety of wallpaper downloads, none of which were groundbreaking but which were exceptional in the level of detail and variety available.

More innovative is the "Pandorapedia," a wiki for all things relating to *Avatar* where fans contributed to an encyclopedic rendering of the world of *Avatar* -- in the process achieving a "cool factor" which was unmatched. The Pandorapedia eventually evolved into 695 web pages, each containing detailed information on a topic relating to Pandora. By harnessing the power of user generated content, the site was assured of being dynamic, constantly evolving, and relevant.

An additional innovation came in the form of interactive trailers which integrated social media feeds and provided viewers with the option to click on a character in the trailer to unlock additional content about the character. The trailer also included three "click to purchase" options to purchase tickets.

Overall, the *Avatar* website was a richly imagined world, promising the same from the movie itself and creating a forum on which the early adopters and entertainment influencers could congregate and build a community through the Pandorapedia and other functions.

---

[143] http:/avatarmovie.com

Other innovations that were not strictly digital but synergized with the digital effort included that, with a release scheduled for December 18, 2009, August 21, 2009 became "Avatar Day" with moviegoers able to watch 16 minutes of footage from the film in 100 IMAX 3-D theaters worldwide. Coordinated with this, on the same day a video game based on the film was released by Ubisoft, and action figures by Mattell were released into the marketplace. At the same time what would become the main theatrical trailer was released -- to a whopping 4 million downloads on iTunes alone.

While attending to the website, the campaign also attended to the other main arenas of online activity so that by the time the film was released, *Avatar* had acquired the following:

1.3 Million *Facebook* Fans

800,000 *MySpace* friends

25,000 *Twitter* followers

The *Twitter* campaign included a unique "Tweet to Listen" promotion wherein fans could send a message on *Twitter* and receive in return a download of music from the film. On YouTube, the *Avatar* trailer garnered 11 Million views, photos were available on Flickr (1 Million views) and the promotion created a Typepad blogging community with 4,000 members who blogged regularly about the film.

A consistent pattern of the *Avatar* profile was that it was clearly geared to the 15-24 (and up) demographic. Nothing about it was "dumbed down" for 'tweens or younger, and the presentation of the world of Pandora and the characters created by Cameron was consistently handled in a way that was consistent with this demographic targeting.

JOHN CARTER NEW MEDIA PROFILE

One of the key decisions was that, rather than give *John Carter* a standalone website with its own URL, Disney would place the *John Carter* website on the Disney.go platform; thus it is accessed through the URL www.disney.go/johncarter and thus has strong identification with the

Disney brand -- including a permanent header including mouse ears and other Disney advertising at the top of each web page.

The decision to situate *John Carter* on the Disney.go website was an early decision that had consequences, as it contextualized *John Carter's* online presence as part of the Disney brand of mostly kiddie entertainment. Such would not be true, for example, for *The Avengers*, which would go up on a Marvel website and be contextualized that way; or *The Help* which was presented on a standalone site at www.thehelpmovie.com.

The official *John Carter* website at www.disney.go/johncarter contained the standard elements of a trailer, synopsis, film background, photo gallery, and character images.

The site contained a brief 100 word synopsis and a total of 11 character pages.

> *John Carter:* Born in Virginia and a veteran of the Civil War, John Carter is an honorable and courageous man. However, the war left him dispirited and broken. Accidentally transported to the planet of barsoom, he soon finds his strength and jumping abilities greatly amplified. He must use these newfound powers to survive the centuries old war between the native inhabitants and save this dying world.

> *Dejah Thoris:* Dejah Thoris is the Princess of Helium. She is also a Regent of the Royal Academy of Science and a fierce fighter. She is on the verge of a scientific discovery that could shift the balance of power between Helium and their vile enemy, Zodanga.

The brevity of the character descriptions, and the "fifth grade" style of writing employed, were typical of Disney copy targeted at the 'Tween level or below, and was in clear contrast to *Avatar's* "15-24" demographic focus.

Notably absent from the *John Carter* website was any effort to contextualize the story based on the source material. There was no section devoted to the history of *A Princess of Mars*; nothing devoted to Edgar Rice Burroughs; nor was there any opportunity for fans to interact -- no "Barsoomapedia" (even though there were plenty of fans who would have gladly created a richly detailed wiki that would have rivaled the Pandorapedia).

As for *Facebook*; there not been a single update since January 2011; and the *Twitter* Account for *John Carter* did not yet exist -- and would only be created on June 15, 2011, as the online phase kicked off. In both of these areas, 'Carter lagged far behind *Avatar* at the equivalent stage.

In sum -- in comparison to its most relevant comparable "template" *Avatar, John Carter* had a steep climb ahead if it was to gain enough traction with its digital profile to be able to use those early adopters and influencers to generate and sustain interest in the film.

THE DIGITAL CAMPAIGN KICKS OFF

The campaign in earnest began on June 15, 2011, with an extended interview of Andrew Stanton by Geoff Boucher in the influential LA Times Hero Complex section.[144] This would be followed by the release of the teaser poster the next day, followed by release of other materials culminating with the release of the teaser theatrical trailer on July 15, 2011, online and in theaters on the head of *Harry Potter and the Deathly Hallows*.

In the interview with Boucher, Stanton in answer to the first question casually mentioned doing "a month of reshoots" in April -- an acknowledgment that would be picked up on by other journalists who, in later interviews, would begin to drill down into the issue of reshoots, which are normally perceived as a sign that a production is in trouble. Boucher let the comment pass, however, moving on to other topics -- including the decision by Disney, endorsed by Stanton, to skip the upcoming Comic-con -- a huge San Diego annual geekfest that had traditionally been a "must-do" for fantasy sci-fi films. Carney's thinking on skipping Comic-con as a launch pad was based largely on the fact that there had been a series of high profile geek-friendly films that debuted loudly at Comic-con -- then fizzled at the box office, including *Sucker Punch, Tron: Legacy,* and others. Disney was not the only studio dodging Comic-con 2011: *Warner Bros, DreamWorks, The Weinstein Company* all had

---

[144] Geoff Boucher, " 'John Carter': Andrew Stanton on Martian History, Comic-Con and ... Montey Python?," *LA Times*, 15 Jun 2011, 4 Sep 2012 < http:// herocomplex.latimes.com/2011/06/16/john-carter-andrew-stanton-on-martian-history-comic-con-and-monty-python/>.

films in the pipeline that were suitable for a Comic-con unveiling; all passed. "I think ....the perception is that it's getting harder and harder to stand out amid the din," Stanton said. "We're going to do our special event [Disney's D23 Convention in August] to get some focus and separation. I know some people will read that as a sign we're unsure of our property. It's just the opposite. We want to control how and what is being seen and the way it is presented. So much stuff now is just spit out so fas and the churn of it all. You almost gain nothing by talking about things really early in this day and age."[145]

In various interviews Stanton would make known his notion that it was important to avoid too much 'here's everything' in the promotion -- whether in the trailer or other wise -- and to keep a degree of mystery and intrigue.[146]

> Yes, I hate that. I feel that the audience is smarter than that. They've heard me rant this way too many times, but I said, "Give them some credit." I now hear anybody—I don't care what their age is, what their demographic is, where they come from—when they show a trailer everything in, I hear somebody whispering, "Well, that's the whole movie; it must not be good." All people see when they see that is you're not confident in what you have and you're afraid. You assume your audience is dumb or won't get it. If I have any say in it, I don't want to go with that. I've been teased way too many times very successfully for most of my career and my youth to know that it can be done, and it can be done every time. It ends up being sometimes a reflection of the people doing that they can't do it, so they point at others. We say we want you to see more, but we actually don't. We just want you to have a little bit of a sense that we won't be wasting our time to go on the air.

Keeping in mind Stanton's stature and the latitude and respect he was being given in the marketing -- and likewise keeping in mind MT

---

[145] Kevin Jagernauth, "Andrew Stanton Says No 'John Carter' at Comic-con, Says Film Will "Gain Nothing" by Showing Early," *Indiewire-The Playlist*, 16 Jun 2011, 4 Sep 2012 <http://blogs.indiewire.com/theplaylist/ andrew_stanton_says_no_john_carter_at_comic-con_says_film_will_gain_nothing>.

[146] Peter Sciretta, "Interview: Andrew Stanton Talks 'John Carter'," *Slashfilm*, 11 Jul 2011, 4 Sep 2012 <http://www.slashfilm.com/interview-andrew-stanton-talks-john-carter/>. Also, Steve 'Frosty' Weintraub, "20 Things to Know About John Carter; Plus an Awesome Interview with Director Andrew Stanton and Your First Look at a Thark", Collider, 11 Jul 2011, 4 Sep 2012 <http://collider.com/andrew-stanton-interview-john-carter/101272/>

Carney's inexperience and workload issues--it is clear that the paucity of publicity for *John Carter* up until the point of the launch of the new media phase of the campaign was attributable to both.

THE TEASER POSTER

Online, the teaser poster debuted in the immediate aftermath of the LA Times interview. Stanton's hand could be seen more clearly in this poster, than would be the case in future posters. The color scheme reflected the color scheme of the title treatment of the movie, and the banners that were released were precisely aligned with the title treatment in the movie itself.

The reaction to the poster was decidedly mixed. Sandy Schaefer in *Screen Rant* offered: "John Carter Teaser Poster Reveals Little,"[147] and while the poster definitely had some adherents who felt that it was stylish, brooding, and "teased" without telling too much -- commentary generally trended negative. Kevin Jagernauth of *Indie Wire's The Playlist* called it "deeply uninteresting" and observed:[148]

---

[147] Sandy Schaefer, " 'John Carter' Poster Reveals Little About the Mars Adventure," *ScreenRant*, 15 Jun 2011, 4 <http://screenrant.com/john-carter-teaser-poster-sandy-119682/>.

[148] Kevin Jagernauth, "Deeply Uninteresting Poster for 'John Carter' Bows," *Indiewire-The Playlist*, 15 Jun 2011, 4 Sep 2012 <http://blogs.indiewire.com/theplaylist/deeply_uninteresting_poster_for_john_carter_bows>.

With "John Carter Of Mars" recently dropping half of its title to simply "John Carter" and now with the first poster being unveiled, it seems Disney is hell bent on making sure audiences don't know this movie takes place in outer space. Instead, if we were to take a guess, the movie appears to be about Taylor Kitsch's quest to get a tribal tattoo (oh wait, that's just the awful font treatment given to the title).

Ethan Anderton at *Firstshowing.net* called it "dark but not thrilling."[149] Christopher Rosen II at *Movieline* suggested that the "JCM" logo should stand for "Just Confused Marketing."[150] As for viewer comments, this first day round of comments from *ComingSoon.net* posted on June 15, 2011, the day it was released, being generally representative of the tenor of the response:[151]

Jon: Sweet! God I hope its good.

Qpf9c8p: poster looks great! until I saw the Disney logo

Bob: Might as well be a GAP ad. Seriously, what's the point? The poster is just as bland as the film's new title.

ST: the poster is bland like the title just like Bob said.

MDWarrior: Eh, it's all right. If they took the "Mars" out of the title and left the "John Carter", why is the "M" still on the poster? It's just going to confuse people.

Starcream: W/ the Disney logo, a shirtless Taylor Kitsch & just the bland "name-only" title...fangirls are going to think this is a sequel to "John Tucker Must Die."

Much better received were the concept art drawings released simultaneously and showing the actual otherworldly designs from the movie. The fact that these concept art pieces were so well received, while the poster was not, created an opportunity for a course correction going

---

[149] Ethan Anderton, "First Teaser Poster for Disney's 'John Carter' is Dark But Not Thrilling," *FirstShowing.net*, 15 Jun 2011, 4 Sep 2012 < http://www.firstshowing.net/ 2011/first-teaser-poster-for-disneys-john-carter-is-dark-but-not-thrilling/>.

[150] Christopher Rosen II, "Let's Decode the 'JCM' in New John Carter Poster," *Movieline*, 15 Jun 2011, 4 Sep 2012 <http://movieline.com/2011/06/15/lets-decode-the-jcm-in-new-john-carter-poster/>.

[151] ComingSoon.Net Staff Report, "The Teaser Poster for John Carter," *Coming Soon.net*, 15 Jun 2011, 4 Sep 2012 <http://www.comingsoon.net/news/movienews.php? id=78668>.

forward that would have skewed the next poster more in the direction of the concept art that was achieving such a favorable reaction. This opportunity was not taken.

At *Facebook*, the release of the teaser signaled the resumption, for the first time since January 2011, of *Facebook* updates, with a total of 8 updates issued during the month. Simultaneously (and belatedly), as the teaser poster was released, the *John Carter Twitter* account was launched. A total of 9 tweets were released between June 15 and June 30. By June 30, *John Carter* had 40 followers on *Twitter*. By contrast, *John Carter's* main competition, *The Hunger Games*, released 40 tweets during the period 15-30 June. What is more important, *The Hunger Games* had launched its *Twitter* account 7 months earlier in December 2010 and by June, when *John Carter* was launched, had over 50,000 followers. The following chart compares the two.

	John Carter	Hunger Games	John Carter Advantage (Deficit)
TWITTER			
Launched	Jun 15, 2011	Dec 10, 2010	
Tweets as of June 15	0	212	-212
Followers as of June 15	0	55,450	-55,480
Tweets June 15-30	9	40	-31
Followers as of June 30	52	62,400	-62,348
FACEBOOK			
Launched	Nov 28, 2010		
Posts in Jan 2011	0	0	0
Posts in Feb 2011	1	0	1
Posts in Mar 2011	1	7	-6
Posts in Apr 2011	1	10	-9
Posts in May 2011	1	20	-19
Total Posts as of May 30	10	37	-27
Total Fans	2,340	45,450	-43,110

Was the fact that *John Carter* lagged behind in Social Media as of June 30, 2011, 9 months prior to release, a "fatal flaw" in the online component to the promotional campaign?

It was definitely a flaw, but not necessarily a fatal one. As will be shown, there are examples of successful *Twitter* campaign -- notably Disney's own *The Avengers* -- who launched as late as five months prior to release.

But in the case of *John Carter*, the question arises: Disney obtained the property in 2007 and greenlit the film for production in 2009. It was widely understood that, while the books had been in print continuously for 100 years and had been a key inspiration for everyone from Carl Sagan to George Lucas and James Cameron -- they did not have a large, active, current fan base like, for example, *The Hunger Games* or the *Twilight Series*, or *The Avengers* for that matter. Logic would dictate that a 250M tentpole film in *John Carter's* position would need to "try harder" than the established competition with built-in audiences, but the opposite seems to have been true.

Indeed, if anyone could afford to be lax in a situation such as this, it would be *The Hunger Games*. Given the immense current popularity of the Suzanne Collins books and the relatively low cost of production -- at $80M roughly one third that of *John Carter* -- Lionsgate might have assumed that it could "coast" in the early phases of its campaign; but it did the opposite. It got its campaign started in plenty of time; it attended to it diligently and creatively, and by June 30, 2011, was already establishing a lead of devastating proportions over Disney and the hapless *John Carter*.

JULY 2011 -- THE TEASER TRAILER

By the time the first trailer for *John Carter* was released on July 14, 2011, theatrical movie marketing had evolved to the point where the release of a theatrical trailer was considered a major event among the universe of fans and influencer media who established the "buzz" for a given film. For example, the release of the *Lorax* trailer caused it to spike from an *IMDB* MovieMeter ranking of 2,464 to 274. In the case of *John Carter*, the release of the first trailer caused a spike from a rank of

1,355 to 190. *IMDB Pro* monitored 8 article placements about the movie the week before the trailer; the week of the trailer's release, this spiked to 130 articles.[152]

Given the foregoing, the release of a trailer is a key moment in which digital best practices call for reputation monitoring and management systems to be fully deployed and countermeasures in place.

The *John Carter* teaser trailer debuted in front of Harry Potter in theaters and on the internet on July 14. This was the trailer with Peter Gabriel music that had finally satisfied Stanton in that it played up the mystery and romance, teasing the audience without spoon feeding them. Online, the release of the trailer was "news" primarily on movie sites catering to the geeks and film influencers. Reaction to the trailer was mixed. A representative sampling can be found on *Collider.com*, all on July 14th:[153]

> *OHOO*: Following the onslaught of cowboys and aliens trailer followed by conan the barb. Kitsch looks like conan while the horse back riding scenes is too reminiscent of cowboys and aliens chase scene, you can only use one location until you covered all the angles. Now that both trailers are out JCM just shot itself in the foot for releasing a trailer so close to the release of cowboys and aliens fresh on everyones mind

> *JLC*: Far more "real" than what I was anticipating. I was thinking more along the lines of *Avatar*, but it clearly isn't that. I think that's a good thing since it will lessen the comparisons.

> *Jay:* I like that it does have a realistic like look to it, but i need to see more before I get really excited for it.

> *John Conor:* so avatar+terminator type of deal...what else did they throw in their.....oops my bad the story dates back before these movies haha

> *Shane:* so this is a remake of Princess of Mars with Traci Lords cause it looks a lot like it in fact scene for scene

---

[152] *IMDB Pro*, "*John Carter* (2012) MovieMeter: Data Table View," accessed 2 Sep 2012 <http://pro.imdb.com/title/tt0401729/graph-data>

[153] Matt Goldberg, "Teaser Trailer for John Carter," *Collider*, 14 Jul 2011, 4 Sep 2012 <http://collider.com/john-carter-trailer/96574/>.

Skivingtong: The fact that they shied away from calling It John Carter of Mars feels as if they're not willing to go all the way with the source material.

Shaunx: AVATAR + Prince of Persia + Cowboys and Aliens + 300 = JOHN CARTER

Rockslide: I just finished reading Princess of Mars, somewhat in anticipation of this, and somewhat just to see one of the origin points of so many sci-fi elements. Its funny to think that many people will believe John Carter is ripping off so many other stories when in fact it was the original

Steven: I really like that song, but I dunno how I feel about the film from watching the trailer... it doesn't seem to sell the idea that John Carter is transported to a unique and fantastical world. I think filming in a real location might have been a detriment to the film....

Saadgkhan: Its looks lot better than I've expected!

dpramroop: why isnt this guy the Prince of Persia

Tk421: I sincerely hope this film turns out well. The cast abounds with great actors and Andrew Stanton is solid. However, the costume designer needs to be castigated for making John Carter's outfit look nearly exactly like Jake Gyllenhal's on Prince of Persia. This movie already has the originality hurdle to leap with audiences in terms of story, it does not need to draw derision for it's costuming choices as well.

nevinx: ...ups we just remade Scorpion King.
But please bring the money you can to our time wasting facilities.

MDFaraone: I think the stupidest thing about this movie is the BORING name that they cut it down to, whose brilliant Idea was that. The original title was perfect : John Carter of Mars , it juxtaposes a common familiar name with something otherworldly and makes the mind pause for a moment to ponder it....might as well be "Jimmy Carter"

Perhaps more significant than the mixed quality of the response to the trailer, was the muted quantity of the response. *Collider.com*, for example, logged a total of only 19 comments on the first day of the trailer's release. On the same site, *Avenger* had 88 comments on the same site on the opening day of its first trailer.[154] This light response was

154 Matt Goldberg, "First Trailer for *The Avengers*," *Collider.com*, 11 Oct 2011, 3 Sep 2012 <http://collider.com/the-avengers-trailer/111404/>.

consistent with the level of response on other influencer movie sites and was an "early warning" indicator to Disney.   It was also a foreseeable outcome based on the minimal amount of publicity in the months leading up to the trailer release.   There is no indication that Disney undertook any reputation management countermeasures once the trailer was out, and the mixed reaction had begun.   A close study of first day reaction to the trailer across the internet shows no sign of Disney having done more than toss the trailer into the internet swamp and let the reaction play out without intervention or engagement.[155]

But while the reaction to the trailer was less than optimal -- at least is was not wholly negative, and a mixed reaction to the first teaser trailer was a manageable result -- not good, but not devastatingly problematic.

Meanwhile, it was an event not directly within the *John Carter* sphere that would erupt in August, and it was this event that would, more than anything else, cause the explosion of negative buzz that would eventually overwhelm and envelope *John Carter*.

---

[155]   It is possible to take historical readings of an event such as this. All but a very few of the articles published that day are still online; the comments are still viewable; and social media monitoring and reputation management software have the ability to take historical "snapshots" covering a given day or date range.   Such historical readings for the entirety of the *John Carter* campaign are available to anyone with the software.

THE LONE RANGER FIASCO AND D23

When Rich Ross took over from Dick Cook as Disney Studio Chief in October of 2010, all indications are that he would have pulled the plug on *John Carter* just as he did on *Captain Nemo: 20,000 Leagues Under the Sea*, save for the fact that *John Carter* was too far advanced at the time with principal photography less than 90 days away. All the main cast had been signed to 'pay or play' contracts;[156] all the contracts were in place for special effects -- the *John Carter* horse was out of the barn.

Now, 18 months later, in the summer of 2011 with the Online Phase of the *John Carter* campaign just being activated, Ross was engaged in a struggle with Jerry Bruckheimer and Gore Verbinski over the budget of *The Lone Ranger*, which was set to go into production in October 2011 for a release date of December 21, 2012. The budget of $250M was the issue -- a budget that between Bruckheimer, Verbinski, and star Johnny Depp was more a function of "above the line" costs than, as was the case in *John Carter*, where it was animation/VFX costs that drove the budget to $250M.[157]

---

[156] A 'pay or play' contract, which is the standard for lead actors in Hollywood, obligates the studio to pay for the contract regardless of whether the film goes into production.

[157] "Above the Line" costs are the costs for the literary property, screenwriters, producers, director, and cast. "Below the Line" costs refer to the actual 'wind and grind' of film-making -- crew, equipment, special effects, and so on. *The Lone Ranger* -- with Depp, Verbinski, and Bruckheimer on board -- had a heavy "Above the Line" load, whereas *John Carter* did not.

To show he was serious, Ross pulled the plug. Breaking the news, *Deadline Hollywood* ran with the headline: *"SHOCKER! Disney halts 'The Lone Ranger"* with Johnny Depp and Gore Verbinski."[158]   Within the article, there was what would turn out to be a fateful reference to *John Carter:*

> This had to be an incredibly tough call for Disney's Rich Ross and Sean Bailey, but they have several huge live-action bets on the table already. Budget busters include *John Carter*, the Andrew Stanton-directed adaptation of *John Carter of Mars* with *Friday Night Lights'* Taylor Kitsch in the lead role, which has a budget that has ballooned to around $250 million . . .

The very first version of the report placed the *John Carter* budget at $300M, and later revised it to $250M, evidently doing so after receiving urgent assertions from Disney that $250M was the correct number. The $300M figure, however, was already embedded in the consciousness of many studio watchers by the time the change was made, and would spawn other references to $300M as the final cost. Unfortunately, in correcting the figure and setting it at $250M, Disney did nothing to correct the misimpression that the cost had gotten as high as $250M by "ballooning" due to out of control production and "costly reshoots."

And so it was that *John Carter* became a piece of collateral damage in the reporting about the shut-down of *The Lone Ranger*, and would forever onward from that date be branded in the media and, eventually, the public consciousness as an out-of-control production that "ballooned" to $250M (or $300M) from an original intended budget of $150M, as announced in 2009 at the time Taylor Kitsch was signed. This was not how the $250M budget actually came about, and was an unfair rendering of what had happened -- but the narrative exploded onto the internet in the wake of *The Lone Ranger* announcement.

Stanton would later vehemently and credibly contend that he stayed on budget from day one based on this approval before the start of shooting. But that didn't matter in August 2011, because the seeds of the "out of control production" story that would ultimately bring down *John Carter* more than anything else, were now planted.

---

[158] Mike Fleming, "SHOCKER! Disney Halts 'The Lone Ranger' With Johnny Depp and Gore Verbinski," *Deadline Hollywood*, 12 Aug 2011, 4 Sep 2012, http://www.deadline.com/2011/08/shocker-disney-scraps-johnny-depps-lone-ranger/

The $250M reference was not the only seed.

Another important seed came from a lengthy "edit bay interview" of Stanton which was released through multiple outlets timed to coincide with the release of the first teaser trailer in July 2011, a month before the announcement about *Lone Ranger*.

For the edit bay interviews, about 30 journalists were taken to Barsoom Studios in Berkeley,[159] where they were given an introduction by producer Jim Morris that included the trailer, selected scenes, a viewing of art and costumes, and a lengthy presentation by Stanton. The journalists in attendance were armed in advance with questions about the reshoot because of Stanton's casual comment in the June 15 LA Times interview in which he talked about having done a "month of reshoots" -- an attention getting number in an industry where anything more than a "pickup day" or two is regarded as sign of a "troubled production." *Collider.com* published the complete interview, unedited:[160]

> I've always seen live action as the adults: They really get to make the movies, and we're just kids here doing our little thing. I've always wanted to give it the intelligence and everything. That's a bad trap you fall into, and the shocking thing when I got out there was like, "Oh my God, we actually know how to do it better on a lot of things back here [at Pixar]." I think some of that isn't because people are bad at their job but that people are stuck in a certain way that it's always been done. You can say that about any system. Pixar had this luxury of being ignorant and young and not knowing how it's done. We saw from afar how we thought movies were made, and we used logic—turns out that's not used that often.

The line that stands out is, "Oh my God, we actually know how to do it better on a lot of things back here." This was echoed by Stanton in other interviews--the notion that the venerated Hollywood system of live action film production was inferior and that Pixar had evolved a better

---

[159] The premises are owned by the Saul Zaentz Media Company. The journalists viewed Stanton's Power Point presentation there, then were bused to Pixar for lunch in a room where they were surrounded by props, costumes, and production art.

[160] Steve 'Frosty' Weintraub, "20 Things to Know about JOHN CARTER; Plus an Awesome Interview with Director Andrew Stanton and your First Look at a Thark," *Collider.com*, 11 Jul 2011, 4 Sep 2012 <http://collider.com/andrew-stanton-interview-john-carter/101272/>.

way of doing it.   It was a notion that conformist establishment Hollywood would resent. But Stanton wasn't finished:

> One of the other things that I realized is animation...you draw it, you put your own voice on it, you cut it, and you don't like it, and you do it again. You do it every six months over three to four years. Every time you do that, that's the equivalent of a reshoot, so I've been taught how to make a movie with four reshoots built in every time. And you wonder why our movies are good? It's not because we're smarter, it's not because we're better, it's because we are in a system that recognizes that you don't go, "Oh my God, okay, I'm going to paint this, but I can only touch the brush once and I'm only going to make one stroke. That stroke's asked, and we're done; we're not making this painting." I get to try it, play it, don't like that, play it again, no, play it again, record it—most creative processes allow for somebody to go off into their shack, their studio, their recording booth, and try stuff until they figure it out and find it. This is such an expensive way to make something creative, which is a movie. People freak, and they want to hold it all in. They want to see, "Can you be really smart and think about it some more and plan some more? Just do it once. Or maybe twice." Most places now aren't even letting you think about it; they're like, "Just do it! Maybe you'll luck out." We planned the bejesus out of it here. I've never met people who plan more than we do, and we do it four times over. You have no excuse: It's got to be good. I never had to argue, but my explanation to Disney when they were going, "Why do we have to reshoot, and why is this number so bad?" I said, "You're taking somebody who's learned how to do it three to four times and do it once." I tried to be as smart as I could and raise the bar as high as I could with the script before we went shooting knowing I wasn't going to get these same iterations, then tried to be as smart as I could about doing the reshoots. It's still less than what I'm used to. You start to understand the logistical problem trying to do that. It's such a gypsy culture: You don't get to keep the same people. They're not in that building; you can't grab them on a Thursday and go, "What if we do this?" All your actors are gone off. It's a real conundrum, and believe me, we're trying to think if we do another one, how can we improve upon what we've learned? We've managed to seduce some of that with our thinking on this, but there's huge room for improvement. It's a gnarly problem; I get it.

Although Stanton never directly says it -- clear from the subtext is that while he thinks the "Pixar process" is superior, and it is the only film-making process he knows or trusts, it was not possible to approach *John Carter* as if it were a Pixar project.   The best that was possible was a hybrid, and Stanton clearly found that frustrating, and although he never comes right out and says that his creative process was compromised, a observer can't help but wonder how much the "gnarly problem" affected his creative process. By Pixar standards, one could argue, *John Carter* was being forced into the marketplace essentially "half-baked." No one would admit that, but the logic is inescapable.

For the journalists, the elements for the explosion of negativity were all now in place. There was the notion -- incorrect but firmly implanted -- that the film had been budgeted at $150M and then "ballooned" to $250M because of reshoots made necessary by an inexperienced director; meanwhile the director was asserting that via Pixar he had figured out a "better way" that he was applying to live action filming; and Disney was making strange decisions (the title change) and producing and releasing marketing materials that were not resonating.

It was a toxic brew indeed.

THE D23 PRESENTATION AND ITS AFTERMATH

After the release of the teaser trailer in July, the next major event in the campaign would be the presentation at the Disney D23 convention in August.[161] This was intended to replace participation in the Comic-con convention in San Diego which was the traditional launching pad for sci-fi and superhero movies. The D23 Convention, on Disney turf in Anaheim, was an opportunity to showcase the film in a more managed environment--however the context, instead of sci-fi geekdom, would be an environment where it would be promoted alongside Pixar's *Brave*, *The Muppets*, Tim Burton's *Frankenweenie*, Sam Raimi's *Oz The Great & Powerful*, and Marvel's *The Avengers* to an audience of mostly journalists who would report on what they saw.

The presentation of *John Carter* was part of a two hour and forty minute presentation of the overall Disney lineup, both animation and live action, on Saturday morning, August 21, 2011. The *John Carter* portion was largely a replay of the edit bay presentation made two months earlier in Berkeley, with the exception that this time Stanton was joined by

---

[161] "D23" refers to the year Disney was founded, 1923.

actors Taylor Kitsch, Lynn Collins, and Willem Dafoe. Disney showed the journalist the same package that had been shown at the "Edit Bay" interview -- the now familiar teaser trailer, a clip of *John Carter* arriving on Mars and meeting Tars Tarkas; his scene with Dejah Thoris in her chambers just before her wedding to Sab Than; the white ape coliseum sequence. Additionally, one new scene was added, with John Carter being shown comically attempting escape from Woola while chained in the Thark nursery.

The press reaction to the presentation was muted. Jeff Otto writing for Indiewire/The Playlist reported, a "lukewarm"[162] response, while another Indiewire Blogger, Anthony D'Alessandro, wrote: "Of all their reels at D23, *John Carter* received the most muted response--especially compared to the rousing applause awarded *The Avengers*."[163] ; The hugely influential (in sci-fi circles) *Ain't It Cool News* ran a headline that included "The Agony of John Carter" and called it "stunningly flat" with a "strangely dour" tone;[164] At *Hey U Guys.com*, Ezequiel Gutierrez reported, "I'm not sure what it is about this project, but I feel nothing."[165] Devin Faraci at *Badass Digest* called it "John Carter of blahs,"[166] while at *Collider* Tommy Cook lamented its "somber,

---

[162] Jeff Otto, "D23: 'John Carter,' 'Timothy Green' Receive Lukewarm Responses," *Indiewire/The Playlist*, 21 Aug 2011, 4 Sep 2012 <http://blogs.indiewire.com/theplaylist/d23_john_carter_timothy_green_receive_lukewarm_response_oz_and_frankenweeni#>.

[163] Anthony D'Alessandro, "Disney D23: Box Office Outlook for 2011-13, John Carter's Marketing Challenge, Muppets Make Comeback," *Indiewire*, 22 Aug 2011, 4 Sep 2012 <http://blogs.indiewire.com/thompsononhollywood/disney_d23_muppets_john_carter_pixar_oz_great_and_powerful#>.

[164] Mr. Beaks, "Mr Beaks Beholds the Agony of John Carter and the Ecstasy of the Muppets at D23," *Aint It Cool News*, 22 Aug 2011, 4 Sep 2012,< http://www.aintitcool.com/node/50924>.

[165]Ezequiel Gutierrez, "D23 -- Disney's Live Action Panel + "John Carter" and "Muppet" Footage Description/reaction," *Hey U Guys*, August 23, 2011, http://www.heyuguys.co.uk/2011/08/23/d23-disneys-live-action-panel-john-carter-and-muppet-footage-descriptionreaction/

[166] Devin Faraci, "D23 Expo Report: JOHN CARTER of Blahs," *Bad Ass Digest*, 20 Aug 2011, 4 Nov 2012, http://badassdigest.com/2011/08/20/d23-expo-report-john-carter-of-blahs/

melancholy" tone and noted, "it's just a guy fighting and jumping over giant CGI monsters."[167]

The issue of which clips were shown is, perhaps more than any other marketing element, a function of the coordination and relationship between Disney marketing under MT Carney, and the *John Carter* production under Andrew Stanton and producers Jim Morris and Lindsey Collins.

Stanton had a well established and often repeated tendency to refrain from showing "too much too soon" and the choice of scenes for D23 and the edit bay interviews reflects both Stanton's personal preferences, and the realities of heavy CGI post production in which the most complicated, CGI intensive scenes are typically not ready until much closer to the release date of the film.

As it turned out, the one aspect of the D23 presentation that reflected the conflict over high VFX content was the scene of *John Carter* and Tars Tarkas battling a giant white ape in the Thark coliseum. That scene was, at the request of Carney, fast tracked so that the first half of the scene could be included at D23.

Unfortunately, of all scenes to be chosen to showcase VFX and action, this was perhaps the worst one, not because the scene itself was lacking -- but because it was Burroughs' coliseum scene from 1912's *A Princess of Mars* that inspired George Lucas to mount an extremely similar scene in *Star Wars: Attack of the Clones*, a scene that was very familiar to everyone except, perhaps, Carney and her marketers. There was every reason to believe that the scene from *John Carter*, presented largely without explanation or context -- particularly so in light of Stanton's decision to mount the scene with production design and art direction that accentuated the similarities to Lucas' scene--would be viewed as derivative and that is indeed what happened, with many of the journalists citing *Attack of the Clones* and, more generally, the "strip-mining" of Burroughs by everyone from the creators of Flash Gordon to James Cameron.

---

[167] Tommy Cook, "D23 Live Action Recap," *Collider.com*, 20 Aug 2011, 4 Nov 2012 <http://collider.com/d23-recap-the-muppets-john-carter-oz-the-avengers/110675/>

About the best piece of "buzz" that *John Carter* was able to claim coming out of D23 was a flurry of articles written about how Willem Dafoe and the other actors had been required to learn to play their role in motion capture suits on 3 foot high stilts in the Arizona desert. This minor nugget seemed to capture the imagination of a number of journalists, and was a potential angle for helping stress the diligence and commitment to realism and acting performances that Stanton brought to the project, since this meant that Taylor Kitsch, for example, was actually acting against Willem Dafoe in his scenes with Tars Tarkas, as opposed to giving his lines to a "tennis ball" or some other eye-line device.

But there was no doubt that, coming out of D23, *John Carter* had now officially transitioned into the "troubled" promotional zone. The film had gone from being an anticipated sci-fi tentpole without any measurable negatives as recently as of April, to a film that was now the object of a relentlessly negative narrative that varied greatly from any narrative the studio would have willingly put forward.

There was clearly a problem.

What would Disney do to counter the problem?

MEDIA SILENCE FROM BARSOOM

There is no definitive reading on when, precisely, M T Carney knew it was "game over" in her tenure at Disney. Most estimates from those knowledgable place it as likely coming in the aftermath of D23, in the early fall of 2011.

Carney being preoccupied with resuming her life in New York is certainly one explanation for what happened after D23 to *John Carter* publicity. There may be other factors as well. But regardless of why, what happened was that after D23 the Disney publicity machine again went silent about *John Carter* -- this time inexplicably so, because the release was now only 7 months away. There was another in-house marketed film under Carney's supervision that was ahead of *John Carter* in the pipeline, and was occupying staff and resources -- *The Muppets*. There was also *The Help* and *War Horse* to consume resources -- but whatever the reason, in the weeks and months after D23, a baffling (for a $250M "tentpole" release) period of "radio silence" ensued -- a remarkable period of three months during which promotion for *John Carter* came to a complete standstill.

To place what Disney marketing did, or did not, do in the aftermath of the less than stellar reviews of the D23 presentation, it is helpful to make some comparisons to *John Carter*'s stablemate, *The Avengers*, which also debuted footage at D23 and which was slated for release on May 4, 2012, 8 weeks after *John Carter.*

First, the reaction to *The Avengers* presentation at D23 was substantially more favorable than the reaction to *John Carter.* On *Slashfilm*, Germain Lussier reported, "*The Avengers* looks like it's going to kick ass."[168] Ezequiel Guttierez of *Hey U Guys* [169] wrote that the film "could be everything Avenger fans have been waiting for." Matt Holmes at *WhatCulture.com*[170] reported on the "thunderous ovation" the footage from *The Avengers* received, and *Joblo.com*[171] reported, "The film looks terrific, and yes, my expectations are pretty damn high." The reaction was not 100% rave, but it was clearly and irrefutably far stronger and more positive than the reaction to *John Carter.*

So, the argument could be made that coming out of D23, if anything, *John Carter* was the film that needed a high intensity marketing effort to counter the negatives that were piling up, and to make up for the fact that it was entering the marketplace with no large preexisting fan base. And *The Avengers*, riding a positive buzz en route to an expected successful release, might be forgiven for taking its foot off the pedal and relaxing slightly, confident in its position.

---

[168] Germain Lussier, "New Footage From 'The Avengers' Revealed [D23 Expo]," *Slashfilm*, 21 Aug 2011, 4 Sep 2012 <http://www.slashfilm.com/footage-the-avengers-revealed-d23-expo/>

[169] Ezequiel Guttierez, "The Avengers" Footage Description and Reaction," *Hey U Guys*, 21 Aug 2011, 4 Sep 2012 < http://www.heyuguys.co.uk/2011/08/21/d23-the-avengers-footage-description-and-reaction/>.

[170] Matt Holmes, "New THE AVENGERS Footage Shown at Disney's D23 Expo," *What Culture!*, 21 Aug 2011, 4 Sep 2012 <http://whatculture.com/film/new-the-avengers-footage-shown-at-disneys-d23-expo.php>.

[171] Jimmy O, "D23: A Full Report From Disney's Version of Comic-Con!," *Joblo.com*, 21 Aug 2011, 4 Sep 2012 <http://www.joblo.com/movie-news/d23-a-full-report-from-disneys-version-of-comic-con>.

The opposite happened. *The Avengers,* secure in its market position and with 9 months until its release, came out guns blazing. During the week after D23, article placements emanating from the film's publicity team included 140 buzz generating press placements comprising more than 20 different topics, all generated by official release of information on behalf of the film. The week after that; 120 placements on 40 different topics or releases of information. In all, between the end of D23 and the first week of October, *The Avengers,* with a comfortable nine months until its release, placed 390 media placements, never leaving the media or public consciousness.[172]

John Carter, acutely insecure in its market position and with only 7 months until its release, went silent. During the week after D23 the number of publicity placements emanating from the studio? Zero. And the next week? Zero. And the week after that? One -- a lone release of "new Helium Airship Design Concept Art" which was picked up by a handful of outlets.[173] In all, between the end of D23 and the first week of October, *John Carter* generated 5 media placements monitored by IMDB.

Once again, *John Carter* had drifted into an inexplicable "media silence" mode that would not end until an extensive interview of Andrew Stanton would appear in the October 17 edition of the New Yorker -- an interview that would stir up further woes for the now seriously troubled and largely invisible *John Carter* promotional campaign.

---

[172] *IMDB Pro,* "*John Carter* (2012) MovieMeter: Data Table View," accessed 2 Sep 2012 <http://pro.imdb.com/title/tt0401729/graph-data> ; *IMDB Pro,* "*The Avengers* (2012) MovieMeter: Data Table View," accessed 2 Sep 2012 <http://pro.imdb.com/title/tt0848228/graph>; *IMDB Pro,* "*The Hunger Games* (2012) MovieMeter: Data Table View," accessed 2 Sep 2012 <http://pro.imdb.com/title/tt1392170/graph-data>. As an additional data point -- during this same window of time, *The Hunger Games,* the principal competition for *John Carter* in March, achieved 276 placements according to *IMDB Pro.* So the "score" -- *Avengers* 360, *Hunger Games* 276, *John Carter* 5.

[173] SciFi Mafia Staff, "New Airship Concept Art from Disney's John Carter," *SciFi Mafia,* 15 Sep 2011, 4 Sep 2012 <http://scifimafia.com/2011/09/new-airship-concept-art-from-disneys-john-carter/>. Bryan Kritz, "Helium Airship Concept Art for Upcoming Sci-Fi Film John Carter," *The Daily Blam,* 13 Sep 2011, 4 Sep2012 <http://www.dailyblam.com/news/2011/09/13/helium-airship-concept-art-for-upcoming-sci-fi-film-john-carter>.

What about *Facebook*? During the same period, the *John Carter Facebook* page produced the following posts to the *Facebook* page:[174]

> August 23, 2011: "Let's test your knowledge of the Barsoomian language: do you know the word a Thark would use to say "Earth"?
>
> September 19, 2011: "Show your support for the city of Helium with these concept art wallpapers of Dejah Thoris's homeland at dusk." (with downloadable graphic of Helium at Sunset.)
>
> October 14, 2011: "Your ships cannot sail on light in Virginia>" - Dejah Thoris (with downloadable graphic of Barsoomian airship)

As an indication of how far behind *John Carter* was, and how damaging the inattentiveness and lack of marketing was -- the Internet Movie Data Base maintains weekly "MovieMeter" rankings which track the number of hits in the *IMDB* movie page and forums for any film, and from that generate a ranking. Going into D23, *John Carter*'s ranking, as of the week of August 21, was 899. The next week, August 28, it went to 804 presumably reflecting the D23 coverage. Then, as the radio silence descended, it's weekly rankings plummeted from 804 on August 28 to 1545 on October 2.

The Avengers, by contrast?

The Avengers went into D23 ranked 17 on August 21. It came out of D23 ranked 15 on August 28 and never dropped more than 12 spots to 27, as a continual flow of articles, images, video clips, and more continued to emanate from the marketing team.

How could it be, one might ask, that two "stablemate" films, both tentpole franchise efforts at the highest budget level, both from the same studio and both about to be released in roughly the same time frame, could have such a radically different media placement profile?

One interesting clue: In the week after D23, worked leaked out through *Deadline Hollywood* that Disney had fired the entire Marvel Marketing department, starting with Dana Precious, EVP of Worldwide Marketing and including Jeffrey Steward, VP of Worldwide Marketing

---

[174] The John Carter Official *Facebook* Page, Nov 28, 2010, 2 Sep 2012 <https://www.facebook.com/JohnCarterMovie>.

and Jodi Miller, Manager of Worldwide Marketing.[175]   This was a step that had been rumored ever since Disney acquired Marvel in 2009. Disney's official line was that Disney marketing would be taking over the marketing and handling the release of *The Avengers* and future Marvel movies.

Thus, as if *John Carter* needed one more nail in its release coffin, Disney marketing -- which had been struggling horrifically with *John Carter* even without the added burden of being responsible for *The Avengers* -- now had *The Avengers* on its plate.

But more trouble was coming.

THE NEW YORKER INTERVIEW

One piece of the *John Carter* promotion puzzle that came directly from MT Carney was an arrangement which Carney put in place to have *The New Yorker* run an extended profile of director Andrew Stanton by Tad Friend.[176] Friend visited Stanton at his home in Mill Valley, on the set of reshoots at Playa Vista, and accompanied him to the June 2011 test screening in Portland, Oregon.

The article, while generally favorable to Stanton, referred to him as "having a midlife crisis, an aberrant fling with a two-hundred-and-fifty-million-dollar trophy film."

More important was this passage:

> Even as Stanton banked on that confidence, he knew that Disney didn't fully share it. He'd always planned to make a *John Carter* trilogy, but the studio hadn't yet green-lit a sequel, and didn't seem eager to discuss the topic. It also nervously lopped "of Mars" off the film's title, to lower the barrier between women filmgoers— who are famously averse to sci-fi—and Taylor Kitsch's smoldering aura. Disney's caution was perhaps understandable; earlier this year, the studio's "*Pirates of the Caribbean: On Stranger Tides*" grossed

---

[175] Nikki Finke, "Disney Fires marvel's Marketing Department," *Deadline Hollywood*, 23 Aug 2011, 4 Sep 2012 <http://www.deadline.com/2011/08/disney-fires-marvels-marketing-department/>.

[176] Tad Friend, "Second Act Twist", *The New Yorker*, 17 Oct 2011, 4 Sep 2012 <http://www.newyorker.com/reporting/2011/10/17/111017fa_fact_friend>.

more than a billion dollars around the world, but made only a small profit because it was so expensive to produce and market. "John Carter," which will be nearly as expensive, will have to earn about seven hundred million dollars to justify a sequel.

More than any other single statement throughout the campaign, this was the moment that it all began to fall apart for *John Carter*'s campaign. At *Vulture.com*, an adjunct to *The New Yorker*, Margaret Lyons immediately posted within an hour of the *New Yorker* article appearing:[177]

How Much Does *John Carter* Need to Make to Get a Sequel?

Director Andrew Stanton — the Scheherazade of Pixar, as his *New Yorker* profile calls him — wants to make *John Carter* (formerly known as *John Carter of Mars*) a trilogy, but Disney's only going to go for that if this first film is a success. A huge, huge success, apparently: According to a long, psyche-probing article, "*John Carter* ... will have to earn about $700 million to justify a sequel." That would put it among the 50 highest-grossing films of all-time, above *Wall-E* and *Iron Man* and around the moneymaking machinery of the first *Transformers*. Taylor Kitsch in a loincloth has its appeal and all, but jeez Louise.

This was picked up minutes later by Germain Lussier at *Slashfilm* under the title "John Carter Needs to Make About $700M to Earn a Sequel" in which Lussier wrote:[178]

$700 million would put the film in the top 50 highest grossing films of all time, something Stanton previously experienced with *Finding Nemo*. However, that's a tough mountain to climb for a movie with an unproven lead star, unspecific title and little in terms of general audience buzz six months out from a March 2012 release.

Others picked it up from there, and within hours of the *New Yorker* interview hitting the internet, the notion that *John Carter* would have to earn the highly unlikely figure of $700M just to justify a sequel had put the scent of blood distinctly in the water.

---

[177] Margaret Lyons, "How Much Does John Carter Need to Make to Get a Sequel," Vulture.com, 10 Oct 2011, 4 Sep 2012 <http://www.vulture.com/2011/10/john-carter-mars-andrew-stanton-box-offic.html>

[178] Germain Lussier, "'John Carter' Needs to Make About $700 Million to Earn a Sequel," *Slashfilm*, 11 Oct 2011, 4 Sep 2012 <http://www.slashfilm.com/john-carter-700-million-earn-sequel/>

As *Slashfilm's* German Lussier acknowledged, such a figure was not entirely out of reach. *Finding Nemo* at $867M, was number 27 on the all-time Top 50 list. And *Wall-E*, at $521M, was at number 90, not too far behind. But the preposterousness of launching a film with as tough a marketing proposition as *John Carter* with a "par" level of box office set at $700M reeked of Hollywood hubris and made the film an inviting target. The fact that the marketing had been as weak as it was thus far, only added fuel to the gathering firestorm of negativity.

From this point on, everything about *John Carter* would be judged not just as one of the movies coming to the screen in 2012 -- it would be seen as a film that personified Hollywood excess -- it had become "Disney's Folly."

And so *John Carter* prepared to enter the all important final push of the campaign beginning November 30, 2011. Rather than being positioned for success, it was positioned for disastrous failure. Virtually everything had gone wrong that could go wrong. The title change in May had started the negativity; the first poster in June and trailer in July had failed to excite, it had skipped Comic-con, D23 had fallen flat; tales of a month of reshoots had led to disclosure of a "ballooning" $250M budget; then Disney had gone completely silent between the last week of August and mid-October, and the *New Yorker* comment about $700M being needed for a sequel to be greenlit had set off a chain reaction that had, finally and forever, altered the perception of the film from that of an anticipated sci-fi classic, to that of a bloated monument to Hollywood ego and excess that was doomed to failure by those egos and excesses. Now the game was to wait in anticipation and watch Disney's Barsoomian Titanic sail into the iceberg awaiting it.

The one saving grace was that all of this was happening outside of the view of the vast majority of the moviegoing public, most of whom had never even heard of the film. But those who had heard about it, and were writing about it, were the all important influencers and they had gradually become convinced by the ongoing series of blunders, miss-steps, substandard marketing materials, and media silence from Disney that *John Carter* was a train wreck unfolding in inexorable slow motion.

Within Disney, MT Carney knew that her stewardship as Disney President of Worldwide Marketing was coming to an end, and she was "okay with it." She had never moved to California from New York, returning each week to Manhattan to be with her children. Now it was just a matter of time until the announcement was made, and her focus was increasingly on what would be next for her.

In October, a key Carney assistant, Ayaz Asad, was promoted to Senior Vice President, Marketing. At 35, Asad was young, but clearly a mover within the Disney organization. He had graduated from USC with a degree in economics in 2003, and had begun his career at Disney shortly thereafter, first in the audit department, then as a Director of Brand Marketing, a post he held from 2005-2010. When Rich Ross had taken over in October 2009, he had emerged from the shakeup as a Vice President of Global Marketing Strategy and Communications, a promotion that signified he'd successfully navigated the house cleaning that Ross's arrival had triggered, and that he was viewed by Ross as part of the solution, not the problem. With Carney increasingly disengaged, it would fall to Asad and others to rescue the campaign, if indeed it could be rescued.

Battered and buzzless, with a newly minted senior VP in charge and with MT Carney's attention elsewhere, *John Carter* staggered toward the final stage of the campaign.

PART THREE

JOHN CARTER 2012

THE FINAL PUSH BEGINS

Joseph E. Levine famously said, "You can fool all of the people all of the time ... if the advertising is right and the budget is big enough." While today's blindingly fast, social media-driven word of mouth has altered the equation somewhat since Levine made the statement, the fact remains unaltered that money and message are both needed to get the job done for a movie at the top level of budget and hence, investment.

Buffy Shutt in "Research and the Movies" writes:[179]

> Marketers must create a visceral, nearly tribal need to attend one movie over the three or four other new movies opening on a specific Friday; over the five or six holdover movies from two to four weeks earlier, one specific movie over all other entertainment choices -- renting a DVD, going to a concert, staying in to watch The Sopranos, choosing to attend one specific movie over everything else in life they could be doing....a lot of money is at stake and a movie can only be launched once theatrically. Once. There are no do-overs in movie marketing.

Because a theatrical campaign builds to a particular date, and because there are no do-overs, it shares many of the characteristics of a political campaign. Just as political campaigns constantly monitor the feedback to the candidate and his or her appearances and statements, so too does a theatrical campaign need to keep an ear to the ground and listen to the feedback that is available.

---

[179] Buffy Shutt, "Research and the Movies," *Design Research, Method and Perspectives*, edited by Brenda Laurel, (MIT Press, 2003) 294.

In the early phases of a "final push" theatrical campaign, the main mechanisms for measuring feedback are online evidence of "buzz" which comes in the form of articles and the comments responding to those articles, tweets mentioning the movie, *Facebook* posts, message board posts on movie and entertainment message boards, and posts on other microblogs and social media sites. A percentage of the overall theatrical campaign budget is allocated for research and this research provides those managing the campaign with real-time readouts of how the creative and other materials being released are faring.

Research is also typically conducted prior to the release of materials to the public. Trailers, posters, taglines, and other materials are all typically focus group tested, and many studios hire multiple design and trailer cutting houses to create completely different campaigns, which are then tested with focus groups before final decisions are made.

Apart from various forms of online monitoring via reputation management and social media monitoring software, four weeks prior to the release of a film the studios begin to get "tracking numbers" provided under contract and accomplished the old fashioned way, via telephone interviews of likely theater goers.

All of this is designed to ensure that once a campaign launches its final push, the studio has at its fingertips the kind of feedback that will allow it to recalibrate and respond as necessary if the campaign is failing to achieve the desired resonance among potential filmgoers.

The *John Carter* campaign's "Online Phase" would end, and the "All Media" phase would begin, during the last week of November 2011, with the key launch event being the release of the full theatrical trailer on November 30, 2011. Covering the final 100 days of the campaign, this is the portion of the campaign where as much as 80% of the marketing budget, estimated at $100M, would be spent, with the campaign making the transition from an existence defined almost entirely by a presence on the internet among influencers, to an existence that would include all areas of mass, mainstream media in such saturation that, if successful, it would result in more than 80% of Americans knowing plenty about *John Carter*, with at least 6 million Americans being so highly motivated to see the film that they would view it in theaters on opening weekend.

ANOTHER MISFIRE

As the final all-media phase of the campaign launched in the waning days of November, the campaign was once again coming off of a period of media silence. Since D23 in August, a paltry total of 45 publicity placements monitored by IMDB. By comparison, during the same period its main competition *The Hunger Games* logged over 1100 placements, and its stablemate *The Avengers* logged over 1400 placements.

The date when Disney broke the media silence was November 23. Not coincidentally, November 23 was the release date for *The Muppets* -- an event which freed up internal in-house personnel who had been working on *The Muppets* and would now turn their attention to *John Carter*. The first salvo was the release of an image of *John Carter* facing a Great White Ape in the Thark arena -- an image that would become the dominant image for all of the promotion that would follow. Disney chose to release the image initially through one outlet only, the summer preview issue of Entertainment Weekly.[180] But the striking image was quickly replayed across the web on more than 50 outlets.

Accompanying the picture release was a brief interview with Andrew Stanton discussing the white apes:

---

[180] Adam B. Vary, "'John Carter': Taylor Kitsch fends off a fearsome white ape -- EXCLUSIVE FIRST LOOK", *Entertainment Weekly*, 23 Nov 2011, 3 Sep 2012 <http://insidemovies.ew.com/2011/11/23/taylor-kitsch-john-carter-white-ape-first-look/>.

They're sort of an oversized gorilla in the books, and they're kind of ubiquitous. They're littered everywhere through at least the first several novels. ....We needed a scene where Carter was going have to get out of his execution sentence in order to move the story forward, and we thought what better than having to go up against this formidable creature?

As with many of the misfires in the campaign, there was a foreseeable negative outcome of the release of this particular image. That foreseeable outcome was that those journalists familiar with the iconic arena scene from *Attack of the Clones* would look at this and think "derivative" unless something was done to pre-empt this response. A simple way of pre-empting it would have been for Andrew Stanton, in the accompanying interview, to talk about how this scene, written by Edgar Rice Burroughs in 1912, was the source of and inspiration for the *Attack of the Clones* scene. Since the Stanton interview was released with the picture, any responsible journalist who would want to mention the similarity, would at least have to offer Stanton's counterpoint. The alternative to this pro-active "inoculation" was to simply hope no one noticed the similarity.

Disney took the second option -- unfortunately, the similarity was noticed. One of the first to pick up the story, publishing within an hour of the EW story going up, was *Geek Tyrant*, where Joey Paur set the tone of much that would follow:[181]

> This is a story I've been waiting to see brought to the big screen for a long time, and I'm not excited about it. Neither are a lot of other people, and that's not a good sign.....The image above comes from Entertainment Weekly and it looks like a scene right out of *Star Wars.*

Minutes later Matt Goldberg at *Collider.com* would publish the image and a link to *Entertainment Weekly*, with commentary that included the following:[182]

---

[181] Joey Paur, "New Image from Disney's JOHN CARTER," *Geek Tyrant*, 23 Nov 11, 4 Sep 2012 <http://geektyrant.com/news/2011/11/23/new-image-from-disneys-john-carter.html>.

[182] Matt Goldberg, "New Image From John Carter," 23 Nov 2011, 4 Sep 2012 <http://collider.com/john-carter-movie-image/128060/>.

John Carter is rumored to have an insane budget and while the movie comes out in March, Disney has held off on the marketing and hasn't built awareness beyond the trailer from July, an edit bay visit, and showing clips at D23 (clips the rest of us haven't seen). Obviously, there's still time to get everyone's attention, but when you think about how much lead time the studio gave to The Muppets compared to a movie based on the less well-known John Carter of Mars, it's a little difficult to understand why we're just now getting another image. Hopefully, we're about to see a lot more and get a better sense of what Stanton's conjured.

A few minutes later, Russ Fischer at *Slashfilm* posted:[183]

So, yeah, it's a little bit like something out of the *Star Wars* prequels — I could see a few lightsaber-wielding Jedi facing down that thing. We haven't seen much at all from this movie, and while the trailer left some people pretty cold, I think this is just the beginning of the wave of alien creatures that are going to be revealed from the film.

A MOVIE ABOUT AN APE . . .

A larger question which would only get larger as the campaign progressed, was whether the coliseum battle scene between John Carter and white apes, which is not central to the story and conveys nothing of the story's context, should be afforded such prominence in the marketing. Without context, it simply conjured up images of slaves and gladiators and fantastic beasts at a time when, most marketers would argue, "it's got cool CGI creatures" is not enough to motivate viewers to part with $12-15 to view a film in theaters.

By the end of the day on November 23 a total of 32 movie and entertainment sites had picked up the story and run the image, each generating comments and chatter. Once again, the issue of reputation management would come into play. Disney's "early warning" system (the influencer media) was in place; this "digital focus group" had seen what Disney had offered up, and now that focus group was speaking.

---

[183] Russ Fisher, "New Image From 'John Carter' Shows a Giant Toothy Beast', *Slashfilm*, 23 Nov 2011, 4 Sep 2012 <http://www.slashfilm.com/image-john-carter-shows-giant-toothy-beast/>.

Reaction to the released image was tepid at best. Apart from citing the Star Wars 'lookalike' issue; commenters gave a collective "meh" to the image. First day reaction to what would become the central image using standard "Sentiment Analysis" software of the campaign produced a "positive/negative sentiment ratio" of 6/4, which was dramatically lower than the 9/1 that an opening salvo like this would hope to generate.[184]

On *Facebook*, Disney broke a month of silence, not posting the white ape image, but instead posting the kind of random tease that would typify the *Facebook* campaign: "Zodanga: a nation of the red men of Barsoom, at war with Dejah Thoris's beloved Helium."[185] The post drew only 11 comments. On that same day, a second post appeared (one of only a handful of days in the entire campaign when more than 1 post appeared on the *John Carter Facebook* page: "126 days until *John Carter* arrives. Share the countdown, and learn more about Barsoom, Edgar Rice Burroughs, and the legend of John Carter." This drew a total of 31 comments. It was only two days after posting the white ape image at IGN that Disney posted it on *Facebook*, drawing 64 comments.

The woes and missteps were continuing to mount for *John Carter*.

. . . IN A DRAB, DUSTY, DREARY DESERT

Next, on November 25, Disney released six images from the film. Curiously, all the images, except for a shot of a Helium warship sporting blue pennants, were taken from desert scenes and featured a color pallet that was extremely reminiscent of *Prince of Persia*, and which represented a very tiny sliver of the rich visual elements within the overall film. The white ape scene as well, previously released, also was limited to the

---

[184] Sentiment Analysis identifies the Fan or Follower's attitude toward a brand by using variables such as context, tone, emotion, among others. A commonly used reference is "positive/negative sentiment ratio" which expresses the ratio of positive to negative brand references. There are a variety of software programs available, as well as companies specializing in Sentiment Analysis. All major corporations in the US conduct sentiment analysis on the brands and products; movie studios, with the acute challenge of a one-shot, no do-over marketing campaign have perhaps the strongest need of all types of companies to conduct and make use of the results of Sentiment Analysis.

[185] Official John Carter *Facebook* Page, <https://facebook.com/johncartermovie>.

"desert" look . All images were daylight exterior; no images contained any major sets or production design (other than the Helium flyer); the one image of a Thark showed Tars Tarkas against a brown backdrop that caused him to be almost camouflaged and hardly visible; and the one image of Dejah Thoris was an ill-chosen one that made the "incomparable one" look thick waisted (which Lynn Collins was not), and showed her only in profile from a distance.

On November 28, 2011, Disney debuted what would become the main *John Carter* poster through iTunes. The poster featured a new tagline: "Lost in our world. Found in another." The poster, produced by BLT Communications, was designed by artists Andrew Witt (a former Marine), Nguyen Nguyen, and Ryan Osga based on concepts that emanated from MT Carney's marketing team at Disney.

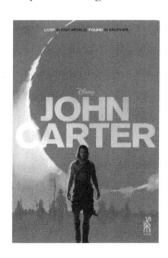

One of the first reactions came from Alex Riviello at *JoBlo.com*, who ran the poster under the headline: "John Carter of Uglytown"[186]

> The new poster for JOHN CARTER is here and it's really, really red. It might be better than the last one but honestly, anything would be. It's still as bland as can be, nothing that you'd expect for a film that was supposedly a thrilling tale about an immortal being facing giant aliens.
>
> JOHN CARTER hits theaters March 9. Will anyone care?

Gregory Ellwood observed:[187]

> **Red-orange is not a great color scheme for a movie campaign (aka, 'That was one bad poster')**
>
> Again, Disney (and possibly Stanton) took the brand idea for "John Carter" too far with the film's poster . . . It created a retro-esque campaign look that made the film look even less appealing to the under 25 demo . . . from a marketing perspective they [Disney] looked at it as a brand first and not a movie . . . . From the first teaser trailer to the first poster to the outdoor advertising to the final poster and almost every piece of marketing material in-between, too much of the "Carter" campaign was fashioned as a brand campaign, not a movie campaign. The studio did everything possible to try and sell those words "John Carter" in your face as something to associate with fantastic imagery while forgetting the need to sell either a marketing hook or the movie's storyline.[188]

The Film Informant, a site which rates movie posters and offers fans the opportunity to rate them as well, gave the poster a devastating 0.8/10 (that's zero point 8 out of 10), while fans gave it 5.6/10. The critique:[189]

> You might mistake "JC" for a cartoon judging from this botched new teaser poster, which marks a confusing tone change after the first one-sheet and teaser trailer. For a movie set on the red planet,

---

[186] Alex Riviello, "John Carter of Uglytown", *Joblo.com*, 28 Nov 2011, 4 Sep 2012 <http://www.joblo.com/movie-news/john-carter-of-uglytown>.

[187] Gregory Ellwood, "What went wrong with 'John Carter'?," HitFix, 12 Mar 2012, 4 Sep 2012 <http://www.hitfix.com/blogs/awards-campaign/posts/what-went-wrong-with-john-carter>.

[188] HItFix, March 12, 2012, http://www.hitfix.com/blogs/awards-campaign/posts/what-went-wrong-with-john-carter

[189] TFI Staff, "John Carter - Poster 2", The Film Informant, 28 Nov 2011, 4 Sep 2012 <http://thefilminformant.com/2011/11/john-carter-poster-2/>.

bright orange makes little sense, and a purple title character isn't helping. A blah logo design begs the question, what happened to the much cooler logo from the teaser trailer?

Ironically, the poster came from one of the most successful graphic design houses in Hollywood -- BLT Communications who had done posters for Disney as well as other studios, and whose theatrical poster output in 2012 in addition to *John Carter*, included *Brave*, *Safe House*, *The Dictator*, *Battleship*, *Prometheus*, *The Avengers*, *Spiderman*, *Total Recall*, and more. *John Carter*, seen among these other posters, clearly stands out -- but did it stand out in a way that would be effective?[190]

Poster designers in external houses like BLT work under the supervision of the creative media director of the studio, in this case Frank Chiocchi. Chiocchi had come to Disney in January 2011 from Universal, and reported to MT Carney while maintaining liaison with Andrew Stanton. Chiocchi is one of the most highly respected creative directors in the business.

Given the combination of BLT's and Chiocchi's credentials, the question arises -- who was the driving force behind the creatives that were starting to come out. Was it Stanton, or Carney, or someone else?

Much later, after the film had been released, at least one Carney surrogate was widely quoted as saying that Stanton's stature was such because of his Pixar success that he was given full final approval over all key art and trailers, and that he and Carney had multiple arguments that "ended with the brash department head almost reduced to tears", with Stanton "winning every battle" and summing it up: "They throw petals at his feet . . ."[191]

Professionals close to Stanton, and Stanton himself, say otherwise, claiming that while he was engaged on the marketing, mainly in consultations with Chiocchi, he had little direct contact with Carney and that the relationship with Chiocchi went smoothly and professionally,

---

[190] BLT Communications, "John Carter," 4 Sep 2012 < http://bltcommunications.com/ Explore/TheatricalPrint>.

[191] Claude Brodesser-Akner, "The Inside Story of How John Carter Was Doomed by Its First Trailer," *Vulture.com*, 13 Mar 2012, 4 Sep 2012 <http://www.vulture.com/2012/03/ john-carter-doomed-by-first-trailer.html>.

with reasonable give and take on all sides. "We didn't always agree on which direction to take every step of the way, but there was never serious contention," Stanton said of the studio's marketing. "The truth was everyone tried their very best to crack how to sell what we had, but the answer proved elusive."[192]

Regardless of where it was coming from -- one thing that was clear is that the peculiar choices that dogged the *John Carter* marketing creatives were unlikely to be a result of the Chiocchi, Tamusaitis, or the artists at BLT Communications.

Meanwhile, the poster hit with a thud.

The fact that many of those commenting on the poster referred to it as a "teaser poster" reflects the fact that, for a final theatrical poster for a film based on an unknown property, the imagery was exceptionally oblique. For a hundred years the same material had been conceptualized by book cover artists in a manner that was completely different, emphasizing fantastic aliens, swashbuckling adventure, and always -- John Carter *and* Dejah Thoris. The absence of Dejah Thoris from the primary poster was a strategic decision, not an accident: Disney had deemed that *John Carter* was a "boys" movie targeted at young boys age 10-14; it was an "adventure" brand in development; and the presence of Dejah Thoris would muddy the waters.

Dejah Thoris was out, and she would never appear on a single poster except once, in the distant background, a tiny unrecognizable figure on a thoat.

Things were about to get worse.

---

[192] Drew Taylor, "Andrew Stanton Reflects on the Box Office Failure of John Carter", *Indie/Playlist*, 10 Sep 2012, 11 Nov 2012 <http://blogs.indiewire.com/theplaylist/andrew-stanton-reflects-on-john-carter-20120910>

"That Trailer" is Unveiled

Andrew Stanton had learned from Pixar co-founder Steve Jobs the mantra that "you only get one chance to make a first impression," and for millions of Americans their first impression of *John Carter* would be the trailer that appeared on *Good Morning America*, the morning of November 30, 2011. Disney and ABC touted in advance that this would be the "World Premiere" of the trailer, and for the influencers who had been following the saga of the film, this was must-see television.

A number of outlets commented on the advisability of Disney choosing *Good Morning America* for the premiere of the trailer, wondering how Disney marketing had selected this particular demographic for a movie like *John Carter*. In fact, the choice of *Good Morning America* reflected perfectly the decision by MT Carney to target boys ages 10-14, since this would reach the Moms, and some Dads, who were needed to get those "tween" boys to the theater. So from Disney's point of view; it was a logical choice -- however to the observers who were still looking at *John Carter* as a four quadrant mass appeal film with demographics similar to *Avatar* or *Prometheus*, the choice seemed strange indeed.

After having promoted the event in advance as the premiere of the full theatrical trailer, Disney decided instead to show only a 45 second cut-down of the two minute trailer -- with the impact of the first 11 seconds being diminished by the fact that it was shown by having a camera point zoom in on the big screen over Times Square.[193] The decision to go with a 45 second TV spot instead of the two minute trailer -- even though it had been trumpeted loudly as the premiere of the full trailer -- reflected two factors; first, the exigencies of network morning television, and second, Disney's focus on the wider GMA audience and failure to consider the early adopter and influencer audience that would also be watching. Proclaiming that what would be shown was the full trailer, and then showing a 45 second clip degraded by the first 11 seconds being shot off the Times Square screen, might have slipped unnoticed past that wider audience who was getting its first taste of the movie -- but it did not play well with the influencer audience.

Matt Goldbert of *Collider.com* wrote "The trailer (or at least the cut that aired on *Good Morning America*) is short and not sweet . . ." and then a few hours later: "2nd UPDATE: Disney has asked us to refer to this as a "sneak peek" . . . which is the idiotic world of double-marketing we live in. If you want to see the full trailer in all its wonder, it will run tonight at 9:00 PM PST on IGN."[194] All across the internet, the influencer sites put out stories in the first hour after the GMA airing, only to subsequent update the stories at Disney's request, redefining the GMA event after the fact as a "sneak peek" of the trailer, not the trailer debut that had been promised. *That* was now scheduled for 9PM PST tonight.

Another blunder had occurred.

On *Twitter*, Andrew Stanton responded to a barrage of tweets asking if what was shown on GMA was actually the full trailer:[195]

> @andrewstanton: "@IllusionOfLife: Was the trailer on GMA the full cut or will we get a longer version online later today?" Long version on Kimmel and online.

Besides the issue of how Disney had chosen to unveil the "sneak peek," there was the matter of the trailer itself. Many commentators

---

[193] Robin Roberts, "Friday Night Lights Star Taylor Kitsch Shows Official Trailer for John Carter" *Youtube "ABC News" Channel*, 30 Nov 2011, 2 Sep 2012 <http://www.youtube.com/watch?v=Swf9pVGVW30>.

[194] Matt Goldberg, "'Sneak Peek' at New Trailer for JOHN CARTER," Collider.com, 30 Nov 2011, 12 Sep 2012 <http://collider.com/john-carter-movie-trailer/102418/>.

[195] Twitter, Andrew Stanton Feed, <http://Twitter.com/AndrewStanton>.

simply posted the GMA sneak peek without comment; a few acknowledged that it was better than the teaser trailer released in July, but by far the majority who voiced any opinion at all, voiced concern. Katy Rich at *Cinema Blend.com* encapsulated much of the commentary:[196]

> The brief bit they've shown, though, is emphasizing the massive spectacle and battle scenes of the Mars world that Stanton has built . . . It's still hard to look at this, with its alien creatures and flying spaceships and man in a loincloth, and assume that anybody beyond hardcore sci-fi audiences will go for it. What I think will make *John Carter* work is the story, pounded out relentlessly by Pixar veteran Stanton, and it's hard to get a sense of that in a trailer that seems to be all about spectacle.

Finally 16 hours later, after more than 50 media outlets had weighed in on the "sneak peek" version, resulting in social media reactions that skewed negative yet again, the full trailer appeared online on IGN, and on TV on Jimmy Kimmel Live, where Kitsch was a guest.

The full version of the trailer opens with an aerial shot of the Thark coliseum, then cut to Tars Tarkas and *John Carter* seen from behind entering the arena -- a shot that directly resembles a specific and very famous shot from the arena scene from *Attack of the Clones*.[197] A voice is heard: "Let them be crushed," then Carter is seen battling a white ape. The white ape opening occupies the first 30 seconds of the trailer, ending with Carter leaping over the ape and slaying it. While the trailer was criticized for not specifying where the action is taking place, there are meant to be clues that it is on another planet including Tars Tarkas' line: "When I saw you I thought that something new can come into this world...", and Dejah Thoris: "You...are...John Carter of Earth," as well as the graphics cards reading: "Lost in our world, found in another."

Harry Knowles of *Ain't It Cool News* was one of those who liked the new full trailer: "I just got finished watching this trailer about a half dozen times. I'm actually really intrigued. It is most definitely aesthetically its own thing. Very curious to see how this JOHN

---

[196] Katey Rich, "New John Carter Trailer Previewed on Good Morning America," *Cinema Blend*, 30 Nov 2011, 4 Sep 2011 <http://www.cinemablend.com/new/John-Carter-Trailer-Previewed-Good-Morning-America-28116.html>.

[197] DisneyMovieTrailers, "John Carter Trailer,", *Youtube*, <http://www.youtube.com/watch?v=nlvYKl1fjBI>.

CARTER re-imagining will go."[198] Another one of those who found the trailer encouraging was Joey Paur at *GeekTyrant.com*, who until the release of this trailer had been using words like "underwhelmed" and "unimpressed" but who now wrote: "I really want this movie to be good. I will say this is the best trailer I've seen so far, and I'll admit, it actually ended up getting me a little excited to see the movie."[199]

A more typical mixed reaction came from Angie Han at *Slashfilm*, who wrote:[200]

> I wasn't blown away by that first trailer and this morning's preview of this new trailer didn't impress me much either. So I'm surprised and pleased to find that I like this longer trailer more, though it's possible that the anticipation just has me feeling more generous. We get a great look at the scope and beauty of this world in this video, and there's no denying that it all looks very pretty. On the other hand, star Taylor Kitsch still doesn't appear to have anything terribly interesting to do, and the dialogue is still painfully generic.

The chatter in social media was equally mixed. Keywords that appeared with regularity including "confusing," "spectacle," "cheesy" -- but also "epic" and "fun."

By the time the dust had settled, the initial response to the trailer reflected a positive/negative sentiment ratio of 6.5/3.5 which, while not a complete disaster, was a far cry from the 9/1 ratio that would have signaled broad acceptance of the trailer.

On December 3, Scott Mendelson made a sharp case for Disney's shortcomings, saying of the new trailer:[201]

---

[198] Harry Knowles, *Aintitcool.com*, December 1, 2011, http://www.aintitcool.com/node/52128

[199] Joey Paur, "The Sci-Fi Film JOHN CARTER gets a New Full Trailer!" *Geek Tyrant*, 30 Nov 2011, 4 Sep 2012 <http://geektyrant.com/news/2011/11/30/the-sci-fi-film-john-carter-gets-a-new-full-trailer.html>.

[200] Angie Han, "'John Carter' Trailer - 'Wall-E' Director Andrew Stanton Goes Back to outer Space, This Time with Tim Riggins," 30 Nov 2011, 4 Sep 2012 <http://www.slashfilm.com/john-carter-trailer-2/>.

[201] Scott Mendelson, "Going Broke Chasing Boys: Why Disney ditched princesses and spent $300M on John Carter," *Hollywood News*, 3 Dec 2011, 4 Sep 2012 <http://www.hollywoodnews.com/2011/12/03/going-broke-chasing-boys-why-disney-ditched-princesses-and-spent-300-million-on-john-carter/>.

. . . it so painfully feels like a Mad Libs male-driven fantasy blockbuster that it borders on parody. It's no secret that Disney thinks it has a boy problem. One of the reasons it bought Marvel two years ago was to build up a slate of boy-friendly franchises. And the last two years have seen an almost embarrassing attempt to fashion boy-friendly franchises (*Prince of Persia, Tron: Legacy, The Sorcerer's Apprentice, I Am Number Four, Fright Night*, and *Real Steel*), only half of which were even as successful as their alleged flop *The Princess and the Frog* (which obviously grossed 'just' $267 million on a $105 million budget because it starred a character with a vagina)......Now we have *John Carter*, which allegedly cost $300 million (if not more). It's being released in March, where only one film (to be fair, Disney's *Alice In Wonderland*) has ever even grossed $300 million. Hell, in all of January-through April, there have been just five $200 million grossers (*The Passion of the Christ, Alice In Wonderland, How to Train Your Dragon, 300*, and *Fast Five*). So you have yet another film that basically has to shatter all records regarding its release date in order to merely break even. But that's okay, thinks Disney, because John Carter is a manly science fiction spectacle so it is surely worth risking the bank. Disney is so desperate to not only chase the young male demos that it is willing to risk alienating the young female demos that has netted it billions of dollars over the many decades.

The less than spectacular launch of the All Media phase of the campaign notwithstanding, the situation was not yet hopeless. Many of those who had been following the *John Carter* story seemed to be on the fence, with the trailer having left them undecided but still willing to give the film the benefit of the doubt. For most, that benefit of the doubt was offered courtesy of their trust in Andrew Stanton, for whom they had a high degree of respect after *Finding Nemo* and *Wall-E*. True, there was cause for concern -- but with 100 days remaining, there was time to get it right.

IT BECOMES PERSONAL

Prior to the unveiling of the trailer on November 30, 2011, I had paid at best cursory attention to the promotion of *John Carter.* I'd seen the teaser trailer released in July 2011, which I had found to be encouraging, and had read perhaps a half dozen articles at various times about the film in progress. When *Avatar* came out I had been startled at the similarities to Burroughs' work, and had written an article for ERBzine about it, but that had been about it.[202]

Coming into the unveiling of the main theatrical trailer 100 days before the March 9 release date, I had no thoughts of being anything other than an interested observer to the campaign -- an Edgar Rice Burroughs fan rooting on a movie that, regardless of whether or not it turned out to be a perfect adaptation, would have the potential to introduce my old friend Edgar Rice Burroughs to millions of new fans and in so doing refresh Burroughs' legacy going into its second century.

---

[202] Michael D. Sellers, "Heady Days for Edgar Rice Burroughs Fans: *Avatar*, ERB, and John Carter of Mars," Erbzine, 10 Jan 2010, 3 Sep 2012 < http://www.erbzine.com/ mag30/3038.html>.

But . . . the unveiling of the trailer was a bumpy one. What had been hyped in advance as debut of the full theatrical trailer on *Good Morning America* didn't turn out to be that at all. The full trailer finally did premiere sixteen hours later on Jimmy Kimmel and thankfully it was better than the cut-down version shown that morning. I checked on YouTube to see how the full trailer was being received, and discovered an ongoing argument between viewers who complained that it seemed to be a "ripoff of *Avatar*" and those trying to set the record straight about which story came first, and who ripped off whom. The same argument was being played out in comment threads on various of the entertainment sites that I checked. I left a few comments here and there, but otherwise just read.

Online, Disney was being second guessed for both the content of the trailer, and the handling of its release.

Then there was the disheartening discovery of just how lame the publicity for *John Carter* had been -- and how badly the film was being outclassed by both the *Hunger Games* and *Avengers*. I felt helpless, and discouraged.

By Saturday, December 3rd, an idea was beginning to form.

I had been a fan of Edgar Rice Burroughs since I was 12, and I was a blogger -- but other than the article about *Avatar* and ERB, I hadn't written much about Burroughs. As a filmmaker I had always wanted to do a Burroughs adaptation -- but my station in Hollywood as an "indie" filmmaker making movies at budgets of a few million dollars or less had made it unlikely that I would ever get that chance.

Meanwhile, there were things about Burroughs I had always been interested in exploring. I had, for example, felt that his books achieved a level of deeply satisfying wish-fulfillment that truly set them apart from all other books of its kind, and yet he was widely written of as a "pulp adventure" writer in a manner that seemed to me to fall short of truly understanding his genius. This had always been just an impression I'd had, but life had never presented me with an opportunity to think deeply about it or write about.

What if ....

The next 100 days would be a period, I knew, where I would be thinking more about Edgar Rice Burroughs than I had in a number of years. And others would be too. Maybe this was the right time to try for a little repayment of a debt owed to the grandmaster who had filled me with hope and confidence about what is possible in life, just at the time in adolescence when feeling such inspiration can propel you into adulthood in a positive way. I was sure that the path I had taken in life was in some way affected by, if not inspired by, the "ERB magic." Maybe it was time to try and do something positive for ERB and his legacy.

Added to this was the fact that I knew a few tricks of the blogging trade that would make it possible to easily, and without putting much time into it, aggregate all of the articles on *John Carter* that were now starting to come out, and create a "John Carter Newsfeed" that could be promoted to entertainment journalists and bloggers as a one-stop-shop for *John Carter* information, and which should -- if my thinking was correct -- result in greater replay and online amplification of the articles that were now beginning to appear with regularity.

On Saturday, December 3rd, I purchased the URL www.thejohncarterfiles.com and started creating a blogsite. I chose the name *John Carter Files* because I had in mind that when the film's theatrical run was over, I would hopefully have assembled a good collection of background material on Burroughs, Barsoom, and John Carter, and this could remain online as a kind of resource archive for anyone stumbling across *John Carter* in the future.

All day I roamed the internet finding pieces of background information and plugging them in to the blog -- a page for each character, a page on Edgar Rice Burroughs, links to all the Burroughs fan blogs that were out there, links to Edgar Rice Burroughs Inc., links to the project Gutenberg text of *A Princess of Mars*, examples of artwork through the years. It was a Burroughs fanboy feast and I was having a blast.

By the time the end of that first day, I had a decent looking little blogsite up and running and had written and published the first substantive post: "*John Carter* Inspired *Avatar*, not vice versa -- let's set the record straight."[203]   I had also done my first aggregated "News About John Carter" newsfeed. Not bad for a Saturday on the couch.

It felt good to strike a blow for old ERB.

THE BURROUGHS COMMUNITY

As the theatrical trailer was released on November 30, 2011, a very interested party was Jim Sullos, President of Edgar Rice Burroughs, Inc., the publishing company that the entrepreneurial minded Burroughs had created in 1923.   Almost 90 years later, the company continued to manage the rights to Burroughs' creations, operating from the same small Spanish style bungalow on Ventura Boulevard in Tarzana that Burroughs had built in 1926, and where he had written many of the *Tarzan* and *John Carter* novels.

In those days, Ventura Boulevard was not paved, and Burroughs would ride his horse to work; today, the boulevard is eight lanes wide with dense commercial structures on both sides.   The small bungalow, largely unchanged since 1926, stands as a quaint anachronism and a window into an earlier era.   From the street it is almost obscured from view by a large walnut tree in a gated front yard that is almost a jungle-like tangle of trees, vines, and shrubbery.   Adding to the sense of myth and mystery is the fact that Burroughs' ashes are buried without markings at the base of the walnut tree.

Sullos is an accountant by trade.   After college and graduate school at Columbia University, he had joined the accounting firm of Windes & McClaughry in his native Long Beach.   He spent his entire career with the firm, and from the mid 1990s counted Edgar Rice Burroughs, Inc. among the clients he served. His role included that of trustee and a member of the board of directors. When he reached mandatory retirement at age 62 in 2001, Sullos began divesting himself of clients. A trim and spritely 73 years old today, Sullos recalls: "When I was a 36-year-

---

[203]Michael D. Sellers, "John Carter Inspired *Avatar*, not Vice Versa", The John Carter Files, 3 Dec 2012, 3 Sep 2012 < http://thejohncarterfiles.com/2011/12/john-carter-inspired-avatar-not-vice-versa-lets-set-the-record-straight/>

old partner, I voted for mandatory retirement without ever thinking I'd be that old. The time went just like that," he says.[204]

As a longtime and trusted ally, Sullos was tapped to become President of the company on May 1, 2008, in a restructure that would make Burroughs' grandson, Danton Burroughs, the Chairman of the company. Tragically, that same day Danton Burroughs, who had been the keeper of the flame for the Burroughs legacy for the last 36 years, died of heart failure. Burroughs' death occurred a day after a fire at his home destroyed a room full of priceless family memorabilia, leaving Burroughs broken-hearted. "It was tragic and unexpected," says Sullos.

In addition to the "official" Burroughs office in Tarzana, at the time of the release of the first trailer in July 2011, there was a nationwide network of Burroughs fan groups which, while not large in terms of absolute numbers, nevertheless represented a potential ally for Disney, with more than a thousand active participants spread among a half-dozen organizations and email lists, many of whom were academicians, journalists, and writers who have written extensively on Burroughs and were seasoned, excellent interview subjects. The roster of groups included the Burroughs Bibliophiles, founded in 1960 and with a lineage that could be traced back to 1947; Erbania, started in 1956; the National Capital Panthans, the Chicago Muckers, and others.

Among the more prominent of the "ERBophiles", were Bill Hillman, a retired college professor from Manitoba whose weekly "ERBzine" fanzine at www.erbzine.com has grown over the years into a 10,000 page online archive of everything from a detailed timeline of Burroughs' life and collection of his letters, to a collection of virtually all of the art by Burroughs' illustrators; Bob Zeuschner, a philosophy professor at Pasadena City College and author of "ERB: The Exhaustive Scholars and Collectors's Descriptive Bibliography; George T. McWhorter of Louisville, Kentucky, the curator of the Burroughs memorial collection at the University of Louisville Library; David Bruce Bozarth of Houston, Texas, moderator and webmaster for the ERBlist Listserv email group and author of the exhaustive "Barsoom Glossary"; Scott Tracy Griffin, a Hollywood actor and writer, Laurence Dunn of

---

[204] William Cock, "Don't Mess With Tarzan", Erbzine, 1 Sep 2008 1 Nov 2012 <http://www.erbzine.com/mag35/3557.html>.

London, President of the Burroughs Bibliophiles Fan Group; and Henry Franke III, the longtime Editor of the Burroughs Bulletin Magazine. Additionally, there were various bloggers who maintained fansites relating to Burroughs and Barsoom - Jeff Doten, an artist who had worked on the failed "Carson of Venus" project, maintained www.barsoomia.org; Diana Cole maintained www.jcofmars.com; Mike Carembat maintained www.johncartermovie.com, "MCR" maintained www.jcomreader.blogspot.com, and Bill Hillman, in addition to his Erbzine efforts, maintained www.cartermovie.com. Other ERBophiles maintained other sites, including Phil Normand's www.recovering.com which specialized in creating replica dust jackets for many of the Burroughs books.

The attitude of the Burroughs community toward the film was one of cautious optimism; cautious because the many disappointing (from the perspective of Burroughs' fans) Tarzan screen adaptations had taught them to expect Hollywood to alter fundamental aspects of the characters and story in ways that would probably result in less than total satisfaction from the ERB community. But there was also optimism, in part because "hope springs eternal" but also because at least some recognized the Burroughs community was aging and new blood was needed to keep the unique Burroughs brand of romance and visionary adventure from slipping toward oblivion.

Within the Burroughs community the full trailer, when taken in combination with the earlier teaser trailer, showed promise, as seen from the Burroughs fan perspective; the movie clearly contained elements of the frame story from the novel with Burroughs himself a character learning of Carter's adventures through a journal left to him by Carter; it showed Carter arriving on Mars much as in the book; it contained brief depictions of Tharks that seemed true to the original; Dejah Thoris and John Carter seemed appropriate in terms of costumes and design, with the only deviation being the presence of reddish tattoos on Dejah Thoris that seemed to be Stanton's interpretation of how to present the "red Martians" of Burroughs' creation, plus substantially more clothing than Burroughs describes -- a nod to Disney realities that surprised no one. There was a brief glimpse of what seemed to be the pivotal Warhoon attack scene from the novel; the flyers and aircraft, while not perfectly in synch with what Burroughs had described, were close enough to satisfy most, and the shots of John Carter leaping showed him reaching a height of about 40 feet which was reasonably close to Burroughs description capping Carter's leaping ability at 35 feet vertically, and 100 feet laterally.

While the fan organizations tended to focus on the adaptation with a mixture of optimism and caution, for Jim Sullos and ERB Inc. it was less about the nuances of the adaptation and more about the success or failure of the release. After 100 years, John Carter was finally about to be introduced to a massively wider audience than had been the case at any time since the heyday of the sixties revival, and for the first time on film. Conservatively, even if the film did not do well, at least 30 million moviegoers worldwide would see the movie and at least some of those would be interested in the legacy on which the film had been constructed. That alone was progress.

But *John Carter* was not a one-off, it was the beginning of a series, and the financial and other rewards for the company Burroughs founded in 1923 would multiply if the film did well. A trilogy (indeed, the story outline of the trilogy was already complete), and then a series that could go on indefinitely. That in turn would spark interest in Burroughs' other properties, most notably the Carson of Venus series which had its own charms.

For ERB Inc., at stake was nothing less than millions of dollars and the future of the Burroughs brand, and legacy of Edgar Rice Burroughs himself.

THE FINAL 100 DAY PUSH BEGINS

The release of the trailer vaulted *John Carter* from #986 on the *IMDB* Movie Meter to #67, and in the week of the trailer release *IMDB* monitored 400 news articles and blog posts about the movie, but the surge was short-lived. The very next week, December 11, 'Carter fell to #130, and the week after, all the way to #501. Only 30 articles were monitored during the week of December 11. Meanwhile, throughout this whole period *The Hunger Games* was steadily climbing from #32 on December 11 to #14 on January 1.

On *Facebook, The Hunger Games* had multiple pages for each District in the movie; updates were being published at least daily; 900,000 fans had already signed up, and each post that was published were generated 1000 or more comments. By contrast, *John Carter* had no "special" pages; updates for the entire month of November totaled a paltry 6; only 1 update generated more than 100 comments and even the posting of the new poster on November 29--a major event for any theatrical campaign -- drew only 68 comments and 84 shares.[205]

---

[205] The Official John Carter *Facebook* Page, 28 Nov 2012, 4 Sep 2012 <https://facebook.com/JohnCarterMovie>; The Official Hunger Games *Facebook* Page, 20 Jul 2010, 4 Sep 2012

The day after the trailer appeared, Disney released three new banners that had a distinctly different look than the main poster. These banners, and a poster that would soon be released that matched them in style, were not produced by BLT Communications, the design house the created the main poster, but were rather the result of in-house efforts at Disney.

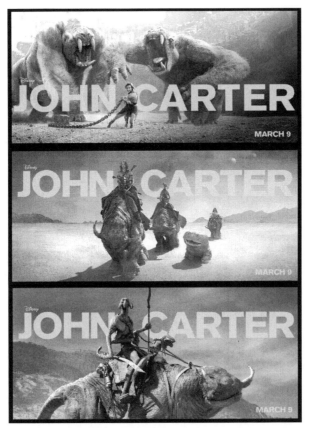

Like the trailer, which had featured Carter vs the white apes as the dominant "takeaway" image, the banners featured the white apes and other creatures against a desert environment. Strikingly, there was no image of Dejah Thoris; nothing suggesting romance; nothing suggesting science or technology; and most of all no images of any of the human Martians who would figure prominently in the movie and the projected series. Reaction to the banners was largely swamped in the reaction to the trailer, which was still fresh and prompting commentary that was mostly neutral, with positives leading negatives 2 to 1, which was a far cry from the 8 or 9 to 1 that would have signaled broad acceptance. The early vote was in: the campaign was not working.

Meanwhile *The Lorax*, Universal's animated Dr. Seuss feature starring Danny Devito, was set for release a week ahead of *John Carter* and released its trailer on December 6, a move which brought the film up to #373. Perceived as both a sequel to the successful *Dr. Seuss' Horton Hears a Who*, which had opened at $45M en route to a $154M domestic gross, and an encore by the *Despicable Me* team, the Universal picture bore watching as, if strong, it could eat into *John Carter's* opening weekend number, particularly with the 'tween/family demographic that Disney had decided to pitch to as the core audience for *John Carter*. In most "buzz monitoring" categories it looked relatively non-threatening, but the 210,878 *Facebook* fans was alarming.[206] *The Lorax* was clearly leveraging *Facebook* better than any of the films except *The Hunger Games*.

As of December 11, *John Carter's* profile, compared to its main competition, looked like this:

RELEASE DATE	TITLE	IMDB RANK	IMDB LIKES	IMDB MSG BOARD PGS	FB LIKES	POS/NEG SENTIMENT	GRADE
Mar 2, 2012	The Lorax	373	4550	2	210878	7/3	B
Mar 9, 2012	John Carter	140	3200	10	42560	6/4	B-
Mar 16, 2012	21 Jump Street	729	4950	7	52509	8/2	B
Mar 23, 2012	Hunger Games	32	52504	50	67902	9/1	A+
Mar 30, 2012	Wrath/Titans	635	4850	4	1507	7/3	B

Based on the chart, it was clear that *John Carter* was light years behind *The Hunger Games* and there was no hope of overtaking it, or even competing with for the March buzz. That battle had been lost.

But there was hope in that *John Carter's* position as of December 11 was competitive with the rest of the March competition and thus it was

---

[206] *The Lorax* Official *Facebook* Page, 10 May 2010, 3 Sep 2012 <https://www.facebook.com/theloraxmovie> *IMDB Pro* MovieMeter Data Table, *"The Lorax* (2012)"* 3 Sep 2012 <http://pro.imdb.com/title/tt1482459/graph-data>.

in position, with a solid promotional campaign going forward, to have a solid shot at the $55M - $60M opening it would need to be considered a success and generate a sequel. Such an opening would give it two strong weeks before *The Hunger Games* arrived.

The key question was -- would the campaign going forward become more surefooted and find ways to resonate with the audience that would be paying increasing attention to it now that it was in the final push?

Or would the misfires continue?

Adding to *John Carter* woes was the fact that the bar for *John Carter* was considerably higher than for any of the other films. Its budget of $250M stood in stark contrast to *21 Jump Street* ($40M), *The Lorax* ($70M) *The Hunger Games* ($100M), and Wrath of the Titans ($150M).[207] Based on budget, it was clear that *John Carter* should be occupying the position on the chart occupied by *The Hunger Games,* and the fact that it was in among the pack, while costing more than twice as much as most of the films, was reason for concern.

BREAKING DOWN THE BOX OFFICE CHALLENGE

A theatrical campaign is targeted on achieving certain opening weekend figures and after that, while the campaign continues in a sustaining mode, it is reviews and word of mouth that will propel a film to either fade quickly, follow the normal pattern of earning 35% the opening weekend and 65% over the remainder of the run, or develop legs so that the opening weekend ends up being less than 35% of the total.

What figures did *John Carter* need to get?

First, although there had been speculation since the October New Yorker article had come out that *John Carter* might need "as much as $700M" to break even and generate a sequel, the reality was that no "sequel-ready" film earning more than $400M worldwide had ever failed to generate a sequel. Indeed, the sequel "trigger" point is a far more

---

[207] All figures for budgets and box office gross are from Box Office Mojo, which is generally considered to be the most authoritative source for this information. <http://boxofficemojo.com>. To access the budget, theatrical gross, and other information for a given film, enter the title of the film in the search bar at the home page of Box Office Mojo.

complicated calculation than simple breakeven, particularly for Disney, where film franchises are a "wave generator" creating streams of income throughout the Disney ecosystem. Among serious analysts, there was confidence that a figure of $500M global gross would easily justify a sequel.

Breaking that number down -- if $500M was the trigger point, that meant that, if *John Carter* followed a pattern of 40% of its income coming from the US, and 60% overseas, it would need $200M total from the US domestic box office, and if the standard pattern was for domestic opening weekend to be 35% of the domestic total -- that meant *John Carter* needed a $70M opening weekend to be on track for $200M domestic gross and $500M global gross.

While $70M would be an unequivocal "win", there were other paths to $500M global total. Andrew Stanton, for example, had a track record of creating films which had "legs" -- *Finding Nemo*, for example, ended up with a pattern in which the first weekend was only 20% of the final domestic total, far better than the norm of 35% of the total coming from opening weekend.[208] And with *Wall-E*, the figure was 28%.[209] So if Stanton's patterns held up, opening weekend might end up being just 25% of the final domestic total. Thus an opening weekend of $50M, with the same kid of "legs" that Stanton had produced with *Finding Nemo* and *Wall-E*, could generate a $200M domestic gross.

The other factor was that increasingly, major action/CGI films were doing relatively better overseas, to the point that a 40-60 split was now becoming a 33-67 split for many films. This pattern, if it held true, meant that the US domestic total might not have to reach $200M in order for a $500M global total to be achieved -- the figure might end up being closer to $167M.

In the end, with all variables taken into consideration, for *John Carter* to be certified a "hit" by the entertainment media on opening weekend, it

---

[208] Box Office Mojo Staff, "Finding Nemo", 4 Sep 2012, <http://boxofficemojo.com/movies/?id=findingnemo.htm; http://boxofficemojo.com/movies/?page=weekend&id=findingnemo.htm>.

[209] Box Office Mojo Staff, "Wall-E", 4 Sep 2012, <http://boxofficemojo.com/movies/?id=wall-e.htm>

would need an opening at least in the mid $60M range. Anything in the $50M range would be considered inconclusive, and anything below $50M would be considered a failure given the high budget and marketing cost. Below $40M, for a film with production and marketing cost of $350M, would be regarded by the media as a disaster of epic proportions.

At this stage, in December, the few early projections that were available had the film opening at $25M.

December 16, 2011: The Air Wars Begin

On December 15 Disney released the IMAX poster for *John Carter*, initially exclusively via Fandango but within minutes other sites began to pick it up and replay it.[210]

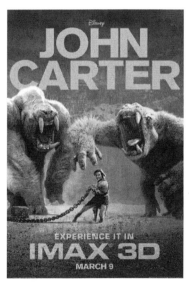

---

[210] Peter Dimako, "New John Carter Movie Poster has Taylor Kitsch in Monstrous Trouble," Upcoming Movies.com, 15 Dec 2011, 3 Sep 2012 <http://www.upcoming-movies.com/Articles/new-john-carter-movie-poster-has-taylor-kitsch-in-monstrous-trouble/>.

Like the images released a few days previously, the IMAX poster was created in-house at Disney. Its emphasis on the white apes and the arena scene would be a consistent feature of the in-house materials that Disney would generate for the entire run of the campaign, including the posters, the banners, and the trailers and TV spots.

On December 16, the TV campaign launched with two spots: ""Warhoon" and "Awakening."

In "Warhoon"[211], the spot begins with a line of green martian "Warhoon" warriors appearing on a canyon ridge with John Carter in the foreground:

This opening image immediately creates a "western" feel -- the cliff, the Warhoons (Indians?), even the handle of the sword John Carter has sheathed in his back looks like the butt of a rifle and the Thark fighting harness looks like a bandolier. The spot then reverses to show John Carter and Dejah Thoris, with John Carter saying "get her of here" against a background of a cracked desert floor. Dejah Thoris is carried away, then Carter turns and faces a charging horde of of Warhoons with the martian hound Woola loyally beside him.

Disney began placing this spot on male demographic shows -- notably the college football bowl games, as well as news broadcasts.

---

[211] Disney Movie Trailers Staff, "John Carter Warhoon TV Spot," *Disney Movie Trailers Channel Youtube*, 19 Dec 2011, 4 Sep 2012, <http://www.youtube.com/watch?v=HV4tekTPQbQ>.

In "Awakening," the spot begins with John Carter waking up in the desert (8 seconds of a 30 second spot is devoted to this), then follows with a mixture of shots balancing mystery (John Carter and Dejah in the temple of Iss), action, and spectacle -- ending with the ubiquitous white ape scene.[212]

Along with the two spots, Disney released two images, both again featuring the "dusty west with creatures" look that by now had come to characterize the film.

The critical question was: what would be the reaction to the TV spots?

Very little, as it turned out.

After the surge of chatter on December 1, the volume had quickly leveled off.

---

[212] Disney Movie Trailers Staff, "John Carter Awakening TV Spot," *Disney Movie Trailers Channel Youtube*, <http://www.youtube.com/watch?v=AbTdSQuCB5Q>.

Worse yet -- the TV spots released on December 16, and playing steadily on multiple networks during the week that followed, *barely had an impact at all.*

Where was the bump?

Other than a 'mini-bump' on the 16th, the day the TV spots began playing, there was nothing to indicate that the TV spots were having an effect.

The holidays came and Disney continued to play the same two TV spots with significant frequency.

Meanwhile at Disney, worldwide marketing president MT Carney was clearing out her desk and getting ready to make what would be her final trip back to New York, ostensibly for the holidays but in reality it was a permanent move. The New York based Carney had never moved to Los Angeles, returning home each weekend to be with her children in Manhattan, and by December she and Rich Ross had agreed that he would make the announcement in early January, and that she need not return.

Back at Disney, the campaign went forward on auto-pilot through the remainder of the holidays. By the end of December, *John Carter* TV spots had been playing for two weeks, largely on male-oriented programming, particularly the college bowl games and other sporting events.

During December, a frequent sentiment that was emerging among the influencer media was that the writer or commentator wasn't sure about the movie based on what he or she was seeing, but given that it was Andrew Stanton who was directing, there was reason for hope. Stanton was definitely not a "brand" to the public in the way that James Cameron was, but he *was* a brand to the movie intelligentsia who drive buzz and the question of whether or not he should be touted in the advertising ("From the Academy Award Winning Director of *Wall-E* and *Finding Nemo*", or "The Live Action Debut of the Academy Award Winning Director of *Wall-E* and *Finding Nemo*") was a critical one.

But both Stanton and Carney had agreed that the campaign would not tout "from the Director of *Finding Nemo* and *Wall-E*." Both felt that it could send a confusing message, given Stanton's reputation as a

Pixar director. Meanwhile, however, as December dragged on and the campaign failed to generate excitement, and bloggers and writers and commenters across the web referred again and again to Stanton as a primary reason for having interest in the film, the question arose -- should the campaign reconsider its initial decision?

The idea of highlighting Stanton in the promotion was given further boost by the fact that his Pixar stablemate Brad Bird's live action debut with *Mission Impossible: Ghost Protocol*, had just been released to positive reviews and box office, making the topic: "Can Pixar Directors move successfully into live action?" one that had significant potential.

At Collider.com, Brendan Bettinger wrote:[213]

> I have not yet connected with the story, but I give Andrew Stanton, the writer/director behind WALL·E, the benefit of the doubt. *Mission: Impossible – Ghost Protocol* finally proved once and for all that an animation director—and specifically a Pixar graduate in Brad Bird—can make the leap to big-budget live-action successfully. Stanton has the material, passion, and skills to follow suit.

Others wrote in a similar vein, but at Disney, it was the holiday break; MT Carney had already disengaged; *John Carter* was not at the forefront of any top-level thinking, and the opportunity to launch the "Pixarians go for live action" thrust passed.

THE JAPANESE TRAILER -- AN OPPORTUNITY LOST?

Ironically, the one event over the holidays that generated positive chatter on entertainment outlets was the discovery by *Ain't It Cool News'* Harry Knowles on 23 December of a Japanese *John Carter* Trailer initially uploaded without fanfare or awareness in the US by a Japanese YouTuber on 15 December. Knowles posted an embed of the Japanese trailer with positive comments about its contents on 23 Dec at 9:17 PM CST.[214] Immediately, other influencer media outlets began to pick up on the story.

---

[213] Brendan Bettinger, "Japanese Trailer for John Carter," *Collider.com*, 26 Dec 2011, 5 Sep 2012 <http://collider.com/john-carter-trailer-2/134204/>.

[214] Harry Knowles, "Japanese John Carter Trailer Begins to Show the Shape of the Story," *Ain't It Cool News*, 23 Dec 2011, 5 Sep 2012 <http://www.aintitcool.com/node/52394>.

Unlike the US trailer which opened with John Carter in the arena battling white apes, and generally left the audience with no clear sense of where the action was taking place, or how John Carter came to be there, the Japanese trailer spent 45 seconds, almost half of its entire length, setting up John Carter on Earth.   This was a decision which clearly resonated across the entire range of those following the film.

The trailer quickly became the first clear "hit" with influencer media, who embedded the trailer with favorable comments.   Brendan Connelly at *Bleeding Cool.com* raved about it, calling it a "Superb new trailer"[215] and other commentators welcomed the answers the trailer provided to the question -- how did John Carter get to Mars? -- a question that had been completely ignored in the main Disney theatrical trailer and the TV spots it had spawned.

Nick Newman at *The Film Stage* summed it up:[216]

> If there's one consistent issue plaguing the two trailers and TV Spots for *John Carter*, it's a lack of context. When an audience is being sold a movie, it usually helps to get a wider breadth of information on its plot, characters, and tone, but the first of those characteristics has been missing this entire time . . .   Anyone who wanted to see that is in luck... so long as they speak Japanese. An international preview for Andrew Stanton's live-action debut has popped up . . .

There was more.

At Slashfilm, Russ Fischer weighed in favorably, applauding the fact that the Japanese trailers showed "more of the framing story, and of the moments in which John Carter is actually transported to Mars."[217]

---

[215] Brendan Connelly, "Superb New Trailer and Intriguing Concept Art for John Carter," *Bleeding Cool.com*, 24 Dec 2011, 5 Sep 2012 < http://www.bleedingcool.com/ 2011/12/23/trailer-concept-art-for-john-carter/>.

[216] Nick Newman, "International 'John Carter' Trailer Provides More Backstory," *The Film Stage*, 23 Dec 2011, 5 Sep 2012 <http://thefilmstage.com/trailer/international-john-carter-trailer-provides-more-backstory/>.

[217] Russ Fischer, "'John Carter' International Trailer Shows More of Carter's Trip to Mars," *Slashfilm*, 23 Dec 2011, 5 Sep 2012 <http://www.slashfilm.com/john-carter-international-trailer/

Comicbook Movie,[218] Geek Tyrant,[219] Hey U Guys,[220] and dozens of other key influencer media sites weighed in favorably, ironically making the bootlegged Japanese trailer not intended for US audiences the first solid hit with the US influencer audience.

The influencers were playing their role as a feedback mechanism.

Was anyone at Disney listening?

BLEAK HOLIDAYS

Other than the ripple of positive buzz based on the Japanese trailer, the news was bleak. Steady airplay of the two TV spots released on December 16 was having almost no measurable buzz affect. Meanwhile, throughout December on *Twitter*, the official @JohnCarter account was tweeting less than once a day.[221] From the moment of the release of the trailer on November 30, signaling the launch of the main campaign, until the end of December, Disney's official @JohnCarter account tweeted a total of 12 times, and two of those were retweets of Andrew Stanton, the film's director, who was far more active on *Twitter* than Disney was, and who, it seemed, was helping the film measurably by regularly tweeting updates like: "Day one of our mix is over, and Mars is shining bright. A good sign." Stanton was also doing a regular Friday night Q and A with fans on *Twitter* that didn't appear to be being managed by Disney in any fashion -- it was just the director hanging out and taking questions from excited fans--virtually the only real "buzz" that was being generated anywhere in social media.

---

[218] Wolvie CBM, "Great New Footage Featured in International Trailer for Andrew Stanton's John Carter," *ComicbookMovie.com*, 23 Dec 2011, 4 Sep 2012 <http://www.comicbookmovie.com/fansites/Wolvie09/news/?a=51791&t=Great_New_Footage_Featured_in_International_Trailer_For_Andrew_Stantons_JOHN_CARTER>.

[219] Joey Paur, "John Carter - Japanese International Trailer Shows off New Footage," *Geek Tyrant*, 23 Dec 2011, 4 Sep 2012 <http://geektyrant.com/news/2011/12/23/john-carter-japanese-international-trailer-shows-off-new-foo.html>.

[220] Ken J. Lloyd, "Brilliant New Trailer Introduces a New Side to John Carter," *Hey U Guys*, 26 Dec 2011, 5 Sep 2012 <http://www.heyuguys.co.uk/2011/12/26/brilliant-new-trailer-introduces-a-new-side-to-john-carter-and-plenty-more-mind-blowing-action/>.

[221] Official John Carter Twitter Account, "@JohnCarter", 15 Jun 2010, 5 Sep 2012 <http://Twitter.com/JohnCarter

On *Facebook*, the story was the same. A total of 11 posts to the *John Carter Facebook* page in the same 30 day period, and *John Carter*'s *Facebook* "like" count was hovering around 55,000.[222] *The Hunger Games* continued to vastly outdistance *John Carter*, with more than a million "likes", and *The Lorax* continued its dominance of *John Carter* on *Facebook* with more than half a million "likes" as of the end of December. Each "like" in turn represented another *Facebook* user profile which, when viewed, would show *The Lorax* as something that the profile holder was a fan of, and each like represented a *Facebook* wall feed that would receive the *Facebook* updates from *The Lorax* page and display them to friends. Thus the multiplier effect of having 10 times as many "likes" as *John Carter* was substantial, and increasingly, *The Lorax* was looking like a contender who would pose a genuine challenge as it entered its second weekend on March 9.[223]

---

[222] Official John Carter *Facebook* Account, "John Carter", 28 Nov 2010, 5 Sep 2012 <https://facebook.com/JohnCarterMovie>.

[223] Official *Lorax Facebook* Site, "Dr. Seuss' The Lorax," *Facebook*, 10 May 2010, 5 Sep 2012 <https://www.facebook.com/theloraxmovie>.

THE JOHN CARTER FILES

As December progressed, I re-read, for the first time in twenty years, the trilogy that forms the basis for *John Carter* and the hoped for sequels: *A Princess of Mars*, *The Gods of Mars*, and *Warlord of Mars*.

One of the things that Edgar Rice Burroughs' stories provide is escape from everyday worries -- an opportunity to be transported to a world that is vividly imagined, and where the hero is like you -- only better, stronger, smarter, and more capable -- what Gore Vidal called the "dream-self" in an essay written in 1967.[224]   Vidal wrote of how that "dream-self" that Burroughs created so artfully fulfilled an important purpose:

> How many consciously daydream, turning on a story in which the dreamer ceases to be an employee of I.B.M. and becomes a handsome demigod moving through splendid palaces, saving maidens from monsters.....although this sort of Mittyesque daydreaming is supposed to cease in maturity, I suggest that more adults than we suspect are bemusedly wandering about with a full Technicolor extravaganza going on in their heads.

While Vidal speaks of a self-generated extravaganza -- how much better to be able to plug in to the extravaganza that Burroughs created with such verve?

Vidal goes on to write of Tarzan and John Carter:

---

[224] Gore Vidal, "Tarzan Revisited," *Esquire*, December 1967, 4 Nov 2012 <http://www.erbzine.com/mag16/1653.html>.

All of us need the idea of a world alternative to this one. From Plato's Republic to Opar to Bond-land, at every level, the human imagination has tried to imagine something better for itself than the existing society. Man left Eden when we got up off all fours, endowing most of his descendants with nostalgia as well as chronic backache. In its naive way, the Tarzan legend returns us to that Eden where, free of clothes and the inhibitions of an oppressive society, a man can achieve his continuing need, which is, as William Faulkner put it in his high Confederate style, to prevail as well as endure . . . . The individual's desire to dominate his environment is not a desirable trait in a society which every day grows more and more confining. Since there are few legitimate releases for the average man, he must take to daydreaming. James Bond, Mike Hammer and Tarzan are all dream-selves, and the aim of each is to establish personal primacy in a world which in reality diminishes the individual.

As December progressed, I found that my re-immersion in the world of Barsoom after being absent these many years was providing an escape from the troubles of my life that I hadn't felt in some time. It came at a time when I faced a unique array of problems, some externally generated, most of my own making -- one in particular had dominated my spirit for months and threatened to crush it -- and reacquainting myself with John Carter and his indomitable "We still live!" spirit strengthened my own, and reminded me that the "Burroughs magic" was not confined to the workings of the adolescent mind.

Each morning I spent an hour updating *The John Carter Files*. One of the functions I built into the blog was an automated aggregator which would seek out all articles across the web that mentioned "John Carter" and place them into a single blog post, with each article having a 250 character introduction and a link. Each morning I ran the aggregator and sifted through the results, deleting all the results that had nothing to do with the movie and then reading the haul that remained. When an article was particularly interesting, I created a separate post for it; the others I would leave in the main "John Carter News Today" post. If an article was negative but in a reasonable and intelligent way, I would leave it in. If an article was over-the-top or mindlessly hostile (and there were plenty of these) I simply deleted it.

In this way, without spending an inordinate amount of time, I was able to post a daily digest of *John Carter* news and commentary. Then, time permitting, I would write a post or two of my own - then go off about my business on my fanboy interest.

I was surprised, and pleased, to see traffic to the site grow significantly. From a standing start on December 4, it was pulling in more than 1,000 visitors a day by mid-December. A good number of them were themselves bloggers and journalists who found the daily newsfeed a useful tool for keeping up with the campaign.

Meanwhile I monitored the campaign.

Gradually, it became increasingly apparent that the campaign simply was not catching fire. The creative materials -- trailers, TV spots, posters -- seemed strangely tone deaf. There was negativity in the articles and comments that I was reading online -- complaints ranged from the confusing nature of the trailer and TV spots, to the fact that it looked like a clone of *Prince of Persia* or, worse, was this years' *Cowboys and Aliens*. The comparisons--unfavorable for the most part--to *Avatar* and *Star Wars* were frequent as well.

If Burroughs summoned up my "dream-self", Disney's problems with the campaign summoned up my "work-self", and I found myself beginning to contemplate the troubled campaign not just from the perspective of a anxious fan, but, increasingly, from the perspective of my "day job" which, for more than 20 years, had involved creating and producing films, and being responsible for theatrical marketing campaigns. My initial experience had been overseas, releasing major studio films in the 1990's in the Philippines -- an English speaking archipelago with a population of 100 million substantially "Americanized" potential viewers spread through 7,200 islands. Later I released a dozen indie films in the US. Nothing in my experience compared to a project on the scope of *John Carter*, but I knew the process and started to view it from a professional perspective.

As the "air war" began, with television spots appearing regularly on multiple networks from December 16 on, I began to monitor social media in hopes of seeing a surge, and in the process became aware of the fact that there was no measurable uptick in chatter about *John Carter*. Moreover, the campaign's official accounts on key social media outlets *Twitter* and *Facebook* were oddly inactive.

On December 27th I found myself in a movie theater where the *John Carter* trailer played, and at the end there were snickers of derisive laughter, and a catcall or two.

On December 29 I found myself examining the output by Disney on *Twitter* and *Facebook* for what was then the first 30 days of the 100 day final push. There had been a total of 10 Tweets by @JohnCarter since the trailer premiere a month earlier. On *Facebook*, 11 posts:

On the official *John Carter* website, there had been no changes. There were a few games to draw viewers back, and a "Martian translator" device -- but other than this, nothing. No blog, no news updates, no wiki, no message board, no forum. It was bare bones and flat.

Dec 30, 2012	The new #JohnCarter trailer is here
Dec 2, 2012	Want more #JohnCarter? Head to Apple to check out some new art. http://di.sn/JCOutdoor
Dec 5, 2012	RT @AndrewStanton: Day one of our mix is over. And Mars is shining bright. A good sign.
Dec 8, 2012	#JohnCarter screenwriters @AndrewStanton, mark Andrews, and Michael Chabon all still have the John Carter drawings they did as boys.
Dec 12, 2012	RT @AndrewStanton: Happy Monday! Week #2 of 'Carter mix begins!
Dec 12, 2012	"There are large regions of Mars that are compatible with terrestrial life."
Dec 15, 2012	Check out the new #JohnCarter @IMAX poster.
Dec 16, 2012	Watch two new #JohnCarter TV spots on @YahooMovies.
Dec 23, 2012	From now through Monday, Kiip is giving #JohnCarter fans a chance to win big in a mobile gaming competition.
Dec 27, 2012	On Barsoom, #JohnCarter is caught in a war between two societies: Zodanga and Helium. Which side would you fight for?

Meanwhile, the relentless negativity -- most of it relating to *John Carter's* budget level and dim prospects for profitability -- was dominating the media narrative that was now reaching into the mainstream media -- a narrative that desperately needed to be changed.

I couldn't shake the feeling that opportunities were being missed. The same TV spots were playing over and over -- and neither the TV spots, nor the trailers, nor the posters did anything to create context or fire the imagination.   No mention of Edgar Rice Burroughs or the heritage of the film, no mention of Andrew Stanton's involvement.

An idea began to form. Was it possible that I might be able to in some fashion have a voice at Disney?   Was it crazy to think that might even be a possibility? Was this just the "Mittyesque daydream" that Gore Vidal had written about:[225]

> Until recently I assumed that most people were like myself: day-dreaming ceases when the world becomes interesting and reasonably manageable. Now I am not so certain. Pondering the life and success of Burroughs leads one to believe that a good many people find their lives so unsatisfactory that they go right on year after year telling themselves stories in which they are able to dominate their environment in a way that is not possible in this over organized society.

Was I telling myself a daydream in thinking I might be able to gain a voice in the campaign?

Probably.

But the daydream persisted.

Was it such a stretch?

I considered the output of the official *John Carter Twitter*, *Facebook*, and official website since November 30; 10 tweets, 11 *Facebook* posts, and almost no updates.   Then I considered the output of my "hobby blog" since December 4: 26 "John Carter News" aggregation posts, and 45 other articles. Daily visitors to the site numbered in the thousands, and since many of them were journalists and bloggers who were replaying

---

[225] Gore Vidal, "Tarzan Revisited," *Esquire*, December 1967, 4 Nov 2012 <http://www.erbzine.com/mag16/1653.html>

articles they found there, perhaps what I was doing could be considered significant. Or not.

Trying to convince myself, I printed out a list of my output -- not including the daily aggregated newsfeed -- since December 4:

4 Dec	John Carter inspired *Avatar*, not vice versa
4 Dec	Interview with Michael Giacchino,
4 Dec	The language of John Carter's Barsoom
4 Dec	How to count in Barsoomian
4 Dec	Military ranks on John Carter's Barsoom
4 Dec	Barsoomian Proverbs
4 Dec	The White Ape of Barsoom
4 Dec	Map of Barsoom
4 Dec	Project Gutenberg text of "A Princess of
4 Dec	Andrew Stanton on Edgar Rice Burroughs
4 Dec	Tars Tarkas, John Carter's fierce Ally
4 Dec	Incomparable Dejah Thoris of Helium
5 Dec	Who is John Carter?
6 Dec	Andrew Stanton on reshoots
6 Dec	Video: 100 Years of John Carter
8 Dec	Two great studio stills of Lynn Collins
9 Dec	Who is John Carter - Part 2
9 Dec	"Is John Carter Just an *Avatar* Clone?"
10 Dec	John Carter is #6 on list of Top 25
10 Dec	14 Facts about the Movie John Carter
11 Dec	Andrew Stanton on the John Carter books
11 Dec	Barsoomian, Dolthraki invented languages
12 Dec	Dominic West trained with swords...
13 Dec	$700M Global Gross for a Sequel? Really?
15 Dec	The John Carter Imax Poster .....
16 Dec	John Carter / *Star Wars* comparisons?
16 Dec	ERBophiles are excited for March 9!
17 Dec	Dear John Carter Trailer Team....
17 Dec	Lynn Collins on the Pixar Process
18 Dec	Hear Michael Giacchino's John Carter
18 Dec	Carl Sagan on Edgar Rice Burroughs
19 Dec	Woola Wallpaper -- free download
20 Dec	My advent on Mars
21 Dec	Andrew Stanton's dream for John Carter
23 Dec	Salt Lake City Weekly on John Carter
23 Dec	John Carter Japanese Trailer offers clues.....
27 Dec	Kate Erbland: New Trailer ...
28 Dec	Cheeta dies at 80?
28 Dec	The plot thickens - was Cheeta a cheater?
29 Dec	Taylor Kitsch: Reluctant Hero

In all there were 40 posts in 26 days, and these did not include the 26 aggregated newsfeed posts--one each day with 10-20 articles in it. As I looked at the output and compared it to Disney's entire social media and digital marketing output, the idea of a "seat at the table" didn't seem so far-fetched. I wasn't just a random person off the street, I told myself -- I was a fellow industry professional with some credentials in theatrical releasing, admittedly modest (so modest, in fact, I could imagine someone at Disney complaining "what kind of a bottomfeeder indie lowlife producer is this guy?") but enough that, when coupled with my status as a specialty blogger and knowledge of Burroughs and Burroughs fans.......well, I could daydream about getting in the door at Disney.

After all, Burroughs taught me how to daydream.

The next day I put in a call to Jack Scanlan, a longtime motion picture publicist and a senior member of the Publicist Guild whom I knew to be well connected, resourceful, and persistent when persistence was called for. Jack had worked on dozens if not hundreds of major theatrical releases -- and he and I had worked together on the smaller theatrical releases of my indie films. I thought that if anyone could help me get a hearing at Disney, he could.

A bit shy about confessing to my "daydream", I told him about *The John Carter Files*, then gradually warmed to the task of explaining to him my concerns about the campaign. Finally I shared my fantasy of a "seat a the table" with Disney. Did he know anyone there? What did he think? He agreed to take a look at *The John Carter Files*, then said he would read the memo and get back to me.

The truth was, after 22 years and 20 films--and in spite of living literally in the shadow of the gates to Disney Studios in Burbank--I really didn't have any contacts inside Disney. It would be easy to say that this is because of cloistered nature of Disney Studios, but the truth is my world is the indie world, so to me, "Hollywood" was basically gritty North Hollywood, where I had lived for many years -- rows of small houses owned by film editors and grips and gaffers and VFX artists who worked from project to project and used their houses as ATMs to get through the tough times. They had kids and college and alimony and they dealt with these everyday challenges from a position of far less certainty than equivalent professionals in other industries did. They worked a movie and then chased after the next opportunity, then worked again and waited again.

The next day Scanlan called back, excited. He was impressed with *The John Carter Files*, and he was going to call Arlene Ludwig, head of west coast publicity for Disney Studios.

"Can you draft up a memo, something I can forward to Arlene and use for talking points when I talk to her? I need it right away -- this is the last chance to call her until after the New Year. I need it today."

"I'll have it to you in an hour."

An hour later I pushed "send" on an email that, for better or worse, was throwing my indie hat into the studio ring. In a very diplomatic way, it outlined what I thought were key messaging points that were being missed, and which if used properly could position the film in a positive way that was being missed. I sketched an idea for how to draw on the heritage in a way that would create an aura that the film story is "special"; that Burroughs and Stanton were both assets that could be used to change the narrative about the film, and I included quotes that were powerful endorsements of the material from Carl Sagan, Ray Bradbury, Arthur C. Clarke, and others -- suggesting further avenues for differentiating the product and making it seem less generic, more weighty and unique. There was more -- specific proposals for articles, videos. Scanlan read it right away and got back to me with good notes reflecting his experience and good judgment. I made the edits, then sent the memo back to Jack. Nothing will come of it, I thought, after sending him the re-draft. But at least you gave it a shot.

Happy New Year indeed.

SCANLAN BOBS AND WEAVES

On January 2nd Jack spoke to a secretary at Disney who told him that Arlene Ludwig was on vacation. He then decided that he would try and take the memo to "whomever was her Vice President". After some maneuvering, he got an appointment with a "tcmp secretary" who agreed to see him only after he had insisted that he had an "Urgent Document" that had to be "hand-delivered" and a receipt obtained. This got him onto the lot, after which he basically "stormed the Ivory Towers" at Disney, going first to the secretary with whom he had spoken previously, and in the process learning that Ludwig was not on vacation -- she had retired. Scanlan insisted that he be allowed to deliver the memo to Ludwig's immediate Vice President, which the temp secretary reluctantly agreed to. But when Scanlan got to that VP's office he discovered that she had just been fired and two secretaries were busy cleaning out her possessions.

"Who is in charge now?" Jack asked.

"Ryan Stankevich," one of them answered. "Go see her."

Jack then found his way to Ryan's office and got as far as Janna Bettencourt, her assistant. He introduced himself as a publicist representing the *John Carter Files*, who in turn had connections to hundreds of motivated fans, including college professors and the like, through ERB, Inc. and the ERB fan groups. Janna relayed that info by phone to Stankevich as Jack stood in the outer office. He waited. Finally Janna told him that Ryan had agreed to meet on January 11th.

Mission accomplished without actually delivering the memo to anyone, Jack left, still holding onto the memo.

"Nothing's easy, is it?" I asked him after he'd told me the whole convoluted story. "Thank you."

Jack had delivered, and I was pleased about that -- but was a little concerned at being characterized as officially representing the ERB fans.

"I don't officially represent the fans."

"*The John Carter Files* has fans, lots of them. You officially represent them."

"I'm talking about the ERB fans, the ones that have been out there forever. I don't officially represent them."

"You're splitting hairs. You've got a meeting. Do you want it or not?"

I did.

January 8, 2012: MT Carney is Fired

As the New Year arrived at Disney, Rich Ross was already looking for MT Carney's replacement. Her departure, while not unexpected, would be a rocky moment for Ross, who had selected her as an out-of-the-box choice a mere 18 months earlier. Her departure would not be seen as simply a routine replacement -- it was a rebuke of Ross's leadership and judgment.

Since his arrival in October 2010, Ross had been dutifully implementing Disney CEO Bob Iger's vision for the studio. Under the previous regime -- Chairman Dick Cook, Production chief Jim Gallagher, and Marketing chief Oren Aviv -- the focus had been on creating new franchise worthy projects in-house. But first with Pixar, then with the acquisition of Dreamworks in February 2009, Iger had been working toward a redefinition of the studio as a distribution hub for pre-existing strong brands that would eventually include Jerry Bruckheimer Films, Pixar, Dreamworks, and Marvel, with a diminished focus on in-house production, particularly in the live action space.

In the 18 months of Carney's tenure, her operation had yet to produce success as the marketing machine for Disney/Dreamworks/Marvel/Pixar/Bruckheimer. *Prince of Persia* had been the first test and had fared weakly in the US, adequately overseas; then *The Sorcerer's Apprentice*, which flopped. Step *UP 3D* then underperformed; *Secretariat* performed weakly; *You Again* flopped; then *Tangled* did well, *Tron: Legacy* did a solid $400M worldwide; and *Gnomeo and Juliet* did $100M domestic. From that point on, however, it went downhill.

Dreamworks, due to concerns about Carney and the 'Disney marketing machine' under her, had built its own marketing team by the time its first release through Disney was offered. The same was true of Bruckheimer, and to some degree with Lasseter and Pixar -- with the result that 8 of 14 releases were under the three self-managed operations. Carney was left in charge of *African Cats*, *Prom*, *The Lion King 3D*, *The Muppets*, and *John Carter*. Of these, only *John Carter* was a $250M "tentpole" release.

The net result of all this was that as of the end of 2011, the marketing 'mojo' at Disney was in the producers' offices with individual brands, not the studio marketing team. Carney's tenure was over; and *John Carter*, lumped in among the motley group of in-house projects, was not getting anywhere near the same kind of focus and quality creative attention that the films of Bruckheimer, Dreamworks, and Marvel were getting.

In sum -- Disney's "distribution model" was foundering and Ross's own tenure was in jeopardy--and this was even before the expected *John Carter* debacle unfolded.

It was against this backdrop that Ross would have to announce the departure of MT Carny, a departure that would constitute an admission of a failed experiment and would really represent the beginning of the end for Ross.

The timing of the announcement had not been finalized, but over the weekend of January 7-8 Nikki Finke at Deadline got wind of the shakeup and wrote: "After more than a year and a half in the job, and speculation since her arrival that she was going to be canned, I can confirm that MT Carney is officially out as President of Worldwide

Marketing at Walt Disney Studios." [226] Finke quoted an unnamed Disney source as saying that *John Carter* was a "perfect microcosm" of what went wrong under Carney's brand management oriented regime. Speaking of the decision to remove "of Mars" from the title:

> It's based on a big geek book. You are taking a piece of very well known classic source material and taking the marketing hook out of it. It's like putting it through the deflavorizer. It's like a perfect microcosm of what went wrong.

The report in Deadline came on the same day that the New York Times ran an in-depth article entitled "In Hollywood's Clubby Culture, a Disney Marketer's Rapid Downfall" -- a portrayal of Carney as victim of insider Hollywood which included the following description of her mandate:[227]

> Mr. Ross charged her with shaking up Disney's marketing approach, and she quickly did just that, reallocating funds from traditional media to new media, conducting an extensive review of Disney's overall ad-buying process, jettisoning dozens of staff members and overseeing a chic redesign of the marketing division's office space.
>
> One major contribution, according to her supporters, involved organization and planning; rather than making decisions on marketing at the last minute and having everyone work on every movie, Ms. Carney successfully lengthened the planning process and split her staff into various pods of focus.
>
> "She arrived to a lot of status-quo, grossly inefficient executives surviving on legacy relationships, and she responded with guns blazing," said the Disney executive who spoke on the condition of anonymity.

The next day, January 9, Disney confirmed Carney's exit, publishing Carney's memo to her staff which read in part: "

---

[226] Nikki Finke, "EXCLUSIVE: MT Carney Out as President of Worldwide Marketing at Walt Disney Studios," Deadline Hollywood, 8 Jan 2012, 5 Sep 2012 <http://www.deadline.com/2012/01/m-t-carney-out-as-president-of-worldwide-marketing-at-walt-disney-studios/>.

[227] Brooks Barnes, "In Hollywood's Clubby Culture, a Disney Marketer's Rapid Downfall," New York Times, 8 Jan 2012, 5 Sep 2012 <http://www.nytimes.com/2012/01/09/business/media/the-downfall-of-m-t-carney-disneys-marketing-manager.html?pagewanted=all>.

> After much consideration, I have decided to leave the Disney family to return to my own. It is terribly hard to leave, but I have been constantly torn between my kids and my job, and like all good Hollywood movies, the kids have to win. This has been a remarkable journey and I look forward to seeing your continued brilliance everywhere,

For battered *John Carter,* Carney's departure signaled a new and intensified round of media negativity. Only hours after Disney confirmed Carney's exit, the Wrap led the way with a much read and highly cited article entitled "Disney's $250M 'John Carter' Gamble: Otherworldly Hit or Cosmic Bomb?"[228] The article set the tone for the veritable avalanche of negative reports that would follow:

> The exit of Disney marketing president MT Carney on Monday creates yet more drama around "John Carter," the $250 million sci-fi epic that may be the biggest studio gamble since "Avatar." The film doesn't hit theaters until March, but reports are rampant that "John Carter" has gone over budget and required costly reshoots. A lackluster early trailer didn't help the buzz and now, without a marketing executive to lead the global rollout, the pressure on "John Carter" is more intense than ever. "It doesn't just have to open big -- it has to be one of the top grossing films of all time," a rival studio executive told TheWrap.
>
> A film of this size and scope typically requires a marketing budget of roughly $120 million, adding to the price tag. All eyes are on Disney to see if the studio can turn the lead character from Edgar Rice Burroughs' once beloved, now largely forgotten 11-volume Mars series into a $700 million blockbuster. Only one March release, "Alice in Wonderland," has ever exceeded that benchmark, and it was able to rack up over $1 billion globally ......

There was another aspect to the article in The Wrap which struck at the heart of the issues facing the *John Carter* campaign. MT Carney during her tenure at Disney had made a practice of hiring outside consultants to oversee particular films. In some cases this reflected demands by a major producer; in other cases Carney herself initiated the hiring. In the case of *John Carter,* however, Carney herself was overseeing the campaign. Against this background, the article continued:

---

[228] Brent Lang, "Disney's $250M 'John Carter' Gamble: Otherworldly HIt or Cosmic Bomb?" *The Wrap*, 9 Jan 2012, 5 Sep 2012 <http://www.thewrap.com/movies/article/disneys-250M-john-carter-gamble-cosmic-bomb-or-otherworldly-hit-33532>.

Compounding those challenges is the ouster of Disney's controversial president of movie marketing Carney, who had been overseeing "John Carter"s' rollout. The movie opens in two months, but with Carney out and Disney still searching for her replacement, it will be left to the studio's i-house team to handle the opening.

The studio has not hired an outside marketing consultant for "John Carter," nor does it plan to......

So with nine weeks to go until release date, and with the campaign thus far failing to generate any demonstrable buzz -- and with MT Carney now gone -- Disney leadership elected to leave the campaign on the same "auto-pilot" it had been running on since mid-December when Carney had left for New York and her family.

Meanwhile, on Friday, 6 January, the working level members of the *John Carter* marketing team attended a Nielsen test screening of *John Carter* in Sherman Oaks, just "over the hill" from Hollywood. Each group attending had to include at least one boy aged 10-15. The format was the standard one for test screenings -- the same that had been used at the earlier Portland screening.

Among those in the audience was Rebecca Baeder Garland, a teacher from Long Beach, and her husband and fifteen year old son Isaac. Garland liked movies and had been to a half dozen test screenings previously. She knew nothing about *John Carter*, but enjoyed the atmosphere at test screenings and the chance to react to a film at an early stage when her comments might actually have effect. Her husband and Isaac had been reluctant participants, but Rebecca, knowing that having Isaac along was a requirement, ensured that both came along.

Aside from not knowing anything about John Carter or Edgar Rice Burroughs, Garland also was not a sci-fi fan. She would later say that she had difficulty relating to the "strange worlds" and "strange characters" of sci fi. As the movie began and the prologue showcasing the Helium/ Zodanga conflict unfolded, she was thoroughly confused. The Heliumites and Zodangans looked the same as far as she was concerned (she missed the red flags for Zodanga, blue flags for Helium), and by the time the segment ended all she had gotten from it was that there was a confusing war on Mars.

But for her, and the great majority of the rest of the viewers, the confusing nature of the opening prologue was quickly forgotten as the story then began to unfold in deft, sure strokes. Garland found herself enjoying immensely the introduction of John Carter, particularly the series of quick cuts depicting him resisting Powell and the 7th Cavalry. And with his arrival on Mars, she found herself swept up in a story that she found entertaining and emotionally satisfying. Her son Isaac, who had been reluctant to come, had an equally positive reaction.

By the time the film was over, the Long Beach teacher was thoroughly in love with it. It was not a perfect film, but in her estimation it had tremendous heart and a unique quality about it that set it apart from other action blockbusters. She filled out her questionnaire eagerly and turned it in, along with those of her husband and son. All gave the film "highly recommended" status; all had enjoyed it thoroughly and were curious to learn more about where the story had come from.

Among those at the screening for Disney were Ryan Stankevich, head of publicity for all live action films, Samantha Garry, head of digital marketing, and Ayaz Asad, Executive VP and de facto head of the marketing campaign. For all, it was their first time seeing John Carter. The questionnaires, quickly tallied, showed a strong "recommend" store in the mid 80's -- a clear "win" for any film.

That night, Garland looked up Edgar Rice Burroughs and found her way to the project Gutenberg text of *A Princess of Mars*, and read the original book Friday night and Saturday morning. Then, doing something she had done previously after test screenings, she went to the Internet Movie Data Base (IMDB) message board for *John Carter* and posted "I saw *John Carter* at a Nielsen screening and loved it!"[229]

In true internet fashion, the knives came out and the denizens of the board immediately accused her of concocting the entire episode -- claims were made that it was too late for test screenings, that she must be lying,

---

[229] Rebecca Baeder Garland, "I saw John Carter at a Nielsen Screening and Loved It!" *IMDB*, January 8, 2012, <http://www.imdb.com/title/tt0401729/board/flat/193293774?d=193293774#193293774>.

and that this was all a cynical ploy from Disney. Garland patiently responded, providing the kind of detail that could only come from having seen the movie, and over the course of the weekend posted numerous detailed comments which gradually convinced those on the message board that she had indeed seen the movie. The accusations that she was lying gradually gave way to acceptance, and as word spread, the questions multiplied, with Garland answering each question patiently, and in enough detail to lay to rest any questions that she had not seen the movie. It was, in effect, the first online review of *John Carter*, and it would make waves.

A Visit to Disney Studios

Over the weekend of January 7-8, as Disney Chairman Rich Ross scrambled his executives to prepare the announcement for MT Carney's departure, and as Rebecca Baeder Garland entertained questions about *John Carter* on the *IMDB* Message Board, I was finalizing a "white paper" briefing document which I sent to Ryan Stankevich early Saturday morning, January 7. The paper was something that I had hammered out with Jack Scanlan over the previous week, and was intended to lay out an agenda for the meeting that included possible fan liaison initiatives, but also allowed for strategic discussion of the overall campaign. It was thirteen pages and represented the best work I could do. Sections included an overview of the "messaging points" that were guiding my work on *The John Carter Files*; an overview of the fan organizations; an overview of the "buzz" to date with charts and figures showing 'Carter's position relative to the competition; and finally suggestions for how I might be able to work with Disney to mobilize fan support to counter the negativity of the narrative that was unfolding in mainstream and social media.

Later that same Saturday, I checked the *IMDB John Carter* message board. There are dozens of movie message boards across the internet -- but none with the prominence or intensity of IMDB, and many fans, when contemplating an upcoming film, will check out the *IMDB* board for that film to see how the buzz is running. In the case of *John Carter*, it was a pretty brutal place where proponents of the film (mostly ERB fans but also Stanton fans and other sci-fi fans) were constantly fighting what amounted to a pitched battle with the *"John Carter* will flop" brigade, who were scornful of the movie, the marketing, or both.

I came across the thread started by Rebecca Baeder Garland and read it, intrigued. Clearly she had truly seen the movie, and as the day progressed and she answered more and more queries, it occurred to me that her Q and A was evolving into what was, potentially at least, the first bona-fide published review of the movie. I knew from studying search terms that *"John Carter* review" and "john carter advance review" were already among the highest searched terms relating to *John Carter*, and I was certain that getting a favorable review up on the internet would result in substantial views and commentary. This might be, it seemed to me, the first opportunity for *The John Carter Files* to make a strategic level contribution to the narrative. I published: *"John Carter Advance Review: Test screening reviewer posts "I saw John Carter at a Nielsen screening and I loved it!"*[230]

A few hours later (and a few hours after Deadline.com had posted the story that MT Carney had been fired), I received a reply from Ryan Stankevich at Disney to my email, sent Saturday morning, containing my briefing:

> Thank you very much for this – you are definitely an expert on the subject and we're excited to meet fellow fans of Burroughs and JOHN CARTER! I did coincidentally see your post today regarding the preview screening feedback and having been at that screening I can tell you that the report is dead on. It played extremely well, which we were all really excited to witness on Friday.

---

[230] Michael D. Sellers, "Test Screening Reviewer Posts 'I Saw John Carter at a Nielsen screening and loved it!' and Sends Message Board into a Frenzy," *The John Carter Files*, 8 Jan 2012, 5 Sep 2012. http://thejohncarterfiles.com/2012/01/test-screening-reviewer-posts-i-saw-john-carter-at-a-neilsen-screening-and-i-loved-it-2/.

We're looking forward to the meeting and hearing more about how Disney and the ERBophiles can work together on this campaign. Thanks so much for reaching out.

My reaction came in several waves. First -- good, at least someone at Disney is reading *The John Carter Files*. Next -- good thing that my Rebecca Baeder Garland's report is "spot on" . . . and it was definitely a positive thing that Stankevich was communicating in an enthusiastic, encouraging way. All of that was good.

But there was another subtext to the message that was easy to read -- *"We're looking forward to the meeting and hearing more about how Disney and the ERBophiles can work together on this campaign."* As a professional wordsmith, it could be assumed Stankevich was careful with her words, and those words were clearly positioning the meeting not as a strategic discussion of the campaign -- rather as a fan liaison meeting, and she was making sure I understood that. It wasn't a brush off, but it was gently putting me in my place and setting the parameters. Fan liaison. Stankevich clearly saw it as a "courtesy call" with the fans, which she was willing to do first of all as a courtesy to fellow publicist Scanlan, and secondly because, if I was a channel to the fan groups, it was important to show respect even if the fan community wasn't large.

Anyway -- that was her attitude going into the meeting, so it was good to know that was the starting point. Perhaps. with Jack Scanlan's help, I could turn it around in the meeting. It was worth a try.

JANUARY 11, 2012

Stankevich's offices were on the lot at Disney Studios in the building closest to the corner of Alameda and Hollywood Way, the "Seven Dwarfs Building" with statues of Sneezy, Sleepy, Dopey, Doc, Happy, Bashful, and Grumpy.

The meeting took place in a modern, casual meeting room with a couch and comfortable chairs in modern design surrounding a low coffee table. Stankevich's assistant Janna Bettencourt showed us to the room, and a few minutes later Stankevich arrived with Samantha Garry, whom she introduced as Director of Digital Marketing.

At the outset, Stankevich and Garry both acknowledged the advance "white paper" that I had sent, claimed to have read it, and Garry in particular offered comments agreeing with the analysis of *John Carter*'s position among the March releases. Specifically Garry with my assessment of the problems with the level of buzz, and positive/negative sentiment ratio -- acknowledging that my numbers and Disney's numbers were in alignment.

While there was some discussion of the overall status of he campaign, it was clear that in the view of Stankevich and Garry, the meeting was not meant to be a forum for a substantive strategic discussion of the issues of the *John Carter* campaign; rather, it was a courtesy call with Disney showing respect to the ERB fan community, and indicating an open attitude toward that community.

"What, specifically, can we do for the fans?" Stankevich asked no less than three times during the meeting.

Each time I tried to get across the idea that it wasn't so much Disney doing something for the fans -- it was Disney empowering the fans by giving them a role to play and a sense of connection to the campaign. I emphasized that the fans are in essence awaiting their instructions -- and while it was one thing for me and JCF to give them instructions, if they understood that Disney was actually calling upon them to do something that could actually help the campaign -- they would feel that they were a part of it and would respond very favorably.

I eventually gave up on moving the conversation into the "fellow professionals" discussing the campaign zone. But Scanlan didn't give up so easily; he bravely tried to steer the conversation back to that zone, emphasizing what I could do for the campaign on a strategic level, bringing up the "seat at the table" concept, which was met each time with a polite, "Well, we'll have to see about that," which I mentally translated as, "Not in a million years."

Even when it came to fan initiatives, it was difficult for me to get any real traction. Stankevich evinced respect for the fans, but also noted: "The fans of the books are always the hardest to please," which was, I knew, a true statement but one which did not preclude the ability to mobilize the fans of the books, a mobilization that had already happened at the behest of *The John Carter Files*, but which could be greatly amplified if Disney would get behind specific programs for fan engagement that had been outlined in the briefing.

Of the programs that had been offered in the briefing, one seemed to be more interesting than the rest to Stankevich, and that was the "home town story" program -- a publicity project wherein Burroughs experts could be interviewed by their hometown newspapers and/or TV stations with a story that basically ran: "While Disney's *John Carter* is just another Hollywood epic sci-fi film to most, to one local resident [insert name of ERBophile expert] it is the culmination of a lifetime of waiting for this particular sci-fi classic to make it to the silver screen." I offered to provide a list and contact information for potential interviewees, some of whom were suitable for national publications, others for regional value.

On the digital marketing and social media side, I attempted to engage Garry, who was responsible for *Facebook*, *Twitter*, and all "digital" marketing, on ways to improve the performance of the 'Carter social media component to the campaign. I got nowhere. Garry graciously and politely assured me that they had everything well in hand; that a big push was coming soon, possibly by the first week of February, and that while the shortcomings identified in the briefing were accurate, all were being addressed and there was nothing I, *The John Carter Files*, or the fans could do, or needed to worry about.

I wondered aloud, politely and diplomatically, why simple thing like *John Carter* digital wallpapers for computer desktops had not been made available; or other simple digital promotional giveaways such as a countdown calendar, had been made available -- noting that I had the capacity to create such things and could do so on short order if that would help. Don't worry, was the repeated response -- we have it all under control. Big things are coming.

Eventually, realizing that the meeting, while cordial, was going nowhere, I shifted gears and did what I could to simply obtain useful information. Stankevich confirmed that *John Carter* would have a Super Bowl ad and this would signal the beginning of the truly big push over the last month of the campaign. Other points made by Stankevich and Garry included the fact that although *John Carter* only had 2000 *Twitter* followers this didn't mean that much, since the Disney Pictures Twitter Account had over a million followers and no one but Disney had that kind of studio-wide following; after all *Pirates of the Caribbean: On Stranger Tides* only had 10,000 followers, and look what it did. Stankevich also talked about the Disney moms and dads who were being reached by the promotions on the Disney channel, and confirmed that "tween boys" were indeed considered the key demographic, and they were reaching them through the Disney Channel.

The most important point made by Stankevich was that Disney had conducted a number of test screenings in December and that the test screenings had gone extremely well. "We know we've got a great movie," Stankevich said, and indicated that decisions had already been made to do advance "word-of-mouth" screenings in the final week prior to the release of the film, based on the confidence in the film. In fact, it seemed to me that the subtext of much of what Stankevich was saying was -- *it's a good movie, and good movies find their audience. Don't worry. It will be okay.*

But such an attitude was worrisome because even with good word of mouth and good reviews, films in release follow very predictable patterns of dropoff and decline, and if Disney marketing and publicity did not get a minimum "critical mass" of audience to see the movie opening weekend, word of mouth would not save it unless the WOM was so good (as in 'once in a decade good') that it completely transformed the equation. To me, it seemed like Disney was relying too much on Stanton to produce a miracle. I thought of it like a baseball analogy in which to be a "success" a film has to score a run and the marketing campaign is the first batter, the film, once released, is the second. If the marketing campaign does its job, the film itself comes up to bat with a runner in scoring position at second base and all that is needed is a "single" and the project is successful. But if marketing fails abysmally, the film itself is then left with the need to hit a home run all on its own to score the run. Disney seemed to be increasingly content to just send Stanton (the film itself) up to the plate with no one on base and expect the director to hit a home run.

In the end, having been politely but firmly rebuffed in all substantive areas, we said our goodbyes and headed back through the studio labyrinth to our car.

"What do you think?" Scanlan asked.

"They listened politely and showed us the door," I replied. "There won't be a seat at the table."

Scanlan wasn't so sure -- he is indefatigable and not inclined to take no for an answer when he's committed to making something happen. On my side, I felt that not only was Stankevich not seriously considering such a thing -- I was pretty sure that her entire attitude and handling of the meeting were solidly in alignment with what her Disney bosses would consider to be the right way to handle such a situation.

"So what are you going to do?"

I thought about it.

It had been a game enough effort to get taken seriously by Disney, but in the end, it had been my Burroughsian "dream-self" who had believed it might be possible to get a seat at the table, and now the reality was here, and that reality that my quest had been a Walter Mitty fantasy, and now I had been put back in my place, gently and politely to be sure, but there was no doubt that the dream of having a strategic voice was just that, a dream.

Toldja, I said to myself. *You were kidding yourself.*

Deal with it.

"Oh well," I said. "I'll keep blogging. You never know, maybe something good will happen."

FALLING FARTHER BEHIND

As January rolled on, the drumbeat for *The Hunger Games* steadily increased on all fronts while the *John Carter* campaign haltingly moved forward in fits and starts. On the publicity front, through the entire month of January, *John Carter*--moving into the final stages of its campaign prior to a March 9 release--generated a total of 170 article placements. By contrast, Disney's *The Avengers*, not due out until May 4, generated 520 placements and *The Hunger Games*, 'Carter's chief rival for March buzz, generated 540 placements.[231]

The disparity between *John Carter* and *The Hunger Games* was even more apparent on *Facebook*, where *John Carter* managed to add only 11,183 new fans with 14,156 "talking about" the movie, in contrast to *The Hunger Games* who within the month of January alone added 775,000 new fans and logged 451,000 "talking about."[232] The same pattern repeated itself throughout the social media universe -- *Twitter*, blogs, message boards

[231] *IMDB Pro*, "*John Carter* (2012) MovieMeter: Data Table View," accessed 2 Sep 2012 <http://pro.imdb.com/title/tt0401729/graph-data> ; *IMDB Pro*, "*The Avengers* (2012) MovieMeter: Data Table View," accessed 2 Sep 2012 <http://pro.imdb.com/title/tt0848228/graph>; *IMDB Pro*, "*The Hunger Games* (2012) MovieMeter: Data Table View," accessed 2 Sep 2012 <http://pro.imdb.com/title/tt1392170/graph-data>.

[232] The Official John Carter *Facebook* Page, "John Carter," 28 Nov 2010, 5 Sep 2012 <https://facebook.com/JohnCarterMovie>; The Official Hunger Games *Facebook* Page, "*The Hunger Games*", 10 May 2010, 5 Sep 2012 <https://facebook.com/TheHungerGames>.

were all buzzing for *The Hunger Games*, while *John Carter* remained mired in what, when held up next to *The Hunger Games* efforts, seemed like a sleepwalking trance. Particularly vexing to *John Carter* enthusiasts was the flatness and lack of verve in the *John Carter Facebook* postings. For the entire month of January, the *John Carter* stories and updates on *Facebook* consisted of the following 15 posts:

Date	Full Text of Post	Comments	Shares
Jan 2, 2012	The River Iss (with photo)	27	26
Jan 3, 2012	What is the Barsoomian Word for Earth?	0	0
Jan 6, 2012	You've been sent a Barsoomian message. Click below to translate.	64	3
Jan 11, 2012	Get a better look at Woola and the thoats in the new John Carter International Poster	80	217
Jan 12, 2012	Play Lost Symbol and uncover exclusive John Carter Art	121	116
Jan 13, 2012	John Carter "Awakening" TV Spot	32	165
Jan 14, 2012	On Barsoom, John Carter is caught in a war between two societies: Zodanga and Helium. Which side would you fight for?	127	35
Jan 17, 2012	50 Days	107	300
Jan 19, 2012	In John Carter, Taylor Kitsch did 98% of his own stunts, including an 85 foot jump during the learning to walk sequence.	53	15
Jan 23, 2012	Accidentally transported to Barsoom, John Carter reluctantly begins a journey to save his newfound world.	95	174
Jan 24, 2012	Is your name John Carter? Sign up now for an invitation to an advance screening.	26	2
Jan 25, 2012	Translate this message	25	4
Jan 26, 2012	Have you unlocked the exclusive concept art in Lost Symbol Levels 1-3?	6	0
Jan 27, 2012	Woola would find John Carter anywhere on Barsoom	94	137
Jan 30, 2012	Watch a 20 second sneak peek of the John Carter Super bowl ad.	82	65

By contrast while *John Carter* was logging only 939 comments and 1259 shares for the month of January, *The Hunger Games* during the same period logged 14,939 comments and 13,749 shares. *The Lorax*, who would emerge to become an even bigger threat to *John Carter*, logged five times as many comments as *John Carter* (3,956 to 939) and four times as many shares (4,337 to 1,259).[233]

As problematic as the lack of buzz, was the fact that what buzz there was for *John Carter* skewed negative with an overall positive/negative sentiment ratio holding at 7/5 -- while *The Hunger Games* was holding on to a 9/1 ratio and *The Lorax* was running at 8/2.

By the end of January -- by every measure available, *John Carter's* promotional posture was weak and getting weaker, while *The Hunger Games* rolled on like the juggernaut that it was, and *The Lorax* -- set for release a week ahead of *John Carter* -- was gaining momentum and showing signs that it would pose very significant problems for *John Carter*.

RICKY STRAUSS TAKES OVER

The devastatingly poor influencer and social media performance of the *John Carter* campaign in January played out against the backdrop of Disney's announcement on January 13 that Ricky Strauss had been hired to replace MT Carney as President of worldwide marketing. Strauss was a veteran of Sony Pictures and most recently had served as President of Participant Media -- whose recent release "The Help" had been a success for Disney and Dreamworks. In reporting Strauss's hiring, industry trade bible Variety called him a "familiar face", but noted that in hiring Strauss, Disney Studio chief Rich Ross was not backing off his demands for innovation -- demands that had led him to hire MT Carney from outside the circle of Hollywood marketers 18 months earlier. Marc Graser in Variety wrote:[234]

> ... it's not as though Ross is abandoning his demand for innovative film campaigns. Strauss' mandate will be to carry out Ross' wish to

---

[233] Official John Carter *Facebook* Account, "John Carter", 28 Nov 2010, 5 Sep 2012 <https://facebook.com/JohnCarterMovie>; Official *Lorax Facebook* Site, "Dr. Seuss' The Lorax," *Facebook*, 10 May 2010, 5 Sep 2012 <https://www.facebook.com/theloraxmovie>.

[234] Mark Graser, "Disney names Ricky Strauss head of marketing," *Variety*, 13 Jan 2012, 5 Sep 2012, < http://www.variety.com/article/VR1118048612?refcatid=13&printerfriendly=true>.

make marketing dollars work more efficiently by stretching beyond traditional ad buys and physical marketing materials.......Hiring of Strauss is not a change in direction for Ross, who still made "outside-the-box" thinking a key. As Participant Media president, Strauss shepherded the company's unique, socially conscious campaigns that turned to social media and partnerships with brands and organizations to target specific auds.

Now the job of reinventing Disney's marketing belongs to a guy who knows the old ways, too.

On the day Strauss was hired, the *John Carter* campaign had 8 weeks to go until opening day, and was by any measure in deep trouble. As the next major Disney release, and a $250M production investment, a decision had to be made -- would Strauss get a mandate to shake up the campaign and try to right the ship while there was, arguably, still time to make an impact?

Or was the *John Carter* too far gone to be saved?

On January 19 Kim Masters, in an article in the industry bible *The Hollywood Reporter*, launched the latest and most potent iteration of the "out of control production" narrative that had yet appeared. In an article entitled "Mega Movies + New Directors = Big Drama" Masters wrote of *John Carter*.[235]

> The 3D extravaganza has undergone a complete re-engineering, and the budget, originally $200 million, is widely rumored to have ballooned to $300 million. Industry sources with links to the project believe it might lead to a staggering write-down.....
>
> According to several sources close to the project, the issues plaguing the film also result from a lack of experienced support for the director. One source associated with talent on *John Carter* says Stanton, 46, initially was allowed to pursue his vision with "no checks and balances, no star, no producer, nobody to keep him in check." In December 2010, when he showed a 170-minute cut to executives at Pixar and Disney, they found the story unclear and the characters not engaging. Stanton then began to re-engineer a film that already had been shot, creating storyboards of new sequences and cutting them into the footage. A few months later, he embarked on extensive and costly reshoots. Disney, which had

---

[235] Kim Masters, "Mega Movies + New Directors = big Drama," *The Hollywood Reporter*, 19 Jan 2012, 5 Sep 2012 <http://www.hollywoodreporter.com/news/%20john-carter-taylor-kitsch-47-ronin-keanu-reeves-mission-impossible-283347>.

anticipated *John Carter* as a trilogy, held off on discussing the next installment.

This was precisely the kind of publicity that the project didn't need, and Andrew Stanton, when he read it, did not respond immediately other than a tweet on January 20, which responded to a question: "Any annoying myths about *John Carter* you'd like to dispel?", to which he replied: "Was a DISNEY film that I completed on time, on budget, w/ full support."[236]

At Disney, the focus at the moment the Masters article came out was on a London preview session for UK journalists that was occupying most of the attention of the entire publicity team. No official reaction was issued; and no one from the publicity team contacted friendly journalists to get a counter-story out. As a result, the unchallenged narrative of "bloated, out-of-control production" took root and would begin to spread, to the intense detriment of *John Carter*.

Meanwhile Ricky Strauss, the new head of marketing, turned to a trusted resource, Janet Dubin whose Dubin Market Research Inc., had for years been a quietly successful and trusted resource for cracking the code of difficult marketing propositions like *John Carter*. Dubin's longtime parter Roger Edwards would take the lead in what would be a last ditch effort for Disney's new marketing leadership to find a solution. In the final weeks of January Edwards and Dubin would test market all of the marketing materials and make recommendations for changes.

Would it be possible to right the ship?

Or, as was more likely, was the task handed to Edwards and Dubin the cinematic equivalent of being called in to consult on HMS Titanic after the ship had hit the iceberg?

At a minimum the iceberg was clearly in view at the time Dubin and Edwards got the call.

It was called The Super Bowl.

---

[236] Andrew Stanton, Official Andrew Stanton Twitter Account @AndrewStanton, *Twitter*, <http://twitter.com/AndrewStanton>.

THE SUPER BOWL MASSACRE

The official announcement that it had bought a Super Bowl Ad for *John Carter* came on January 12. For the 2012 Super Bowl, Ads were going for $3.5M, a huge amount to spend but a unique opportunity. More than 100 million sets of eyeballs would be available and most of them not only watched the game intently -- they watched the commercials. In fact, the Super Bowl ads got more attention from many viewers than the game itself -- and ads that clicked with Super Bowl fans would also receive millions of replays online from dozens of sites which aggregated all the ads and conducted audience polls.

For the *John Carter* campaign -- the Super Bowl ad represented an opportunity, one month ahead of release of the film, to change the narrative and create, for the first time, positive momentum for the film.

So ... what would be presented?

Within the Disney marketing team, the decision was made to put forward a sweepstakes ad which would contain a hidden code, which viewers could then send on March 9 to qualify for a sweepstakes gift which would be a trip to the 2013 Super Bowl.

On paper, the idea had at least some merit. Football fans would be encouraged to watch the ad closely in order to qualify for the sweepstakes prize.

But how to embed the code?

It was left to creative director Frank Chiocchi and Joseph Tamusaitis to figure out a way to implement the idea. Disney had purchased a 60 second spot, and this enabled a decision to create a spot that began with a 24 second pull-out from what would emerge as a mosaic of the "JOHN CARTER" title treatment, with multiple moving images playing simultaneously within the title treatment. This created a complex visual in which it would be easy enough to bury the code that audiences would have to dig out in order to qualify for the sweepstakes.

But there was a potential problem.

When a studio books an ad on the Super Bowl, even if it books a 60 second spot, there is a chance that it will get cut to 30 seconds if it comes up in the wrong spot in the ad rotation (typically an injury timeout) and thus Disney would have to submit both a 60 second and 30 second version, and run the risk of it being the 30 second version that plays.

With a 22 second pull-out that couldn't be shortened because of the sweepstakes, the 30 second version was -- and there could be no doubt of this--a stinker. But the commitment to the sweepstakes was a "given" - and so the decision was made to roll the dice and hope that the sixty second ad would play.

For the second half of the 60 second ad, Chiocchi and Tamusaitis decided to depart from previous trailers. While it used the Kashmir cover that had dominated the earlier trailers for the first 30 seconds, the second half of the 60 second trailer used a piece of music by British orchestral composer Nick Ingman entitled, appropriately enough, "Mars." Ingman had worked with Andrew Lloyd Webber and Tim Rice, and was known for bridging the gap between classical and pop. His

"Mars" suite had been initially discovered by Andrew Stanton and director Erik Jessen a year earlier, when they had prepared a 'sizzle reel' (more akin to a director's reel than a trailer, but serving a similar purpose) for which they had used Ingman's "Mars." The music, unlike all of the music used until this point, was orchestral, blending voices, strings, and more, and had an epic, emotional pull to it. It marked a clear departure.

On February 5, 2012, the day of the Super Bowl, *John Carter* fans as well as crew members, cast members, director Andrew Stanton, and just about everyone involved with the film physically or emotionally, were waiting for the ad to play with perhaps more than the usual level of enthusiasm. There was a collective sense that the Super Bowl ad would mark the beginning of the "real push", and that it would contain something new -- a new direction for the TV spots and trailers.

Andrew Stanton was online tweeting to fans, and in his case, as a lifelong New England Patriots Fan, his attention was divided between the game and the prospect of the *John Carter* ad that would play. Hours before game time he tweeted: "4.5 hours until Emperor Belicheck has young Jedi Brady do his bidding." Then: as the game began, a fan tweeted: "Want to see that JC ad now!" and Stanton replied: "Coming up soon ;-)."

Stanton in fact knew what was there -- he had been in discussions with Chiocchi and Tamusaitis and had suggested the Nick Ingman music that carried the second half of the sixty second spot.

Then fate intervened.

In the Super Bowl ad rotation, *John Carter's* number came up in the wrong spot, an injury timeout in the second quarter, and when the ad played -- it was the 30 seconder consisting of 24 seconds pulling out from a mosaic of the *John Carter* title treatment with mini-movies playing within the letters, and 6 seconds of John Carter battling a white ape.[237]

It was a disaster.

---

[237] Disney Movie Trailer Channel Staff, "Disney - John Carter Super Bowl Ad," Youtube, 3 Feb 2012, 5 Sep 2012 <http://youtu.be/V3yzs4OUnlI>.

Stanton, standing by and waiting for the full spot to play, and with thousands of *Twitter* followers monitoring him, went silent, then simply retweeted a tweet that the official *John Carter Twitter* account, scrambling to do damage control, put out:[238]

> @John Carter RT by @AndrewStanton: The #Superbowl had the :30 #JohnCarter spot, but we have the :60. Watch: http://di.sn/eV

For any movie, the cut-down would have been damaging, but for *John Carter*, it was devastating and demoralizing to everyone involved. The one "big moment" that had a chance to reboot the narrative for *John Carter* had passed, and not only had the moment not been seized -- it had been squandered, and yet more damage had been inflicted on the campaign and the movie.

Online, the USA Today-*Facebook* Ad Meter rankings landed *John Carter* in last place among the seven movie ads that played, and in the bottom five overall among all 70 ads that played.[239]

Recognizing the disaster that was playing out, Disney scrambled to make the 60 second version available online as widely as possible. Unfortunately, the online audience is a tiny fraction of the Super Bowl audience. Six months after the 60 second ad appeared online, a total of 423,000 viewer had seen it, less than 1/2 of 1% of the Super Bowl audience.[240]

The big moment to shake things up had passed.

---

[238] Andrew Stanton, Official Andrew Stanton Twitter Account @AndrewStanton, *Twitter*, <http://twitter.com/AndrewStanton>.

[239] Joel Ryan, "Best Super Bowl Movie Ads: The Avengers...and Star Wars," *EOnline.com* 6 Feb 2012, 5 Sep 2012 <http://www.eonline.com/news/291969/best-super-bowl-movie-ads-the-avengers-and-star-wars>>

[240] Disney Movie Trailers Staff, "John Carter: Extended Super Bowl Ad," *YouTube*, 5 Feb 2012, 5 Sep 2012 < http://www.youtube.com/watch?v=7krwq5hZPY0>

FRUSTRATION AND AN IMPULSE

Waiting for the Super Bowl ad to play on February 5, I was one of the many hoping to see something that would reboot the troubled campaign. If ever there existed a moment where a game changer was needed, this was it, and I was holding out hope that Ricky Strauss had shaken things up since his arrival three weeks earlier, and we would see a new direction in the campaign.

Then the ad played.

I watched the 22 second pullout, the 8 seconds of Carter fighting the white ape, and then it was over.

What just happened?

Beside me on the couch was my wife Rena, a film-making buddy Mark Linthecum, and Mark's wife.

"Wow, what was that?" was Linthecum's comment.

I stared at the TV. What the hell?

I had my laptop up and was monitoring the *Twitter* reaction, and what I saw caused my heart to sink. There was almost no spike in the #JohnCarter traffic and what there was, confirmed that the spot was widely viewed as poor -- an impression that would be reconfirmed again and again in coming days as the various Super Bowl Ad rating sites rated it in the bottom 5% of all Super Bowl ads and absolutely last place among the seven movie ads that played during the game.

As the game continued, a sense of defeat settled in.

This was it - game over.

I ran the tracking software and confirmed that the volume of tweeting about the JC commercial was low, and the positive/negative ratio was bad.

This was the worst possible scenario for *John Carter*.

The one thing that had a real chance of turning the tide for the campaign -- a successful Super Bowl ad -- was not to be.

Not only had the Super Bowl ad not helped -- the 30 seconder that aired on TV was so bad that it was just feeding the negativity that was beginning to engulf the campaign. In all probability it had done more harm than good.

The game ended in the early evening in Burbank, and as I watched the New York Giants defeat the New England Patriots 21-17 an idea that had been floating at the back of my consciousness for weeks began to come into focus.

That idea was to gather up all of the available trailers and TV spots that had been released by Disney -- the two official trailers and 8 official TV spots, plus the Japanese trailer which was the only one that included substantial footage of John Carter on Earth -- and make my own damned trailer.

Why bother?

Answer: If for no other reason than to create at least the illusion of feeling like I could do something to affect the train wreck that was unfolding beyond my control.

I knew it was an illusion, but still.....

I explained to Mark what I had in mind. He was game. It occurred to both of us that this was, if nothing else, an intriguing opportunity to cut something with elements from a $250M studio film, a far cry from the elements that were normally available to us for an indie film. It was, simply on the creative level, a fantasy fulfilled to be able to work with this kind of material.

It took about an hour to find all the best available HD material online, download it, and get it organized in Final Cut Pro, the editing software that had become the standard for independent film-makers. some of the material was only available in standard definition -- the Japanese trailer, and one kiddie trailer from the Disney channel that had a moment in it that I knew I wanted to use. We would just have to live with a mixture of HD and SD materials.

Because I had been thinking about it for awhile, I had a very clear outline of how the trailer should be structured. The official theatrical trailer was perceived to be all spectacle and CGI -- and yet I, like any Burroughs fan, knew that there was a story with a beating heart there that wasn't getting communicated by the trailers.

So the plan was:

Act 1 - the first thirty seconds - would be spent introducing John Carter and showing how he gets to Mars.

Act II would run for one minute and would introduce Mars -- and unlike the Disney approach which focused on the white ape scene and other scenes all set relentlessly in a barren desert environment, I wanted to introduce Mars not as a barren, drab desert -- but to start with rich, colorful images of the vibrant societies of Helium and Zodanga, images that had always been dominant in my own mind as he contemplated the Barsoom of Burroughs books. I also wanted to establish and reinforce early in Act II of the trailer the love story between John Carter and Dejah Thoris so as to make clear to the viewer what was causing John Carter to be engaged in the action scenes that would be presented, particularly in act three.

Then in Act III, there would be the final cataclysm of action and romance, leaving everything unresolved.

And finally -- the trailer could not end with John Carter leaping into the charging Warhoons as it had been this ending that created the unintended laughter that I had heard in the theater when he watched the trailer in a packed house. There would need to be a tag at the end that was mysterious, alluring, and which left the viewer wondering about the mystery and magic of Barsoom.

There were two other key elements that I felt were very important to include -- references to both Stanton and Burroughs. The film had a pedigree and the audience needed to know that. There would be two graphic cards: "From the Director of *Wall-E* and *Finding Nemo*", and "From the Epic Tale That Inspired 100 Years of Film-making." I felt strongly that placing these two cards at the beginning of Act II would change the way the audience reacted to everything it saw from that point onward.

We went at it for 8 hours, well into the night, and then it was done. Our impression when we finished it was that it was good. It was basically a mashup of Disney trailer elements, not a completely new trailer -- but one that revealed enough of the story and the characters for the audience to become engaged -- while not giving away spoilers.

At the end of it, we uploaded the trailer to YouTube, set it to "Private", at least for the moment, and called it a day. The next day, February 6, I watched the trailer with fresh eyes and remained convinced it was a substantial improvement. But was it really better trailer, or was this just my own bias causing me to believe it was better?

It occurred to me that a first step, before anything else, would be to "focus group" the trailer, presenting it neutrally to viewers who would rate it side by side with the main official theatrical trailer. If the results came back that our trailer polled substantially better than the theatrical trailer, that would be one thing. If it didn't .... well, we would know.

So on February 7, I posted the trailer to *The John Carter Files* with the following text, which did not expose who had created the trailer or why:[241]

---

[241] Michael D. Sellers, "Poll: John Carter Trailer Survey," The John Carter Files, 7 Feb 2012, 4 Nov 2012 <http://thejohncarterfiles.com/2012/02/survey-which-john-carter-trailer-should-be-playing-in-theaters/>

Poll: John Carter Trailer Survey

The JohnCarterFiles.com is trying to obtain some genuine market feedback regarding John Carter Trailers. We appreciate your thoughtful participation. It has been set so that **only one vote per person is allowed**, so after you vote you just see the results — you can't vote more than once from any one IP Address. We're trying to keep this real. And please do not vote unless you view both trailers and give it some serious thought.

We encourage you to leave comments. This is all about trying to help in any way we can to make this movie have a successful outcome.

Which John Carter trailer makes you more interested in seeing the movie in theaters?

Trailer 1: This is the existing trailer that is playing in theaters now.

Trailer 2: This is a new draft trailer for consideration as an alternative.

Readers were then invited to vote and leave comments. Within hours the trend was clear, and by the end of the first 24 hours total votes were 119/20 in favor of the new trailer. Comments flooded in as well, supporting the new trailer:

> *Khanada T:* The draft trailer is just magnificent!! I love them all but the test trailer pulls some of the best bits together and it, or something similar, should be in theaters. The mention of 100 years inspiring films is huge too!

> *Terry C:* So far the test trailer is the best of them all. Sadly, I don't believe the powers that be have been listening. If they had been listening all this time we would have seen a different direction in the marketing of the film.

> *Rudy:* By far the best trailer is the 2nd draft one-nice to see that it shows that it is 100 years in the making and also gives credit to stanton as director

> *Billy York:* Trailer #2. In the Draft test it shows more of a romantic connection that I think will be very important to bring in the females but enough action to bring in the males.

> *Seymour:* I think the draft trailer is so much better! I like the intro that shows a bit of how he ended up there; it gives context to the rest of the plot. I also like the reference to the fact that the story is 100 years old as well as the mention of the director's credits.

Abraham Sherman: The test trailer is the best of the ones I've seen. It best captures the basics of the story, and it shows the action, gives moments of the romance, conveys the loyalty of Woola, and highlights the selling points of the director and legacy of Edgar Rice Burroughs.

MCR: It looks much better playing up the story and the action scenes and I did like the mention of the story being influential.

Patrick D: Disney, are you paying attention? Good movies are not about mere spectacle, but characters and story. The test trailer gives viewers a much clearer view of those elements. Equally important, it places "John Carter" in context: "The epic tale that inspired 100 years of filmmaking." You've invested too much money in this project for your advertising to fall so woefully short. Do something about it before it's too late!

Nightshadesiris: DEFINITELY THE TEST TRAILER! The most important part is the mention of "From the Epic Tale that Inspired 100 years of Filmmaking." Since that has not been mentioned in any previous trailers, people are writing off this movie as a ripoff and are not interested in seeing it!! Believe me I know this is true – not just by all the negative comments on You Tube, but from hearing it first hand.

I took the post down off the site and contemplated the next move. Was there a legit chance to get Disney to look at the test trailer and contemplate using it?

My reality-self said -- are you kidding?

My dream-self said yes, why not?

By now I had figured out some things about Disney email addresses and so I put together an email with an explanation and links to a password protected page with the trailer poll and the two trailers on it, and sent it to a handful of top Disney executives on the hope that one of them might see something of value. After giving it considerable thought, I did not send it to Ryan Stankevich or Samantha Garry, the two Disney executives whom we had met. My feeling was that they had clearly defined the parameters of the relationship as fan liaison and I had a responsibility to use that channel productively for whatever fan liaison could be achieved. If I tried to use it for this, there was a chance it would almost certainly be considered an "overreach" and could damage whatever fan liaison possibilities existed.

Instead I sent it to the top players in the studio and hoped something good would happen.

I also sent the link to the trailer to members of the film crew from *John Carter* who had corresponded with *The John Carter Files*, and whose email addresses I had. I heard back from several of them -- enthusiastic replies.

I waited, wondering if I would hear anything from Disney.

I didn't hold my breath.

"GREAT FAN TRAILER: THEY GET IT!"

The social media tracking that box office prognosticators had been using thus far is different from the "traditional tracking" that the studios start receiving four weeks prior to release. This traditional tracking is a polling service that all the studios subscribe to, and reflects telephone polls of potential movie goers which establish percentages for "unaided awareness" ("Have you heard of a movie called *John Carter*?); aided awareness ("Have you heard of any big sci-fi movies coming out soon?"), "definite interest" ("Are you definitely interested in seeing *John Carter* in theaters?") and "first choice" ("Of all the upcoming movies, what is your first choice?").

John Carter's figures first came online for the studio trackers on the morning of February 16 and that evening, *Deadline Hollywood* broke the story with an article: 'John Carter' Tracking Shockingly Soft: "Could Be Biggest Write-off of All Time" which reported:[242]

---

[242] Nikki Finke, "'John Carter' Tracking Shockingly Soft: "Could Be Biggest Writeoff of All Time," *Deadline Hollywood* 16 Feb 2012, 5 Sep 2012 http://www.deadline.com/2012/02/john-carter-early-tracking-shockingly-soft-could-be-biggest-writeoff-of-all-time/

Hollywood is in a tizzy over the early tracking which just came online this morning for Walt Disney Studios' *John Carter* opening March 9th. "Not good. 2 unaided, 53 aware, 27 definitely interested, 3 first choice," a senior exec at a rival studio emails me. Another writes me, "It just came out. Women of all ages have flat out rejected the film. The tracking for John Carter is shocking for a film that cost over $250 million. This could be the biggest writeoff of all time." I'm hearing figures in the neighborhood of $100 million. And the studio isn't even trying to spin reports of the 3D pic's bloated budget any more.

To put the numbers in perspective -- four weeks out from the release of a movie at the very top tier in terms of production investment, the marketing in a deep, deep hole. Marketing is a process--and creating awareness is the first step in the process. With an abysmal 2% unaided awareness, *John Carter* was not even remotely "in the ballpark" of where it needed to be at this juncture. Also the huge gap between "unaided awareness" of 2% and "aided awareness" of 53% spoke to the eminently forgettable nature of the title.

On February 21st Chris Lee at *The Daily Beast* ran an article entitled "John Carter: Disney's Quarter Billion Dollar Movie Fiasco,"[243]

> Around Hollywood, Disney's quarter-billion-dollar 3-D epic John Carter holds a dubious renown: it's the film with Avatar-size ambitions that's being greeted sight unseen as the next Ishtar. . . If Hollywood executives don't know who John Carter is, they certainly know what John Carter is. It's the kind of cautionary tale that keeps studio chiefs popping Ambien at night: a vanity project with sky-high expectations and a humongous budget that now seems destined to land with a massive thud at the box office—unless it can somehow rake in more than $400 million to break even. In other words, it's the kind of movie that causes heads to roll.

Andrew Stanton heard the bad news about the tracking on the morning of the 16th as he was just about to depart on a four stop press junket in support of the movie. But what could he do except grit his teeth and grind through it? He had long held that he could only truly be responsible for what happens once audience members were in their seats

---

[243] Chris Lee, "'John Carter': Disney's Quarter-Billion Dollar Movie Fiasco," *The Daily Beast*, 21 Feb 2012, 5 Sep 2012 http://www.thedailybeast.com/articles/2012/02/21/john-carter-disney-s-quarter-billion-dollar-movie-fiasco.html

to view the film, and he truly believed he had created a film that would weave a spell as intensely satisfying to audience members as he had with *Finding Nemo* and *Wall-E*. It was distressing to hear the weak tracking numbers, but it didn't shake his faith in the film itself.

But there were two things he could do, and would do.

First, he was going to come out with guns blazing on the junket on the issue of the supposed "out-of-control-production" which had supposedly "ballooned" to the level of $300M because of "costly unplanned reshoots." That simply wasn't true. He had been waiting for someone from Disney to set the record straight since Kim Masters article had come out on January 19th in *The Hollywood Reporter*. Well, no one had -- and so now he was going to do it.

At the first round-table in Arizona, where the press junket was kicking off, Stanton let go and the result hit the wires the next day, with IndieWire being one of the first to post Stanton's counterpunch under the headline: "Andrew Stanton Says Rumor that 'John Carter' Cost $300M Is A "Complete and Utter Lie"[244]

> To say that the development of Disney's "John Carter" has been scrutinized would be an understatement. The project itself has been in the works for years with a handful of directors (Jon Favreau and Robert Rodriguez among them) working on it, but never quite cracking the sci-fi space epic. However, it was Pixar veteran Andrew Stanton ("Wall-E," "Finding Nemo") who finally got the ball rolling and for his live action debut, he couldn't have asked for a bigger challenge. And indeed he's been closely watched every step of the way, with rumors growing loud as the film shifted release dates, dropped "Of Mars" from its initial title and slowly started earning concerned buzz, with reports showing up in the trades suggesting that his inexperience led to reshoots that pushed the budget to a staggering $300 million (a figure most recently tossed around in The Hollywood Reporter), but Stanton is now fighting back.

> This week, a massive press get-together for "John Carter" was held in Arizona and Movieline was there and found Stanton in a

---

[244] Kevin Jagernauth, "Andrew Stanton Says Rumors That 'John Carter' Cost $300 Million is a "Complete and Utter Lie"," *Indiewire*, 17 Feb 2012, 5 Sep 2012 <http:// blogs.indiewire.com/theplaylist/021712/andrew-stanton-says-claims-that-john-carter-cost-300-million-is-a-complete-and-utter-lie#>.

fighting spirt. Calling reports about the rumored $300 million budget "a complete and utter lie" Stanton insisted the studio was fully behind him: "I want to go completely on record that I literally was on budget and on time the entire shoot. Disney is so completely psyched that I stayed on budget and on time that they let me have a longer reshoot because I was such a good citizen, so I find it ironic that we're getting accused of the opposite."

Similar articles appeared across the web, and Producer Lindsey Collins added her voice to forcefully back up Stanton.[245]

"It's frustrating, because it's wrong," Lindsey Collins, one of the film's co-producers, says of years of trade reports that the film, the first live-action effort from Oscar-winning "WALL-E" director Andrew Stanton, was a bloated, over-budget mess.

"There's no way to talk about it without sounding defensive, but I'm going to sound defensive for a second and say this movie was made on budget," Collins asserted. "I think Disney took a huge leap of faith with us early on and said, Okay, we believe your number and it's higher than we wanted but we believe it so make it for that ... And in fact, in most areas, it came in under, and the one area we came in slightly over was offset by all the underages of the others, so it came within I think two percent of the budget."

The budget they say they hit was $250 million, which went into live shoots in desert locations and massive computer graphic work to create an elaborate world in which a leather-clad Taylor Kitsch, as Carter, leaps into a war between two rival nations and a race of green, horned, four-armed natives. Barsoom, as Mars is called by its inhabitants, is a rocky desert-scape littered with ornate cities, mystical ruins and anachronistic flying machines. And it's one that took over seventy five years of technological development to make believable on the screen.

But while Collins backed up Stanton, no one from Disney had anything to say about it, leaving it to the director and his producers to attempt to set the record straight with a version of the story that was, in fact, essentially correct, at least insofar as any budget Stanton or Collins had been shown was concerned. No one in the production knew what studio overhead or other charges might have been added, and this might

---

[245] Jordan Zakarin, "'John Carter' Producers on Budget Rumors and Creating Mars," *Huffington Post*, 22 Feb 2012, 5 Sep 2012 < http://www.huffingtonpost.com/ 2012/02/22/john-carter-producers-on-budget-rumors-creating-mars_n_1293248.html? ref=entertainment>.

explain Disney's silence -- although as with most other incidents in the *John Carter* rollout, simple inattention and lack of focus seems more likely to be the explanation for the lack of support from Disney.

With that salvo out of the way, Stanton took another damage control step. A fan trailer had been forwarded to him by one of the members of the production team some days earlier, and Stanton had been struck by how well it showcased the film. The trailer was essentially a reorganized mashup of bits and pieces from all the trailers and TV spots that had been released to date, yet it did something that no trailer or TV spot had done previously, and that was to put forward the basic storyline of the film in a compelling way that that captured what Stanton would later call "the DNA of the film we've made."

Throughout the production and promotion of *John Carter*, Stanton had been doing his part by tweeting regularly, including weekly Friday Q and A's with fans that were lively and had caused his *Twitter* following to grow substantially.

On February 19th, three days after the "soft tracking" report had hit, he tweeted:[246]

"Great Fan Trailer. They get it!"

At the the end of the tweet was a link to "view media", allowing the fan trailer to play in the *Twitter* feed.[247]

It would be a tweet that started a chain reaction of rare positivity for the beleaguered film.

---

[246] Andrew Stanton Official Twitter Account, @AndrewStanton, 23 Apr 2009, 5 Sep 2012 <http://Twitter.com/andrewstanton>.

[247] John Carter Files Youtube Channel, "Fan Trailer - The John Carter Files.com", Youtube, 5 Feb 2012, 5 Sep 2012 <http://youtu.be/-BxeHQY1NuM>.

A DELUSION OR A GLIMMER OF HOPE?

As Stanton was tweeting, I was on my couch putting the finishing touches on an article for *The John Carter Files* entitled "Yes, there is a path to success for John Carter."[248] In the article I made the case that woeful as the tracking figures were, there were four weeks to go and there was historical precedent for the type of improvement in the tracking numbers that *John Carter* would need to achieve to have an opening weekend that would be regarded as marginally successful, or at least not the disaster that everyone was predicting.

> The "path to success" for Disney in this situation, being realistic, is to get from 52 "aware" /27 "definitely interested" to 70/40, which would put it a bit higher than Super 8 [which opened at $37M] was tracking coming into opening weekend. Disney can get to this "Aware" number pretty much by brute force — just keep advertising with greater and greater intensity; turn on the publicity machine that will flood the media with articles, interviews, etc and Awareness should go to 70. Definitely interested will increase but likely only to 35 or so (i.e. the same ratio as now, roughly 2/1, Aware/Definitely Interested) unless the quality of the advertising and promotion improves. But another way of looking at it is that to get to 40 definitely interested, Disney only needs to pick up 5 "quality points" with better advertising — that being the five points between 35 Definitely interested (where they will land if they get aware to 70 and nothing changes in the

---

[248] Michael D. Sellers, "Yes, There Is a Path To Success For John Carter," *The John Carter Files*, 19 Feb 2012, 5 Sep 2012 <http://thejohncarterfiles.com/2012/02/yes-there-is-a-path-to-success-for-john-carter/>.

quality of the advertising) and 40, if they do better and convert from Aware to Definitely Interested at a better rate than they are now.

I published the post, then read a heartfelt comment from a reader, Daniel Quesnel in which the author made a plea for "the Community" to rise up and help *John Carter* overcome the deficiencies of Disney's marketing. There was a certain innocence to the writing -- and I found it even more compelling and heartfelt for having that quality. I decided to publish it as a guest blog post:[249]

> I'm not a professional writer but I want to say something. I've been watching the promotion of John Carter, and seeing the reaction. Somehow it seems that even though John Carter is likely a great film and has been getting a lot of positive reviews . . . still it can't get a good box office? Why? I don't really get how it works, when a really good movie is in trouble like this. We need to give this movie hope. I know in my heart, that this movie deserves it.
>
> This is kind of like Bad. vs. Good characters, the Bad Character's are always stronger until the end, but then a Good Character steps in, and gives hope. Disney did their part on advertising, but now it's the Community is the only thing to help Disney. like basically how a Bad Community doesn't give anything to a movie, and bashes on it, and calls it a copycat and everything,. then we have a Good Community which is basically a shield for Disney, and the Good Community basically tells all those people that bash the movie that this movie is based this great book that brought sci-fi to the big screen, you know what i mean?
>
> My point: It's the community that needs to help this movie, not Disney.

I was intrigued by his reference to the "Good Community" and how we had to help. Throughout the brief history of *The John Carter Files*, a community of fans and potential fans had been growing and the tools of the internet and social media provided new opportunities to use our voices, and be heard.

Was there enough of a community now in place to make a difference?

---

[249] Daniel Quesnel, "Letter From a John Carter Fan: What Disney Needs to Do," *The John Carter Files*, 19 Feb 2012, 5 Sep 2012 <http://thejohncarterfiles.com/2012/02/letter-from-a-john-carter-fan-what-disney-needs-to-do/>

The truth was, as the campaign had progressed, I was of two minds about our roles. On the one hand, *The John Carter Files* seemed to be having at least some minor but measurable impact by helping stimulate the appearance and re-posting of more positive articles than would have been the case without JCF -- and it was doing this at a time when positive articles were needed. But on the other hand, realistically, how much of an impact could that add to a $100M marketing campaign?

Answer from my real self: Not much.

Answer from my dream self: Who knows?

Maybe if something happens . . .

Maybe if the fans band together using all the   tools of social media . . . .

I won't deny it -- of course I wanted to be some kind of leader who helped the little guys rise up and make a difference.   That was my ERBian dream-self talking, that inner voice that believed, or wanted to believe, that the little guys weren't helpless in this equation -- that the fans, and the influencer bloggers (who had more in common with fans than they did with corporate Hollywood, after all), could get together and turn the tide. So many of us had waited decades for this film, and now it was slipping away into oblivion.   Maybe we could really do something, really make a difference.....

Nah. Who are you kidding?

Not gonna happen.

You're being delusional, Sellers.

This is big budget, corporate Hollywood, not the indie-ville that you're used to, and you -- even with all the other fans that have showed solidarity on JCF and elsewhere -- are nothing more than fleas riding on the Disney elephant. Be real. The movie is going down. ERB is going down. Your dreams of *John Carter* catching the imagination of the world are just that -- dreams. It's pretty much game over.

I stretched out on the couch and started looking for a Sunday night movie to finish off what had been a frustrating weekend. As I flipped through the channel guide, a text beeped in on my cellphone. I ignored it. Then another came through. And a third.

A flurry of emails were starting to hit my laptop as well.

Curious, I checked email: "Stanton pimped ya!" read one subject line, then inside: "On *Twitter* he pimped your fan trailer!" I checked and found the tweet.

Well that's something, I thought.

It did not immediately occur to me that this could be the start of something substantial. If it had, I would have immediately started monitoring to see what happened next. But I didn't do that. I registered the fact that Stanton had given us a pat on the back, allowed myself to feel slightly pleased, and that was it.

At least you put your money where your mouth is. The director likes your trailer. You weren't completely delusional; your ideas at least made sense to him.

The next morning I saw that Stanton's tweet had been retweeted 32 times, and following some of the retweets, I saw that many of them had been retweeted 20 or more times. Nice.

Then I ran the aggregator program looking for *John Carter* stories for the daily *John Carter Files* News Feed and saw that a few influencer sites had posted our Fan Trailer, or more specifically, had posted articles about Andrew Stanton tweeting about our fan trailer, with an embed of the trailer that would play it on the site.

One of the first was Brendan Connelly, writing in *BleedingCool.com*, posted an embed of the trailer and wrote: [250] "That trailer was sanctioned by Stanton himself, given his blessing via *Twitter*. I think's Kudos with a capital K and U at least, and perhaps even the D."

---

[250] Brendan Connelly, "Fan Film Fanfare -- Akira, John Carter, and Mass Effect," *Bleeding Cool*, 20 Feb 2012, 5 Sep 2012 <http://www.bleedingcool.com/2012/02/20/fan-film-fanfare-akira-john-carter-and-mass-effect/>.

Another blog, *LiveForFilms.com*, posted: "This is a brilliant trailer put together using bits from all the *John Carter* footage released so far. Director Andrew Stanton enjoyed it."[251]

My first thought was that Brendan Connelly was someone who gets read widely . . . was it possible others might pick it up?

I felt a flicker of hope.

But it was just a flicker. It was 16 days until the release and the original hearty band of influencers, who were the ones most likely to pick this up, were being swamped now by the mainstream media that had come late to the game, as would always be the case, only getting into the act at the end but now dominating the narrative and reaching the many millions of potential viewers who only become aware of a movie in the final weeks before it is released. The moment for the influencers had been earlier, much earlier. Realistically, ever since the campaign had moved on to the All Media phase on November 30, their role had shifted from being the dominant voice setting the buzz, to a niche of 'insider' voices with the mainstream media now in the game. Their seeds had been sown prior to the launch of the final push. Seeds that were sown now were just being planted too late.

But still . . . . could they still have an impact?

Dream self: Sure they can.

Real self: Nope. Too late.

Others began to pick it up.

One of those who read about it was Adam Chitwood at *Collider.com*. Chitwood published an article on the morning of the 21st under the

---

[251] Live For Films Staff, "Epic John Carter Trailer is Fan Made," *Live For Film*, 20 Feb 2012, 5 Sep 2012 <http://www.liveforfilms.com/2012/02/20/epic-john-carter-trailer-is-fan-made/>.

headline: "New Fan-made Trailer for JOHN CARTER Sells the Movie Better Than the Film's Previous Trailers," which stated: [252]

> We're merely a couple weeks away from the release of Disney's John Carter and I'm willing to bet that a good deal of the general public still has no idea what this movie is about. The previous trailers and TV spots have tried in vain to sell the film as a big action-adventure pic, but none of that matters if your audience doesn't understand why there are a bunch of CG people monsters hanging out in the desert. A fan-made trailer for the film has recently hit the web and it's leagues better than what the Disney marketing machine has come up with. It clearly sets up the story and rightly sells the Edgar Rice Burroughs adaptation as the precursor to basically the entire sci-fi genre. From *Star Wars* to *Avatar*, Burroughs' source material served as the inspiration for some of the world's most beloved sci-fi stories, and finally the tale that started it all is getting a film adaptation of its own. That's how the movie should have been sold.

The embedded trailer followed the article, as it would on all the sites that picked it up. Readers were not just reading about the trailer -- they could click and view it without leaving the page they were on.

Harry Knowles and Alan Cerna (aka "Nordling") of the geek-centric and highly trafficked movie site *Ain't it Cool News* also saw it and posted: "A Fan-Made Trailer for JOHN CARTER sells the Movie Better Than Any Other Trailer So Far"[253]

> This fan-made trailer seems to do what the official ones have not - sell the legacy of the stories as well as show how good the story is. I like this trailer a lot, and Disney could do worse than just buy this trailer cut from this guy and release it.

The Collider and AICN posts ensured that the story of the fan trailer would "go wide." Within an hour other influencer movies sites were picking up on the story.

---

[252] Adam Chitwood, "New Fan-made Trailer for JOHN CARTER Sells the Movie Better Than the Film's Previous Trailers," *Collider*, 21 Feb 2012, 5 Sep 2012 <http://collider.com/john-carter-fan-trailer/147054/>.

[253] Nordling, "A Fan-Made Trailer for JOHN CARTER sells the Movie Better Than Any Other Trailer So Far," *Ain't it Cool News*, 21 Feb 2012, 5 Sep 2012 <http://www.aintitcool.com/node/53732>

Russ Fisher at *Slashfilm* ran with it under the title: "The Best 'John Carter' Trailer Yet" and noted: "It's a lot better than any of the others, both from the perspective of laying out the story, and for showing the scope of the film."[254]

Neil Miller at *Film School Rejects* noted "If the marketing minds at Disney have proven anything with their campaign for *John Carter*, it's that taking a vacation and leaving their first big movie of the year to the interns and office robots is probably not a good idea...." then went on to say:[255]

> Behold this completely badass fan-made John Carter trailer, which outdoes everything Disney has put out thus far. I'm sensing a trend, here. Perhaps Disney, like anyone would be, wasn't quite clear on how to market such a genre-defiant film. This trailer is far more representative of the movie you should be seeing on March 9.

All within a span of 12 hours, others followed -- *Fused Film, Metacafe, Blastr, Badass Digest, Flick Daily, Live for Film, Hollywood News, Screen Rant,* and more -- so that by the end of the day on the 21st more than 50 movie tracking sites had carried the embedded Youtube trailer, causing a viral bump on YouTube.

By February 22nd the number of sites carrying the trailer had grown to more than 100, and now mainstream media outlets were picking up on it. At *Wired*, Angela Watercutter posted: "Fan Trailer for John Carter Tops Studio's Best Efforts," and wrote: "the new video uses footage we've already seen before, pulled from fan site The John Carter Files. But it's far more engrossing than the actual studio trailers we've seen to date — right down to the "epic tale that inspired 100 years of filmmaking" tag line."[256]

---

[254] Russ Fischer, "The Best John Carter Trailer Yet," *Slashfilm*, 21 Feb 2012, 5 Sep 2012 http://www.slashfilm.com/fanmade-trailers-john-carter-trailer-liveaction-akira/

[255] Neil Miller, "Movie News After Dark: John Carter, Doctor Who . . . ," *Film School Rejects*, 21 Feb 2012, 5 Sep 2012 <http://www.filmschoolrejects.com/news/movie-news-after-dark-john-carter-doctor-who-oscar-and-other-manly-things-also-john-carter.php>.

[256] Angela Watercutter, "Fan Trailer For John Carter Tops Studio's Best Efforts," *Wired*, 22 Feb 2012, 5 Sep 2012 <http://www.wired.com/underwire/2012/02/fan-trailer-john-carter/>.

Fox MovieFone's Mike Ryan wrote: "pay the guy who made this a few thousand dollars for editing Disney's footage together better than Disney did and get it out there. Everywhere."[257]

The Hollywood Reporter ran an article that said in part: "this is the kind of trailer that should have been out there in the first place, something that gives you a sense of the story and the scope. In fact, one person in the office here just had his mind switched and now wants to see the movie."[258]

Eventually the LA Times[259] and CNN[260] wrote about it, exploring the phenomenon of a fan-generated trailer having an impact on the promotion of the film.

Visitors to the *John Carter Files* quadrupled overnight, with page views spiking to 50,000 a day before leveling off in the 30,000-40,000 range.

On *YouTube*, the views began to pour in, 21,000 in the first day from the embed on *Ain't It Cool News* alone, and by the end of the second day it had registered 100,000 views overall and was outdrawing the official trailer by a 2 to 1 ratio. In terms of "likes", it drew a ratio of 92 likes for each "dislike" -- 8 times better than the official trailer and six times better than the official trailer for *The Hunger Games*.

Watching the reaction unfold, I was under no illusions that what was happening around the fan trailer could have enough impact to right the promotional ship for Disney. But it was clearly having some impact,

---

[257] Mike Ryan, "John Carter: 6 Ways To Fix the Poor Marketing Campaign," *Fox Moviefone*, 22 Feb 2012 <http://news.moviefone.com/mike-ryan/6-things-john-carter-marketing_b_1294083.html

[258] Boris Kit, "Fan-Made Trailer for 'John Carter' Could be Better Than Official One (Video)," The Hollywood Reporter, 22 Feb 2012, 6 Sep 2012 < http://www.hollywoodreporter.com/heat-vision/john-carter-fan-trailer-disney-293944>.

[259] Dawn Chmielewski, "Fans create unofficial new trailer for Disney's John Carter', LA Times, 24 Feb 2012, 6 Sep 2012 < http://latimesblogs.latimes.com/entertainmentnewsbuzz/2012/02/fan-creates-new-trailer-for-disneys-john-carter.html

[260] Henry Hanks, "Fans Create Their Own Trailer for John Carter," *CNN Geek-out*, 27 Feb 2012, 6i Sep 2012 <http://geekout.blogs.cnn.com/2012/02/27/fans-create-their-own-trailer-for-john-carter/>

causing some degree of uptick in the media coverage of the film--at last there was something positive being written about it.

I began to daydream again.

What if fans, with the tools of social media at their disposal and supported by bloggers and creative professionals, were able to "change the narrative" about *John Carter*. It was a long shot -- but then, to use a word Burroughs had liked, the whole "damphool" enterprise was a long shot.

Perhaps, after all, belief in self and the ability to affect outcomes was not just a daydream or an indulgence in personal fantasy. Perhaps you have to be a dreamer in order to believe in the possibility of having an impact and going for it to do something. Perhaps that dream-self was not just an indulgence -- perhaps it was an essential persona that all those who "dream big" and go on and do it possess.

Or maybe I just couldn't tell the difference between fanciful fiction and cold Hollywood reality.

THE PREMIERE AND THE TWEET REVIEWS

Disney normally holds its premieres at the company owned El Capitan Theater on Hollywood Boulevard but Oscar preparations made that impossible for the *John Carter* Red Carpet Premiere on February 22, so the L.A. Live Theater became the venue, with the after party held in the ballroom of the JW Marriott Hotel.

Coming six days after the unveiling of Nikki Finke's *"Shockingly Soft Tracking"* debacle, the premiere faced an uphill struggle but Disney, recognizing the grimness of the situation and knowing the film itself wasn't a stinker, partially lifted the embargo they had placed on dozens of journalists who had viewed the film at the press junket in Arizona, allowing them to tweet about the film, but not write full reviews yet. This turned out to be one of the few shrewd moves of the campaign, as Disney and Stanton were rewarded on the day of the premiere with a "floodlet" of favorable tweeted mini-reviews about the movie that were picked up by the entertainment media and replayed throughout the eco-system. This, plus the positive chatter about the fan trailer and a new unofficial "Mondo" poster by J.C. Richards that far outclassed the previous official posters, plus premiere buzz (what's to criticize about a premiere?) added up to a better day than the campaign had seen in quite awhile, if ever.

260

At *ScreenRant*, Sandy Schaefer posted "'John Carter': Fan-Made Trailer, Mondo Poster, & Early Reviews," saying:[261]

> Disney is pushing hard for its *John Carter* adaptation to become a ticket-selling smash when it hits theaters next month, but early tracking results are not boding well for the film's box office prospects. Many people have chalked that up to the bulk of the movie's marketing material, which has mostly painted the classic sci-fi literary adaptation as a bland "Disney-fied" variation on such effects-heavy blockbuster properties as Star Wars and Avatar (and other thematic descendants of author Edgar Rice Burroughs' trendsetting *John Carter* source material, ironically enough).
>
> Today, however, we have new material in the form of a nicely structured fan-made mashup trailer, a beautiful Mondo poster, and the release of several entertainment journalists' *Twitter* reactions to *John Carter* (spoiler: they're largely positive). All of these items suggest that director Andrew Stanton's adaptation may turn out much better than Disney's official marketing campaign has indicated.

At the premiere, after the screening Taylor Kitsch was feisty when anyone probed him about the publicity. "We made a f---ing great movie. It's such wasted energy if I worry about what a million people I don't know are going to think. I'm excited for people to enjoy the journey."

Producer Jim Jacks, who'd had the film at Paramount, praised Taylor Kitsch to anyone who would listen, and claimed Stanton's ending was "better than the book."

Twitter reaction in the hours after the film screened was the best yet, with strong positives across the board. "John Carter is much better than you're expecting it to be," tweeted *Slashfilm's* Peter Sciretta. *Hitfix's* Drew McWeeney tweeted, "I am no longer in danger of being killed for saying that I quite liked *John Carter*."

Other mini-review tweets rolled in praising the film:

> JOHN CARTER is a great movie. For 2 hours I was transported to another time and place. Can't wait to see it again. Don't miss it.
>
> — Steven Weintraub (@colliderfrosty) February 22, 2012

---

[261] Sandy Schaefer, "'John Carter:': Fan-Made Trailer, Mondo Poster, and Early Reviews,", *ScreenRant*, 22 Feb 2012, 4 Nov 2012 <http://screenrant.com/john-carter-trailer-poster-reviews-sandy-156030/>.

Also the effects were amazing. The action scenes inspiring. And the music was fantastic. Seriously....JOHN CARTER is not to be missed.

— Steven Weintraub (@colliderfrosty) February 22, 2012

I am no longer in danger of being killed for saying that I quite liked "John Carter."Full reviews are still embargoed, though.

— Drew McWeeny (@DrewAtHitFix) February 22, 2012

The best parts of JOHN CARTER are Woola and Dejah Thoris. A generation will be ushered into puberty by Lynn Collins.

— Devin Faraci (@devincf) February 22, 2012

John Carter (aka John Carter of Mars) is MUCH better than it looks. A great sci-fi film. Plan on seeing it!

— John Campea (@johncampea) February 22, 2012

The tweets, passed about on smartphones among those at the premiere after-party, bolstered what two days earlier was expected to be a funereal mood, generating high spirits that carried many of the key players well past midnight at the Marriott.

Could it be that the tide of negativity was turning?

Throughout the last week of February and first week of March a struggle for control of the narrative played out in a way that underscored the sense of inevitability and doom on the one hand, and last-ditch-maybe-this-can-be-saved optimism on the other. On the positive side, on blogs and in social media there was a ripple of positivity that had proved elusive up until this moment. There were were a number of elements that converged to help make this happen: The lifting of the tweet embargo was generating positive digital word-of-mouth as journalists tweeted mostly favorable quotes about the movie; the Andrew Stanton-endorsed fan trailer eventually would land on 400 media outlets; the unfolding press junket was being used by Andrew Stanton and producer Lindsey Collins to fire back at those pushing the "Hollywood-out-of-control" storyline, and the new Mondo movie poster by artist J.C. Richard arrived featuring the sense of scope and wonder that had been lacking thus far in Disney's promotion of the film.

For me, seeing the fan trailer spread to 400 media outlets in a matter of days caused the 'stop fantasizing, be real' voice inside my head to go quiet. I began to hold out hope that the fans, properly organized and motivated, might actually be able to make a difference in the final weeks before release.

As the influencer and social media swung positive, while the mainstream media continued to savage the film, I wrote "How Motivated Fans Can Make A Difference." The article began:[262]

> Frankly, this should have been smooth sailing. One of the beloved novels ever being adapted by the genius director of Wall-E with plenty of budget to get it right, a great cast, state of the art special effects....what can go wrong? When we started this site, we imagined that by now, a little more than two weeks out, John Carter would be tracking like gangbusters en route to a $60M-70M opening weekend, sequels would be almost assured, and long suffering ERB fans would be on the verge of a once in a lifetime moment of something pretty close to pure ecstasy.
>
> Instead, two weeks out, we are having to endure a constant onslaught of bad news. The tracking is bad; interest is low; critique of the promotion is getting very bloody. The latest is Newsweek saying that the buzz around Hollywood is that John Carter is Disney's Ishtar — and if you aren't old enough to remember Ishtar, that was the all time epic big studio fail. Being compared to Ishtar is basically apocalyptic. On the other hand, every advance review that has slipped out into the blogosphere has been favorable and then some. The film itself seems poised to deliver the kind of great viewing experience that you'd expect when you put Edgar Rice Burroughs and Andrew Stanton into a petri dish for four years.
>
> The question is this: In this day and age of social media, we the fans have more power than ever at any time in the past. We can say things, do things, that have impact far beyond our own geographical community.
>
> Is it possible that a grassroots #gobarsoom effort could really make a difference?

[262] Michael D. Sellers, "How Motivated Fans Can Make a Difference," *The John Carter Files*, 21 Feb 2012, 6 Sep 2012 < http://thejohncarterfiles.com/2012/02/john-carter-can-motivated-fans-actually-make-a-difference/>.

The post then went on to list things that fans could do that, collectively, could have an impact. It talked about checking the local multiplex to ensure that *John Carter* lobby displays were prominently featured; using the "share" features on *Facebook*, *Twitter*, and other social media and bookmarking outlets to amplify the positive narrative; monitoring and contributing positivity on *IMDB* and other movie message boards; reaching out to local media to generate "hometown stories" about fans rallying to the film based on the beloved 100 year classic (a process JCF would support with B roll and in other ways); Retweet Andrew Stanton's tweet and link to the fan trailer, using hashtags properly to ensure as wide an audience as possible.

The next day JCF announced the "#GoBarsoom Digital Grassroots Media Campaign."[263] The idea was to give fan tools and support to help them reach out to their local media and give "hometown interviews" while directing the media to a digital online press kit on *The John Carter Files* that would "full range of materials about Edgar Rice Burroughs, the history of *John Carter* as a book series, the history of efforts to make it into a movie — plus art examples, quotes from people who were influenced by ERB (Carl Sagan, Ray Bradbury, James Cameron, etc).

The storyline for the interviews was to be the same one Jack Scanlan and I had pitched to Disney: "For many, the opening of Disney's *John Carter* is just another movie, but for local fan [Insert Name] it's the culmination of decades of waiting to see his boyhood hero John Carter on screen." All of this, plus the digital press kit included HD videos that could be downloaded so that the media outlet has everything it needs to craft a good story.

Meanwhile, Social Media monitoring software showed a measurable improvement in the positive/negative sentiment ratio surrounding *John Carter* during the period in which the fan trailer, tweet reviews, and premiere were all happening. Clearly the efforts by Stanton, the fans, and the tweets by reviewers were moving the needle -- could this be a turning of the tide?

---

[263] Michael D. Sellers, "Announcement: The #GoBarsoom digital grassroots media campaign for John Carter," *The John Carter Files*, February 22, 2012, http://thejohncarterfiles.com/2012/02/announcement-the-gobarsoom-digital-grassroots-media-campaign-for-john-carter/

Or just a temporary, unsustainable bump?

On the same day, Disney Australia released what appeared to be the full great white ape scene that had dominated the trailers and TV spots to date followed by a two minute montage that had a distinctly different feel from anything that had been released previously -- more epic, with the same Nick Ingman "Mars" music that had been used in the second half of the largely unseen (because it only ran online) SuperBowl 60 second ad. This two minute piece after the ape scene was, in fact, the "sizzle reel" created not by marketing professionals but by the film-makers themselves, a year earlier. [264]   Erik Jessen, one of the editors on Eric Zumbrunnen's team, had been the primary cutter of the piece, which the team had made long before the official promotion began. The "sizzle reel" garnered some favorable publicity online.

But......

It was reaching tens of thousands of people and 4-5 million moviegoers would have to buy tickets and see the film in theaters across the country.

Where were they going to come from?

On February 26, for the Oscar pre-show spot, almost two full weeks before the release, Disney began running "critics" TV spots filled with random review quotes that no longer tried to sell the film on its own merits or do a better job conveying the film's essence, instead drawing mainly from the "Tweet" mini-reviews that had come out since Disney had decided on February 21 to lift the embargo partially and allow tweets. Many observers saw this as Disney in effect throwing in the towel as far as doing a better job of conveying the essence of the film's story, and indeed, it was almost game over at this point.

The review quotes, which built to a climax that ended with "First Blockbuster of the Year" followed by (could it be anything else) a clip of John Carter fighting a white ape, drew fire from some of the journalists

---

[264] ComingSoon.Net Staff, "Extended John Carter Clip and Sizzle Reel," *ComingSoon.net*, 24 Feb 2012, 6 Sep 2012 <http://www.comingsoon.net/news/movienews.php?id=87440>.

quoted, and hoots of derision from others, particularly for the "First Blockbuster of the Year" climax.[265]

A few days later, on February 28, Disney released the third and final theatrical trailer, this one ordered up by new marketing chief Ricky Strauss.[266] The final trailer was greeted with a collective sigh.[267]

> "Who is that?" So villain Mark Strong asks in the opening line of the latest trailer for John Carter, thus echoing the sentiment of pretty much every non-sci-fi-nerd who is not John Carter. The film opens in less than two weeks and, according to recent tracking, awareness and interest for the film is dismally low for a $250+ budgeted film. Confirming those tracking numbers, last night, following a John Carter TV spot, I was drawn into this brief conversation:
>
> "What is this place supposed to be?"
>
> "Mars."
>
> "Oh, that's Mars? I was wondering why he was in a weird desert. Why is he on Mars?"
>
> "I... I don't know. He was in the Civil War, and somehow he ends up on Mars. It was a series of books."
>
> "What? Why does he have the most boring name imaginable?"
>
> "I don't know."
>
> This so-called "final" trailer for John Carter makes no attempt at clearing any of that up. Like with the previous trailers, Disney is so intent on showing off their effects that you can't taste any of the actual meal under all the overwhelming CGI ketchup they dumped out.

[265] Brad Brevett, "Is 'John Carter' this Year's Waterworld?," *Rope of Silicon*, 27 Feb 2012, 7 Sep 2012 < http://www.ropeofsilicon.com/is-john-carter-this-years-waterworld/>.

[266] DisneyMovieTrailers Staff, "John Carter - Trailer 3," *Youtube Disney Movie Trailers Channel*, 29 Feb 2012, 7 Sep 2012 <http://youtu.be/XavXWxqZvLY>.

[267] IWatchStuff Staff, "Final 'John Carter' Trailer Shows You Its Nonspecific CGI Things One Last Time," *IWatchStuff.com*, 28 Feb 2012, 7 Sep 2012 <http://www.iwatchstuff.com/2012/02/final-john-carter-trailer-shows-you-its.php>

In the mainstream media, this article in *The Weekly Standard* captured the situation clearly and was reflected in hundreds of newspapers and media outlets as the release date approached.[268]

> Stanton chose to attempt to make a realistic epic full of special effects in the Pixar way—a method that involves a lot of reshooting, rewriting, and rethinking as the movie is being made. As a result, it appears *John Carter* may have cost Disney as much as $250 million to make, but in this case the money was spent on a movie with no major stars, an unproven director, and based on a "brand" with meaning only to science-fiction geeks......
>
> What this means is that *John Carter* has become the latest in an endless series of tsk-tsk subjects of Hollywood-run-amok articles and books, as pop-culture spending excesses seem always to generate a kind of thrilled and sickened fascination on the order of reading about the Madoff family.

Tsk-tsk indeed.

Was there any hope of changing the outcome?

---

[268] John Podhoretz, "Buzz in the Air", *The Weekly Standard*, 25 Feb 2012, 7 Sep 2012 <http://www.weeklystandard.com/articles/buzz-air_631894.html?page=2>.

FINALLY: THE FILM ITSELF

On February 27, the LA Times Hero Complex was sponsoring an advance screening in Burbank of *John Carter*, with Andrew Stanton to be present for a Q and A after the film. Jack LesCanela, a reader of *The John Carter Files*, had scored a ticket for me so a few days prior I put the word out via email to a member of the *John Carter* film crew that I would be at the screening.   My email got forwarded up the chain and eventually landed in Andrew Stanton's in box, with the result that on Oscar Sunday, February 26, I opened my email to find a message from Andrew Stanton:

> Dear Michael
>
> I'd very much like to meet you after the Q&A after the Burbank screening. I'll stick around to find you. Thanks so much for the trailer you have done.
>
> You managed to capture the true movie we have much better than anyone else (so far.) I'd love to hear if you have any other wonderful underground trailers that I could help you virally spread.
>
> See you tomorrow night!
>
> Andrew

I was thrilled.

On one level this was just a kindly pat on the back to a fan who had done something nice for the film, and I didn't want to read too much into it. But on the other hand, it was as if there a guerrilla alliance was forming between fans and the film-makers to use the tools of social media and try and make a difference.

I had studied the elements that are present when something goes viral, and one of the most important was precisely what had happened with the fan trailer -- there needed to be an endorser who gets the video or blog post out into a much larger channel than would otherwise be possible. Maria Aragon had just been a 10 year old playing around making YouTube videos until Lady Gaga saw her cover of "Born This Way" and tweeted about it. The result: 52 million hits.

Nothing on that scale had happened to us, but Stanton's tweet had been the difference between the trailer being hardly noticed, and generating 100,000 hits and 400 news articles in a matter of days. If he were an ally providing amplification, and it seems he was, perhaps there was hope that the efforts could become meaningful.

But, sadly, the harsh reality was that the time for the influencers to influence had passed. The damage had been done; the narrative was set.

The raw numbers were humbling.

The Fan Trailer had garnered 100,000 views and hundreds of highly favorable comments on YouTube in a matter of days, and the story had been carried on 400 media outlets and sites. It had generated credibility for JCF, and had, along with the tweets and the Mondo poster, helped contribute to a measurable improvement in the positive/negative sentiment ratio on blogs, *Twitter*, and *Facebook*. The fans, with zero budget, had moved the needle. But more was needed and Disney needed to be able to take this "gift" and do something with it.

Meanwhile, though, for every person who saw the fan trailer online or read about the favorable tweets on an entertainment blog, there were 100 potential moviegoers receiving an advertising or publicity impression that was either the "more of the same" movie trailers from Disney, or "John Carter will bomb" articles in the press.

The sad truth was that *John Carter* needed to find 4-5 million paying fans on opening weekend to keep from being labeled a failure and at this point, with the release so near, the positive "buzzlet" that was rippling through blogs and social media circles was being swamped by mainstream negativity.

Too little too late.

We were trying to stem a tsunami with a teacup.

On February 27, as the lights went down at the opening of the Hero Complex screening of *John Carter* in Burbank, I experienced an emotional moment as I absorbed the reality that after playing privately in my head for forty years, Edgar Rice Burroughs' world of Barsoom, and characters like John Carter, Dejah Thoris, Woola, and Tars Tarkas were about to be revealed onscreen. There was something very personal about my relationship with Burroughs, his characters, and his world, and I'm nor ashamed to admit that I was brought to tears by a mixture of anticipation, poignancy, and pride at finally seeing my boyhood dreamworld come alive on screen.

Barsoom, as drawn by Edgar Rice Burroughs, becomes more than a setting -- it becomes a character. As John Carter, for the love of "the incomparable" Dejah Thoris, finds himself in a position very much like King Arthur to gradually unite the warring factions of all the planet's cultures, Barsoom becomes an otherworldly Camelot -- a place of dreams, of honor, and of possibilities. I am convinced that it is for this reason - this deeply emotional context - that dreamers like Carl Sagan and Ray Bradbury both spoke of their own dreams of going "home to Barsoom."

Now it was here, realized on screen, after 100 years of existing in the imaginations of so many.

The movie began to play.

I was aware in advance of certain of the strategies that Stanton had employed, so I was not surprised at the prologue on Barsoom even though in the novels, Burroughs had carefully revealed Barsoom to the reader only through John Carter's eyes, a technique which caused the exposition to be doled out in manageable bites rather than all at once.

I found the prologue easy enough to follow but wondered what the takeaway would be for audiences unfamiliar with the world being depicted -- would it be confusing to them? But the Barsoomian prologue was over quickly, and then it was on to John Carter in New York City sending a telegram to the young Edgar Rice Burroughs, then young Burroughs arriving at Carter's estate only to find his uncle dead, and then, seven minutes into the story, it was on to the "real story of John Carter, thirteen years earlier in Arizona, just prior to being transported to Mars.

Three beginnings, I thought, seemed a bit dangerous: Barsoom prologue, ERB frame story, then Carter in Arizona. But I found the opening captivating and when, fourteen minutes in, Carter awoke on Mars and began his comical attempts to adapt to the lower gravity there, I sat back and prepared to enjoy, for the first time in cinema, the thrilling ride of an Edgar Rice Burroughs novel brought to life on screen.

But it didn't quite turn out as expected.

It was a thrilling ride -- no question about that. But the experience was not quite the uniquely *Burroughsian* ride I was expecting. I would later describe it as being as if I had gone to my hometown after decades away and made a pilgrimage to the Italian restaurant I had loved as a child. The restaurant was still there; it looked the same, the name was the same. But a new chef had taken over and the cuisine was no longer homestyle Italian, but a very delightful modern fusion cuisine, which tasted great and was presented beautifully -- but left you wondering: "Where's my lasagna?"

While this was a mild disappointment as a fan, as a film-maker I was conscious of how much Stanton did retain of the original, and I found myself being mostly grateful for that. I had read most of the screenplays of the previous *John Carter of Mars* attempts, and I felt that even though this one had substantial changes, it was the closest of them all in its faithfulness to the basic setup of getting John Carter to Barsoom, and the world he finds when he gets there. The "world build" in particular was faithful -- Helium, Zodanga, Tharks and Red Martians, airships and flyers, swords and radium pistols--it was all there, lovingly rendered.[269]

As a devotee of the books, I knew that my viewing experience was skewed by the fact that at each step of the way, particularly on a first viewing, I found myself automatically comparing what was on the screen to the book, a process that interfered with the normal psychology of watching a movie. I understood this "background static" problem, and accepted it, and deferred my final judgment on the movie -- it would take a number of viewings to reach a point where I could simply go on the journey Stanton was offering, without constantly referencing the somewhat different journey that Burroughs had implanted in my mind. Of all the changes, the two that had the most profound effect for me were the conversion of John Carter's character from knight errant to damaged-goods-hero-in-need-of-redemption, and related to that - the use of a technology (Thern medallion) to transport Carter to Mars. The latter was more than the layering of a scientific element -- it changed a major dynamic of the story because John Carter, rather than having been spiritually transported to Mars to begin a new life there that he seemed somehow destined for, had instead been in essence kidnapped to Mars and placed there with a piece of technology in his hand that could, if he learned how to use it, return him to Earth. This created major shifts in John Carter's relationship to Barsoom; his motivation; and his goal as he understood it for much of the film

There was much to think about .

But vastly more important in my view than my personal reaction to the movie was -- how would audiences and critics react? The audience at the Hero Complex screening seemed to genuinely enjoy it, and when afterwards Mark Linthicum and I taped exiting viewer comments we had no trouble finding strongly positive reactions. [270]

But was it strongly favorable enough?

---

[269] The conversion of Zodanga into a mobile city was a deviation, and one which I thought must have been suggested by the fact that Burroughs, who went so far as to give latitude and longitude coordinates for the city states of Barsoom, had inadvertently given two different locations for Zodanga in two different books.

[270] http://www.youtube.com/watch?v=orGXOMqi8yo

It was now twelve days until the release; Disney had essentially thrown in the towel at the idea of trying to better explain the movie in trailers and TV spots, and was now just using fifteen second "Critics" spots, urging viewers to believe that the critics loved the movie.

Would they?

For a typical, well-promoted action adventure blockbuster, a middling critics response and B+ Cinemascore viewer response would be enough, coupled with strong promotion, to generate a box office success.

Sadly, the elements were arranged differently for *John Carter*.

The weak promotion had left the film in a situation where it needed an absolute home run from Andrew Stanton to have a chance.

Stanton had hit two home runs previously. *Finding Nemo* and *Wall-E* had been huge hits with both critics and fans. At Rotten Tomatoes, *Finding Nemo* had scored an astonishing 99% critics rating and 81% audience rating, and *Wall-E* had scored 96% with critics and 89% with audiences.[271]

The only hope for *John Carter* was for him to hit another home run.

Having just seen the movie, I just wasn't sure whether he'd pulled it off. It was good -- but a home run? It was hard to tell.

As the Hero Complex screening and Q and A with Andrew Stanton came to a close, I watched as fans swarmed the director and Disney handlers tried to get him through the crowd and out of the theater. I realized that Stanton's "I'll stick around to find you" was about to get overwhelmed by reality, and was on the verge of exiting when Ryan Stankevich from Disney spotted me and said hello. I mentioned to her that I'd gotten an email from Stanton saying he'd like to meet me after the screening. Ryan pushed through the crowd, calling out to Stanton that "Michael Sellers is here." For a moment I was afraid he wouldn't

---

[271] Rotten Tomatoes Staff, "Finding Nemo", *Rotten Tomatoes*, Accessed 7 Sep 2012, <http://www.rottentomatoes.com/m/finding_nemo/>; Rotten Tomatoes Staff, "Wall-E," *Rotten Tomatoes*, Accessed 7 Sep 2012 <http://www.rottentomatoes.com/m/wall_e/>.

recognize the name, but he did recognize it and immediately broke away to greet me.

In the conversation that followed, Stanton -- who seemed in no hurry -- thanked me and the fans and said, "you're the only ones who've figured out what the DNA of the film is and gotten it into a trailer." He asked if there were additional trailers in the works. I admitted that it was difficult, due to the paucity of available materials but said I would try to come up with more. "Get me anything you can and I'll tweet it and get Favreau to tweet it and we'll get it out there. This really helps."[272]

I promised to give it my best shot.

The Disney handlers hustled Stanton off, and I was left wondering how we could possibly do another trailer, given that we had already used up almost all of the available material.

Still, it felt a little bit like being "on the team."

It was, as my father used to say, "better than a poke in the eye with a sharp stick."

---

[272] Jon Favreau, who was the last director attached to direct the failed Paramount version of *John Carter of Mars*, was a staunch ally of the project and a 'Twitter Hound" with more than 1.5 million followers.

THE CRITICS WEIGH IN

The critical response to *John Carter* unfolded in several phases, beginning with the partial lifting of the embargo on February 21 that allowed journalists who had attended Disney-sponsored advance screenings to tweet brief comments while stopping short of publishing actual reviews.

Coming as it did on the same day that articles such as The Daily Beast's "Disney's Quarter Billion Dollar Movie Fiasco," the mostly favorable tweets coming mainly from sci-fi oriented or second tier critics were a welcome injection of positivity into the poisonously negative broth that was the media environment for *John Carter* at that point.[273]

By February 26, Oscar Sunday, Disney had collected enough tweeted accolades to be able to release its first "critics" spot at the end of the Oscar pre-show.

---

[273] Chris Lee, "'John Carter': Disney's Quarter-Billion-Dollar Movie Fiasco," *The Daily Beast*, 21 Feb 2012, 7 Sep 2012 <http://www.thedailybeast.com/articles/2012/02/21/john-carter-disney-s-quarter-billion-dollar-movie-fiasco.html>.

But it was on March 2, the date the embargo for full interviews was lifted, that the first wave of actual reviews hit and the verdict with the first 10 reviews in: 80% "Fresh", 20% "Rotten." From *Rotten Tomatoes*: [274]

FRESH

Total Film: A handsome new sci-fi adventure that feels rather familiar.

IGN: Disney's adaptation of Edgar Rice Burroughs' *A Princess of Mars* knocks it out of this world.

Badass Digest: It took a hundred years to get on screen, but Edgar Rice Burroughs' classic pulp story gets there right... mostly.

Digital Spy: When John Carter moves up the gears it's an accomplished blockbuster packed with pulse-racing action.

Matt's Movie Reviews: Epic in scope and stunning in imagery, John Carter is an old school blockbuster....

WhatCulture: Lovingly made pulp fantasy

HitFix: John Carter does pulp fiction right and on a grand scale

SFX: Lynn Collins' feisty Dejah Thoris is the best sci-fi kick-ass princess since Princess Leia

ROTTEN

Quickflix: An Underwhelming Epic

Fan the Fire: The story veers between interesting, boring, and borderline incomprehensible.

Reading the first batch of reviews, I was concerned. There was nothing wrong on the surface with an 80% critics rating -- but these were only first reviews, the ones from minor reviewers and/or those with a special emphasis on sci-fi or geek culture films. Plus, he positive reviews were positive enough to be graded "Fresh" - but they weren't unqualified raves.

True, the positive reviews did contain at least some statements of unbridled enthusiasm: "Some of the stuff that Stanton pulls off in *John Carter* is mind-blowing," enthused *Badass Digest's* Devin Faraci, "There

---

[274] Michael D. Sellers, "John Carter "Rotten Tomatoes" rating currently at 80% "Fresh","*The John Carter Files*, 2 Mar 2012, 7 Sep 2012 <http://thejohncarterfiles.com/2012/03/john-carter-rotten-tomatoes-rating-currently-at-80-fresh/>.

are a few sequences that feel simply classic, like we'll be referring to them for years to come. There's one scene, where John Carter stands alone (well, with Woola) against a rampaging army of nine foot tall, four armed Tharks, that is an all-timer."

Drew McWeeney at *Hitfix* offered praise of the CGI Tharks: "The Tharks, led here by Tars Tarkas (Willem Dafoe), are compelling creations. By a few scenes into their time onscreen, I stopped thinking about the technical trick involved in bringing them to life and simply accepted them as real."[275]

More importantly, the negative reviews went straight to the issues that had worried me after his first viewing on February 27, and a second viewing that same day, March 2, at a screening for Edgar Rice Burroughs Inc and a group of Burroughs fans.

At *Quickflix*, Simon Maraudo wrote:[276]

> *John Carter*, for all of its pricey spectacle, is a mostly impenetrable picture unlikely to please children nor adults. .... This film tells of two human-ish tribes at war on Mars (or, as they call it, Barsoom). When the leader of the Zodanga tribe, Sab Than, (Dominic West) is gifted with a powerful ray by the planet's omnipotent watcher (Mark Strong), he begins to wipe out the people of Helium indiscriminately, much to the chagrin of their princess Dejah (Lynn Collins). Meanwhile, the CGI Martians of Thark keep to themselves, betting on which army will ultimately prove victorious, but hoping they'll just wipe one another out. If you're keeping up, I commend you.
>
> The script, penned by Stanton, Mark Andrews, and author Michael Chabon, does not ably construct this universe (a framing device involving a young Edgar Rice Burroughs pays off in the end, but only further confuses us in the beginning). So much time is spent explaining the lay of the land, little is left to craft memorable characters, or involve us in the struggle, or show us why it might be a bad thing for Sab Than to rule Barsoom (for all the to-ing and fro-ing we do across the planet, we don't much get to see how

---

[275] Drew McWeeny, "Review: 'John Carter' does pulp science-fiction right and on a grand scale," *Hitfix*, 2 Mar 2012, 7 Sep 2012 <http://www.hitfix.com/blogs/motion-captured/posts/review-john-carter-does-pulp-science-fiction-right-and-on-a-grand-scale>.

[276] Simon Miraudo, "Barsoom brawl -- John Carter Review," *Quickflix*, 2 Mar 2012, 7 Sep 2012 <http://blog.quickflix.com.au/2012/03/02/barsoom-brawl-john-carter-review/>.

the place actually works, or what the people living there even do. See also: *Thor*). Kitsch is likable as a reluctant hero, and Collins works her Princess Leia shtick nicely, but the antagonists are a non-entity.

However, once all the confusion regarding names and locations in the first half fades away, we are treated to a series of fairly thrilling action sequences. The film's extravagant $250 million budget *can* be seen on the screen in the mostly sumptuous special effects. Who knows? Perhaps the sequel – if we ever get there – will fill in the gaps and expand on John Carter's legend now all the expositional heavy-lifting has been done. But is that an acceptable excuse for an epic to be *this* underwhelming?

The good news -- it wasn't completely negative. But the charge that the film's exposition heavy opening was confusing was not unexpected, and doubtless was going to become a theme. And indeed, the other hostile review (which upon a full reading revealed itself to be mixed-negative), delivered a strong punch to the gut of the film along the same lines:[277]

Amidst the CGI environments and constant plot machinations, the story veers between interesting, boring and borderline incomprehensible. The latter instances usually involve Mark Strong's staring villain Matai Shang, whose presence is given almost no context until right near the end, at which point his explanations are watery at best.

Meanwhile, reviews aside -- the drumbeat of negativity in the journalistic articles was increasing. Bloomberg News, for example, ran with: "Disney Hopes 'John Carter' doesn't become 'John Doe.'[278] Dozens of other similar articles were appearing daily.

Steadily over the next few days, the critics had their say, and on Rotten Tomatoes the rating began a steady decline. By March 4, it was at 72%; March 5 it was 69%, and by March 7 it was flirting with dropping below the 60% threshold, after which it would no longer bear the "fresh" rating, and would be labeled rotten.

---

[277] Martin Roberts, "Film Review: John Carter," *Fan The Fire*, 2 Mar 2012, 7 Sep 2012 <http://fanthefiremagazine.com/blog/film/film-review-john-carter/>.

[278] Bloomberg Staff, "Disney Hopes 'John Carter' Doesn't Become 'John Doe'," *Bloomberg Businessweek*, 2 Mar 2012, 7 Sep 2012 <http://www.businessweek.com/news/2012-03-02/disney-hopes-john-carter-doesn-t-become-john-doe>.

Under normal circumstances, not obtaining spectacular reviews would not be a crippling outcome for a movie such as *John Carter.*

The Lorax, which opened surprisingly strong on March 2 at $70.2M (tracking had it opening at $45-50M) did so with a 56% critics rating, making it "Rotten", and an audience rating of only 68% -- clear evidence of a strong and successful marketing campaign.[279]

But nothing about the *John Carter* situation was "normal." It had cost a whopping $350M to make and market; it was the target of relentless sniping from multiple quarters; it was saddled with an extraordinarily weak marketing campaign, and as a result of all this, the stakes were raised and the critics' reaction was more important than it would otherwise have been.

On March 4, Disney played one last card -- releasing the first 10 minutes of the movie (minus the opening Mars prologue) on the internet. The first comments were largely favorable -- far more so than had been the case for any of the trailers. But coming as late as it did, and being available only online, unless it went massively viral it was not going to be a game-changer.

Meanwhile, there was now a new issue that was generally being viewed as yet another hurdle -- *The Lorax* was over-performing so much that it now seemed likely that *John Carter*, tentpole epic with a $250M budget, would not even win its opening weekend.

The Lorax had opened at $70.2M, well above tracking which had it at 45-50M, and a 40% dropoff would mean it would book $42.2M on its second weekend and it looked highly unlikely that *John Carter* could beat that. While all cards had been played -- there was one final factor that might just save *John Carter*: red hot overall box office.

For the year, Box Office Gross was running 16% ahead of same period 2011 and there had been at least three major cases of tracking being way off -- *The Lorax*, which tracked at $45M and did $70.2M, *Safe House* with Denzel Washington which tracked in the low 20's and opened

---

[279] Rotten Tomatoes Staff, "Dr. Seuss' The Lorax," Rotten Tomatoes, Accessed 7 Sep 2012 <http://www.rottentomatoes.com/m/the_lorax/>.

at $40.1M, and *The Vow* which tracked in the low 20's and opened at $41.2M.

Was it possible that all of the reports, all of the analysis, even the gut feel of it all would turn out to be wrong and *John Carter* would somehow fool everyone and over-perform versus the tracking as those three films had? That would mean an opening as high as $50M if it doubled the tracking as *Safe House* and *The Vow* had.

Was there reason to believe it could happen?

Was there still a best case outcome that would keep *John Carter* from being pronounced DOA?

As the reviews poured in, I watched the "Fresh" rating plummet and realized there was going to be no *deus ex machina* in the form of critics raves to overcome the campaign shortfall. I held to the hope that it would open at $40M which, with legs, would give it an outside chance of making it to $150M domestically -- then if foreign was huge, it could still reach $500M.

I looked at all the factors-- tracking as predicted by the tracking polls; recent history of tracking polls missing low (*The Lorax*, *Safe House*, *The Vow*); macro factors (Box Office running 16% ahead of last year); and X factors that might not be being captured by the analysis.

What X Factors?

Disney Moms and Dads -- were they being captured by the tracking or online monitoring? Could they give it a boost?

Answer: "yes" to the tracking, which was old technology, calling selected likely filmgoers which would probably encompass the Disney moms, and "no" to online buzz -- maybe the busy moms weren't as active on the internet as other segments, so they might be under-represented. They could boost it by a few million.

What about Boomer ERB fans -- men (and women) now in their 50's and up, who had discovered ERB via the Ace and Ballantine paperback reprints in the sixties? They might not be showing up either in the online monitoring or the tracking polls. Another booster of a few million.

And finally there was the late buzz -- the wavelet of positive word of mouth that had been building online since the fan trailer and tweet reviews had started having an impact on February 21. Was there enough there to move the needle? Or was it too little, too late?

In response to Stanton asking for more "underground trailers", Mark Linthicum and I had set out to cut another trailer, but it wasn't easy. Expectations were high -- and yet we only had access to the materials that Disney had released, and all of those materials had sound and image tied together so we were stuck not only with the limited images, but if we cut a standard trailer we would have to live with the soundtrack that was already attached to each piece of film. This had been alright for the first trailer because that one was basically a re-arrangement of many different Disney pieces. Having done that once, doing it again would be repetitive.

We tried a number of approaches, but none seemed to really offer anything substantially different enough from what was out there, or from what we had already released, to warrant releasing.

Almost out of ideas, we decided to try something that would not be, precisely, a trailer, but would simulate an Opening Titles sequence that would set up the "Heritage" of the film, and then offer an images-and-music-only trailer flowing out of the opening titles.

For the music bed we chose Nick Ingram's 'Mars' -- the track that had been used in the un-aired second half of the Super Bowl TV Spot, and in the sizzle reel cut by Erik Jessen, one of the film's editors, which had been released by Disney on February 24. The music began with a very slow, emotionally laden melody and my thought was to have the beginning of the trailer play like an opening title credit sequence with cards that laid down the unique heritage of the film that was about to follow. We also inserted images from the original artwork for the first book publication of *John Carter*. As the evocative, melodic strings played, the cards came up:

> IN 1912 EDGAR RICE BURROUGHS GAVE US THE GIFT OF MODERN SCIENCE FICTION.
>
> HIS STORY OF A VIRGINIA CAVALRY OFFICER TRANSPORTED TO MARS .....

......HAS INSPIRED THE GREAT SCIENTISTS AND STORYTELLERS OF OUR TIME

CARL SAGAN   JAMES CAMERON   ARTHUR CLARKE   STEVEN SPIELBERG   RAY BRADBURY   GEORGE LUCAS JANE GOODALL JERRY SIEGEL

WALT DISNEY PICTURES PRESENTS

ON THE 100TH ANNIVERSARY OF "*A PRINCESS OF MARS*"

A FILM BY ANDREW STANTON

BASED ON THE VISIONARY NOVEL BY EDGAR RICE BURROUGHS

The cards laid out beautifully, and they created just the right mood for the first shot, the iconic shot of a flyer approaching, with Helium in the background. It was a shot that had been used in all the trailers, but watching it come up after reading the cards that preceded it created -- at least for me -- a completely different reaction. It seemed epic, special, laden with meaning because of its origins and the impact it had had over the years.[280]

But there was no denying the fact that it took 45 seconds to get to that first image from the film. No one to my knowledge had ever made a trailer that took that long to get to the visuals from the movie.

---

[280] Michael D. Sellers, "John Carter Fan Trailer 2 "Heritage"," *Youtube JohnCarterFiles Channel*, 2 Mar 2012, 7 Sep 2012 <http://youtu.be/OzPVYy7LHIo>.

The remainder of the trailer used images and music only, no dialogue or sound effects, and with the help of the powerful, emotional orchestral score, laid out enough of the story to create, we hoped, intrigue.

It wasn't exactly a trailer -- but it was true to the underlying marketing narrative that I felt strongly had been missed, and was "from the heart" for sure. Plus it was all we had. And so we released it on March 2, publishing it on YouTube and sending it along to Andrew Stanton. Jack Scanlan, who had become the volunteer publicist for the #GoBarsoom Digital Grassroots Media Campaign, put it out to key outlets who had covered the first trailer.[281]

While it didn't have the immediate impact of the first trailer -- it did get coverage in over 200 outlets and garnered six figure views. In fact, in the final week prior to release, the two fan trailers together managed to almost as many views as the official trailer.

We had given it our best shot.

After putting out the second trailer, there was little I could do in the final days except find positive reviews and post links to them. And there were plenty of positive reviews coming in.

> *Houston Chronicle:* "Thrilling John Carter well worth the wait."
>
> *MSN:* "...first movie of it's kind in a very long time and I'd willingly sit through it again for a second or even third time."
>
> *Village Voice:* "A lively, visually crafty pleasure."
>
> *View London:* Intelligent script, strong characters...superb performances."
>
> *Miami Herald:* "Ridiculously fun!"
>
> *Salt Lake Tribune:* "A Rousing Sci-Fi epic."

But just as surely as there were positive reviews in abundance, so too were their negative ones and as the release date approached, the overall critics ratings continued to fall -- not a nose dive, to be sure, but a gradual slide. On March 8, the day before the release, it dipped into "Rotten" territory at 58%.   Worse -- it was the "Top Critics" who were savaging the film.

> *Variety's Peter Debruge (March 6)* : To watch John Carter is to wonder where in this jumbled space opera one might find the intuitive sense of wonderment and awe Stanton brought to Finding Nemo and Wall-E.

> *New York Post's Lou Loumenick (March 7):* "It's hard to care about anything going on in this shapeless would-be franchise, which lurches from scene to scene without building any real excitement."

> *Arizona Republic's Bill Goodykoontz (March 7)* : Somehow, despite that boatload of talent, the movie never really comes together.

> *EW's Owen Glieberman (March 7):* "Nothing in John Carter really works, since everything in the movie has been done so many times before, and so much better.

> *AP's Christy Lemire (March7):* "Yes there's life on Mars and it's deadly dull."

> *Salon's Andrew O'Hehir (March 7):* "You can feel Stanton struggling to bring the confidence, wit and style of "Wall'E" and "Finding Nemo" to bear upon this leviathan, but he can't quite pull it off.

> *Chicago Tribune's Michael Philips (March 8):* " The major problem here is one of rooting interest. I hate to sound like a mogul, or a focus group ho, but at the center of this picture is a flat, inexpressive protagonist played by a flat, inexpressive actor."

Then, miraculously it seemed, on March 8, Global Financial News Service predicted a $57M opening. Could it possibly be true? By the end of the day on March 8, all of the predictions were in, and they ranged from the $57M from Global Financial News, to the LA Times at $22.5M.

57.0 | RTT NASDAQ
38.9 | Box Office Mojo
29.5 | Screen Crave
30.0 | Variety
30.0 | Hollywood Reporter
29.0 | Coming Soon.net
26.0 | Entertainment Wkly
25.0 | Boxoffice.com
25.0 | LA Times

Meanwhile, the reviews continued to come in. Overall, the critic's rating was dropping but not precipitously. The complaints from the top critics were by far the most strident:

> *New Yorker's David Denby:* "A mess."[282]

> *Washington Posts's Ann Hornaday (March 8)* "Gets off to such an incoherent start that it takes almost the entire, interminable two-hour-plus running time to catch up."[283]

> *Newark Star-Ledger's Stephen Whitty:* "Whenever the fighting stops and two people have to stand and talk, all the air goes out of everything. Suddenly, it feels as if we're in an empty theater, watching a dusty old sword-and-sandal epic."[284]

And:

> *LA Times Betsy Sharkey:* "Yep, everything you're heard is true. The movies is a big-budget bomb. The visuals are great, but the storytelling is stale and the leads are lost."[285]

Reading the reviews, I was struck by how many of the naysayers made reference, as the LA Times did, to the narrative of failure that had predicted the film would be an overpriced bomb -- it was as if there was a merging of popular chatter and serious criticism.

What difference did the chatter about the budget make to a reviewer?

Theoretically none. But there it was, again and again on the page, references that seemed to support the conclusion that the reviews were being influenced by the toxic anti-hype that had been circulating.

---

[282] David Denby, "John Carter Review", New Yorker, 9 Mar 2012, 5 Sep 2012 <http://www.newyorker.com/arts/reviews/film/john_carter_stanton>.

[283] Ann Hornaday, "John Carter Review," Washington Post, 9 Mar 2012, 4 Sep 2012 <http://www.washingtonpost.com/gog/movies/john-carter,1170714/critic-review.html>.

[284] Stephen Whitty, "John Carter Review," Newark Star Ledger, 9 Mar 2012, 5 Sep 2012 <http://www.nj.com/entertainment/movies/index.ssf/2012/03/john_carter_movie_review.html.

[285] Betsy Sharkey, "John Carter Review," Los Angeles Times, 9 Mar 2012, 5 Sep 2012 <http://www.latimes.com/entertainment/news/movies/la-et-john-carter-20120309,0,136941.story>.

Even so, it was by no means all complaints. In fact if anything was becoming apparent, it was that *John Carter* was polarizing -- critics had strong feelings in both directions.

> *Mania.com's Rob Vaux:* "John Carter is an absolute romp."[286]

> *Nerdist's Luke Y. Thompson:* "John Carter is a science-fiction epic worth cheering, one where however much they spent, it all went to throw amazingly huge and awesome things onscreen in the service of a story that some are actually calling too complicated."[287]

> *St. Louis Post Dispatch's Mathew DeKinder:* "This is an old-fashioned movie told with cutting-edge technology and while it's easy to be cynical...it is refreshing to see a movie that approaches its subject with an authentic, wide-eyed sense of wonder."[288]

> *Film School Rejects' Robert Levin:* "Visionary and philosophical, with the sort of complex allusions to death, immortality, and the destruction of civilizations that you don't expect from a $250M film."[289]

As March 8 ended, I sat with my laptop, watching for a hoped-for surge in positive internet chatter that never came. If there was going to be a box office miracle the next day, it wasn't going to come from social media users. I was pretty sure there wasn't going to be a miracle.

---

[286] Rob Vaux, "John Carter Review," Mania.com, 9 Mar 2012 4 Nov 2012 <http://www.mania.com/mania-review-john-carter_article_132346.html>.

[287] Luke Y. Thompson, "John Carter Sends a Red Stater to the Red Planet", *Nerdist*, 9 Mar 2012, 4 Nov 2012 <http://www.nerdist.com/2012/03/lyt-review-john-carter-sends-a-red-stater-to-the-red-planet/>.

[288] Matthew DeKinder, "John Carter: Sci-Fi Fun From the Age of Pulp" 9 Mar 2012, 4 Nov 2012 <http://www.stltoday.com/suburban-journals/illinois/life/matdekinder/review-john-carter-sci-fi-fun-from-age-of-pulp/article_b7c10fa2-1853-5d81-aa0c-db49dd80a5cd.html>

[289] Robert Levin, "Box Office Be Damned, John Carter is a Cinematic Wonder," Film School Rejects, 9 Mar 2012, 5 Nov 2012 <http://www.filmschoolrejects.com/reviews/review-box-office-be-damned-john-carter-is-a-cinematic-wonder-rlevi.php>.

Opening Day

Almost 100 years to the day after *Under the Moons of Mars* had first appeared in *All-Story* magazine, the long delayed journey of Edgar Rice Burroughs' original classic made its way to cinema screens in the United States and 58 countries around the world.

For Andrew Stanton, the final weeks of the promotional campaign had been alternately exhilarating and exhausting. There had been the press junkets in mid February in Arizona and New York, followed by the premiere of the movie on February 21. After a few quick days at home in Mill Valley north of San Francisco, he returned to Los Angeles on February 25 for Oscar weekend. He attended the Oscars on February 26, then on the 27th visited the set of *Star Trek 2* before attending the Hero Complex *John Carter* Screening in Burbank and doing a Q and A there. On February 28th he gave a TED talk, about which he remarked : *"I've never rehearsed so much for so little face time since my wedding."* Then it was off to London for more press and the London premiere, then Moscow for more press and a premiere. Exhausted, he flew back to Mill Valley on the 6th and settled in to wait, watch, and see what happened.

He was buoyed by a steady stream of effusively favorable reviews that friends and *Twitter* followers sent him. But he couldn't help but be aware of the negative reviews that were out there too, and he knew that *John Carter* was not going to be the kind of love fest with critics that *Finding Nemo* and *Wall-E* had had been.

'Carter, as he referred to the movie, was different than those two. Some people just didn't get it.

Clearly there were those -- critics and fans alike, who deeply loved the movie. The word of mouth screenings over the last two weeks prior to release had already generated fans who had seen the film 2 or more times prior to opening day and were shouting about it on the internet in every way they could. Stanton's *Twitter* feed was filled with tweets from fans and critics which Stanton retweeted:[290]

> @gpaulwills: "Loved John Carter! Fantastic job! I'll be sharing the film with my kids someday. Felt like a 10 year old again!"
>
> @fisherbaird: Spread the word, people of Earth. Just saw John Carter and it's crazy goddamn good. Enter-effing-taining from beginning to end.
>
> @damonlindelof: Why is everyone so surprised JOHN CARTER is totally awesome? I went with high expectations and they were SURPASSED. Epic. Fun. SEE IT.
>
> @halhickel: just got out of the most gloriously realized pulp science fantasy I've ever seen. And a hell of a good time to boot. JCM!
>
> @solat78: just watched JC. My dad would have loved it! Thx u 4 making the movie he always wanted. Miss u dad!
>
> @dannytrs: Just saw JC. Thanks to you we can no longer say "They don't make 'em like they used to, anymore
>
> @jfangsky: Saw JOHN CARTER. Mind blown. See it on the big screen. Then see it again. In awe of @andrewstanton 's craftsmanship.

Then the day finally came.

Would the experts be right -- *John Carter* would tank? Or would there be a surprise?

---

[290] Andrew Stanton Official Twitter, "Andrew Stanton @andrewstanton", 8 Oct 2009, 7 Sep 2012 <http://twitter.com/andrewstanton>.

FRIDAY, MARCH 9, 2012

The day began at midnight and the reports from midnight screenings weren't good. As usual Nikki Finke in full-on "*toldja*" mode at *Deadline.com* led the way reporting the box office demise:[291]

> *FRIDAY 8:30 AM:* The studio is expecting only $24M-$30M despite a whopping budget of $250M, and this start of $500K midnights is weak considering that cost. Rival studios tell me that foreign numbers are starting out soft as well. Disney is uncharacteristically mum despite planning a gigantic worldwide day-and-date push for *John Carter* with all the frills no matter how dismal its prospects look. All in, this could mean a $100M writeoff for the Walt Disney Co. Box office for this bomb is making rival studios just a little too gleeful considering that probably 1,000 of their Hollywood brethren were gainfully employed during a dismal economy.

In the case of *John Carter*, the weak midnight showing figure could only presage that the day would not hold a big favorable surprise for the film. Meanwhile, Finke continued her updates:

> *UPDATE 8:50 AM:* Disney just told me that *John Carter* has made $13M so far overseas with the biggest news from 3D sci-fi-loving Russia where the movie had the highest opening day in history with $6.5M. The studio is reporting solid starts in Asian markets. But rival studios are warning me of soft starts in Europe.

> *2ND UPDATE, 9:15 AM:* Disney wants me to know that *The Avengers* trailer that broke records online last week is going up on *John Carter* in theaters this weekend. It's a blatant attempt to use the enormous anticipation for the Marvel movie to pump up what box office predictions say are the sagging fortunes of *Finding Nemo* and *Wall-E* director Andrew Stanton's live action turkey. *John Carter*'s biggest problems, aside from the fact that no women want to see it, is its inability to attract young males — which is Marvel's sweet spot.

> *4TH UPDATE, FRIDAY 5:30 PM:* Nothing changed. My sources are still predicting box office results for Walt Disney Studios' *John Carter* (playing in 3,749 theaters) around $9.5M to $11M today and $27.5M to $33M for the weekend. For a smaller budget film, that

---

[291] Nikki Finke, "101.2M Worldwide: But 'John Carter's $30.6M Weak Domestic Weekend Lags #1 'The Lorax'; Eddie Murphy Bombs Again," Deadline Hollywood, 9 Mar 2012, 7 Sep 2012 <http://www.deadline.com/2012/03/john-carter-weak-500k-midnight-shows/ >.

would be considered a good opening — but not one costing $250+M.

For most of professional Hollywood, by the end of the day on Friday the jury on *John Carter* had come in. *Deadline* and *Box Office Mojo* were reporting a Friday gross of $9.8M which projected to a weekend total in the $25-30M range that had been widely predicted. That was enough to spell doom for the film, even if it achieved the good (but not spectacular) word of mouth that early audience tracking showed it could expect.

Was there anything left to hope for?

Would there be a word of mouth miracle?

On Saturday, *John Carter* received an unexpected bump up to $12M that even Nikki Finke had to acknowledge reflected better than expected word of mouth. In her Sunday morning update she wrote:[292]

> *John Carter* finished a feeble #2 considering its whopping $250+M cost. Friday's domestic box office numbers for director Andrew Stanton's actioner came in even weaker than predicted but rival studios tell me the loincloth epic experienced an unexpected double-digit bounce on Saturday. Clearly word of mouth, like the 'B+' CinemaScore from audiences, is helping although reviews were decidedly mixed.
>
> To summarize: this flop is the result of a studio trying to indulge Pixar... Of an arrogant director who ignored everybody's warnings that he was making a film too faithful to Edgar Rice Burroughs's first novel in the Barsoom series *A Princess of Mars*... Of the failure of Dick Cook, and Rich Ross, and Bob Iger to rein in Stanton's excessive ego or pull the plug on the movie's bloated budget ... Of really rotten marketing that failed to explain the significance or scope of the film's Civil War-to-Mars story and character arcs and instead made the 3D movie look way as generic as its eventual title... Disagree all you want, but Hollywood is telling me that competent marketing could have drawn in women with the love story, or attracted younger males who weren't fanboys of the source material. Instead the campaign was as rigid and confusing as the movie itself, not to mention that 'Before *Star*

---

[292] Nikki Finke, "$101.2M Worldwide: But 'John Carter's $30.6M Weak Domestic Weekend Lags #1 'The Lorax'; Eddie Murphy Bombs Again," Deadline Hollywood, 11 Mar 2012, 7 Sep 2012 <http://www.deadline.com/2012/03/john-carter-weak-500k-midnight-shows/>.

Wars, Before *Avatar* tag line should have come at the <u>start</u> and not at the finish.

Although the US media was obsessed with the domestic gross, dollars were dollars and the foreign numbers were far from a disaster. While *John Carter* grossed only $30.2M in the US, it took in $70.6M internationally in 58 countries representing 80% of the international market. As weak as the US opening was, it was abundantly clear that JC was no "Mars Needs Moms", which took in $39M total worldwide for its entire run.

The *Hollywood Reporter* acknowledged as much, first reporting that the film had come nowhere near the type of box office that it needed, given its budget, but adding:[293]

> The good news for Disney was that *John Carter* received a B+ CinemaScore and was up 25 percent on Saturday, reflecting positive buzz. The film played best to older fanboys, but needed an equally strong showing from younger males. On Saturday, families turned out as well, making up 20 percent of the audience.

> Nearly 60 percent of the audience was over the age of 25, according to exit polls conducted by Disney, while 64 percent of those buying tickets were males....

> Internationally, *John Carter*--headlining Taylor Kitsch--opened particularly strong in Russia, grossing roughly $17 million, and did good business in Asia as well. It's European performance was mixed.

Still, no matter what the window-dressing, the reality was that *John Carter* was now officially labeled a mega-flop.

On Sunday, the same day that most casual box office watchers see the first weekend results, The New York Times' published a lengthy article by Brooks Barnes under a headline that reconfirmed and amplified the flop narrative: "Ishtar Lands on Mars." Other reports followed the same tone, and the buzzards that had been circling for weeks began to feast.

---

[293] Pamela McClintock, "Box Office Report: 'John Carter' Earns Weak $30.6 Mil domestically, $101.2 Mil Globally," *The Hollywood Reporter*, 11 Mar 2012, 7 Sep 2012 <http://www.hollywoodreporter.com/news/box-office-report-john-carter-dr-seuss-lorax-298377>.

For those rooting for the film, it seemed that the pre-ordained flop narrative had played a role in the film's demise.

From Mill Valley, Stanton tweeted bleakly: "Thanks to everyone who ignored the schadenfreude and went to "Carter this weekend. you're the best."[294]

About the same time Stanton tweeted about Schadenfreude, I was writing and posting an article about it: "John Carter and Big Budget Schadenfreude, or How $100M Global Gross in the first 3 days gets Labeled an Iconic Hollywood Flop."[295]

The article attempted, as best I could, to make sense of the psychology behind the gleeful reporting of the demise of the film. Stanton had given heart and soul and five years of his life to the movie; others had worked on it for years and it was clearly a labor of intense, passionate film-making. Why were people so "thrilled and sickened" to watch something like this happen?

I found a quote from James Shenton which seemed to capture some of it:[296]

> There's something oddly satisfying about seeing a big-budget movie flop. Whenever we hear about these ambitious, special effects-laden extravaganzas going down in flames we get an odd feeling of schadenfreude. But why is this? Does it stem from the fact that we feel manipulated, almost exploited, by the movie industry? Perhaps. After all, movie studios make a lot of coin from tweaking our emotions, be it through adrenaline-filled action films or mawkishly tear-jerking weepies. Perhaps the best reason for our guilty pleasure at seeing a big-budget movie flop is the fact that we

---

[294] Andrew Stanton Official Twitter, "Andrew Stanton @andrewstanton", 8 Oct 2009, 7 Sep 2012 <http://twitter.com/andrewstanton>.

[295] Michael D. Sellers, "John Carter and Big Budget Schadenfreude, or how 100M gross in the first 3 days gets instantly labeled an iconic Hollywood flop," *The John Carter Files*, 11 Mar 2012, 7 Sep 2012 <http://thejohncarterfiles.com/2012/03/john-carter-and-big-budget-schadenfreude-or-how-100m-gross-in-the-first-3-days-gets-instantly-labeled-an-iconic-hollywood-flop/>.

[296] James Shenton, "Box Office Flops -- More Than Meets the Eye?," Ezine Articles, Accessed 11 Mar 2012 <http://ezinearticles.com/?Box-Office-Flops---More-Than-Meets-the-Eye?&id=296370>.

feel like we won a battle. We caught Hollywood trying to pull a fast one by releasing a bad movie and trying to hype it anyway — and we weren't fooled. Gotcha. Better luck next time.

Digging deeper, I found a 2007 study by Norman T. Feather entitled: "Envy, Resentment, Schadenfreude, and Sympathy: Reactions to Deserved and Undeserved Achievement and Failure."[297] That study too seemed to suggest that the explosion of glee and lack of empathy related to a sense that justice is achieved by the failure. I wrote:

> The answer, it would seem comes back to the notion that schadenfreude erupts when there is a felt perception that the failure restores balance, that a form of justice is achieved by the failure. In this case, Disney is seen as being properly rewarded for foolishly investing mega-dollars in a questionable property, and then shoving the resultant product down the throats of unwilling potential audience goers with mind-numbing, relentlessly obtuse marketing. To the Schadenfreudist, an epic fail is the only just reward for such epic hubris, and thus the narrative is pre-determined and nothing short of an outright "win" at the box office will derail that narrative.

Still, reflections about Schadenfreude aside, the facts were the facts, and *John Carter* was not going to be the recipient of a box office miracle. Opening weekend had come and gone, and even with $100M in worldwide revenues, the verdict was "flop."   As far as the mainstream was concerned, it was game over for *John Carter*.

But elsewhere, outside the box office obsessed circles in journalism, something was stirring.

John Carter needed 20 million viewers worldwide to see the film on opening weekend, and that hadn't happened. But 10 million *had* seen the film.   And for some of those, the Burroughs-Stanton collaboration was working a certain magic.

Fans were starting to speak.

---

[297] N.T. Feather, "Envy, Resentment, Schadenfreude, and Sympathy: Reactions to Deserved and Undeserved Achievement and Subsequent Failure," SAGE Journals, Accessed 11 Mar 2012 <http://psp.sagepub.com/content/28/7/953.abstract>.

THE FANS GET ORGANIZED

Edgar Rice Burroughs had always forged an emotional connection with readers who responded to his unique blend of wish-fulfillment adventure and imaginative discovery. His influence on creative minds from Bradbury to Cameron is well documented. He was the most read author on the planet during the first half of the 20th century, and his creation Tarzan is arguably the single best known literary character ever created. In the sixties, another generation -- including Steven Spielberg, James Cameron, and George Lucas -- had discovered Burroughs, and been profoundly impacted by him.

Now, at last, Burroughs' Martian universe had been portrayed on cinema screens worldwide and, even if box office results were far below what was needed for the business enterprise of *John Carter* to be labeled a success -- there was, now, a substantial body of filmgoers numbering in the millions who had just been introduced to Burroughs universe via Stanton's interpretation of it, and who liked what they saw.

Precisely because the marketing had not prepared them for what to truly expect from the film, many were caught by surprise at what they discovered onscreen. These newly minted *John Carter* fans went on *Facebook* and *Twitter*, blogs and message boards, and shared what they had experienced:[298]

---

[298] Michael D. Sellers, "Readers Describe How They Discovered John Carter: Some great stories, would love to hear more," The John Carter Files, 19 Jul 2012, 7 Sep 2012 <http://thejohncarterfiles.com/2012/07/readers-describe-how-they-discovered-john-carter-what-about-you/>.

Debbie Banway: I knew nothing of Burroughs before seeing the film, and I had doubts based on the trailers I had seen.....I loved the story. The themes of a reluctant hero haunted by tragedy, a stranger in a strange land with new abilities, and trying to figure just where in the world he was. As the movie progressed I saw loyalty, friendship, honor, and doing the right thing for the right reasons. And the best was yet to come because there was an interplanetary love story that made me swoon. It was unabashedly romantic and such a treat.......

Khanada Taylor: I loved John Carter and I'm beyond anxious to see it again, and again! It is one of those films that you'll hunger for seeing more than once......You really hate when it ends and you don't want to leave those worlds......I think it's a film that needs more than one view to really grasp, since it's so different from anything else...... I fall to my knees and raise my arms to the red planet, begging to go back...

Sparky Santos: I literally knew nothing about ERBs books or the John Carter character prior to viewing the movie. On opening day I convinced a coworker to go see the film with me and we were both blown away. There are few films that have pulled me in, tugged at my heart strings and made me feel excited like JC did. It's kind of hard to describe really. I immediately took friends and family to see it and all enjoyed it......Then I started to see that immense negativity in the press and how it was failing at the box office and I became indignant.

Shari Armstrong: I almost missed the movie because I hadn't seen that it was opening earlier, I hadn't seen any trailers or ads. I saw someone post online that they saw it opening weekend. I took our two older kids (10 and 7) and one of their friends to a matinee. The kids were mesmerized and our 7 year-old son's first word when it was done was simply an excited, "Again!" It was fantastic. So, I started making plans to see it again, this time when my husband could join us. My husband enjoyed it as much as I did. John Carter has something for everyone, action, adventure, humor, friendships, and a non-sappy love story (for someone who doesn't like chick flicks, this is important). I pre-ordered the DVD, and we haven't bought a full price DVD in years, since getting Netflix.

Beyond affection for the movie, the unfolding of events that weekend spurred an additional level of emotional reaction in many of the viewers -- a fan's sense of indignation at what seemed like an injustice. A film which to many seemed to be "special" in so many ways, was having its reputation destroyed before their eyes via a media savaging that, in the view of many fans, took on the characteristics of a lynching.

Erik Jessen was one of the senior members of Eric Zumbrunnen's *John Carter* editorial team. Jessen had been attached to the Paramount *John Carter of Mars* project, so his history on the project was among the longest of any of the crew, and as an editor his engagement with the story was intimate and intense. He knew all the twists and turns that had resulted in the finished product, and he was proud of what had been accomplished. He had also been the author of the "sizzle reel" released to favorable reviews on February 24th.

On the morning of March 14, Jessen started a *Facebook* group with the long and grassroots sounding name: *Take me Back to Barsoom! I Want a John Carter Sequel!* He added fellow crew member Sarah Smith as a fellow administrator, then sent an email to me via *The John Carter Files* "Contact Us" feature:

> Would you mind mentioning a *Facebook* group that I started? It's called Take Me Back to Barsoom! I Want John Carter to Have a Sequel! People can just enter Barsoom or John Carter, and it should pop up. Most of the Emeryville crew are members already. THANKS!

When I received the email, I was intrigued. "Emeryville Crew" referred to Pixar and the production crew of the movie, and in reflecting on it, this seemed like a further evolution of the fan/film-maker alliance that had started with Stanton tweeting about the fan trailer.

Could this amount to something?

I checked out the group on *Facebook* and joined.[299] There were 60 members, and as Jessen had said, most were from the films' "working level" production team. I announced it on *The John Carter Files*:[300]

> John Carter may have encountered serious headwind in its opening weekend at the US Domestic box office (foreign sales were better, though), but that has only served to motivate a group of fans and

---

[299] Erik Jessen, "Take Me Back To Barsoom! I Want a John Carter Sequel!", *Facebook Group*, 14 Mar 2012, 7 Sep 2012 <https://www.facebook.com/groups/backtobarsoom/>.

[300] Michael D. Sellers, "John Carter Fans and Film Crew Form Facebook Group," *The John Carter Files*, March 14, 2012, http://thejohncarterfiles.com/2012/03/john-carter-fans-film-crew-form-take-me-back-to-barsoom-facebook-group-to-lobby-for-a-sequel/

members of the John Carter production team to form a *Facebook* Group called "Take Me Back to Barsoom! I Want John Carter to Have a Sequel!" The purpose of the group — as the name states — is to provide a venue for fans looking for a sequel to Disney's John Carter to let their voices be heard. If you are logged in to *Facebook*, this link will take you there. Or within *Facebook*, just type in Barsoom and it should pop right up. We'll report more on this as we learn more about it — but want to get the link out there without further delay. Sign up an show your support for John Carter!

After tweeting the story and posting it to social bookmarking sites like Reddit, Stumbleupon, Digg, and a half dozen others, I went back to the original post on *John Carter Files* and saw that it was being tweeted by others now, and reposted on *Facebook*. Plus on *Twitter*, Jessen and company were tweeting the existence of the group as well. A few hours later Forbes blogger Mark Hughes picked up the story:[301]

> Fans of the new John Carter film take heart — there is a new Facebook group calling on Disney to have faith in the franchise and move forward with a sequel. The group is spreading their message on *Twitter*, encouraging fans of the film to retweet the message and to join the *Facebook* group.

Over the next 24 hours several dozen media outlets picked up the story and by the time Germain Lussier at *Slashfilm* reported on it the next day, membership had reached 2,000 and was climbing quickly.[302]

Curious about context, I researched to see if group such as the one that was now blossoming on *Facebook* had sprung up after other movies which had questionable starts, as *John Carter* had. My research turned up that in the case of *Prince of Persia*, which many were comparing *John Carter* to in terms of appeal and box office outcome,[303] a *Facebook* page calling

---

[301] Mark Hughes, "John Carter Fans Start *Facebook* Group Calling for Sequel," *Forbes*, March 14, 2012, http://www.forbes.com/sites/markhughes/2012/03/14/john-carter-fans-start-facebook-group-calling-for-sequel/

[302] Germain Lussier, "'John Carter' Fans Demand a Sequel, Launch *Facebook* Campaign," *Slashfilm*, 15 Mar 2012, 7 Sep 2012 <http://www.slashfilm.com/john-carter-fans-demand-sequel-launch-facebook-campaign/>.

[303] *Prince of Persia* opened on May 28, 2010, and earned $30.1M on its opening weekend (*John Carter* earned $30.2M) en route to a domestic total of 90.8M and global total of $335M -- both figures slightly higher than John Carter.

for a sequel had been started but had fizzled with only 419 "Likes" achieved.[304]

Another "comparable", Van Helsing ($300M Global Gross), had a group calling for a sequel that fizzled at 167 members.

With 2,000 members in a day, it was clear that something was afoot in the fan sector.[305]

Could fans actually make a difference?

The *Firefly/Serenity* Browncoats group on *Facebook* had played a key role in resurrecting the series and getting a movie made, and research showed that this group had grown to 50,000 after three years, and that had been sufficient to become a factor in studio decision to make Serenity. And of course there was the fabled history of how *Star Trek* fans, long before there was internet or social media, had achieved success.

Given the beating that *John Carter* had taken, and was continuing to take in the media, the fact that a fan movement seemed to be coalescing was, if nothing else, one bit of good news in a sea of misery -- misery that was about get substantially worse in a matter of days.

---

[304] Author Unknown, "Give Us a Sequel of Prince of Persia Movie," *Facebook*, 27 Nov 1910, 7 Sep 2012 <https://www.facebook.com/pages/Give-us-a-sequel-of-Prince-of-Persia-Movie/170148259673826>.

[305] Author Unknown, "Universal Studio! We need- Van Helsing 2," *Facebook*, 29 Oct 2010, 7 Sep 2012 <https://www.facebook.com/JoinUsForVanhelsing2>.

THE DOOMSDAY SENTENCE

For the Edgar Rice Burroughs community and fans of *John Carter*, Monday, March 19, 2012 is a day that will live in infamy -- the day that Rich Ross broke with longstanding Hollywood and Disney practice and, with *John Carter* only 10 days into its run and the film still unreleased in major foreign territories including China and Japan, announced that Disney was taking a $200M write-down due to the poor performance of the film. The early statement of the write-down was released minutes after the stock market closed:[306]

> In light of the theatrical performance of *John Carter* ($184 million global box office), we expect the film to generate an operating loss of approximately $200 million during our second fiscal quarter ending March 31. As a result, our current expectation is that the Studio segment will have an operating loss of between $80 and

[306] The Deadline Team, "Disney Expects $200M Loss For John Carter," *Deadline Hollywood*, 19 Mar 2012 5 Nov 2012, < http://www.deadline.com/2012/03/disney-expects-200m-loss-for-john-carter/>.

$120 million for the second quarter. As we look forward to the second half of the year, we are excited about the upcoming releases of *The Avengers* and *Brave*, which we believe have tremendous potential to drive value for the Studio and the rest of the company.

That the announcement was a shot heard round the world. Within hours of the announcement, the labeling of *John Carter* as the "flop of the century", "greatest flop in Hollywood history", was complete. It took *John Carter* from the status of "just another high profile box office failure" to "epic flop of the century" all in the space of twelve hours.

By the afternoon of March 20th, according to Google News there had been more than 2,000 articles released in the United States alone. Every television channel and most radio stations carried a story about the debacle. The *New York Times* wrote of "science fiction megaflop John Carter", and added that the film "will go down as one of the biggest flops in Hollywood history."[307]   *CBS* led with: "*John Carter* is now officially a flop of galactic proportions."[308] *Hollywood Reporter* wrote of the "catastrophic performance" and labeled the movie officially as what amounted to a money wasting debacle.[309]

Social media exploded, spiking to a level that three times higher than at any other point in the history of the *John Carter* campaign. *John Carter* finally had "buzz" -- only it was toxic, radioactive buzz that would effectively kill off any chance the film might have had to gain momentum during the remainder of its theatrical run -- a run which at the time of the announcement had only completed 10 days out of a typical 100 day theatrical journey, with more than 50% of theatrical revenues and all revenues from all other sources still to be collected, and thus vulnerable and negatively impacted by the announcement.

---

[307] Brooks Barnes, "$200 Million Write-Down for 'John Carter," Disney Says," *The New York Times*, 19 Mar 2012, 7 Sep 2012 <http://mediadecoder.blogs.nytimes.com/2012/03/19/200-million-write-down-for-john-carter-disney-says/>

[308] CBS Staff Report, "Disney Set to Lose $200M on 'John Carter'," *CBS Los Angeles*, 19 Mar 2012, 7 Sep 2012< http://losangeles.cbslocal.com/2012/03/19/disney-set-to-lose-200m-on-john-carter/>.

[309] Paul Bond, "'John Carter' Will Cost Disney $200 Million in Operating Losses," *The Hollywood Reporter*, 19 Mar 2012, 7 Sep 2012 <http://www.hollywoodreporter.com/news/john-carter-cost-disney-millions-301704>.

Some journalists raised an eyebrow or two at the tactic of making such an unprecedented announcement so soon after the release. Veteran entertainment journalist Sharon Waxman at the respected outlet *The Wrap* wrote:[310]

> I can't think of a similar announcement for a single movie in recent history. In fact, most studios try to bury losses for individual pictures in their financial statements. And they always argue that long-tail revenue streams mitigate a weak box office.

Waxman's comment highlights the fact that *John Carter* was getting special treatment -- as in special *negative* treatment -- by its own studio. it is standard practice among studios when dealing with box office disappointments to refrain from making any statements that will damage either the immediate box office performance or the longterm asset value of the film -- recognizing that a film's longterm value is worthy of protection, as is its legacy. Was such an early, unprecedented, and devastating (to the film) announcement necessary?

Did it make good business sense?

Was it required?

First, there can be little doubt that such an announcement about any film made 10 days into its release would have a chilling effect on theatrical revenue over the remainder of the theatrical run. Other than morbid "stare at a car wreck" fascination -- who would want to invest $12 or $15 in seeing the movie now firmly labeled "biggest flop of all time?" Avoiding stigmatizing a film as a mega-flop helps the studio earn as much revenue as possible from the film.

As Waxman noted, it is hard to come up with a "similar announcement for a single movie in recent history."

Given the lack of precedent, what was the justification for such an early and devastating announcement?

No explanation was offered by Disney. Arguments broke out among fans and Schadenfreudists and those attempting to defend the decision

---

[310] Sharon Waxman, "Rich Ross and the 'John Carter' Debacle -- Disney Takes It on the Chin," *The Wrap*, 20 March 2012, 7 Sep 2012 <http://www.thewrap.com/movies/column-post/rich-ross-and-'john-carter'-debacle---disney-takes-it-chi-36389>.

cited the notion that the *John Carter* box office performance was so devastatingly bad that it rose to the level of a "material event" which, as a public company, Disney was required to disclose without delay.

The question arises -- was there precedent for the announcement?

What has Disney announced in similar circumstances during the Iger years?

The most obvious comparison is 2011's *Mars Needs Moms*, also a fiscal Q2 release -- and a film whose total global gross of $39M (against a budget of $150M) was far worse than *John Carter's* $280M global theatrical gross. Interestingly, that announcement -- made "normally" at the routinely scheduled quarterly investor conference call on May 9, 2011, created an awkward re-arrangement of the call. Normally on the quarterly calls, investor relations chief Lowell Singer introduces Disney CEO Bob Iger, who gives a broad brush "state of the company" overview before turning the call over to Chief Financial Officer Jay Rasulo to go through the numbers. But on the Q2 2011 call, with *Mars Needs Moms* as the '800 pound gorilla in the room', the call began with Singer introducing Rasulo first, before Iger, so that Iger could be spared the ignominy of having to deliver the news about *Mars Needs Moms*.[311] The transparency of this maneuver, with Iger letting his CFO do the squirming, was a solution of sorts, but not a satisfactory one, and suggests part of the motivation for making the announcement early.

A second corollary is Disney's *The Sorcerer's Apprentice*, which carried a price tag of $150M and opened disastrously at $17.4M en route to a domestic total of $63M and global total of $215M. No special announcement of a write-down was made; the only reference was to an "unspecified write down" included in subsequent earnings reports.[312]

So, why was *John Carter* handled so differently?

---

[311] Walt Disney Company Staff, "The Walt Disney Company Q2 FY 2011 Earnings Conference Call," The Walt Disney Company Presentations and Events, 10 May 2011, 8 Sep 2012 <http://cdn.media.ir.thewaltdisneycompany.com/2011/q2/q2-fy11-earnings-transcript.pdf>.

[312] Brooks Barnes, "Disney's Earnings Better Than Expected," New York Times, 11 Aug 2011, 11 Sep 2012 <http://www.nytimes.com/2010/08/11/business/media/11disney.html>.

One factor was that, clearly, Disney CEO Iger did not want to have a repeat of the previous year's uncomfortable situation on the quarterly earnings conference call. An early statement would remedy that by getting the bad news out of the way early, effectively re-setting the bar for quarterly earnings expectations so that when Iger and Rasulo would face analysts and investors in May, the likely outcome would be a report that exceeded analysts' expectations--expectations that would have been re-set by the May 19 announcement.

But there was another factor.

Ten months earlier Iger had begun a dialogue with George Lucas for the acquisition of Lucasfilm and the *Star Wars* franchise. That dialogue had largely been on hold -- nor specifically because of *John Carter*, to be sure, but on hold nonetheless. Iger was eager to make a deal with Lucas and saw Lucasfilm and *Star Wars* as everything that *John Carter* was not--a ready-made, off the shelf franchise that would play to Disney's strengths as an optimizer of value, and eliminate the risk and heavy lifting associated with a "grow your own" franchise.

Disney's acquisition would be announced in October 2012, and Iger would at that time say that the earnest phase of negotiation began "six months ago" -- placing it in the time frame of the *John Carter* announcement. Iger would say of Lucasfilm and *Star Wars*:[313]

> We just announced a pretty big acquisition last week from Lucasfilm, and it's not often that we're working on two big ones at a time. . . . we have received feedback and in put from just about every sector of the ... of society on this, which is actually something that we've taken note of, because what it does is it confirms what we believed when we announced the acquisition, and that is that this is an immensely popular franchise, not just in the United States, but for the world, not just for kids but for generations, it's something that remains relevant and of interest to so many people, and that makes us feel great.

---

313 John Erlichman, "Disney's Iger on Fourth Quarter Results, Outlook", Bloomberg News, 8 Nov 2012, 9 Nov 2012 < http://bloom.bg/VJvNF9; http://www.bloomberg.com/video/disney-s-iger-on-fourth-quarter-results-outlook-l93Ju5jvQQG29VW1T3fn2Q.html; http://thejohncarterfiles.com/2012/11/bob-iger-interviewed-on-bloomberg-talks-hasbro-and-lucasfilm/>

Meanwhile -- regardless of whether or not the Lucasfilm acquisiton was a prime consideration in the timing of the unprecedented "doomsday pronouncement" about *John Carter* -- the March 19 announcement definitely had the effect of smoothing Iger's path for the May 8 quarterly earnings conference call. By the time that call came, precisely because of the early announcement, *John Carter* was "old news" and Iger was able to speak in the normal order with no need to even mention *John Carter*. Instead, even though *Avengers* was not technically part of the quarter being reported (it had just been released on May 4, 2012, part of fiscal Q3, not Q2), it allowed Iger to lead with:[314]

> There are many exciting things happening across our businesses, starting with *The Avengers*, which as all of you know shattered industry box office records, achieving the biggest domestic opening weekend of all time, with $207.1 million. The movie set new opening weekend records in several other countries as well, bringing its worldwide box office gross to more than $700 million to date.

Aside from smoothing the way for the quarterly earnings call, the early announcement arguably minimized any impact on the stock price by "getting out of the way" the bad news as early as possible. Impact on Disney stock was in fact minimal.

Third, it got the announcement of the write-down done on Rich Ross's watch, which Iger knew was about to end. It would not be a burden that Ross's successor would have to bear.

Thus from a purely "corporate" perspective (which, Iger could argue, is the only perspective that mattered) sacrificing *John Carter* arguably made sense.

True, it would stigmatize the film, diminish its earnings, and extinguish any remaining hope for the film to gather momentum in the remainder of its theatrical run, especially overseas where it had yet been released in the second and third largest markets, Japan and China. But corporate considerations trumped any quaint concern for the film itself

---

[314] Walt Disney Company Staff, "The Walt Disney Company Q2 FY 2012 Earnings Conference Call," The Walt Disney Company Presentations and Events, 8 May 2012, 8 Sep 2012 <http://cdn.media.ir.thewaltdisneycompany.com/2012/q2/q2-fy12-earnings-transcript.pdf>.

or its constituents -- including royalty participants such as the Edgar Rice Burroughs Family, Edgar Rice Burroughs, Inc., and the key filmmakers.

As for whether the *John Carter* performance truly was, or was not, a "material event" requiring immediate disclosure, it is an undeniable fact that at the same time that the announcement was being made, Disney's CFO Jay Rasulo was privately assuring the financial analysts who follow Disney financial performance that it was *not* an event that would substantially effect the bottom line or posture of the company, specifically conveying:

1) Disney Corp is a huge corporation. 93% of operating revenues come from something other than films (TV, theme parks, travel) and only 7% come from Walt Disney Studios.

2) The $200M write-down is meaningful only within that 7%, not the overall 100% equation. To the larger Disney Corp, it is nothing more than a pinprick and will be quickly absorbed.

The analysts dutifully replayed these talking points. Influential Harold Vogel told the *L.A. Times* that the company could easily absorb the loss. "It's the equivalent of a ding on the side of your car. You wish it didn't happen, but at the end of the day the car drives fine."[315]

Other analysts:[316]

> *Drew Crum* (Stifel Nicolaus) Rating: Buy. While discouraged by another large film loss (last year it was *Mars Needs Moms*) we're not deterred and continue to focus on the positives including Media Networks + Parks."
>
> *Barton Crockett* (Lazard Capital Markets) Rating: Neutral. Change to FY 2012 EPS: -15 cents to $3.04. "While the loss over the life of the movie is larger than the $140M we had been anticipating, we were not overly surprised by this news." But the projection that the Studio unit will end up with a loss of between $80M and

---

[315] Dawn Chmielewski, "Disney expects $200-million loss on 'John Carter'," LA Times, 20 Mar 2012, 7 Sep 2012, <http://articles.latimes.com/2012/mar/20/business/la-fi-ct-disney-write-down-20120320>.

[316] David Lieberman, "Disney Analysts Remain Unshaken by 'John Carter' $200M Write Down," *Deadline Hollywood*, 20 Mar 2012, 7 Sep 2012 <http://www.deadline.com/2012/03/disney-analysts-remain-unshaken-by-john-carter-200m-write-down/>.

$120M this quarter "suggests to us that the balance of the studio performance was worse than we had modeled."

Michael Nathanson (Nomura Securities) Rating: Buy. Change to FY 2012 EPS: -6 cents to $2.90. "We do not expect the weaker film results to affect any of the business segments (e.g. we did not anticipate strong consumer products revenue related to *John Carter*) … one-off charges at the Studio segment are not indicative of the overall health of the company's core businesses – namely the Media Networks and Parks. We view any pullback in the stock around this higher film loss as an enhanced buying opportunity."

Spencer Wang (Credit Suisse) Rating: Outperform. Change to FY 2012 EPS: -7 cents to $2.91. "Disney shares could come under some modest pressure from this news, although the financial impact is relatively modest in the context of Disney's overall operations.

Todd Juenger (Bernstein Research). Rating: Outperform. Change to FY 2012 EPS: -6 cents to $2.97. "We have concluded this is a blip investors should ignore….This is a very different kind of a miss than, say, if theme parks generally (or one of the capital projects specifically) was off-track, cable networks were off-track or consumer products was off-track. …

The analysts' reports created the "takeaway" Ross and Iger were looking for -- that *John Carter* was a bump in the road or a ding in the side of the Disney car, but nothing more, and in the process the announcement re-set the bar of corporate expectations so that when the quarterly figures did come out in May, there would likely be no "hit" to be absorbed because the hit would have been taken back in March.

Disney dropped less than 1% and quickly recovered.

But from the perspective of *John Carter* and all those who had an interest in its final outcome, the announcement irrevocably conveyed the idea that the film enterprise was a complete bust; that Disney had completely given up on the film and the franchise; that no word of mouth miracle could now be considered nor was Disney interested in nurturing the longterm legacy of the film a la *Blade Runner* and *2001*, two sci-fi films that got off to rocky starts at the box office and with critics but went on to be regarded as classics. The inevitable takeaway from the announcement was that Disney was washing its hands of *John Carter*, period. And it was doing this a mere 10 days into its release and before it had been released in the 2nd and 3rd largest foreign markets.

If anyone expected Ross or Disney marketing to take any of the blame, they were wrong, as Ross's only comment was:[317]

> Moviemaking does not come without risk. It's still an art, not a science, and there is no proven formula for success. Andrew Stanton is an incredibly talented and successful filmmaker who with his team put their hard work and vision into the making of 'John Carter.' Unfortunately, it failed to connect with audiences as much as we had all hoped.

Thus after his team had executed what many observers were calling the worst marketing campaign in history, Ross laid all of the blame for the failure on the movie itself, and made no acknowledgment of the studios' role in marketing it competently.

In the aftermath of the March 19 announcement, conspiracy theories that blamed Disney for deliberately tanking *John Carter* sprang up and ranged from Richard Hoagland's outlandish claim on Coast to Coast radio [318] that a cabal within Disney had done *John Carter* in to keep the public from learning about Mars' ancient civilization and technology, to dozens of theories put forward on blogs and message boards, all concluding the same thing, which is summed up by a post on *ReelRanting*: "I must conclude that someone high up in Disney had it in for this film or someone behind it and did everything he could to ensure its failure. Someone not only starved it of the oxygen of publicity; he poisoned it with bad publicity. When else has a studio ever come out and said: "Our film is crap. Stay away. *John Carter* was murdered."[319]

Conspiracy theories aside, Barton Crockett, an analyst for Lazard Capital Markets who followed Disney closely on a daily basis, wrote:[320]

---

[317] Brooks Barnes, "Ishtar Lands on Mars," *New York Times*, 13 Mar 2012, 7 Sep 2012, <http://www.nytimes.com/2012/03/12/business/media/ishtar-lands-on-mars.html?pagewanted=all>.

[318] George Noory, "Mars, Ancient Life, and John Carter," *Coast to Coast Radio*, 2 Apr 2012, 7 Sep 2012 <http://www.coasttocoastam.com/shows/2012/04/02>.

[319] David S. Zondy, "Who killed John Carter?," Reel Ranting, 12 June 2012, 7 Sep 2012 <http://reelranting.blogspot.com/2012/06/who-killed-john-carter.html>.

[320] David Lieberman, "Disney Analysts Remain Unshaken by 'John Carter' $200M Write Down," *Deadline Hollywood*, 20 Mar 2012, 7 Sep 2012 <http://www.deadline.com/2012/03/disney-analysts-remain-unshaken-by-john-carter-200m-write-down/>.

....the projection that the Studio unit will end up with a loss of between $80M and $120M this quarter suggests to us that the balance of the studio performance was worse than we had modeled.

The "balance of the studio performance" refers to the rest of the films released by Disney during the quarter, and thus Crockett's statement implied that for *John Carter's* failure was being exaggerated so that other performance deficiencies of other films could be bundled into the $200M figure and, because of the bundling, would not have to be specified. *John Carter* was, therefore, providing protective cover for other deficiencies. Coming from an analyst who tracked Disney performance daily and was in regular contact with Disney financial executives, this is a view which carried weight.[321]

On a psychological and emotional level, Iger in particular was "over" *John Carter*. It was Dick Cook's baby and thus an orphan; it had become a stain on the company; he (Iger) had brought in Marvel which gave Disney all the boy franchises it could ever want and now he had Lucasfilm and *Star Wars* firmly in sight. Making the announcement would clear the air of the stench of *John Carter*, and team Disney could refocus on what remained -- and what remained included *The Avengers*. Iger was the author of the Marvel deal; it represented the direction he was taking the studio; 'Carter was baggage.

But if Disney had let go, the fans had not.

On *Facebook*, the *Back To Barsoom Sequel Group* had grown to 6,000 members, and an intense phenomenon of multiple viewings of the film in cinemas was unfolding. As of March 30, two fans -- sisters Daria Brooks and Madeline Gann--had seen the film 10 times in theaters, and there were many who had seen if 5, 6, or 7 times.

The question remained an open one: Were these fans the "pitiful few", a tiny niche that would never be able to make a difference, or did

---

[321] David Lieberman, "Disney Analysts Remain Unshaken by 'John Carter' $200M Write Down," *Deadline Hollywood*, 20 Mar 2012, 7 Sep 2012 <http://www.deadline.com/2012/03/disney-analysts-remain-unshaken-by-john-carter-200m-write-down/>. The practice of using one film to cover losses from others, just like the practice of burying an individual film's performance in aggregate quarterly studio financial reporting, is well-established in Hollywood.

they represent something larger, and potentially more important, as the curtain on the *John Carter* theatrical debacle began to close?

It was too soon to tell.

A Tale of Two Trajectories

CASE STUDY: HUNGER GAMES VS JOHN CARTER

Two weeks after *John Carter* opened, Lionsgate's *The Hunger Games* brought in a whopping $155M at the domestic box office in its debut weekend, making it the third highest opening weekend ever, just behind *Harry Potter and the Deathly Hallows Part 2* ($168M), and *The Dark Knight* ($158M). *The Hunger Games* was clearly every bit the huge hit that analysts and fans had been predicting.

By contrast, "battered" *John Carter*, struggling in the aftermath of Disney's $200M write-down announcement with its newfound status as "biggest flop in cinema history" brought in $5M, bringing its domestic total to $65M after three weekends, and a slightly better global total of $234M.

Worse yet for Disney, *The Hunger Games* cost $80M to make and $50M to market, while *John Carter* cost $250M to make and $100M to market.

How did such disparity occur?

The tale of the tape: In one corner was *The Hunger Games* at $130M total cost (production and marketing) and $214M total BOG after one weekend, and in the other corner *John Carter* at $350M total cost $234M total BOG after three weekends.

Given the fact that Lionsgate had the easier marketing task due to the large and active current fan base, a case could be made that *John Carter* was the "Avis" of the situation and must "try harder." Yet the opposite was true. Lionsgate left nothing to chance and approached the campaign with all the thoroughness and sense of urgency that Disney lacked in its campaign for *John Carter*.

The writing was on the wall 12 weeks out. At that time, *The Hunger Games* had almost 1,000,000 *Facebook* Fans who were burning up the movie message boards with their chatter about the film. *John Carter* at the equivalent point before its release had approximately 40,000 *Facebook* fans. The same general percentages held true for *Twitter* Followers and other social media measures. Did this just happen because *The Hunger Games* was a current literary phenomenon? Or was there some artfulness involved in the *The Hunger Games* social media marketing that was lacking in the case of Disney and *John Carter*?

Another chart as of January 5, this one showing social media buzz and positive/negative sentiment ratio:[322]

Release Date	Title	IMDB Rank	IMDB Likes	IMDB Msg Pages	Facebook Likes	Pos/Neg Sentiment	Sequel	Grade
Mar 2, 2012	The Lorax	1741	6255	3	270159	8/2	Yes	
Mar 9, 2012	John Carter	386	4204	13	62970	6.5/3.5	No	B+
Mar 16, 2012	21 Jump Street	606	7443	9	56281	8/2	No	B
Mar 16, 2012	Mirror Mirror	622	7133	8	642	8/2	No	B
Mar 23, 2012	1000 Words	4290	290	2	244		No	B-
Mar 23, 2012	Hunger Games	26	72190	60	878229	9.5/.5	No	A+
Mar 30, 2012	Wrath/Titans	12	6186	6	2107	7/3	Yes	A-

---

[322] *IMDB Pro*, "*John Carter* (2012) MovieMeter: Data Table View," accessed 2 Sep 2012 <http://pro.imdb.com/title/tt0401729/graph-data> ; *IMDB Pro*, "*The Hunger Games* (2012) MovieMeter: Data Table View," accessed 2 Sep 2012 <http://pro.imdb.com/title/tt1392170/graph-data>.

What was The Hunger Games doing so differently?

The Hunger Games social media and digital marketing was on a completely different level from the social media and digital marketing that Disney put forward with *John Carter*. With *The Hunger Games*, there were for example 13 *Facebook* pages representing each of the districts in the film. It was set up so that fans could become virtual citizens of each district – and because the large novel fan base was familiar with the context – and because of various other "cool factors", it worked.

There was no equivalent for *John Carter* even though Barsoom boasted the same kind of opportunity. The problem: Disney would need to educate the potential audience first, in order for audiences to know. And it never made the effort. Plus, Disney never tapped into the existing *John Carter* fan base who would have been ready and willing to participate in creating and populating different pages, or a "Barsoomapedia" Wiki.

On *Twitter*, for *The Hunger Games* Lionsgate created both the official @TheHungerGames account as well as @TheCapitolPN, a *Twitter* account for *The Capitol*, the central city in the story.[323] The account @TheCapitolPN acted as a "welcoming site to Panem, the Capitol, and its 12 Districts", often tweeting stories, warnings and encouragement in character. Lionsgate's efforts in this regard again resonated with fans, and this amplified the buzz. The "cool factor" was clearly there. Between the two *Twitter* Accounts, *The Hunger Games* had over 400,000 by opening day.

Meanwhile, the single *John Carter Twitter* account, @JohnCarter, topped out at an anemic 9,400 followers and three weeks into the release, had managed a total of only largely uninspiring 240 tweets – such as: "Which *John Carter* character was the most exciting to see on the big screen?", or "*John Carter* is now in theaters; are you going?" And not only did the account put out very few tweets (something it can do via automation, meaning no one has to "mind the store" to simply put out tweets), it hardly did any retweeting at all — and retweeting is an essential

---

[323] *The Hunger Games*, "@TheHungerGames," *Twitter*, Accessed 12 Sep 2012 <http://twitter.com/TheHungerGames>; *The Hunger Games*, "@TheCapitolPN", *Twitter*, 29 Aug 2011, 12 Sep 2012 <http://twitter.com/TheCapitolPN>

tool to generate buzz. For the entire 7 day period prior to opening day, *John Carter* put out 23 tweets, of which 5 were retweets.[324]

By contrast, the official *Twitter* account @TheHungerGames with 380,000 followers put out over 40 tweets just on opening day, and over 100 in the final week; while the secondary @theCapitolPN account put out an equivalent number and an unofficial account @Hungergames put out even more. Collectively, the output of *The Hunger Games Twitter* accounts generated numerous real interactions with fans and a real sense of an event. Disney's far lower output appear to be a series of tweets that were programmed into a computer in December and just allowed to broadcast at specified times up to the release.

Spam, essentially.

Going through the motions?

As a result — "Hunger Games" mentions on *Twitter* reached 1 million in the last month while *John Carter* mentions never reached a tenth of that.

The *Facebook* comparison is even more striking.[325] As with *Twitter*, the *John Carter Facebook* page confined itself to putting out occasional (not even daily — less than that) canned "spam" announcements that could have been written months earlier, and probably were. For examples, here are all the updates of the *John Carter Facebook* page in a 1 week period (16-23 Mar):

> "In the film, Edgar Rice Burroughs is the nephew of John Carter. He inherits his uncle's journal, which details Carter's journey to a strange, new world."

> "Leave a Thark his head and one hand and he may yet conquer." - Tars Tarkas"

---

[324] John Carter, "@JohnCarter," Twitter, 15 Jun 2011, 7 Sep 2012 <http://twitter.com/johncarter>.

[325] Disney Staff, "John Carter (2012)", John Carter *Facebook* Page, 28 Nov 2010, 7 Sep 2012 <https://Facebook.com/JohnCarterMovie>; Lionsgate Staff, "*The Hunger Games* (2012), *The Hunger Games Facebook* Page, 28 Feb 2011, 7 Sep 2012 <https://www.facebook.com/TheHungerGamesMovies>.

"The actors playing the nine-foot tall, green Tharks had to learn to walk on stilts to film the scenes with John Carter, giving the correct eye-line for the dialogue."

"Did I not tell you he could jump?" -Tars Tarkas

"Bring Barsoom home with these *John Carter* items from the Disney Store."

It is hard to imagine a more unimaginative and lackluster performance. And it was not any better before the release — it was the same "spam-like" stuff, interchangeable with whatever was being tweeted, all feeling, as one observer put it, "as if it had been written months earlier by a single intern in some Burbank Starbucks."

The Hunger Games, by contrast managed at least daily updates; had all kind of special offers, free downloaded games that were actually fun, inside activities with plenty of "cool factor."

The unmistakable "takeaway" for anyone visiting the two *Facebook* pages was that *John Carter Facebook* and *Twitter* effort was a half-hearted endeavor with no serious senior level focus having been placed on it. There was nothing "cool" about it. Meanwhile the *The Hunger Games' Facebook* and *Twitter* effort was hip, run by cool people, and so the takeaway, of course, was that the movie must be cool and worth seeing.

John Carter did perform better than Lionsgate overseas. Why?

One factor was that Disney's overseas divisions generally did a far better job than the home office.

Examples:

1. The Domestic official *John Carter* website, buried on the second layer of Disney Go, was probably not even in the top five of official *John Carter* websites. The UK Site, the Australian Site, the Singaporean Site, and the German site were all better in terms of accessibility, features, and overall impact.

2. The Japanese Trailer was widely considered to be far better than any of the official Disney trailers put out by the US marketing team.

3. Individual country-specific promotions in a variety of countries all had stronger impact and appeal than anything Disney US did.

4. In other words — did the other Disney divisions, far from home and outside the specter of what was g0ing on in Burbank, manage to do a better job?

The disparity was even harder to understand when consideration is given to the fact that MT Carney was brought on board in 2010 to head Disney marketing precisely to strengthen the digital component and achieve a "new paradigm" balance between digital and traditional means of promotion.

LAST TRIP TO BARSOOM

It might have been expected that the announcement from Disney of the $200M write-down, coupled with the subliminal (or not so subliminal) message that Disney was done with *John Carter* would have discouraged the fan on *Facebook* and elsewhere calling for a *John Carter* Sequel. But in fact, the opposite happened.

On *Facebook*, the group's membership continued to grow and in fact the growth rate accelerated in the immediate aftermath of the March 19 announcement. 5,000 members became 7,000 even as *John Carter* was entering the final phase of its theatrical run -- meaning far fewer audience members were discovering the film each week.

On April 11 one of the members of the *Facebook* group, Daria Brooks, who had seen the film 14 times in theaters, volunteered on a message board that she was going to go to Disney-owned El Capitan

Theater in Hollywood for the final showing there on the night of April 19.[326]

The thought occurred: Instead of the curtain coming down on a final showing with a handful of stragglers watching the film, perhaps with social media promotion it could be transformed into a proper sendoff that would show respect for the film, and send a message.

On April 12 "Last Trip to Barsoom" was announced on *The John Carter Files* and *Facebook*.[327] The stated goal was to give the film a solid sendoff. Over the next week, fans in cities around the world put together groups to attend the film in solidarity on April 19th.

> On *Twitter*, Andrew Stanton tweeted: "See Carter 1 last time on the big, bold screen today. "Kaor!" to all you wonderful folks attending the El Cap screening tonight! #gobarsoom

Composer Michael Giacchino also tweeted support for the endeavor, and in Los Angeles, Disney star Daryl Sabara who plays the young Edgar Rice Burroughs in the film tweeted that he was going to El Capitan on the 19th. Another cast member, Evelyn Dubuq, came to the screening as well, as did Edgar Rice Burroughs, Inc. President James Sullos and a contingent from ERB, Inc.

In the end the 225 paying customers made it the largest audience of any night in the theatrical run at El Capitan.

Meanwhile, around the world, fans in groups of 5, 10, or in some cases as many as 50, converged on theaters on the same night. In the US there were groups attending in most major cities and even in some smaller venues such as Oklahoma City, Fargo, Tallahassee, there were groups who went in solidarity.

---

[326] El Capitan is a single screen, 800 seat classic theater that is company owned by Disney and is used by Disney for premieres and special events. Its schedule is locked in advance and so it was established prior to the start of the *John Carter* run that John Carter's run would end on April 19th to make way on April 20th for Disney Nature's "Chimp."

[327] Michael D. Sellers, "Last Trip to Barsoom: Join us For Closing Night of the John Carter run at El Capitan in Hollywood," The John Carter Files, 12 Apr 2012, 7 Sep 2012 <http://thejohncarterfiles.com/2012/04/last-trip-to-barsoom-join-us-for-closing-night-of-the-john-carter-run-at-el-capitan-in-hollywood/>.

By the time "Last Trip to Barsoom" was over, it was clear that *John Carter* indeed had developed an entrenched and passionate fan base that was beginning to view themselves as the "Trekkies" of 2012.

THE DVD RELEASE FINALLY PROVIDES A "WIN"

Six weeks later on June 5, 2012, *John Carter* was released in the US on Blu-ray/DVD and when the numbers came out, it had done what it had failed to do at any point in its theatrical run -- come in first place among all films released that week. It beat the two other wide releases -- *Safe House* and *Act of Valor* -- and was, for the first time, recipient of a modicum of respect in the media.

In the aftermath of the DVD/Blu Ray release, the fan group passed through the 10,000 member barrier and as the summer progressed, continued to add new members at a rate of 300 per week.

John Carter, it seemed, might be buried under a mountain of negativity and disengagement from Disney -- but it wasn't dead, not in an absolute sense.

No one could predict where the fan activism would lead, or whether the positivity of the fans would result in anything other than the creation of an ongoing passionate, but ultimately niche community.

But what was clear was that the combination of Andrew Stanton and Edgar Rice Burroughs had resonated; a community of new fans had been created; ERB's legacy would not vanish -- at least not now.

THE EDGAR RICE BURROUGHS LEGACY

Edgar Rice Burroughs had been the most popular author of the first half of the twentieth century, but coming into the release of *John Carter*, the Edgar Rice Burroughs fan community consisted primarily of aging Baby Boomers (or older) who had discovered Tarzan and *John Carter* via the paperbacks of the 1960s. Prior to the release of *John Carter*, the number of active ERB fans[328] worldwide was unlikely to exceed a few hundred thousand.

Over the course of its theatrical run, a total of 20 to 25 million viewers saw the film in theaters.

The Blu-ray/DVD release expanded those numbers.

Did the movie produce new fans who would extend the legacy of Edgar Rice Burroughs? Or were they simply movie fans?

On July 19, members of the *Facebook* fan group began to post their introduction to the movie and, in many cases, described how the movie led them to the books:[329]

Justin Russell

I literally knew nothing about ERBs books or the John Carter character prior to viewing the movie...There are few films that have pulled me in, tugged at my heart strings and made me feel excited like JC did. ..I immediately took friends and family to see it and all enjoyed it..... I have since read the first three books and I tell people about it any chance I get.

Keith Rightmyer

I first heard of the movie through a trailer either in a theater or during the Superbowl (I only watch for the commercials!). I remember that I was interested but didn't really learn much from the spots, so I researched the name "John Carter" on the internet to learn about his roots. I honestly wasn't aware that E.R. Burroughs wrote anything other than Tarzan. The information I found and the additional TV spots intrigued me enough to make sure I saw it in the theater on opening weekend. Boy, was I glad I did! I thoroughly enjoyed the movie. The action and adventure was exactly what I look for... Having just whet my appetite, I sought out the books that this film was drawn from and delved further into the worlds of Barsoom, Jasoom and John Carter.

---

[328] Defined as fans who had read the books in the last 10 years.

[329] Michael D. Sellers, "How Fans Describe Their First Encounter with Barsoom," *The John Carter Files*, 19 Jul 2012 4 Nov 2012 <http://thejohncarterfiles.com/2012/07/readers-describe-how-they-discovered-john-carter-what-about-you/>

Deb Cates

I did not know anything about John Carter until it was confirmed in the press that the film was in production- then, I only heard about it because my husband, a long-time ERB fan and collector of fantasy, sci fi, and comics, started talking about it. When we saw the first trailer in theaters together, he squeezed my arm and started bouncing. My husband does not "bounce." "It's John Carter!! It's John Carter!!", he said. I wasn't sure what to make of the trailer. It looked like *Prince of Persia*, which I saw and with which I was not much enamored. However, my husband got advance screening passes and I went with him to see it, not really expecting anything. I laughed. I cried. I tensed up. I breathed sighs of relief. I fired off a million questions under my breath. When it was over, I repeated the Barsoomian phrase "och ohem octais whis Barsoom" over and over in my head for weeks. (I am a linguist and I love fantasy languages). I could not believe the movie "flopped", because it is the best film I have seen in theaters in a long time. Thank God for project Gutenberg- I downloaded and read the first three John Carter books over the course of three days.

Lance Salvosa

When I heard that Andrew Stanton was going to adapt *A Princess of Mars* for the big screen, something inside me clicked. I remember being at an old friend's house over ten years ago, marveling at the army of titles that rested on his bookshelf. Although I found the title a bit cheesy at the time, my friend put his foot down in its defense. "Don't knock it," he said sternly. "It's really good." So last year, I began spelunking in various bookstores, only to find it wasn't in circulation. When I finally found a copy, I found myself savoring every line and every chapter. All the while getting drawn deeper into a world I had never heard about and yet, never wanted to leave. One book wasn't enough; I had to have the rest of them. And from the tortured nobility of Tars Tarkas to the cackling laugh of Issus to the innocent fearlessness of Carthoris, the books have remained very treasured gems on my shelf. Best of all was the timeless mystery and white-hot courage of John Carter himself. He didn't know how old he was; he only knew what mattered. And there was something stirring and meaningful about that. The movie just didn't meet my expectations. It surpassed them COMPLETELY. All of the romance, all of the big-hearted action. IT was ALL THERE.

These are just a few samples; there are hundreds more online at *The John Carter Files*.

There can be no doubt -- in spite of the negativity, in spite of the largely bungled opportunity -- the legacy of Edgar Rice Burroughs will undoubtedly grow, and not be diminished, as a result of Disney's *John Carter*. An estimated 50 million viewers worldwide have seen the movie either in theaters or on Blu-ray/DVD since it came out, and as a direct result of this, there are new Edgar Rice Burroughs fans everywhere. Disappointment over the handling of the movie and its outcome cannot, and should not, obscure this fact.

Even so, it's hard to look at this situation from the perspective of a Burroughs admirer and not wonder ....if only.

If only indeed.

ACCOUNTABILITY: WHAT WERE THEY THINKING?

One of the great American corporate success stories is FedEx, a company built on the premise of reliability and on-time performance. Within the FedEx system, every time a flight departs even one minute late, or any other error occurs, an investigation is carried out which identifies what went wrong and assigns responsibility on a percentage basis to the various company components that were involve in whatever went wrong. For example, an investigation might find that a late arrival was 50% due to a maintenance issue, 30% flight operations, and 20% ramp operations. This system has had much to do with FedEx's corporate success, and is an ingrained part of the culture.

What of the *John Carter* debacle? Where does the responsibility lie? The major players in the *John Carter* drama were, from top to bottom, Robert Iger, Dick Cook, Rich Ross, MT Carney, and Andrew Stanton. Many others played important roles but these five are the ones who made the decisions that ultimately produced the outcome.

There are many in the fan community who, terribly disappointed with the outcome of the release of *John Carter*, want to believe that there were active, intentional efforts to cause the film to fail for any number of reasons. In carrying out the research, the output of which is *John Carter and the Gods of Hollywood*, I did not find any credible evidence to support such a theory. What I found was a "perfect storm" of competing priorities and personalities that led to decisions at various steps in the process which, when taken in aggregate, produced the outcome that we observed.

The following attempts to summarize the accountability of each of the major "players" and offer a theory as to "what they were thinking" when they made the decisions they did.

DICK COOK

What is he accountable for?

Dick Cook was responsible for the decision to acquire the rights to *A Princess of Mars*; the decision to offer the picture to Andrew Stanton; the decision to green light the film at a whopping budget of $250M; and the decision to give Andrew Stanton something very close to full creative control over the screenplay, casting, and the production of the film. What could Cook have done that might have changed the outcome?

First, rather than allowing Stanton to staff the production with enabling producers he might have introduced a senior studio-oriented producer into the equation as a means of retaining a higher degree of studio control over the production. Second, he might have questioned the budget level and either pushed back, insisting on a plan that would achieve the film at a lower cost, or at least insisting on some "name" leads to help lower the risk of the film once it's budget had gone as high as it did. He chose not to do any of these things, instead choosing to support Andrew Stanton and his team almost unconditionally.

What was he thinking?

The whole *John Carter* episode occurred in part because Cook happened to reach out to Andrew Stanton, who was then in post production on *Wall-E*, at a time when Stanton had *A Princess of Mars* on his mind due to the fact that Paramount had just released the property back to the Burroughs estate and he was a fan of the property. Making such a "check-in" call was pure Cook -- he is regarded in creative Hollywood as one of the all time "good guy" executives who knows how to interact with creative talent, appreciates their perspective, and knows how to nurture them.

Aside from the fact that it was Cook's basic human nature to check in with talent, the call to Stanton also reflected Disney-Pixar factors. Having recently acquired Pixar, Stanton was a hugely important creative talent in Cook's universe -- perhaps as meaningful as, for example, Johnny Depp was to the *Pirates of the Caribbean* franchise (a franchise that began in a conversation between Cook and Depp).

When Stanton floated *A Princess of Mars*, it was not purely 'I want to do this next' -- he floated it as a fan, saying that this is a property Disney should consider on its own merits. But he also signaled his interest in directing it and, by extension, his interest in testing the live action waters as a director.

Cook knew the Burroughs' property from the 80's and 90's when Disney had it. On the face of it, the idea of Disney reacquiring the *A Princess of Mars* had merit. Disney needed boy-friendly franchises, and in the right hands, this could be one. Plus Disney needed to keep Stanton "on the reservation" at Disney. And so it was an easy decision to acquire the rights and offer the post to Stanton, thus keeping Stanton in the fold with Disney and creating the potential of a boy friendly franchise that was in line with strategic needs. It also helped kept the Disney-Pixar relationship in a good place.

Thus Cook's likely thought process in acquiring the rights and launching the project is easily understood.

But what of the decisions regarding the script, production, casting, and budget?

Here it is somewhat more difficult. It appears that casting decisions came first, while Michael Chabon was rewriting the script and hence before a final budget could be prepared. If this sequence applies -- casting first, then budget -- it helps explain why the studio might not challenge Stanton on the "no stars" approach. If on the other hand the budget decision came first, then the question becomes -- did Cook consider the idea of casting more "bankable" talent as a bargaining chip in the budget negotiations with Stanton and the producers? Imagine the decision to make the original *Pirates of the Caribbean,* on the one hand with Johnny Depp, and on the other hand without Johnny Depp.

Cook accepted the higher budget and Stanton's choices in large part because, first of all, it was in his "DNA" to support talent and enable them, and secondly because in this particular case, it was difficult to make a case of "comparable" films and how they did because the two comparables that mattered most -- Andrew Stanton's two previous films -- had made enough to succeed even with a budget of $250M. In essence Cook concluded that Stanton had earned the right to make the film the way he wanted to at a budget of $250M.

Cook was "all-in" with Stanton. That's who he was, and how he operated. He was true to himself.

One can't help but wonder what the promotion of *John Carter* would have looked like had Cook remained at the helm of Disney Studios long enough to see through to conclusion the project that he had initiated.

ROBERT IGER

What is he accountable for?

Iger was responsible for the firing of Dick Cook, and the hiring of Rich Ross to replace him. He set an agenda for Ross that included a mandate for Ross to undertake substantial changes to the way the studio promoted and marketed its projects. He either instigated or confirmed the decision to deny *John Carter* the kind of all-out marketing push (including merchandising, licensing, and cross promotions) that its $250M budget all but demanded. He either instigated or authorized the unprecedented announcement on March 19, just 10 days into the theatrical run, of a $200M write-down -- an action that produced the highest spike in publicity and chatter about the film, all to the film's disadvantage as it was still in the early phase of its earning cycle.

What was he thinking?

As CEO of the Disney parent corporation, of which the studio division represented only 7% in operating revenues, Iger's focus was on managing entire Disney ecosystem in such a way as to maintain the confidence of the Wall Street analysts who in turn affected the confidence of investors and thus performance of Disney stock. He set the overall model and philosophy of the various divisions, and worked on making the acquisitions and personnel appointments to enable those divisions to operate successfully according to his overall vision for the company. He left intense focus on individual film projects to the head of Disney Studios and thus he cannot be regarded as having been a "hands on" participant in the production and release of *John Carter*.

In the fall of 2009, at a crucial time for the *John Carter* project, Iger fired Cook, and chose Rich Ross to replace him. He did so with the intention of re-fashioning the role of Disney Studios, turning it into a distributor of established brands Dreamworks, Pixar, Marvel, Jerry Bruckheimer Films, and Disney. Iger felt Cook had to go in order to achieve the "new order" he was trying to implement. Cook wasn't precisely an anachronism -- but there was a "throwback" quality that Cook and the studio represented and that Iger wanted to transform with fresh blood and "fresh thinking"--if reducing the role of studio chief to "coordinator in chief" can be considered fresh.

It is unclear whether Iger thought much about *John Carter* (of Mars) until quite a bit later, as the film was making its way through post production. In interviews after the film came out, he claimed to have developed a "sense" that it wasn't going to succeed, well before it came out. And it must be remembered that Iger's courtship of George Lucas and his infinitely more attractive Star Wars franchise began in May 2011, when *John Carter* was in post production.

In the end, Iger's contribution to the *John Carter* situation was probably limited to three elements: First, the acquisition of Marvel was a project that Iger keenly pursued and, once successful, removed whatever remaining luster *John Carter* held for the studio. Secondly, he chose Rich Ross to replace Dick Cook, in the process removing *John Carter*'s main ally and replacing him with Ross, who had no allegiance or personal connection to the film. Thirdly, Iger appears to have participated in or at least sanctioned the decision to limit marketing support to *John Carter* to something less than an all-out tentpole effort -- a decision that was entirely consistent with his overall view of the film and his greater interest in acquisitions like Marvel and, soon, Lucasfilm. All three of these decisions made sense from Iger's perspective; all three ultimately hurt *John Carter*.

RICH ROSS

What is he accountable for?

Ross was appointed head of Disney Studios in October 2009, two months before *John Carter* was scheduled to go into production, and remained the studio chief until April 20, 2012, when he was fired. Ross had no responsibility for the green-lighting of *John Carter* or the casting. He was in a position, had he chosen to, to require a downsizing of the budget (as he subsequently did with *The Lone Ranger*). But Ross's main accountability is in the area of marketing. He was responsible the hiring of MT Carney; the decision to forego an all-out marketing approach that would have incorporated merchandising, licensing, and cross promotions; the decision to advance the *John Carter* release date by 3 months from June 8, 2012, to March 9, 2012, and he was responsible for creating, or failing to create, a sense of urgency in the marketing of *John Carter*, and in particular has a degree of responsibility for the campaign's responsiveness, or lack of responsiveness, when it became apparent that the initial approach was not working.[330]   He is also accountable, in concert with Robert Iger, for the decision to make the "doomsday" announcement on March 19, 2012, claiming a historic $200M write-down attributed to *John Carter*.

What was he thinking?

Much has been made that Ross didn't have ownership of *John Carter* because it was Dick Cook's baby, and to a certain extent that may have entered into it. But when Ross took over in October 2009, *John Carter's* release date was 20 months away, set for June 8, 2012, and that was too far out to simply become "not my problem." It seems much more likely

---

[330] Ross would not have been responsible for formulating the specific response or change in course, but he would have been the one responsible for insisting that a change in approach be pursued -- something that did not happen.

that Ross considered it to be a problem, but not one that could be solved by pulling the plug since it was too close to being fully mounted, with a start date of January 2010.

Aside from *John Carter* per se, there was also the issue of Ross's understanding of his own mandate. He was given a strong directive by Iger to clean house and retool the Studio, bringing it more in line with the rest of Disney Corp and eliminating many of the aspects that made it unique within the larger organization. The studio was to become more of a distribution hub serving client producers, and less a content generator directly via in-house productions. *John Carter* was an in-house production, and although it had been produced by key Pixar talent (Stanton and producers Morris and Collins), it was not a Pixar film and thus John Lasseter, while a friend of the project, was not in the same position of Spielberg with Dreamworks, Feige with Marvel, or Bruckheimer with his films. *John Carter* did not have a champion or high-profile producer demanding focus and attention the way the other films did --- nor did it have a dedicated topflight marketing consultant working for it as the films with client producers did.

Ross fired department heads liberally and, particularly in the case of marketing, brought in an outsider with a clear "shake things up" mandate. He made young producer Sean Bailey head of production and brought in MT Carney to take on the marketing position that was evolving into a coordination job as the marketing hub for Pixar, Dreamworks, Marvel, Jerry Bruckheimer Films, and Disney. In that context, Carney's credentials as someone who knew marketing, and was particularly adept at digital and new media marketing, made sense to Ross.

As the campaign unfolded, and failed to connect -- what was Ross thinking? All indications are that he eventually came to consider *John Carter* a Pixar vanity project which he was willing to let sink or swim largely on the shoulders of Andrew Stanton. He did not "light a fire" under anyone in marketing or otherwise communicate a sense of urgency or that "failure is not an option." He had made the decision long ago, confirmed by Iger, to not "throw good money after bad" by unleashing the kind of all-out marketing campaign that, for example, *The Avengers* was to be the beneficiary of. He knew that, given *John Carter*'s budget, this decision all but doomed the release to failure unless Stanton pulled a rabbit out of the hat with a film that registered 90%++ with both critics and audiences.   He knew this -- but felt the decision was justified in the larger overall scheme of things. In his view the marketing was adequate enough so that Stanton, if he had delivered a film with critic and audience approval in the 90's, could have succeeded.   In the end, Ross seems to have been thinking: This is Andrew Stanton's baby and the entire existence of the project is an appeasement to Stanton, Lasseter and Pixar.   We will give them enough support so that if they deliver a home run with the critics and fans, it will be a success. And if it falls short of that, well -- the studio had supported the film with a $250M production budget and $100M marketing spend.   Any failure would be mainly on Stanton, not the studio.

MT CARNEY

What is she accountable for?

MT Carney bears primary responsibility for the change of title from *John Carter of Mars* to *John Carter*, and shared responsibility for moving up the release date by three months into a March slot, as opposed to a June slot. She is responsible for deciding to handle *John Carter* herself, rather than bring in a consultant, even though she lacked experience and had a very full plate. She is responsible for the substandard level of effort that went into the *John Carter* campaign -- and thus for items such as the lameness of the *Facebook*, *Twitter*, and social media campaigns, the weakness of the website, and the low output of publicity. The failure of the campaign to react and respond when it became apparent that the creatives were not connect with the audience is technically her responsibility, although she was fired on January 8, 2012, sixty days before the release and thus was at the helm of marketing only until then.

As to the disastrous creatives, there is less than total clarity on her role versus Andrew Stanton's role in the major tone-setting creative decisions that led to the weak trailers, posters, and other materials that failed to capture the imagination of potential filmgoers. She clearly bears at least some of the responsibility for the judgments that are reflected in the materials that were produced.

What was she thinking?

It's pretty easy to imagine how Carney, a rising superstar in New York whose company Naked Communications had been highly successful and received accolades from all quarters, entered Hollywood filled with confidence that the skills that had served her so well up to that point, would serve her just as well in Hollywood.

She understood on one level that movies were different from BMW's or packaged goods -- but at the same time, basic principles were basic principles and everything she knew taught her that her skills as a brand strategist should work for movies as well as they had worked for other products. Indeed, in all likelihood she felt like she understood some things that the old school movie marketers didn't understand, and could use that understanding to good effect.

When she arrived at Disney, the projects for which she had responsibility were were hurtling at her at breakneck speed, forcing her into what Sharon Waxman called a "baptism by fire." *Prince of Persia* came first and opened weakly; then the *Sorcerer's Apprentice,* imbued with Carney's own tagline "It's the coolest job ever", flopped. *Step UP 3D* then underperformed; *Secretariat* performed weakly; *You Again* flopped; then *Tangled* did well, *Tron: Legacy* did a solid $400M worldwide; and *Gnomeo and Juliet* did $100M domestic. All of these were on Carney's plate., and all of them were in the pipeline ahead of *John Carter,* demanding attention and focus at a time when Carney was trying to simultaneously implement staffing changes, philosophical changes, and changes in how things were done. *John Carter* did not have a Bruckheimer, Spielberg, or Feige demanding attention, and with all that was on her plate and her lack of experience, MT Carney did not immediately come to grips with *John Carter* or its issues.

Until January 2011, *John Carter* was still scheduled for release in June 2012, after *The Avengers.* The decision, made in January 2011, to move *John Carter* forward to March 9, replacing Frankenweenie who would not be ready for a March release, was made with Carney's concurrence and seems to have been the ringing of the bell that caused it to finally become, front and center, a focus of concern for her.

She then became engaged in the planning that led up to the June/ July 2011 launch of the teaser poster and trailer, but in that process she came to realize that Andrew Stanton was going to have a very significant say in the creative materials, and his ideas did not mesh well with hers. In the end, the materials that came out reflected an uneasy coordination between the studio marketing team, and the film-maker. Carney surely felt that she was being blocked by Stanton from creating the materials she wanted to create for the film.

More importantly, during the run-up to the June/July launch of the teaser materials, Carney became convinced that removing "of Mars" from the title was a key to achieving a positioning that would allow success occur. The decision to drop "of Mars", which turned out to be probably the single most fateful decision of the campaign, was "all MT Carney." She believed it was the right choice -- a choice that would open up a wider demographic. That turned out to be a bad decision -- but she believed in it, and believed it would help the picture.

In MT Carney's case, there was another thread that mattered, increasingly as the campaign moved beyond the summer of 2011 and into the fall. By the fall of 2011 she had, on a personal level, made the decision that Hollywood was not the answer. She journeyed back to New York each weekend to be with her children, whom she adored. Her friends were in New York; her world was New York, and Hollywood was not responding to her insights, strategy, and style in a way that was psychologically or emotionally satisfying. She attempted to deal professionally with her responsibilities in Hollywood, including John Carter, but the writing was on the wall and her heart wasn't in it.

In the end, she was distracted much of the time, and she made some critical miscalculations based on her belief in an application of principles that just did not transfer to theatrical film marketing the way she thought they would.

While it is easy to criticize Carney's bad judgment calls and the *outcome* that ensued, her greater accountability would seem to be in simply failing to set up and implement a solid *effort* designed to generate buzz for *John Carter*. She cannot be expected to have attended to every detail of *Facebook*, *Twitter*, Websites and so on -- but she was hired in large part because of claimed familiarity with new media, yet by any reasonable metric the output of her *John Carter* team in the new media and publicity arenas was substandard (and this only refers to the low measurable output, and does not even address quality issues associated with that output.) It seems that the management task of simply keeping up with all the movies in the pipeline, *John Carter* included, proved overwhelming to her.[331]

ANDREW STANTON

What is he accountable for?

Stanton is unique among the five major players in that he clearly and irrefutability gave the film his all -- no one can realistically accuse Stanton of mailing in his performance or not giving the film his best shot. He clearly did that, and acknowledging that he made an all-out, good-conscience effort is a necessary preamble to any critique. He cared, and he gave it his best shot.

With that established -- film-making is by its nature collaborative and a group effort -- but Andrew Stanton had virtually full creative control and was given ample budget support, so he must take responsibility for virtually all of the major creative decisions that led to a film being created that scored 52% with critics and 75-80% with audiences. These scores, while not the scintillating 90%++ percent ratings he had achieved with his previous two films, are not devastatingly bad and, had they been backed by a solid marketing campaign, could have been adequate to the task at hand. But lacking a solid marketing campaign, these results proved inadequate.

There is also the matter of Stanton's accountability for the certain aspects of the marketing. Stanton clearly had major responsibility for the first trailer and thus the first impression of the film. He espoused a "no-spoiler", don't-give-away-too-much philosophy that seems to have

---

[331] Of all the participants, MT Carney most clearly "dropped the ball", but one unknown is -- what sort of guidance was she getting from Rich Ross. Although the precise details of Ross's guidance are not known, it seems reasonable to assume that if Ross had conveyed to Carney a sense of urgency commensurate with 'Carter's budget, surely she would have at least been able to respond with a higher level of output, even if the creatives didn't improve. It seems unlikely that she ever got that kind of push from Ross.

been adopted by Disney marketing -- whether because Stanton had the power to force it on them, or simply persuaded them of it is not clear. But at least some of the responsibility for what was perceived as "incoherence" in the trailers, for example, is traceable to Stanton's often articulated concern that the materials leave much the imagination.

What was he thinking?

Coming into the film, Stanton had shown a green thumb for every single project he had ever either directed, or been strongly associated with as a writer. He believed deeply that he recognized and understood patterns in storytelling that would allow him to achieve the key goal of "make me care", whatever the story or medium. And why not?

And it wasn't that Stanton was an egoist who ignored collaborators. He understood and embraced the need for collaboration and he worked with collaborators to forge a consensus.

Stanton believed the audience was inherently more intelligent than most film-makers give them credit for.

He believed that Burroughs had created a wonderful universe that had inspired him enormously as a teen, and he wanted to recreate that and share it. But he didn't fully believe in the other aspects of Burroughs storytelling prowess. He didn't see Burroughs as having any unique gifts when it came to creating a compelling hero-protagonist, and he felt he could improve on what Burroughs had given. Moreover, he believed that the improvements he planned were precisely the kind of updates that were needed in order to "freshen up" the 100 year old, badly strip-mined material. He did not drill deeply into Burroughs' genius but rather, like so many before him, strip-mined what he could and then let his own imagination take over.

He also had, for many years, harbored an idea of how to start the movie, and that was on Barsoom, in the council chambers. He had shared that idea for an opening with Robert Rodriguez as far back as the early 2000's. He remained committed to that opening, even when the Brain Trust screening in December 2010 produced feedback that it might not be working, and that following Burroughs' approach of revealing Barsoom through John Carter's experience of it might work better. He truly felt that was bad advice - one of the few pieces of advice from the Brain Trust that he would reject out of hand.

For the critical opening scenes of the movie, he believed that audiences would, like a child, sense that all they needed to take from the opening prologue on Mars was that there were two forces fighting one another, and a third force had entered it, providing a lethal, game changing weapon to one of them.

And he was right to a large extent, as far as the audiences were concerned. There is little indication that the "confusing opening" was a problem for theater goers. The general audience accepted this in much the manner that Stanton anticipated. The critics, however, did not, and the 52% "Rotten" critics score is largely attributable to this, and to other aspect of the film that flowed from this. Stanton and the film took a pounding from the critics on the charge of "confusing and unengaging" -- a charge that more than anything else can be traced to issues with the opening sequences, and the amount of Barsoomian politics and exposition that was offered up in large doses, particularly near the beginning of the film. A film must generate a "buy-in" moment early on, in order for the audience to become engaged and remain engaged. The confusing opening resulted in many critics never having such a moment, and their view of the remainder of the film was often colored by their expressed irritation with the confusing opening.

Finally, Stanton thought he was going to get a trilogy and he trusted in that, structuring the first film in a way that provided maximum payoff over the projected three film series, but which may have lessened the payoff and narrative efficiency of the first film.

WHAT WOULD WALT DISNEY THINK?

The Walt Disney Company today is nine decades removed from the company that Walt Disney and his brother Roy started in 1923 as the Disney Brothers Cartoon Studio with a series of "Alice in Wonderland" cartoons made under contract to film distributor Margaret J. Winkler. Today's Disney is world's largest media conglomerate in terms of revenue. Many of the decisions and actions taken by Disney principals in the case of *John Carter* reflect those realities.

What would Walt Disney think?

In speaking of his approach to any project, Walt said:[332]

> When we consider a project, we really study it--not just the surface idea, but everything about it. And when we go into that new project, we believe in it all the way. We have confidence in our ability to do it right. And we work hard to do the best possible job.

Who among the participants in *John Carter* lived up to the legacy of those words? Who did not?

Former Studio head Dick Cook and all of those involved in the production of the film itself seem to have acted in a manner consistent with Walt Disney's approach. It is possible to criticize choices made by

---

[332] Just Disney Staff, "Walt Disney General Quotes," JustDisney.com, 4 Nov 2012 <http://www.justdisney.com/walt_disney/quotes/index.html>.

Andrew Stanton, and critics have done just that, but no one has accused Stanton or any of the film-makers of giving it anything less than their best shot. The film-makers "worked hard to do the best possible job."

Can the same be said of the executives who set the policy regarding how the film would be brought into the marketplace, or the marketers who implemented that policy?

When we go into a project, we believe in it all the way.

Did Bob Iger, Rich Ross, and MT Carney act in a manner consistent with Walt's values? Or were the values that determined their actions radically different from those espoused by the founder of the company they represent?

In May 2012 Bob Iger was interviewed by Carol Massar of Bloomberg News and had this to say about *John Carter*:[333]

> *Iger:* They're all our babies and we root for all of them to do well…we're relatively realistic about the prospects of our film when we see enough of each film…I mean, you get a good sense if you've been in the business long enough whether something is going to do well or not, before it comes out, research aside — it's more…it's an instinct. There was a point before Carter came out that I had a very strong sense that it was going to be very challenging….
>
> *Massar:* But at that point you were just too way in, right? you have to run with it?
>
> *Iger:* Yes. we weren't going to not distribute it. nor did we really run away from supporting it fully because i felt that given the size of the investment, we owed it to ourselves, to at least give it the shot that it deserved.
>
> *Massar:* And you never know…
>
> *Iger:* No, you never know…but we had a strong sense…i was very worried about it … not that I wasn't cheering for it …but I was worried about it.

Iger's comments to Massar are revealing on a number of levels. What, for example, is meant by: "*When we see enough of a film…*"?

[333] Carol Massar, "Iger: I Was Worried About John Carter,"Bloomberg News, 11 May 2012, 11 Sep 2012 <http://www.bloomberg.com/video/92465895-iger-i-was-worried-about-john-carter.html>.

It would seem that this could only refer to the December 2010 screening of the 170 minute work-in-progress by Disney studio executives. Yet less than a month later, in January 2011, the decision was made to accelerate the opening by three months. Why accelerate the release date of a film that you feel has problems and which represents a "tentpole" investment? Why not hold to the original date, or even delay that date if necessary so as to "get it right"?

What would Walt have done?

"We work hard to do the best possible job."

MT Carney, brought in under Rich Ross as the head of marketing in part because she was believed to have expertise in new media, produced a digital marketing campaign whose output on critical platforms *Facebook* and *Twitter* was so minimal that it could have been accomplished by one intern working 5 hours a week, and which stood in start contrast to the output of competitors like *The Hunger Games* and even Disney stablemate *The Avengers*.

How does one reconcile such a cataclysmic failure of *simple effort* with the reality of a $250M production investment that by its very nature meant that only an *all-out effort*, producing one of the best outcomes ever for a March release, could succeed.

For *John Carter* to be considered a success, a domestic gross of $200M would be needed, and in the history of Hollywood only 5 films released in January through April had ever grossed that much -- *The Passion of the Christ, Alice In Wonderland, How to Train Your Dragon, 300, and Fast Five.* The task and stakes were clear, and yet simply on the matter of effort, the shortcomings are equally clear. Why?

Speaking in August 2012 at a gathering to honor the Centennial of *Tarzan* and *John Carter of Mars, John Carter* Producer Jim Morris acknowledged that a "perfect storm" of executive decisions and marketing factors, including "three turnovers" within the marketing department during *John Carter*'s campaign, resulted in disappointment.[334]

---

[334] Michael D. Sellers, "John Carter Producer Jim Morris at the ERB Centennial Celebration," *The John Carter Files* 18 Aug 2012, 11 Sep 2012 <http://thejohncarterfiles.com/2012/08/john-carter-producer-jim-morris-at-the-erb-centennial-celebration-closing-ban/>.

What would Walt Disney think?

One cannot help but wonder whether any of the principals other than the film-makers would regard such a question as even relevant. Do the personal values of the company's founder matter any more? Does The Walt Disney Company of 2012 have an obligation to continue to reflect the values of its founder? Or has it evolved beyond that and is it accountable only to Wall Street and its investors -- and not the creators of the intellectual property itself -- the filmmakers and the authors of the material that underlies the film, and their constituencies?

The answer seems clear enough.

Iger himself said it best, and quite clearly:

"The baggage of tradition can slow you down. I'm not going to eliminate that, but I'd like to reduce it significantly."[335]

Indeed.

Iger continues to build Disney's value through acquisition of established brands created by others. It began with Pixar in 2006; continued with Marvel in 2009, and in October 2012 he announced the acquisition of Lucasfilm and the *Star Wars* franchise, simultaneously announcing that a new *Star Wars* trilogy representing the seventh, eighth, and ninth films in the cycle will be produced. Iger's vision for Disney is clear, and it is clear that *John Carter* is not part of that vision. Analysts and stockholders applaud Iger's choices.

The "baggage of tradition" is not an issue.

---

[335] Brooks Barnes, "Is Disney's Chief Having a Cinderella Moment," New York Times, 10 Apr 2010, 4 Nov 2012 <http://www.nytimes.com/2010/04/11/business/11iger.html?pagewanted=all>

IN CONCLUSION

In the end, there will always be those who will say that any attempt to argue for the continuation of the John Carter cinematic franchise is an exercise in futility and a fanboy delusion. But it is not the actual performance of *John Carter* in the marketplace that causes the idea of continuation to seem far-fetched -- the film, after all, earned $300M at the global box office in spite of tragically inept marketing, and spawned a global fan movement. The performance is respectable, but the film is stigmatized as an epic flop. Is there a way forward, or is it truly game over?

I am convinced there is a way forward.

Why?

First, the underlying literary property is exceptional; it inspired arguably the greatest creations of modern science fiction, both cinematic and literary, and has stood the test of time. At a time when the idea of a "global market" hardly existed, Burroughs' books were translated into 58 languages and outsold all others, and the magic within those books is timeless and works its magic today.[336] The "strip-mining" has never thoroughly tapped the true genius of the original, which retains multiple treasures that have yet to be unearthed and presented on screen. Andrew

---

[336] In a focus group study in which 12-17 year old teenagers hooked on current book series including The Hunger Games, Twilight, and the Harry Potter book series were given the opportunity to read A Princess of Mars, the results were overwhelmingly positive. See Michael D. Sellers, "Teen Readers React to A Princess of Mars," The John Carter Files, 13 May 2012 15 Nov 2012 <http://thejohncarterfiles.com/2012/05/video-teen-readers-voice-opinions-on-a-princess-of-mars/>.

Stanton's *John Carter* scratches the surface; much remains.   There are eleven books in the series; an entire planet to explore, filled with fascinating cultures, a detailed and compelling history, and poignant turmoil with John Carter becoming deeply emotionally invested in the dying planet that is his adopted home.

But is it economically viable to continue, either through sequels or a reboot?

Again, the answer is yes.

Why?

In the first place, because there is a substantial fan base in place and ready to support future films.

John Carter yielded close to $300M in global sales with an audience favorability rating of 75%, according to Cinamascore and other exit polling mechanisms. That means that at least 30 million moviegoers saw the movie and 75% said they liked it and would recommend it -- and as the growth of the fan movement has shown, the intensity of the appeal to a core group of highly motivated enthusiasts is especially high.   In excess of 20 million viewers are ready to receive the next film with open arms.   And this is an understated figure because it only addresses those who saw the film in theaters, and ignores the millions more who missed it in theaters but discovered it later on blu-ray or cable TV broadcasts. There is truly an "Army of Barsoom" ready to support any future films, and within this number there is a core group of potential influencers numbering in the tens of thousands including film journalists, bloggers, a social media mavens armed with the tools of modern digital marketing and ready to use those tools.

What market outcome can reasonably be projected for a sequel or reboot?

The evidence is conclusive that Disney's failed promotional campaign depressed the performance of *John Carter*, particularly in the United States, and it is reasonable to assume that a sequel with simply adequate marketing would do better. How much better?

Let's start with the realistic assumption that if John Carter earned $282M global gross with a tiny pre-existing fan base and clueless marketing, then $350M global box office gross for a second film is a reasonable minimum likely projection.

At $350M global box office, *Prometheus* was regarded as a success and quickly generated a sequel. Why? Because it only cost $140M to make, not $250M as was the case with *John Carter*.

Do future John Carter films have to cost $250M each?

Realistically, what budget level could John Carter sequels be produced at? Can a budget of $175M be attained?

Could two sequels be produced concurrently for a total budget of $350M, or $175M per film?

Yes, and here's why.

First, the one-time costs associated with the first film have been absorbed. Prototype development is complete. A second and third film would have to bear none of the one-time development costs that burdened the first film.[337]

Secondly, the first John Carter story is extremely reliant on scenes involving multiple Thark characters, who are created via motion capture CGI, onscreen repeatedly throughout the movie. The animation of these characters, who must be rendered at a level allowing them to seamlessly occupy the screen with live human characters, was the core reason driving up the budget of the first movie, and future installments, if they even remotely follow the stories originated by Burroughs, rely substantially less on having multiple Thark (and hence CGI) characters on screen for extended periods. This too, would produce a savings without sacrificing production value.

But while some savings would be achieved by producing two films concurrently; and some would be achieved by having less Thark screen time to deal with -- in the end, to achieve a budget of $175M would

---

[337] In Motion Picture accounting, the one-time costs for a one-off film are typically adjusted after the fact when sequels are ordered and amortized over the full series. Thus under the normal scenario, sequels would each bear a small, proportionate share of the one-time costs that are currently carried by John Carter. However, since Disney has already taken an extreme $200M write-down and written these costs off, the "normal" procedure would not automatically apply.

require that the filmmakers make a commitment to "be smart" about the story and the production and produce the film to a price point. Would this be creatively stifling? The truth is, it is rare indeed in the history of Hollywood for a live action film's production budget be allowed to "seek its own level" in the way that was the case for *John Carter*. The old verities of the industry need to apply: The business model for a sequel needs to start from an assumption of $175M per film for two films; and then the filmmakers must craft an operating plan that meets this price point. It's not impossible -- savvy Hollywood producers work this way all the time. And at a $175M budget, with a projected minimum global theatrical gross of $350M, *John Carter 2* and *John Carter 3* become interesting business propositions.[338]

Is there more global gross available than the $350M projected as a minimum?

Again, the answer is yes. The global market is expanding at a much higher rate of growth than in the US. Two markets where *John Carter* did extremely well, Russia and China, are particularly noteworthy. According to the Motion Picture Association of America's annual report "Theatrical Market Statistics 2011"[339]

> Each international region experienced growth in 2011. Chinese box office grew by 35% in 2011 to become the 2nd largest International market behind Japan, experiencing by far the largest growth in major markets. International box office in U.S. dollars is up 35% over five years ago, driven by growth in various markets, including China and Russia.

---

[338] Traditionally in Hollywood, the shorthand way of determining whether a film is a success or not is "if global box office equals twice production costs, the film will be profitable." This does NOT mean that profitability is achieved from the theatrical results only. Global Box Office Rather, it means that if a film doubles its budget at the box office, then by the time all revenue streams are in, the net to the studio will be enough to generate a profit after the production investment and marketing costs are recouped. Thus a "floor" of $350M global box office against $175M production cost equals ultimate "profitability" for a film.

[339] Motion Picture Association of America, "Theatrical Market Statistics 2011," Available as PDF Download, Accessed 7 Sep 2012 <http://www.mpaa.org/resources/5bec4ac9-a95e-443b-987b-bff6fb5455a9.pdf>.

Writing of dramatic growth in box office in Russia, Matthew Garrahan writes in FT.com (Financial Times):[340]

> Box office revenues in the country have soared over the past decade to more than $1B, rising at a compound annual rate of 27 per cent since 2006, according to Renaissance Capital, a Russian investment bank. The increase has been fueled by a multiplex construction boom and growing appetite for Hollywood movies, as well as Russian-language productions. "Russia's growth has outpaced established markets and emerging markets like China," says Dave Hollis, Disney's executive vice-president for theatrical exhibition sales and distribution. "It's not just because of higher ticket prices, box office has gone up with more admissions. There's a cultural revolution under way there in terms of people embracing cinema. Russia has become a top-five market for us and for some movies it's even more important than that," says Andy Bird, the chairman of Walt Disney International. "Seven years ago our presence there was two employees working out of a Moscow hotel room."

In addition to their general growth, Russia and China have both shown themselves to be extremely "sequel-friendly," as the following chart illustrates:

CHINA

Film	Original	Sequel
Kung Fu Panda 1/2	26.02M	92.17M
Transformers 2/3	57.22M	172.0M
Pirates Caribbean 3/4	16.97M	70.00M

RUSSIA

Kung Fu Panda 1/2	20.58M	31.83M
Transformers 2/3	18.18M	45.13M

There is more to this than just an expanding box office.

The growth noted above, particularly in Russia and China, means that foreign co-producers in those territories are available to share a

---

[340] Matthew Garrahan, "Film Studios Strike Rich Treasure in Russia," *Financial Times/ FT.com,* 12 May 2011, 7 Sep 2012, <http://www.ft.com/cms/s/0/ c00963d4-7cc2-11e0-994d-00144feabdc0.html#axzz25iCS2dL5>.

substantial portion of the production risk. Disney is already a beneficiary of this type of an arrangement in several of its current films.

For *Iron Man 3*, Marvel entered into a coproduction arrangement with DMG Entertainment,[341] a Chinese coproducer. Dreamworks did the same for *Kung Fu Panda 3*, making Oriental Dreamworks a co-production partner,[342] and other US studios are entering into similar agreements.

With a little effort and imagination, Chinese and/or Russian co-production partners can be recruited to lower the risk for the US Studio Distributor.

So, reasons for continuation include the underlying value of the literary property; the availability of an established, motivated, and digitally savvy fan base; a likely global gross of at least $350M; and the availability of foreign co-producers in countries like Russia and China to lower the risk.

Yet it is undeniable that a sequel or reboot is still considered a long shot proposition, not because of hard economic realities -- but rather because of psychological factors. The film has been labeled by its own studio as an epic failure, with the largest announced write-down in cinema history. The press has passed judgment on it as a failed enterprise. *John Carter* is dead.

What comes next?

In all likelihood, before there can be continuation, there must be gradual rehabilitation of the image and reputation of the film and the underlying property it depicts.

If there is an Army of Barsoom ready to support a sequel, it must first gradually change the narrative about the first film from "epic flop"

---

[341] Jonathan Landreth, "Disney, DMG team up to make 'Iron Man 3' a Chinese Co-production," *LA Times*, 16 Apr 2012, 7 Sep 2012 <http://latimesblogs.latimes.com/entertainmentnewsbuzz/2012/04/iron-man-chinese-co-production.html>.

[342] Richard Verrier, "DreamWorks Animation's 'Kung Fu Panda 3' to be China Co-production," *LA Times*, 16 Aug 2012, 7 Sep 2012 <http://www.latimes.com/entertainment/envelope/cotown/la-et-ct-dreamworks-china-kung-fu-panda-3-20120806,0,17577.story>.

to "beloved classic". Fans and bloggers and others who can comment, write, create fan art, carry out fan activities, and otherwise use their voices and be heard, have the power to gradually accomplish this. It would not be the first time in cinema history that the narrative about a film undergoes such a transformation. Flops-turned-classics include the *Wizard of Oz, Citizen Kane, Blade Runner,* and *It's a Wonderful Life.* None of these films are perfect; none were widely praised on first release; all found a place in history that leaves them regarded today as cinematic gems. The initial financial result of a film is one thing; the final verdict on its worth is another matter altogether.

Even those who object to the Stanton adaptation and only support a reboot, not a sequel, have a role to play, because nurturing the idea the Edgar Rice Burroughs' Barsoom deserves an ongoing life on the screen helps keep Burroughs' legacy alive and moves the conversation forward.

But why does it matter?

Why all this effort in support of one potential film franchise?

John Carter was, after all, "just a movie", one of hundreds released each year. Some succeed, some fail, and those that fail are generally allowed to pass quietly into library status with no one clamoring for a sequel.

Why the special attention for *John Carter?*

Those who have been touched by Burroughs' Barsoom understand that Edgar Rice Burroughs' creation is a global cultural treasure that has shown, over its century long history, a unique ability to capture the imagination and inspire. In our own lives it is natural for us to succumb to the human tendency to let other human beings define what is possible. Burroughs' stories counter this. Through dazzling imaginative transport and ennobling characters his genius evokes a sense of wonder and a realization in real life too, more is possible. The stories inspire a belief that something more awaits us if we just go for it and trust that we have what it takes to keep fighting, in whatever struggle or cause it is that we take up or that life throws at us. This is not the lonely personal observation of one author writing an unlikely book about a bungled film enterprise; it is the observation of profoundly successful creators like Ray

Bradbury, Carl Sagan, and others who found in Burroughs unique inspiration for their lives.

In sum, Burroughs stories do far more than just entertain us -- they touch our souls and remind us that no matter how bleak our circumstances may seem, as John Carter would say: "We still live!" Burroughs' genius illuminates the fertile possibility of life, and urges us to believe in that possibility. There is a timeless, global value in that, and it is something that must not be lost, and is worth fighting for.

In Hollywood, films happen because someone fought for them. Usually it is a lonely struggle behind the scenes by an individual filmmaker, perhaps with a few key associates, who carries the argument forward, refuses to take 'no' for an answer, and eventually prevails.

In the case that is being made for the cinematic continuation of John Carter, that voice is not a lonely one, nor is it happening behind closed doors in Hollywood. Rather it is a collective voice emanating from all the corners of the world. Disparate individuals from vastly different backgrounds and cultures are finding inspiration in Stanton's film, Burroughs' stories, or both. Fueled by that inspiration and empowered by the tools of social connectivity, they are finding each other. Together they are using their voices in ways that are empowered by the technology of the age.

Continue to use your voices; you will be heard.

AFTERWORD BY THE AUTHOR

I would never have undertaken such an endeavor as this book were it not for the fans who emerged and made their voices heard, first on *The John Carter Files*, and later on *Facebook* and elsewhere. They inspired me with their passion and gave me confidence that in making the case for not giving up on *John Carter*, I was not a lone voice - but rather was representative of others who believe there is something special here.

William Faulkner spoke of writing as "agony and sweat." In the case of this book, the agony and sweat will have been worth it if one person -- the right person -- reads the book and thinks: "You know, maybe there's something there -- maybe this *John Carter* thing deserves another look."

Is that person Robert Iger or Alan Horne at Disney?

Possibly.

Is it another U.S. Studio chief?

A key foreign coproducer?

With a very few rare exceptions, the forces keeping a literary property from becoming a major motion picture are much stronger than those enabling it to be produced. "Development hell" became a common term for a reason. Nothing worthwhile is easy, and the hundred year history of the journey of *A Princess of Mars* from the mind of Edgar Rice Burroughs to cinema screens is "Exhibit A" of just how hard it can be. Having a passionate proponent is an essential ingredient.

Fortunately, *John Carter* has many such passionate proponents. I am one of them, but I'm not the only one. There is an Army of Barsoom that feels the same way, and my efforts are not those of a lone individual -- they are the expression of a fan base that is global, vocal, and motivated.

The movement for a continuation of the *John Carter* film legacy will continue. The "closing argument" presented as the final chapter of this book is taken from a longer White Paper document, "The Case for a Continuation of *John Carter (of Mars)*," which can be found online at www.TheJohnCarterFiles.com/white-paper, and which includes a detailed financial operational analysis of the prospects for a continuation.

To find out more generally what is happening in the movement to continue the franchise, go to www.TheJohnCarterFiles.com or visit www.BacktoBarsoom.com.

ABOUT THE AUTHOR

Michael D. Sellers was born in Alabama, the son of an Army officer, and grew up as an "Army Brat" living in various cities in the U.S. and abroad, including Stuttgart, Germany where he discovered Edgar Rice Burroughs in the Post Library as a twelve year old. He was a Magna Cum Laude graduate of the University of Delaware in 1975, where he was a Rhodes Scholarship and Danforth Fellowship finalist. He went on to New York University Graduate Film School, then spent 10 years serving as an operations officer for the Central Intelligence Agency, serving in Warsaw (1980), Ethiopia (1981-83), Moscow (1984-86), and the Philippines (1986-90). His work as a CIA officer specializing in Soviet operations has been cited in non-fiction books that include *The Main Enemy* by Milt Beardon and James Risen; *Inside the CIA* and *Moscow Station* by Ron Kessler, and *The Spy Who Got Away* by David Wise. He was awarded the Intelligence Commendation Medal for service in support of President Corazon Aquino during a violent coup attempt in the Philippines in December 1989. He returned to private life in 1990 and since then has worked as a writer, film-maker, and film distribution executive. His films have been selected for more than 100 film festivals and have won multiple awards. Two films released in 2007 and 2010 and financed via a telemarketing organization retained by Sellers in 2007 came under investigation by the Justice Department for fundraising violations. In 2011 Sellers accepted full responsibility in this matter. For more details about Michael D. Sellers visit www.MichaelDSellersAuthor.com, and his blogs: www.TheJohnCarterFiles.com and www.MichaelDSellers.com.

He is married to Lorena Llevado Sellers and has four grown children, Patrick, Pilar, Kaitlyn, and Michelle.

INDEX

A

Printed in Great Britain
by Amazon.co.uk, Ltd.,
Marston Gate.